The Higher Realism of Woodrow Wilson

WOODROW WILSON

THE HIGHER REALISM OF WOODROW WILSON

and Other Essays

ARTHUR S. LINK

With a Foreword by
DEWEY W. GRANTHAM

VANDERBILT UNIVERSITY PRESS
Nashville · 1971

Copyright © 1971 by Vanderbilt University Press

For
Donald Morrison Meisel, Ph.D., D.D.
Colleague, pastor, and friend

CONTENTS

PREFACE

I have collected these articles and essays at the suggestion of Professor Dewey W. Grantham of Vanderbilt University and the editors of Vanderbilt University Press, who were kind (or rash) enough to say that readers might like to have them available in book form. They have been changed only to standardize capitalization, form of citation, and other matters of style; to smooth out a few rough sentences; to correct whatever errors have been detected; and, in two instances, to eliminate repetitive quotations.

I am grateful for this opportunity to acknowledge my warm thanks to Professor Grantham for very helpful advice in the selection of the contents and for a much too generous Foreword; to Martha I. Strayhorn of Vanderbilt University Press, for careful and patient editing; to Professor Eugene P. Trani of Southern Illinois University, National Historical Publications Commission Fellow with the Wilson Papers, 1969-70, and to my secretary, Kate Nicoll, for kind help in preparing the copy; to Jean MacLachlan, Contributing Editor of *The Papers of Woodrow Wilson*, for reading the galley proofs; to my student, John M. Mulder, for help in preparing the index; and last, but by no means least, to my wife, Margaret Douglas Link, my best collaborator and editor for more than twenty-five years, who suffered through all the stages of these essays.

The dedication is a small token of my affection and regard for the senior minister of the First Presbyterian Church of Princeton, New Jersey, since 1960. In the best Wilsonian tradition, he has given himself totally to his community and congregation.

ARTHUR S. LINK

Montreat, North Carolina
August 4, 1970

FOREWORD

SOON after I enrolled as a graduate student at the University of North Carolina in January 1946, I began to hear about Arthur S. Link. Several of my fellow-students had known him before he completed his doctorate in history at the university in 1945, and it was clear that they viewed him, with considerable awe and a little envy, as an intellectual phenomenon. They spoke of his incredible drive and prodigious memory, while recalling his feat of assimilating the twenty-seven volumes of the American Nation Series in the space of a few weeks. Some of my professors also mentioned this brilliant and brash young man, whose academic precociousness had strongly impressed them. In doing the research for his doctoral dissertation, "The South and the Democratic Campaign of 1910–1912," Link had insatiably exploited archival materials in and out of the region. Nor was that all. He had audaciously announced, even before receiving his degree, that he was beginning a new multivolume biography of Woodrow Wilson, a work which he confidently expected to supersede the eight-volume *Life and Letters* completed by Ray Stannard Baker in 1939. When I met Link, during a research trip which he made to Chapel Hill in 1947, he struck me as being, if possible, even more vital and purposeful than his local reputation had led me to expect. The passing years have confirmed my early impressions, and I have followed his remarkable career for almost a quarter of a century with fascination and admiration.

Arthur Stanley Link was born in New Market, Virginia, in 1920. He grew up in North Carolina and attended the state university in Chapel Hill, graduating in 1941 with highest honors in history. He continued his studies at Chapel Hill, earning the M.A. degree in 1942 and the Ph.D. three years later. Meanwhile, he served as a research assistant in the university's Institute for Research in Social Science; held a Rosenwald Fellowship; taught first at North Carolina State College in Raleigh and then at the University of North Carolina; and, at the urging of his major professor, Fletcher M. Green, spent a year at Columbia University in Henry Steele Commager's seminar. Green and Commager, along with Howard K. Beale of the University of North Carolina and Edward M. Earle of the Institute for Advanced Study at Princeton, were the historians who seem to have had the greatest influence upon Link during the formative stages of his career. Nothing could have been more appropriate than the appointment in September 1945 of the young Wilson scholar as Instructor in History at Princeton University. By that time, he had already published several notable articles, including a significant reappraisal of the Democratic national convention of 1912 which appeared in *The American Historical Review.*

The first volume of the biography of Woodrow Wilson was not long delayed. On the basis of the extensive research which he had done for his dissertation and his use of the Wilson Papers and other manuscript materials during the years 1944–1946, he was able to publish *Wilson: The Road to the White House* in 1947. The book was an impressive performance, as almost all reviewers pointed out. It presented a detailed and authoritative treatment of the critically important period between Wilson's entry into politics in 1910 and his election to the presidency in November 1912. Professional recognition now came to Link with a rush. He was promoted to Assistant Professor in 1948, was made a member of the Institute for Advanced Study in 1949, and in the same year was lured away from Princeton to Northwestern University, where he became Associate Professor of History.

The next decade in Arthur Link's career was a period of spectacular achievement. Books and articles poured from his pen. A new crop of Ph.D.'s emerged from Northwestern bearing the stamp of his tutelage in recent American history. He received several honors· a Guggenheim Fellowship in 1950–51, another appointment to the Institute for Advanced Study in 1954–55, an invitation to deliver the Albert Shaw Lectures in Diplomatic History at Johns Hopkins University in 1956, and selection as Harmsworth Professor of American History at Oxford University in 1958–59. In addition to a dozen articles and *Problems in American History* (1952), a volume which he edited with his colleague Richard

W. Leopold, Link wrote four important books in the 1950s. His *Woodrow Wilson and the Progressive Era, 1910–1917* was published in 1954 as the first volume to appear in the eagerly awaited New American Nation Series, edited by Henry Steele Commager and Richard Brandon Morris. This valuable book on Wilson's first administration was, as the author noted, "in the nature of an outline" of the next several volumes of his biography of Wilson. In 1955, Link published *American Epoch: A History of the United States Since the 1890s,* a work that quickly became the premier general history of the United States in the twentieth century. The next year brought the second volume of the biography, *Wilson: The New Freedom;* in impressive fashion it took Wilson from November 1912 to November 1914. Link's Shaw Lectures at Johns Hopkins were published in 1957 under the title, *Wilson the Diplomatist: A Look at His Major Foreign Policies.* These incisive and provocative lectures enabled him to range far beyond the chronological treatment his biography had made possible and to present a summary account of the President's significant foreign policies during his eight-year tenure in the White House.

Early in 1958, Link made a momentous decision: he agreed to become editor of a definitive edition of Wilson's letters and papers. This ambitious undertaking, which was expected to result in the publication of some forty volumes, was officially approved by the Woodrow Wilson Foundation in 1957. Princeton University became a co-sponsor of the project in 1959, and the following year Link returned to that university to carry on the work of editing *The Papers of Woodrow Wilson* and to accept a position as Professor of History. Meanwhile, he was moving ahead with his biography. The third volume, *Wilson: The Struggle for Neutrality, 1914–1915,* appeared in 1960. The next volume, *Wilson: Confusions and Crises, 1915–1916,* came out in 1964; and a year later, the fifth volume was published under the title *Wilson: Campaigns for Progressivism and Peace, 1916–1917.* Link also published *Woodrow Wilson: A Brief Biography* (1963), a cogent outline of the twenty-eighth President's life and politics, and *Woodrow Wilson: A Profile* (1968), a selection of essays from the writings of Wilson's contemporaries and of later scholars. The editing of *The Papers* took an increasing amount of time, but the project moved forward rapidly and surely. The first volume appeared in 1966 and received extraordinary critical acclaim. Eight additional volumes have since been released.

By 1970, Link had written more than a dozen books and two-score articles, in addition to serving as editor for various other works. He was universally acknowledged as the foremost Wilson scholar and as one of the ablest specialists in the field of modern American history. The second and third volumes of his *Wilson* had been awarded the coveted Bancroft Prize for biography. In 1965, he was given a chair at Princeton, the Edwards Professorship in American History. He was elected president of the Southern Historical Association in 1968. He was also recognized for his outstanding contributions as a lay leader in the United Presbyterian Church, and from 1963 to 1966 he served as a vice-president of the National Council of Churches.

"The biographer," Link observed in 1948, "assumes the greatest obligations and responsibilities of all writers of history." No one can doubt that Link's own comprehensive study of Woodrow Wilson and his times is an example of distinguished historical scholarship. His editing of *The Papers of Woodrow Wilson* may eventually equal or surpass his contribution in writing the biography; but at this point in the Princeton professor's career, his most impressive achievement is the work he has done on Wilson between 1910 and 1917. The five published volumes of the biography are a detailed and authoritative treatment of Wilson and his politics during these years. Indeed, Link's *Wilson* is biography in the grand manner, a study almost epic in its proportions and one that has few parallels in the entire range of American historical literature. His volume in the New American Nation Series, *Woodrow Wilson and the Progressive Era*, is a spirited interpretation of the first Wilson administration and the single best book on the subject.

Link's work on Woodrow Wilson and national politics in the period 1910–1917 is exceptional for several reasons. Link has demonstrated an unparalleled mastery of the political scene in the United States during the Wilson era. His research has been exhaustive, and he has based his biography in large part upon primary sources—manuscript collections, public documents, newspapers and periodicals, and diaries and memoirs. His search for new materials has led him to important sources in German, British, and French archives. Link's style is noteworthy. He writes with great clarity and force, and his narrative moves with impressive momentum. The cultural factors that underlay American politics during the Wilson era are not always adequately analyzed in this "political biography," but the author makes a consistent effort to relate his subject to the period which he dominated. The five volumes of the biography provide a masterly exposition of evidence; they reflect an approach to history and biography that seeks to record how things actually were—*wie es eigentlich gewesen ist*. It may be that Link has too frequently allowed facts to speak for themselves, particularly in the last three volumes, and as a result has failed to employ as often as he might have his great talents as an interpreter. Yet the biography contains many incisive and perceptive judgments.

An important part of Link's history of the Wilson period is its full and well-documented account of the President's famous domestic reforms. He discusses in comprehensive and illuminating fashion the great legislative struggles of Wilson's first term, clearly shows the evolution of the Wilsonian New Freedom, describes Wilson's advisers, and treats his relations with Congress. He analyzes the influence of the South, the role of public opinion and organized pressure groups, and the relationship between national and state politics. He follows the resurgence of the Democratic party after 1909 with a keen eye, and his work constitutes a valuable history of that party during the following eight years.

About half of Link's *Wilson* is devoted to international matters, and here, too, there are some remarkable contributions. All of the important aspects of New Freedom diplomacy during the years 1913–1917 have been covered. Link describes the administration's "Missionary Diplomacy" in Latin America and the Wilsonian policies in the Far East, finding much to criticize in both. His elaborate discussion of Wilson's European policies, beginning with Volume III, is surely the richest in the literature on the subject. He carefully reconstructs the complicated history of the Wilson administration's struggles for neutrality after the war broke out in 1914 and describes in detail the President's campaign for mediation in 1916–17. His lengthy treatment of Anglo-American relations is particularly noteworthy. He challenges the older revisionist interpretation of American neutrality and of Wilson's role during that period. He tends to vindicate American policies, though he is sometimes critical of such Wilsonian advisers as Col. Edward M. House and Secretary Robert Lansing—as well as British and

French leaders—and he denies that the President allowed "any emotional bias" in favor of the Allies to affect his commitment to genuine neutrality before 1917. Link may be too sympathetic toward Woodrow Wilson at this point, but he shows that the American statesman was far more flexible during this troubled period than many other scholars have claimed and that his leadership reflected a combination of moral principle and tactical pragmatism. There are many excellent features of Link's account of Wilsonian diplomacy: his treatment of the role played by Congress, his analysis of sectional and hyphenate elements, his discussion of the preparedness campaign and the election of 1916, his recognition of the relationship between domestic and foreign issues, and his demonstration of the narrow range of alternatives available to Wilson in devising a viable neutrality course.

Nothing in the multivolume work is more interesting than Link's interpretation of Woodrow Wilson himself. He pictures Wilson as a man of vaulting ambition: strong-minded, able, filled with a sense of his own destiny, and eager to guide the American people in great and noble movements. Link is strikingly successful in explaining Wilson's phenomenal emergence as a national figure, in revealing the great power of his domestic leadership, in demonstrating the dominant role he played in the conduct of his administration's foreign policy, and in showing his evolution as a world leader. Long before his re-election in 1916, declares Link, Wilson had developed into a "masterful leader driving his party and Congress and . . . a diplomat of increasing deftness and skill, constantly probing and deploying." He shows that Wilson's progressivism also changed significantly between 1912 and 1916; the limited program of the early New Freedom gave way in 1916 to a much broader and more advanced reformism, essentially that embodied in Theodore Roosevelt's New Nationalism. In his discussion of Wilson's conduct of American diplomacy from 1915 to 1921, Link portrays the President as a realist and a moralist, a man intent upon guiding the American people from provincialism toward world leadership and responsibilities. Thus the Peace Conference of 1919 was a time of heroic striving and great achievement. In fighting for the League of Nations at home Wilson spurned the role of statesman for the nobler role of prophet.

Link began his biography as an iconoclast. In his earlier books and articles he called attention to a less happy side of Wilson's character—to his egotism, exaltation of intuition, indulgence in prejudice, and temperamental inability to co-operate with men who would not follow him unreservedly—and he insisted that some of the President's decisions were dictated by political expediency. These critical notes are softened in the volumes that appeared after 1957. The shift in Link's attitude toward his subject was at least in part the result of his willingness to change his mind about important matters of interpretation and to admit such changes in print. In the preface to the second edition of *Wilson the Diplomatist*, for example, Link carefully listed eight ways in which he would have altered "emphases, interpretations, and details" if he had written the book in 1963 rather than in 1956.

In his study of the Wilson years and in his other writings, Link has been a pioneer in the interpretation of the progressive movement. His account of Wilson as a reform governor was an early contribution to the scholarly literature on progressivism at the state level. His authoritative analysis of Wilson's domestic reforms in the presidency is an invaluable treatment of national progressivism at high tide. Furthermore, he has done much to clarify the evolution of Wilsonian liberalism; his ideas and concepts about the so-called "advanced progressives," the Wilson coalition of 1916, and the persistence of progressivism after 1917 illustrate his keen perception and originality. Link views the progressive movement as a positive force in our national life, one that went far toward reconstructing the American political system and that sought solutions to the difficult social problems spawned by industrialization and urbanization. His interpretation emphasizes the continuity of progressivism, relating the movement of the early twentieth century both to antecedents in the nineteenth century and to reform currents that manifested themselves after 1920. Yet he also argues that "there were many 'progressive' movements on many levels seeking sometimes contradictory objectives." He was one of the first historians to recognize the existence of such a movement in the South and to assimilate it into the historical scholarship concerned with our national politics.

Link's magisterial biography of Woodrow Wilson is clearly his major accomplishment, but in some respects his other writings have had an even greater impact. Among these works are his provocative volume in the New American Nation Series and his luminous Shaw Lectures on Wilson as a diplomatist. These have greatly influenced the study of our recent history, and it is a tribute to their author that so many of his interpretations have been incorporated into the books and articles of other students of the Wilson era. He has also influenced the writing of, as well as the teaching of, United States history through his textbook, *American Epoch.* Now in its third edition, this volume reveals Link's mastery of the historical record, his talent as a synthesizer, and his ability to challenge his readers with broad generalizations and fresh conclusions. While his interpretation of twentieth-century America stresses the prevalence and importance of social conflict, his work is also notable for the emphasis it places upon the durability and adaptability of American institutions. Finally, Link's many articles and essays should not be overlooked, for they constitute a vital and generally neglected contribution to our historical literature.

The essays are important for several reasons. In the first place, they deal with significant topics, and they illuminate aspects of the American past which are dealt with briefly but not fully explored in Link's books. They throw light on Wilson's life before 1912 and on certain features of his presidency, reflect Link's early concentration on the campaign and election of 1912, reveal his long-time interest in southern history and in the interaction of regional and national politics, and frequently touch upon the meaning of the progressive movement. Although many of these articles were written while he was very young and some of them have been challenged by other scholars, they are valuable for their sound scholarship and original interpretations. They show a first-rate historical mind at work, reveal a good deal about the development of that mind, and provide an enlarged context in which to appraise the work of a distinguished recent American historian. The merit of Link's interpretations and generalizations is readily apparent in the several essays on Woodrow Wilson which make up the first section of the book. In these the author not only presents his views on certain Wilsonian attributes and themes that are not elaborated in his biography; he also evinces a greater willingness than is evident in the last three volumes of his *Wilson* to assert his own judgments and conclusions. That is, the essays have given Link an opportunity both to deepen his analysis of Wilson and to enlarge his interpretation of the man. His essay on "Woodrow Wilson and His Presbyterian Inheritance" (pp. 3-20) stresses the profound effect that Wilson's Presbyterian background had upon all his thought and activities. It helps us to understand Wilson's public life as "an example of morality in politics." In his presidential address before the Southern Historical Association in the fall of 1969, Link presented an enlightening and gracefully written paper on "Woodrow Wilson: The American as Southerner" (pp. 21-37). In discussing Wilson's attitude toward his native region in the years before he entered the White House, Link charted the future President's ideological journey from ardent nationalism to eventual discovery of his Southernism and regional self-identification as an American. The brief essay devoted to "Woodrow Wilson and the Study of Administration" (pp. 38-44) suggests Wilson's contribution to the study of that embryonic field in the United States. It is a by-product of the careful editorial work Link and his associates are doing for *The Papers of Woodrow Wilson.* Another essay, "Woodrow Wilson in New Jersey" (pp. 45-59), is a hitherto unpublished paper Link delivered at Princeton as part of the New Jersey Tercentenary celebration in 1964. At once reflective and speculative, it characterizes Wilson's governorship of New Jersey as "the ground of his political apprenticeship" and an example of remarkable executive leadership in state affairs.

Two other essays in this section are broader in scope. "The Case for Woodrow Wilson" (pp. 140-154) throws a good deal of light on Wilson's boyhood and on certain aspects of his later career. It sharply challenges the methods, evidence, and conclusions of Sigmund Freud and William C. Bullitt in their psychological study, *Thomas Woodrow Wilson* (1967). "The Higher Realism of Woodrow Wilson" (pp. 127-139) is particularly significant because, in writing it in 1962, Link attempted to pull together many of his thoughts and convictions about Wilson—in short, as he says, "to clarify my own conclusions about the subject of my life's work." Responding to the sharp criticisms leveled at Wilson by European and American "realists," he undertook a wide-ranging examination of Wilson's ideas and actions as a university president and educator, as a domestic leader concerned with political and economic reform in the United States, and as a world statesman who tried to provide leadership for the reconstruction of the international community. While conceding that Wilson was primarily a Christian idealist, he argued cogently that Wilson was in fact a "supreme realist" in each of his three separate public careers.

One group of essays in this collection focuses on Wilson's leadership as President. In "Woodrow Wilson and the Democratic Party" (pp. 60-71), Link shows that, in the process of establishing control over his own party and pushing his early New Freedom legislation through Congress, the President was forced to make peace with Democratic machines all over the country and, in many cases, to withhold administration support from the more liberal elements seeking to gain power in the states and localities, thereby strengthening the conservative factions. Two articles—"Woodrow Wilson and the Ordeal of Neutrality" (pp. 88-98) and "Woodrow Wilson and Peace Moves" (pp. 99-109)—review Wilsonian diplomacy during the period of United States neutrality and the way in which the American leader's peace initiatives and evolving peace program moved him to the center of the world stage during the years 1916-1919. "President Wilson and His English Critics" (pp. 110-126) was Link's inaugural address as Harmsworth Professor at Oxford. This important paper, lucid and forceful in its argument, reveals Link the essayist at his best. Here he tries to account for the English misunderstanding of Wilson by analyzing various images (often "distorted") of the President formed by English critics. A paper on "Wilson the Diplomatist in Retrospect" (pp. 72-87) contains Link's reflections on this subject more than a decade after the publication of his Shaw Lectures in 1957. In this essay, he describes Wilson's preparation for the role of diplomatist and evaluates his techniques, successes, and failures in dealing with international problems.

The next group of essays is concerned with the campaign and election of 1912. "The Wilson Movement in Texas, 1910-1912" (pp. 155-171) and "Democratic Politics and the Presidential Campaign of 1912 in Tennessee" (pp. 172-199) are representative of several of Link's early articles dealing with the Wilson pre-convention campaigns in various southern states. "During 1911 and 1912," Link writes, "the movement to make Wilson the Democratic presidential nominee swept over the South, and the progressive character of this movement was emphasized by the fact that in practically every southern state the progressive faction of the party rallied wholeheartedly to his support, while the conservatives and reactionaries consistently opposed him." In "The

Underwood Presidential Movement of 1912" (pp. 200–215), Link complements his account of the Wilson movement in the South, characterizes the campaign of the Alabama congressman as a conservative "counter-movement against the flood-tide of Wilsonian progressivism" in the region, and shows how, ironically, the Underwood forces helped nominate Wilson at the Baltimore convention. Southern reaction to the presidential campaign of 1912 is explored from another angle in the interesting essay on "Theodore Roosevelt and the South in 1912" (pp. 243–255). Link shows that, despite Roosevelt's concessions to white supremacy in the South, the Progressive party made little headway in that region. Perhaps the most significant essay among those on the politics of 1912 is "The Baltimore Convention of 1912" (pp. 216–242). In his detailed and absorbing account of the convention, the author presents a revisionist interpretation of the roles played by William Jennings Bryan and other political leaders. Finally, another question related to Wilson's election—the "Negro issue" and the Negro vote—is discussed in "The Negro as a Factor in the Campaign of 1912" (pp. 256–271). Link concludes that a majority of the black voters, bitterly disappointed because of the lily-white movement in Roosevelt's Progressive party and not quite trusting Wilson and the Democrats, probably maintained their allegiance to the Republican party in 1912.

In three of his best-known essays, Link examined aspects of the progressive movement. The first of these, "The Progressive Movement in the South, 1870–1914" (pp. 272–297), is a path-breaking survey of reform ideas, proposals, and legislation in the southern region. Although his definition of progressivism may be too simple, he offers a great deal of support for his contention that there was "a far-reaching progressive movement in the South." A more subtle view of southern progressivism is revealed in "The South and the 'New Freedom': An Interpretation" (pp. 298–308). In this essay, he first advanced the thesis that a group of agrarian reformers in the congressional delegations from the South pushed Woodrow Wilson in the direction of more ambitious federal programs and helped make the President a more thoroughgoing progressive. The third paper, "What Happened to the Progressive Movement in the 1920s?" (pp. 349–369), is unquestionably Link's most famous and influential essay. In a brilliant and provocative interpretation, he presented evidence of progressivism's continuing vitality in the twenties and boldly attempted to establish a relationship between the complex phenomenon historians have called the "progressive movement" of prewar years and the reform manifestations of the postwar decade.

The last four essays in this volume are miscellaneous. "The Cotton Crisis, the South, and Anglo-American Diplomacy, 1914-1915" (pp. 309-329) is a penetrating study of the struggle between a powerful southern pressure group and the Wilson administration and, in a larger sense, of the impact of a world-wide crisis upon regional economic interests. A somewhat technical article on "The Federal Reserve Policy and the Agricultural Depression of 1920-1921" (pp. 330-348) is useful for the light which it throws on the postwar farm crisis and the way it entered into politics. "Laying the Foundations" (pp. 370-388), a chapter from a volume which Link edited under the title, *The First Presbyterian Church of Princeton: Two Centuries of History* (1967) evokes the life of the church during the second half of the eighteenth century. It is an example of its author's interest in local history and in the history of his own denomination. The final essay, "Samuel Taylor Coleridge and the Economic and Political Crisis in Great Britain, 1816-1820" (pp. 389-405), is a study of the social ideas of a Tory humanitarian. Although remote in time and place, it suggests Link's broad interest in social reform and in British parallels and contrasts with progressivism in the United States.

This book contains all of Arthur Link's major essays and a good selection of his less important papers. Scholars who are interested in Woodrow Wilson and in recent American history will find here a valuable and convenient collection of articles originally published in widely scattered journals during the past quarter of a century. Students will discover in these articles a challenging and authoritative commentary on the nation's political experience during the first three decades of the twentieth century. The general reader will learn much from this volume about the leadership of Wilson, the meaning of the progressive movement, and the course of American history in the twentieth century. All readers, I think, will share my conviction that these essays by one of our most talented historians succeed magnificently in opening new and revealing vistas on a vital part of our modern history.

DEWEY W. GRANTHAM

Nashville, Tennessee
June 1970

The Higher Realism of Woodrow Wilson

1

Woodrow Wilson and His Presbyterian Inheritance

I The Family and Religious Inheritance of Woodrow Wilson

I would like to say how happy I am to participate in this significant conference. Perhaps at some future time it may be regarded as historic because it marked the beginning of an organized, formal concern for the long and fruitful Scotch-Irish-American connection. This tiny island of Ireland has made, during the past three centuries, a greater contribution to the character and development of the American people than any other territory of comparable size and population on the face of the earth.

Permit me also to say a brief word about what I hope to do in this lecture. I have not come across the water to talk generally and sentimentally about the Scotch-Irish-American connection, for I have neither the ability nor the disposition for such an effort. I had originally planned to focus on Woodrow Wilson's Scotch-Irish inheritance. But one very poor draft of a lecture along these

This essay was an address delivered in Belfast, Northern Ireland, on September 23, 1965, to a conference on Ulster and America sponsored by the Ulster-Scot Historical Society. It appeared in E. R. R. Green, editor, *Essays in Scotch-Irish History* (London: Routledge & Kegan Paul; New York: Humanities Press, 1969), pp. 1–17, and is printed here by permission of the Editor and Publishers.

lines persuaded me that it is impossible to deal in any separate manner with Woodrow Wilson's Scotch-Irish inheritance. When one begins to talk about Wilson's Scotch-Irish inheritance, one runs squarely into the fact that Wilson had an equally important, if not more important, Scottish inheritance, and that it is literally impossible to separate the two strands in his biography.

What, I asked myself, as I threshed about trying to make a new start, was the one aspect of Wilson's inheritance that stemmed both from Scotland and Northern Ireland and was unique? In other words, why was Wilson different because he was of Scotch-Irish and Scottish descent? The answer is not long in coming to anyone familiar with Woodrow Wilson. He was different from a descendant of German or Anglican English immigrants because he was a Calvinist and a Presbyterian. Every biographer of Woodrow Wilson has said that it is impossible to know and understand the man apart from his religious faith, because his every action and policy was ultimately informed and molded by his Christian faith. This is true, but it is even more important to say that Woodrow Wilson was a Presbyterian Christian of the Calvinistic persuasion. He stands pre-eminent among all the inheritors of that tradition who have made significant contributions to American political history. Indeed, he was the prime embodiment, the apogee, of the Calvinistic tradition among all statesmen of the modern epoch.

Woodrow Wilson, thirteenth President of Princeton University, forty-third Governor of New Jersey, and twenty-eighth President of the United States, was of undiluted Scottish and Scotch-Irish descent, and the sheer weight of historical evidence tempts one to say that he was predestined to be a Presbyterian. His ancestors in Scotland and Ireland had been Presbyterians since the Reformation. His mother, Janet Woodrow, was born in Carlisle, England, on December 20, 1830. Her father, the Reverend Thomas Woodrow, was a Scottish Presbyterian minister who migrated with his family from Carlisle to the New World in 1835–36 and, after a brief and cold sojourn in Canada in 1836–37, settled in Ohio and held pulpits in that state and in Kentucky. Thomas Woodrow, in turn, was descended from Patrick Woodrow, a Roman Catholic priest who became a Presbyterian minister and married at the time of the Scottish Reformation. His descendants down to

Thomas Woodrow were prominent Presbyterian ministers and elders. One of Thomas Woodrow's sons, the Reverend Dr. James Woodrow, was long a professor at the Presbyterian Theological Seminary in Columbia, South Carolina, and the publisher of two of the leading American Presbyterian journals in the late nineteenth century, *The Southern Presbyterian,* a weekly newspaper, and *The Southern Presbyterian Review,* a quarterly.[1]

Woodrow Wilson's father was the Reverend Dr. Joseph Ruggles Wilson, born at Steubenville, Ohio, on February 28, 1822. He married Janet Woodrow on June 7, 1849, and, after holding a pastorate in Pennsylvania, settled in Virginia, where he was a professor at Hampden-Sydney College from 1851 to 1855 and then pastor of the First Presbyterian Church in Staunton from 1855 to 1857. Joseph Ruggles Wilson was afterwards pastor in Augusta, Georgia, a professor at the Columbia Theological Seminary, pastor in Wilmington, North Carolina, and professor at the Southwestern Presbyterian University in Clarksville, Tennessee.

Joseph Ruggles Wilson was the son of James Wilson, who was born near Londonderry on February 20, 1787, and migrated to Philadelphia in 1807. There are Wilsons who bear a striking physical resemblance to Joseph Ruggles Wilson and Woodrow Wilson still living in the Wilson homestead at Dergalt near Londonderry. This cottage is almost certainly the one in which James Wilson was born, although historical research has failed to establish incontrovertible evidence that this is so,[2] or, for that matter, evidence about the parents of James Wilson.

A printer who learned his trade in Gray's Printing Shop in Strabane, James Wilson worked on the Philadelphia *Aurora,* a Jeffersonian newspaper, from 1807 to 1815. He married a Scotch-Irish lass, Ann Adams, whom he met on the boat to America, in the Fourth Presbyterian Church in Philadelphia on November 1, 1808, and seven sons and three daughters were born to this union. The Wilsons moved to Steubenville, Ohio, in 1815, so that

1. Marion W. Woodrow, editor, *Dr. James Woodrow as Seen by His Friends* (Columbia, S.C.: R. L. Bryan Co., 1909), *passim.*
2. Kenneth Darwin to the author, November 11, 1965. Both the Wilson cottage and Gray's Printing Shop are now National Trust properties, the Wilson family having removed to a residence nearby. For descriptions of both these properties, see *Wilson House* and *Gray's Printing Press* (Belfast: National Trust, 1967).

James Wilson could assume the editorship of the *Western Herald and Steubenville Gazette*. He was active in business and in Ohio politics, serving several times in the General Assembly and as associate judge of the Court of Common Pleas. He died of cholera on October 17, 1850.[3]

Woodrow Wilson was born in the Presbyterian manse in Staunton, Virginia, on December 28 or 29, 1856, and grew up in manses in Augusta, Columbia, and Wilmington. Thus he had, as he once put it, "the unspeakable joy of having been born and bred in a minister's family." It was a family bound together by strong ties of love and dominated by a strong-willed father who valued education along with Christian faith. Young Woodrow grew up on family worship, Bible reading, study of the *Shorter Catechism*, and stories of Scottish Covenanters. As he later said in a speech in London on his sixty-second birthday, "The stern Covenanter tradition that is behind me sends many an echo down the years." Admitted to the membership of the First Presbyterian Church of Columbia on July 5, 1873, he also grew up in the bosom of the church, imbibing unconsciously its traditions and faith. Woodrow Wilson's father, Joseph Ruggles Wilson, was not only a distinguished minister but also one of the founders of the Presbyterian Church in the Confederate States of America, re-named the Presbyterian Church in the United States in 1865, and commonly called the Southern Presbyterian Church. Dr. Wilson was Moderator of the General Assembly of that denomination in 1879 and Permanent Clerk and Stated Clerk of the General Assembly from 1861 to 1898. It is possible that Woodrow Wilson attended the meetings in his father's church in Augusta in April 1861 when the decision was taken to form the Southern Presbyterian Church. In any event, he later became his father's right-hand man in correspondence relating to church business and in preparing the minutes of the General Assembly for publication. Dr. Wilson also edited the Wilmington *North Carolina Presbyterian* in 1876–77, and young Woodrow not only helped to edit the paper but also contributed a series of articles in 1876—the first that he ever published.[4] Church

3. Francis P. Weisenburger, "The Middle Western Antecedents of Woodrow Wilson," *Mississippi Valley Historical Review*, XXIII (December 1936), 375–390; Edwin M. Stark to the author, May 3, 1966.
4. They are printed in Arthur S. Link *et al.*, editors, *The Papers of Woodrow Wilson*, 9 vols. (Princeton, N.J.: Princeton University Press, 1966–), vol. I.

leaders were constantly in the Wilson home, and church affairs were a major subject of family correspondence and discussion.

Woodrow Wilson was inordinately proud of his family inheritance and especially of the fact that he, rather strikingly, reunited in his own person the Scottish and Scotch-Irish stock. He knew his grandfather Thomas Woodrow very well and visited Carlisle several times in efforts to find the manse in which his mother had been born and the church in which his grandfather had preached. He of course never saw his grandfather Wilson. Woodrow Wilson constantly referred in speeches and conversations to his ancestry and often remarked playfully about its manifestations in his own personality. To his Scottish ancestors he attributed his introspection, seriousness, and tendency toward melancholy. To his Irish forebears he attributed his occasional gaiety and love of life. Once, half joking, half serious, he told his students at Bryn Mawr College, "No one who amounts to anything is without some Scotch-Irish blood."

II Woodrow Wilson, Presbyterian

Woodrow Wilson's inheritance, both from Scotland and Northern Ireland, and from his own immediate family on the Wilson and Woodrow sides, laid strong foundations for Christian faith in mature life. "*My* life," he told a friend when he was President of the United States, "would not be worth living if it were not for the driving power of religion, for *faith*, pure and simple. I have seen all my life the arguments against it without ever having been moved by them. . . . There are people who *believe* only so far as they *understand*—that seems to me presumptuous and sets their understanding as the standard of the universe." [5] Wilson was apparently never buffeted by strong winds, much less storms, of doubt. His adult faith found expression, among other ways, in family worship, daily prayer, Bible reading—it has been said that he wore out several Bibles reading them—and, above all, active church membership. He and his family were members, successively, of the Bryn Mawr, Pennsylvania, Presbyterian Church, the First Congregational Church of

5. Arthur S. Link, *Wilson: The New Freedom* (Princeton, N.J.: Princeton University Press, 1956), pp. 64–65.

Middletown, Connecticut, the Second Presbyterian Church of Princeton, and the First Presbyterian Church of that same town. He was ordained a Ruling Elder in 1897 and served on the sessions of both Princeton churches.

Wilson and his wife resumed their relationship with the southern Presbyterian denomination in which they had both been reared by moving their membership to the Central Presbyterian Church when they went to Washington in 1913. It was a small congregation, and Wilson loved its simple service—it took him back, he said, to the days when he was a boy in the South. He attended as regularly as possible until 1919, when illness confined him to his home, and he showed his concern in ways large and small. He also developed a warm friendship with the church's pastor, Dr. James H. Taylor, that lasted until Wilson's death in 1924.

Wilson was one of the most thoughtful and articulate Christians of his day. He spoke with increasing perception and power on subjects ranging from problems of the ministry and Christian education to problems of the rural church in an urbanizing society. He was, additionally, a pulpit preacher of moving eloquence and evangelical fervor. He preached only in the Princeton University Chapel, and all but one of his sermons have remained unpublished to this day. They were among the greatest speeches that he ever delivered and, it might be added, some of the greatest sermons of this century.[6]

Now, having established Wilson's religious credentials, so to speak, let us see how his religious inheritance from the Old World and his own additions to that inheritance influenced Woodrow Wilson as a politician and statesman.

6. The following is an incomplete list of these papers, lectures, and sermons: "Religion and Patriotism," Northfield (Mass.) *Echoes*, IX (July 1902), 217–221; *The Young People and the Church* (Philadelphia: The Sunday School Times Company, 1905); *The Present Task of the Ministry* (Hartford, Conn.: Hartford Seminary Press, 1909); *The Ministry and the Individual* (Chicago: Lakeside Press, 1910); "The Bible and Progress," *The Public Papers of Woodrow Wilson, College and State*, edited by R. S. Baker and W. E. Dodd, 2 vols. (New York: Harper & Brothers, 1925), II, 291–302; address to Trenton Sunday School assembly, October 1, 1911, Trenton *True American*, October 2, 1911; *The Minister and the Community* (New York: Association Press, 1912); "Militant Christianity," address before the Pittsburgh YMCA, October 24, 1914, *The Public Papers of Woodrow Wilson, The New Democracy*, edited by R. S. Baker and W. E. Dodd, 2 vols. (New York: Harper & Brothers, 1926), I, 199–209; address before the Federal Council of the Churches of Christ in America, December 10, 1915, *ibid.*, pp. 429–445; address at his grandfather's church in Carlisle, England, December 29,

III Morality and Politics

It is fairly common knowledge that Woodrow Wilson was an honorable man. His integrity was as considerable as his personal ethics were lofty. Before he entered politics, he had already given abundant evidence of integrity as president of Princeton University in risking serious decline in enrollment by greatly elevating academic standards and refusing to change policies in order to please alumni or potential donors. He was the same kind of man in politics. He was incapable, not only of outright corruption, but also of more subtle and dangerous forms of corruption like acceptance of political support when he knew that strings were attached. For example, he nearly wrecked his chances for the presidential nomination in 1912 by literally telling the publisher William Randolph Hearst, whom he abhorred, to go to hell when Hearst offered to support Wilson's candidacy. He also resisted the most insidious temptation that can corrupt a leader in democracy, that of following policies simply because a majority of people seem to favor them. For example, he refused to yield to public clamor for a march through Germany in the autumn of 1918 and proceeded to negotiate for an end to the World War. And, when a senator warned him that he would be destroyed if he did not yield to public demand, he replied, "So far as my being destroyed is concerned, I am willing if I can serve the country to go into a cellar and read poetry the remainder of my life. I am thinking now only of putting the U.S. into a position of strength and justice." [7] More important, he refused later, in 1919–20, to accept the Lodge reservations to the Versailles Treaty and thereby

---

1918, *The Public Papers of Woodrow Wilson, War and Peace,* edited by R. S. Baker and W. E. Dodd, 2 vols. (New York: Harper & Brothers, 1927), I, 347–348; "The Road away from Revolution," *ibid.,* II, 536–539.

For Wilson's chapel talks and sermons, see the notes of chapel talks on April 5, 1891, November 8, 1896, and May 27, 1900, and of talks before the Philadelphian Society, November 2, 1899, and February 20, 1902, all in the Papers of Woodrow Wilson, Library of Congress, Washington, D.C.; baccalaureate addresses delivered on June 12, 1904, and June 11, 1905, *ibid.; The Free Life* (New York: T. Y. Crowell & Co., 1908), Wilson's baccalaureate address in 1907; and baccalaureate addresses delivered on June 7, 1908, and June 12, 1910, manuscripts in the Princeton University Library, Princeton, N.J.

Extracts from and references to these writings and speeches will be made later in this paper without additional footnote references.

7. George F. Sparks, editor, *A Many-Colored Toga; The Diary of Henry Fountain Ashurst* (Tucson, Ariz.: University of Arizona Press, 1963), p. 84.

made defeat of ratification inevitable, even though many of his friends, party leaders, and leaders of public opinion in the United States begged him to accept ratification on Lodge's terms. He simply could not do something that he believed constituted a rank betrayal of America's plighted word and stultification of his own creation, the League of Nations. There is no need to labor the obvious. Let it suffice to say that Wilson set an example of morality in politics excelled by few other statesmen in the modern world.

It is more important to talk about the wellspring of Wilson's morality. The initial source was the somewhat stern ethics that he inherited from Scottish and Scotch-Irish Presbyterianism by way of his family and church. In Wilson's case, as in many others, adherence to a rigid moral code was sharpened and defined by the Calvinistic emphasis upon universal moral law and belief that men and nations are moral agents accountable to God and transgress that law at the peril of divine judgment. This theme runs so strongly through all of Wilson's political speeches as to give the impression that he **was** simply a moralizer who lived rigidly by rules. His constant reference to what he called principles, and his occasional stubborn adherence to them, also suggest that Wilson had thoroughly imbibed the strong legalistic tradition of Scotland and Ireland.

Wilson **certainly** imbibed this tradition in his youth, but he also developed a much more advanced and sophisticated understanding of Christian ethics. He believed firmly, deeply, in moral law and judgment, but he came to understand them in the light of God's love and reconciling work in Jesus Christ. Moreover, he came to see that morality and character were by-products of obedience and to believe that Christ in the Holy Spirit alone gives men power to live righteously. He said these things many times, but nowhere more eloquently than in his baccalaureate sermon at Princeton University in 1905, as follows:

And so the type and symbol is magnified—Christ, the embodiment of great motive, of divine sympathy, of that perfect justice which seeks into the hearts of men, and that sweet grace of love which takes the sting out of every judgment. . . . He is the embodiment of those things which, not seen, are eternal—the eternal force and grace and majesty, not of character, but of that which lies back of character, obedience to the informing will of the Father of our spirits. . . . [In Christ] we are made known to ourselves—in him because he is God, and God is the end of our philosophy; the revelation of the thought which, if we will but obey it, shall make us free, lifting us to the planes where duty shall seem happiness, obedience liberty, life the fulfilment of the law.

Wilson suffered imperfection and mortality like the rest of men. He had a powerful ego and drive toward dominance. He had a tendency to identify his own solution with the moral law. He often sounded like a moralizer. But it is only fair to look at his entire career while coming to judgment about him. When one does this, the record shows a man committed very deeply to fundamental Christian affirmations about moral law, but also enormously flexible about details and methods, so long as they did not violate what he thought was right. He seems to have broken through the iron shell of Presbyterian legalism and come to an understanding of what is called contextual or relativistic ethics entirely on his own. However that may have been, one cannot truly know Wilson without concluding that here, indeed, was a man who tried to live by faith rather than rules in meeting complex moral problems in everyday life. As he put it in his baccalaureate sermon in 1905:

But the standard? It is easy enough to talk of assessing moral values and of increasing the stock of good in the world, but what is good and what is evil, for us individually and for the world? May we not determine that deep question by our experience, candidly interrogated and interpreted—by the peace, the ardour, the satisfaction our spirits get from our own days and their tasks—by the tonic health we get from one course of action, the restlessness, the bitterness, the disappointment and weariness we get from another? . . . You shall not find happiness without health, and health lies in the constant rectification of the spirit, its love of the truth, its instinctive sincerity, its action without fear and without corruption of motive, its self-sufficing energy and independence. It is God's power in the heart. It is the spirit's consciousness of its immediate connection with his will and purpose. It is his saving health, which must be known among all nations before peace will come and life be widened in all its outlooks.

IV God's Providence and the Lordship of Jesus Christ

Wilson was most heavily indebted to his Scottish and Scotch-Irish forebears in his emphasis upon the sovereignty and majesty of God. He literally stood in awe of the Almighty One.

He was not a prig, and he sometimes used words which some Presbyterians would not approve. But using the Name lightly was to him blasphemy against divine majesty. His daughter, Mrs. Eleanor Wilson McAdoo, has told the present speaker about his fearsome reaction when she once repeated a ditty that took liberties with God's name. This is mentioned merely as illustration of Wilson's consciousness, manifested in numerous other ways, that he stood constantly in the presence of a jealous God. He also inherited a rigorous Sabbatarianism from Scotch-Irish Presbyterianism through his family and church. Like a devout Jew greeting the Sabbath, he revelled in the joy of God's holy day. It was a time for reading, family worship, church attendance, and good works, not for labor or travel. Edith Bolling Wilson told the present speaker about an embarrassing moment in Milan, when Wilson refused to attend an opera at La Scala on a Sunday evening. He went only when told that it would be a religious service.

This jealous God was, in Wilson's view, not only the Lord of individuals but also the Lord of history, ruler of men and nations, who turned all things to His own purpose. "The idea of an all-merciful God," Wilson's brother-in-law, Stockton Axson, once said, "was, I believe, to him, a piece of soft sentimentality." This did perhaps characterize Wilson's earlier understanding of God's sovereignty as it had been influenced by his church's stern Calvinism and that of his professors when he was an undergraduate at Princeton. It was also Joseph Ruggles Wilson's view of God as expressed in his sermons, insofar as one can tell from the few that have survived. But the God that the son came to know through his father in conversation and correspondence was different. To be sure, He was the God of the Old Testament, because Joseph Ruggles Wilson, like most Presbyterians of his time, was not ardently Christological in theology. But in the father's view, God was also tender, loving, and merciful. Woodrow Wilson had shed most of the residue of scholastic, hardened Presbyterianism that remained in his own theology by the early 1900s. By this time he had come to the conviction that men know God truly only through Jesus Christ. God's saving work in history, he believed, is most clearly revealed in his work of reconciliation through Christ who is also the Lord of the Ages.

"The providence of God," Wilson told a Trenton, New Jersey, Sunday School convention in 1911, "is the foundation of affairs." Significantly, in the very next breath he linked providence to revelation, saying·

Only those can guide, and only those can follow, who take this providence of God from the sources where it is authentically interpreted. . . . He alone can rule his own spirit who puts himself under the command of the Spirit of God, revealed in His Son, Jesus Christ, our Saviour. He is the captain of our souls; he is the man from whose suggestions and from whose life comes the light that guideth every man that came into the world.

About the irresistibility of God's providential work, another Calvinistic theme inherited from his forebears, Wilson had the following to say in a famous address on the Bible, delivered in Denver, Colorado, in 1911:

The man whose faith is rooted in the Bible knows that reform cannot be stayed, that the finger of God that moves upon the face of the nations is against every man that plots the nation's downfall or the people's deceit; that these men are simply groping and staggering in their ignorance to a fearful day of judgment; and that whether one generation witnesses it or not the glad day of revelation and of freedom will come in which men will sing by the host of the coming of the Lord in His glory, and all of those will be forgotten—those little, scheming, contemptible creatures that forgot the image of God and tried to frame men according to the image of the evil one.

There was power in faith such as this. For Wilson it provided, when plans were succeeding, the strength and joy that come from conviction that one is doing God's work in the world. It also brought courage and hope in the time of his greatest adversity and sorrow, when the Senate wrecked his work at Versailles and, as he believed, the best hope for peace in the world. "I feel like going to bed and staying there," he told his physician, Dr. Cary T. Grayson, after he had received word that the Senate had rejected the treaty for a second time. But later in the night he asked Dr. Grayson to read the marvelous words of 2 Cor. 4:8-9· "We are troubled on every side, yet not distressed; we are perplexed, but not in despair; persecuted, but not forsaken; cast down, but not destroyed." Then Wilson said, "If I were not a Christian, I think I should go mad, but my faith in God holds me to the belief that He is some way working out His own plans through human perversities and mistakes." [8]

To be sure, faith like this carried obvious dangers, the principal one being the temptation to believe that what the self wants to do is what God commands, and that one's opponents are not only mistaken but also of evil heart and mind. It was a particularly acute danger for a person of Wilson's highly combative personality. He often said that he had inherited this trait from his Scotch-Irish ancestors. He might have added his Presbyterian kinsmen both in the Old World and the New, who were eternally fighting among themselves. In any event, Wilson loved nothing better than an intellectual duel or oratorical contest. He always insisted that he abhorred personal controversy. Perhaps he did, but he was drawn into such fights from time to time, and, once engaged, he could give as well as take. Wilson also became entangled in political controversy because of his deep commitment to fundamental principles. Some of the reasons for this passion for principles may have been personal stubbornness, pride, egotism, and a tendency to identify subjective conclusions with objectively right principles. All these factors certainly contributed to his inflexibility to a varying degree. But they alone do not account for his passionate convictions. He, at any rate, believed that they stemmed from the innermost resources of Christian faith: in other words, that they were given. Wilson, having received them, was as bound by them as anyone else, even more bound by them. They were the imperatives of his life. He could not be false to them without betraying God. Another trait that led Wilson into controversy was his unrelenting will, his absolute determination to accomplish objectives that he believed were right. Once again, his motives were no doubt mixed. His will was fired by pride, the egotistical belief that he knew better than others, and the ambition for fame and glory. But it was fired more often by an urgent, compelling sense of duty and destiny that would not let him go and drove him on and on in spite of insuperable odds. The destiny that he saw for himself was in many respects terrible,

8. Cary T. Grayson, *Woodrow Wilson, An Intimate Memoir* (New York: Holt, Rinehart and Winston, 1960), p. 106.

for in the end it led to his physical destruction. But he believed that he could not turn his back upon it because it was the destiny marked out by the sovereign God of history.

And yet it must be said that all leaders who stand and fight for great causes have to run all these risks. And if Wilson succumbed at times to pride and willful egotism, he never forgot for long that he was a servant of Jesus Christ, and that final judgment belongs to God. As he once said in a reflective moment about men with whom he disagreed, "While we are going to judge with the absolute standard of righteousness, we are going to judge with Christian feeling, being men of a like sort ourselves, suffering the same temptations, having the same weaknesses, knowing the same passions; and while we do not condemn, we are going to seek to say and to live the truth." [9]

V Presbyterianism and an Ordered Political System

Woodrow Wilson knew the polity, laws, and procedures of the Presbyterian Church long before he knew those of his state and nation. Thus it is a temptation, particularly to an admirer and practitioner of the Presbyterian form of government, to say that Wilson was profoundly influenced by the constitutional structure and political ethos of the Presbyterian Church. The influence operated, and operated undoubtedly in a powerful way. The trouble in talking about it is that it was indirect and cannot be seen as precisely, for example, as Walter Bagehot's influence on Wilson's ideas about the proper form of parliamentary organization. But we are not totally in the dark, and I think that we are entitled to say that the experience of growing up in the Presbyterian Church influenced Wilson's more general secular political ideology at least in the following ways·

First, it caused him from his youth to have a passion for orderly representative government, for doing political business in a decent way. There is a story that his first constitution was one that he drafted while a boy in Augusta for a baseball association called the "Lightfoot Club." This may be mythological. The first Wilsonian written constitution that has survived is the one that he drafted in the summer of 1874 for an imaginative "Royal

9. In his address before the Pittsburgh YMCA, October 24, 1914.

United Kingdom Yacht Club." Then followed a constitution for the Liberal Debating Club, which Wilson organized at Princeton in 1877; a new constitution for the Jefferson Literary Society at the University of Virginia in 1880; a new constitution for the Hopkins Literary Society, renamed the Hopkins House of Commons, in 1884; a constitution for the Wesleyan House of Commons at Wesleyan University in 1889; and so on down through the Covenant of the League of Nations. The form of government established by these constitutions varied, but all of them demonstrated Wilson's concern for orderly representative government and for making it work.

Second, Wilson inherited from the Calvinistic tradition its repudiation of the rationale of an ordered society based upon birth or wealth. With Wilson, it was an inherited assumption that God is no respecter of persons and calls whom He will to bear rule in Church and State. This was Calvinism's most important contribution to modern political development. In the case of the United States, it was one of the main causes for the development of what would eventually become equalitarian democracy. In Wilson's own case, it was the foundation stone of an unchanging belief in the inherent capacity of all men, generally speaking, for self-government.

Third, Wilson inherited from Scottish and Scotch-Irish Presbyterianism its basic conservatism along with its fundamental equalitarianism. The most important ingredient of this conservatism was the belief in God's sovereignty over the historical process. Men may propose, but God disposes in the end. The second ingredient was belief in election and what it implies by way of responsibility: hence, emphasis upon education. The third ingredient was belief in original sin. All of mankind's works are infected with imperfection and death. These were all fundamental beliefs with Woodrow Wilson, and they shaped and controlled his thinking about the way historical change occurs, the limited possibilities of human progress, and the unlimited power of God to achieve His ends in history.

VI   Christianity, Social Conscience, and Political Action

The most remarkable thing about Wilson as a political leader was the change that occurred in his thinking about the functions of government. Even more remarkable was the way Wilson's views on government paralleled his thinking about the Christian's duty toward his fellowman.

Wilson grew up during the high tide of individualism in the western world. His political heroes were the English and Scottish devotees of laissez-faire; his economic mentors, British and American classical economists. He inherited from scholastic Presbyterianism, both American and Scottish, its pietism, individualism, and almost total rejection of organized social action either by religious or political communities. He seems to have been oblivious of the great movement to reawaken Christian social conscience that began in an organized way in the 1860s and was beginning to leaven religious thought and life by the 1890s. This was true of Wilson even as late as the first decade of the twentieth century. He gained what little political fame he then enjoyed as a critic of the American reformers. William Jennings Bryan and Theodore Roosevelt, and as an advocate of very cautious solutions of economic and political problems.

Wilson's political thought first began to show signs of changing about 1907, and the first sign of this metamorphosis was a significant shift in his thinking about the role that Christians and the church should play in the world at large. He delivered three major addresses on this subject between 1906 and 1909: "The Minister and the Community," in 1906, and "The Present Task of the Ministry" and "The Ministry and the Individual," both in 1909. They revealed that Wilson had not yet altogether shed his earlier pietism and intense individualism. The church's duty, he said, was to save individual souls. Christ was not a social reformer. As he put it, "Christianity, come what may, must be fundamentally and forever individualistic." The minister should "preach Christianity to men, not to society. He must preach salvation to the individual."

Yet we can see a momentous intellectual ferment clearly reflected in the last two lectures. We find Wilson also saying in 1909 that "If men cannot lift their fellowmen in the process of saving themselves, I do not see that it is very important that they should save themselves. . . . Christianity came into the world to save the world as well as to save individual men, and individual men can afford in conscience to be saved only as part of the process by which the world itself is regenerated."

Wilson's movement into the ranks of advanced reform after he entered politics in 1910 is well known. From the beginning of his political career, he was in the forefront of the fight to overhaul the American political institutional structure. During the first two or three years of his presidency he also fought for fundamental changes in national economic policies. But he was notably reluctant before 1916 to support or even to countenance what might be called advanced social reform, that is, legislation for the protection and welfare of disadvantaged groups, at least when such legislation involved the direct intervention of the federal government in economic and social life.

Wilson crossed his political Rubicon in 1916 by espousing and winning adoption of a series of measures, including the first federal child-labor law, one that put national government squarely into the business of social amelioration for the first time. Moreover, he went on during the presidential campaign of 1916 to describe his vision of the new good society in which government would be ceaselessly at work to restrain exploiters, uplift the downtrodden, protect women and children, and defend the helpless and weak. It was nothing less than a vision of the modern welfare state. Again, the significant fact about his vision was its origin, at least in part, in Wilson's Christian social conscience. The awakening, if such it may be called, was caused by Wilson's own broadening political experiences and the social gospel, which was then running at high tide in American Protestantism. It was derived only very indirectly from his more particular Presbyterian inheritance.

VII   America's Mission to the World as Ministry

Woodrow Wilson's whole thinking about foreign policy was shaped by his concept of ministry and his belief in divine providence. Ministry, as he said many times, is Christ's ministry of unselfish service to individuals, societies, and nations. He believed that God had created the United States out of diverse peoples for a specific, eschatological role in history—as one scholar has written, "to realize an ideal of liberty, provide a model of democracy, vindicate moral principles, give examples of action and ideals of government and righteousness to an interdependent world, uphold the rights of man, work for humanity and the happiness of men everywhere, lead the thinking of the world, promote peace—in sum, to serve mankind and progress." [10] Hence foreign policy should not be used for material ends, not even defined in terms of material interests. America's mission in the world was not to attain wealth and power, but to fulfill God's plan by unselfish service to mankind.

These beliefs were all, in their fundamentals, the inheritance of an activistic Calvinism brought to the New World by English Puritans and Scottish and Scotch-Irish Presbyterians. They were also greatly affected by the ecumenical, worldwide missionary movement of the early twentieth century in which Wilson participated as a member of the Presbyterian Church and of the World Student Movement of the YMCA. Wilson came to the presidency in 1913, as has often been noted, with no training and very little interest in the practical details of foreign affairs and diplomacy. Naturally, inevitably, he simply adopted all his assumptions about the nature of the church's worldwide ministry as the controlling assumptions of his foreign policy. And during his first two years in the White House, he and his first Secretary of State, William Jennings Bryan, another Presbyterian elder who shared Wilson's motivation, put into force what has been called "missionary diplomacy" aimed at helping underdeveloped countries work toward domestic order and democracy.

Wilson soon discovered that a diplomacy of helpfulness was immensely difficult, troublesome, and dangerous. He soon learned that it was not always possible to impose even altruistic solutions on other countries. Experience rapidly dispelled Wilson's naïveté. The hopeful, eager diplomatist became the Christian realist, doing what he could in the knowledge that ideal solutions were not always possible. But Wilson's basic motivation and objectives never changed. He struggled to avoid involvement in the First World War in part because he ardently desired to use American power for a noble purpose: mediation of the conflict. He accepted belligerency in 1917 in large part because he then believed that American participation was now the surest if not the only way to lasting peace. He created the League of Nations in part because he thought that it would be the instrument of America's redemp-

---

10. Harley Notter, *The Origins of the Foreign Policy of Woodrow Wilson* (Baltimore: The Johns Hopkins Press, 1937), p. 653.

tive work in the world. And he spent his health and strength in trying to convince Americans that God had laid the burdens of leadership for peace on them. As he said when he presented the Versailles Treaty to the Senate on July 10, 1919:

The stage is set, the destiny disclosed. It has come about by no plan of our conceiving, but by the hand of God who led us into this way. We cannot turn back. We can only go forward, with lifted eyes and freshened spirit, to follow the vision. It was of this that we dreamed at our birth. America shall in truth show the way. The light streams upon the path ahead, and nowhere else.[11]

This paper began with Woodrow Wilson's Scottish and Scotch-Irish inheritance of family and religious traditions. It explored Wilson's own Christian faith and tried to demonstrate that it stemmed essentially from Calvinistic, Presbyterian formulations and affirmations and was the source and motivation of all his thinking about ethics, political and social action, and America's role in the world at large. This discussion has also tried to show how developments, or new emphases, in American Presbyterianism and Protestantism and his own broadening experiences led Wilson into new understanding of the meaning of Christian faith in changing circumstances. If there be any justification for such a lecture to such an audience as this one, it is that in Woodrow Wilson we see almost perfectly revealed the signal Scottish and Scotch-Irish legacy to American society, culture, and politics.

11. *The Public Papers of Woodrow Wilson, War and Peace*, I, 551–552.

Woodrow Wilson:
The American as Southerner

WOODROW Wilson was claimed by southerners as one of their own from the beginning of his career as a publicist and scholar. "Mr. Woodrow Wilson . . .," the Augusta, Georgia, *Chronicle and Constitutionalist* declared in early 1885, "has distinguished himself already by the production of a volume entitled 'Congressional Government.' . . . Mr. Wilson is the son of the Rev. Joseph R. Wilson, who was once the honored pastor of the Presbyterian Church in this city." [1]

"We are glad," said the Wilmington, North Carolina, *Morning Star* at the same time, "that the South has such a student of history and of politics, and that he has been able to present to his countrymen such a capital discussion of the American system." [2]

These were only two of a large number of southern voices that greeted Wilson's entry on the stage of affairs in 1885. That chorus, hailing Wilson the Southerner, swelled in volume with each successive triumph and achievement. Wake Forest College in 1887 and Tulane University in 1898 were the first of many

This essay was the presidential address to the Southern Historical Association in Washington on October 30, 1969. It appeared in *The Journal of Southern History*, XXXVI (February 1970), 3–17, and is printed here by permission of the Managing Editor.
    1. Augusta *Chronicle and Constitutionalist*, March 15, 1885.
    2. Wilmington *Morning Star*, March 12, 1885.

institutions in the United States and Europe to give Wilson honorary degrees. In the first extensive biographical sketch of Wilson ever published, John Bell Henneman of the University of Tennessee—better known for his later career as editor of the *Sewanee Review*—hailed Wilson as a southern scholar and man of letters.[3] When the editors of the *Library of Southern Literature* created their pantheon of regional luminaries, they included Wilson, printing a biographical sketch of him and his bibliography along with two of his essays.[4] Three times he was offered the chairmanship of the faculty of the University of Virginia. And when Princeton University chose Wilson as its thirteenth president in 1902, southern newspapers reacted with lively regional pride. Wilson, the Richmond *Times* boasted, "is a Virginian through and through." [5] He was, other editors said, an Augusta boy, a southern man, and bound to Georgia by tender ties of family.[6] "To Virginia and to the South," the Baltimore *American* added, "the appointment of Dr. Wilson is significant as well as important. It demonstrates the obliteration of sectionalism and the mark which men of Southern birth are making in the North." [7]

It is therefore hardly surprising that southern editors, educators, and public leaders should have been in the vanguard of the movement to make Woodrow Wilson President of the United States. This was true as early as 1906, when George Harvey, editor of *Harper's Weekly*, sent up his first trial balloon by proposing Wilson for the Presidency in a speech before the Lotos Club in New York.[8] One enthusiastic Georgian expressed the opinions of many southerners when he declared that Wilson would "find a solid South behind him" if he made a fight for the Democratic presidential nomination.[9]

3. "X," "The Work of a Southern Scholar," *Sewanee Review*, III (February 1895), 172–188.

4. Edwin A. Alderman *et al.*, editors, *Library of Southern Literature*, 17 vols. (New Orleans, Atlanta, and Dallas: The Martin & Hoyt Co., 1907–1923), XIII, 5881–5901; XVI, 60.

5. Richmond *Times*, June 11, 1902.

6. Augusta *Chronicle*, June 11, 1902; Nashville *American*, June 11, 1902; Atlanta *Constitution*, June 11, 1902.

7. Baltimore *American*, June 13, 1902. For similar comment, see the Charlotte *Daily Observer*, June 12, 1902.

8. Arthur S. Link, *Wilson: The Road to the White House* (Princeton, N. J.: Princeton University Press, 1947), pp. 98–99.

9. Columbus (Ga.) *Ledger*, cited in *Harper's Weekly*, L (May 19, 1906), 716.

However, these were mere harbingers of the regional support that Wilson would evoke when he did make a serious and, of course, successful bid for the Presidency in 1911 and 1912. Wilson, proclaimed a Rome, Georgia, editor, was *"of southern blood, of southern bone and of southern grit."* [10] Another editor emphasized that Ellen Axson Wilson was a native of Georgia and that two of the three Wilson daughters had been born in that state.[11] Indeed, some of Wilson's editorial advocates went so far as to claim that he was the only true southern candidate in 1912, because his chief rival in the South, Oscar W. Underwood of Alabama, was, as one editor said accusingly, "really a full-fledged Yankee, . . . the son of a Yankee soldier, the citizen of that city of the South [Birmingham] owned by Yankees." [12]

It would seem redundant to examine Wilson's credentials as a southerner, so self-validating do they appear at superficial glance and so unanimous have been his biographers in agreeing that the South had first claim to him by birth, rearing, and ideology. The facts of the case, it would appear, are too obvious to admit of any other conclusion.

There is the indisputable fact that Wilson was born in Staunton, Virginia, and reared in Presbyterian manses in Augusta, Georgia, Columbia, South Carolina, and Wilmington, North Carolina. His father, the Reverend Dr. Joseph Ruggles Wilson, was an ardent defender of slavery on biblical grounds. One of his sermons was so fervid in defense of that institution that his congregation ordered it printed.[13] Although of midwestern birth and northern education, Dr. Wilson made his decision in 1861 to go with the Confederacy even though it meant ostracism then and ever afterward by most of his ardently pro-Union family. Woodrow Wilson's first memories were of the Civil War—of Lincoln's election, of the formation of the Presbyterian Church in the Confederate States of America in his father's church in Augusta, of wounded Confederate soldiers and Union prisoners, and of the terror that might strike while Sherman marched north-

10. Rome (Ga.) *Tribune-Herald*, quoted in the Atlanta *Journal*, March 16, 1912.
11. Atlanta *Journal*, March 24, 1912.
12. Claxton (Ga.) *News*, quoted by the Montgomery *Advertiser*, March 30, 1912.
13. Joseph R. Wilson, *Mutual Relation of Masters and Slaves as Taught in the Bible. A Discourse Preached in the First Presbyterian Church, Augusta, Georgia, on Sabbath Morning, Jan. 6, 1861* (Augusta: Steam Press of Chronicle and Sentinel, 1861).

ward from Savannah. Moving to Columbia in 1870, he could see still vivid reminders of Sherman's wrath. At one time soon after the war, Wilson the boy looked upon the face of Lee.

Other facts of Woodrow Wilson's biography constitute an impressive argument in favor of his southernness. As is well known, he was partially educated in the former Confederacy, in private schools in Augusta and Columbia and at Davidson College and the University of Virginia. He enjoyed wide regional contacts through his father, who was Stated Clerk of the General Assembly of the Southern Presbyterian Church all through his son's youth and early manhood. Woodrow Wilson extended these contacts by his marriage in 1885 to Ellen Louise Axson of Rome, Georgia, and Savannah, for Miss Axson came from distinguished ministerial families on both sides and was, besides, related to the great Benjamin M. Palmer and a close friend of the family of the equally great James H. Thornwell.

Piling evidence upon evidence, as it would be easy to do, would only confirm what seem to be well-known facts proving beyond cavil that Woodrow Wilson was a southerner.

To engage in such an exercise, however, would be to indulge in the risky practice, not altogether unknown among historians, of leaping to dubious conclusions on a basis of seemingly obvious evidence. The truth of the matter under discussion lies elsewhere. During his youth and early manhood, when his political opinions and ideology were being formed, Woodrow Wilson not only failed to think and act like a southerner but, in his strident affirmation of American nationalism and condemnation of sectionalism, indeed went far toward repudiating identification with the South.

The first sign of this repudiation was Wilson's decision to withdraw from Davidson College in 1874, after a successful freshman year at that institution, and to go instead to Princeton, a decision made possible because of his father's enhanced fortunes after his move in June 1874 from a professorship at the Columbia Theological Seminary to the pulpit of the First Presbyterian Church of Wilmington. Now that it was possible for him to do so, Woodrow Wilson chose to go to a national instead of what was then a provincial southern college. It might not be amiss to say that it was one of the two or three most important decisions of his early life.

Southerners were back at Princeton in large numbers when

Wilson went there in 1875. He made many lifelong friends during the next four years, but not a single one of them came from the former Confederacy. More impressive is the evidence that we have about Wilson's undergraduate convictions, interests, and reactions. He could dismiss Professor Henry Clay Cameron, a professional southerner, in his diary with the contemptuous remark that the professor of Greek at Princeton was a *"jackass* on the southern question." [14] Wilson was deeply concerned about the election of 1876, but only because the Democratic candidate, Samuel J. Tilden, was a reformer and advocate of low tariffs, not because the outcome of the election might have any special significance for the South. Not a single one of Wilson's undergraduate heroes was a southerner. He published essays on two great builders of empire, William Pitt and Bismarck.[15] As a freshman, Wilson copied a long section on the glories of the American nation into his commonplace book, "Index Rerum." [16] As a sophomore, he prepared a speech on the Union in which he condemned sectionalism, acclaimed the "noble Webster," and concluded by calling on the people of the North and South to join hands "in their great progress with the world and still grander make it 'Liberty and union, now and forever, one and inseparable.' " [17] As a senior, he began an essay on Daniel Webster, comparing the Massachusetts nationalist to his English hero, Pitt.[18] As a law student at the University of Virginia in 1880, he could say that he rejoiced "in the failure of the Confederacy" and that "the damnable cruelty and folly of reconstruction was to be preferred to helpless independence" for the southern states.[19]

"Ever since I have had independent judgments of my own," Wilson wrote, years later, to the Harvard historian Albert Bushnell Hart, "I have been a Federalist (!)" [20] Wilson did not mean that he was a Hamiltonian in politics or economic philosophy. He

14. Arthur S. Link *et al.*, editors, *The Papers of Woodrow Wilson,* 9 vols. (Princeton, N.J.: Princeton University Press, 1966–), I, 191–192; hereinafter cited as *Papers of Woodrow Wilson.*
15. "Prince Bismarck," *Nassau Literary Magazine,* XXXIII (November 1877), 118–127; "William Earl Chatham," *ibid.,* XXXIV (October 1878), 99–105.
16. *Papers of Woodrow Wilson,* I, 117–118.
17. *Ibid.,* pp. 226–228.
18. *Ibid.,* pp. 396–397.
19. *Ibid.,* pp. 618–619.
20. Wilson to Hart, June 3, 1889, *ibid.,* VI, 243.

meant simply what the record about his formative years emphasizes: that he had been a nationalist in his attitude toward the Union and the Constitution ever since he was an undergraduate. One is tempted, indeed, to push these convictions back to what was probably their original source, Wilson's father. Although he supported the Confederate war effort with all outward sincerity, Dr. Wilson was probably one of the group about whom Kenneth M. Stampp has recently written—southerners who were at heart American nationalists during the war and in fact desired the victory of the Union cause.[21] In any event, in the hundreds of letters that Dr. Wilson later wrote to his son, there is not a single instance of repining for the Lost Cause and there is much evidence that Dr. Wilson could not abide unreconstructed rebels.

After withdrawing from the University of Virginia in 1880, Woodrow Wilson spent the next three and a half years growing up in the New South. By and large, he was not entranced by what he saw about him. Wilmington, where he lived while completing his study of law, bored him exceedingly. Atlanta, where he tried to practice law in 1882 and 1883, he found positively revolting on account of its lack of cultural life, crass materialism, and the low state of the ethics of its lawyers.[22] His moral sense was offended by Georgia's convict lease system.[23] He was disgusted by the Georgia legislature's neglect of education and its willingness to endorse the Blair bill for federal aid to education as a means of having public schools without paying for them.[24] Generally speaking, he was appalled and depressed by the South's cultural and educational backwardness.[25]

Wilson's passions during these formative years at Princeton and in the New South were British constitutional history and practices and American national politics, problems, and issues. "Cabinet Government in the United States," [26] written while he was a senior at Princeton, was the first evidence in print of Wil-

---

21. Kenneth M. Stampp, *The Southern Road to Appomattox*, Cotton Memorial Papers, No. 4 (El Paso: Texas Western Press, 1969).

22. For example, Wilson to Hiram Woods, Jr., May 10, 1883; Wilson to R. H. Dabney, May 11, 1883; Wilson to Robert Bridges, May 13, 1883, *Papers of Woodrow Wilson*, II, 348–359.

23. Wilson, "Convict Labor in Georgia," *ibid.* pp. 306–311.

24. Wilson to R. Bridges, c. February 28, 1886, *ibid.*, V, 128n.

25. See, for example, his "Culture and Education at the South," *Papers of Woodrow Wilson*, II, 326–332.

26. *International Review*, VII (August 1879), 146–163.

son's fascination with the problem of responsible leadership in a democratic polity. His first book-length essay, "Government by Debate," [27] written in Wilmington and Atlanta, adumbrated the same problem while giving much attention to strictly national issues. His first book, *Congressional Government* (1885), was an analysis of the irresponsibility of national government by congressional committees. At no time during these important years did Wilson ever evidence any lively interest in the South or in southern problems, except as a usually harsh critic of contemporary southern institutions and life.

Woodrow Wilson matured, or, to use one of his favorite phrases, came to himself between 1883 and 1895. During these years, he did graduate work at the Johns Hopkins University; taught at Bryn Mawr College, Wesleyan University, and Princeton; and published numerous articles and three books in addition to *Congressional Government: The State*, in 1889; and *Division and Reunion* and *An Old Master and Other Political Essays*, in 1893. In this same period, Wilson also did his most important scholarly work: the reading and research for his three-year course on administration at Johns Hopkins, beginning in 1888, and for his undergraduate courses at Princeton, beginning in 1890, on jurisprudence, public law, the history of law, the history of English common law, and American constitutional law.

Ellen Axson Wilson said, during this period, after Wilson had protested one time too many that he loved the South,[28] that her husband was not a southerner in the conventional meaning of that word but was rather an American of southern birth, free of provincialism of any sort.[29] But this does not state the case entirely. It is important to add that Wilson also still sought, often quite pointedly, to deny any particular identification with the South. He assiduously worked to rid his own and Ellen Axson's speech of any vestiges of a southern accent.[30] On every occasion when the matter came up, he declared that, although sympathetic to the South, he was not a southerner, but was rather a son of

27. *Papers of Woodrow Wilson*, II, 159–275.
28. Wilson to Ellen A. Wilson, May 16, 1886, *ibid.*, V, 232.
29. Ellen A. Wilson to Wilson, May 22, 1886, *ibid.*, pp. 250–251.
30. Wilson to Ellen A. Axson, February 8, 17, 1885, *ibid.*, IV, 224, 263–264.

midwestern parents of Scotch-Irish ancestry who was living or had happened to live in the South.[31]

That southern birth, rearing, and partial education left slight marks on Wilson in his maturity can be seen when we apply a few necessarily crude tests of southernness to his thinking about certain issues during the period 1883–1895.

1. *The nature of the Union.* As a student under Stephen O. Southall at the University of Virginia Law School, Wilson heard enunciated the pure doctrines of Calhoun concerning the nature of the Union under the Constitution. The Union, Southall taught, was the creature of the people of the several states, not of the people of some nonexistent nation, and the Constitution was a compact among the people of the several states.[32]

To a limited degree, Wilson assimilated and expounded this traditional southern view. For example, in a review of John W. Burgess, *Political Science and Comparative Constitutional Law,* in 1891, Wilson stoutly defended the compact theory.[33] However, in the same review, and more extensively in *Division and Reunion,* Wilson argued that the tide of nationalism which swept across the North and West had changed the nature of the Union at the very time that the compact view was becoming sectionalized in the South. History, Wilson said over and over, had made the United States a nation by 1860. This conclusion had ripened into deep conviction by 1893. "I hold most decisively, therefore," he wrote in that year,

that the right of secession did not exist at the time the South sought to exercise that right, whatever might have been the rights of a state in the first years of the century. I hold that a Government is what its people and its history make it and that our Government had been made national and indissoluble long before 1861. . . . The northern soldiers were preventing a fatal revolution. They need no further justification than that.[34]

Wilson set forth his mature view of the nature of the Union

31. For example, Wilson to H. E. Scudder, March 4, 1885, *ibid.,* p. 329; Wilson to A. B. Hart, June 3, 1889, *ibid.,* VI, 243.

32. See Wilson's notes on Southall's lecture on the origin and nature of the Union, *ibid.,* I, 621–623.

33. *Atlantic Monthly,* LXVII (May 1891), 694–699.

34. Transcript of Wilson to W. H. Bartlett, May 3, 1893, *Papers of Woodrow Wilson,* VIII, 206.

in the late 1880s most fully in *The State*. It might appear at first
glance that to some degree he had been influenced by southern
traditions in his strong emphasis upon the *federal* character of the
Union and the reserved powers of the states.[35] In actual fact, Wilson
was here only following the two major works of Judge Thomas
M. Cooley, the leading American constitutional authority of the
latter part of the nineteenth century, *The General Principles of Constitutional Law in the United States of America* and *A Treatise on the
Constitutional Limitations Which Rest upon the Legislative Power of the
States of the American Union*. It is more important to note that in
all his writings Wilson agreed with Cooley in affirming that the
war had settled, once and for all, the debate over the ultimate
supremacy of the federal government.

2. *Attitudes toward the Negro.* Wilson is supposed to have been
a southerner most markedly in his attitudes toward the Negro.
However, if he was a southerner in this regard, he belonged to
that tiny minority who were in advance even of the groups whom
Guion Griffis Johnson has called progressionists and paternalists.[36]
As early as 1881, we find Wilson writing hopefully about the
development of a class of sturdy, independent Negro landowners
in the South, advocating compulsory education for Negroes who
did not want to go to school, and applauding independent Negro
political action.[37] Whatever youthful doubts Wilson may have had
about the wisdom of the Fifteenth Amendment and of universal
male suffrage were clearly gone by the time—1885—that he wrote
his first general treatise on democratic government.[38] In the following year, we hear him saying that government had to be responsive
to the desires not only of Americans of old stocks, "but also of
Irishmen, of Germans, of negroes."[39] Ten years later, in his lectures on city government at Johns Hopkins, Wilson would say
that Negroes and the Irish had the best paved streets in Princeton
because they knew how to protect their interests through intelli-

35. *The State: Elements of Historical and Practical Politics* (Boston: D. C. Heath & Co.,
1889), pp. 480–488.
36. "The Ideology of White Supremacy, 1876–1910," in Fletcher M. Green, editor,
Essays in Southern History (Chapel Hill: University of North Carolina Press, 1949), pp. 124–156.
37. "The Politics and the Industries of the New South," *Papers of Woodrow Wilson*,
II, 53–54.
38. "The Modern Democratic State," *ibid.*, V, 61–92.
39. "The Study of Administration," *ibid.*, pp. 369–370.

gent use of the ballot and that it was a good thing for the town that they, rather than the propertied classes, controlled elections.[40]

This is not to argue that Wilson during this period was an ardent champion of civil and political rights for the Negro. It is only to say that he held views on the status of the Negro that would have been considered very advanced in the South at this time and that he absorbed these views, not from the South, but from the nonsouthern academic environment in which he matured.

3. *Attitudes toward government.* Woodrow Wilson as a mature political scientist derived all his attitudes toward government and the role that it should play from his professors at Johns Hopkins, notably Herbert Baxter Adams and Richard T. Ely, and also from the modern positivistic German school of political scientists and economists whose works he read in large numbers. It is not demonstrable that Wilson derived any part of his thinking about political economy from clearly recognizable southern traditions. For example, Wilson and the political apologists of the New South were worlds apart in political philosophy.

To be sure, from his undergraduate days Wilson was a devotee of free trade or low tariffs. However, he derived this philosophy—for such it was—not from the South, but from his English exemplars, Richard Cobden, John Bright, and William E. Gladstone, and from two of his American heroes, Samuel J. Tilden and Grover Cleveland.

As for general thinking about governmental policy, it is no exaggeration to say that Wilson was a principal agent in catalyzing the ferment that would explode into the urban progressive movement of the 1890s. His textbook, *The State,* was widely used and had a strong influence on the generation coming into political leadership. It ended with a heavy attack against individualism, laissez faire, and Social Darwinism, and it listed a wide number of what Wilson called the "ministrant functions" of the modern state.[41] It was not the kind of argument that one would have expected from a man imbued with southern political traditions.

Wilson went through something of a crisis of political identity under the impact of the Populist and labor upheavals of 1892–1893. Before this time, he had counted himself a disciple of Walter

40. Baltimore *News,* February 29, 1896.
41. *The State,* pp. 639–640.

Bagehot, because he shared Bagehot's interest in hardheaded analysis of political institutions and the practical workings of government. Before 1893, also, Wilson had demonstrated a growing faith in majoritarian democracy and the inevitability of progress.[42]

However, under the impact of the seemingly cataclysmic events of 1892–1893, Wilson turned to the conservative Edmund Burke to find political principles to guide himself and the nation through the troubled seas. He also prepared his first lecture on the great Anglo-Irishman at this time. After reading lectures from the Burkeian scriptures, Wilson proceeded in this lecture to preach his own sermon to the American people. On all sides, he said, there are cries for change, but to innovate is not necessarily to reform. Progressive, constructive change has to come, but it must be expedient, that is, prudent because based upon tradition and consonant with prevailing public habit. America in the 1890s, like England a century before, has to be made immune to the "radically evil and corrupting" libertarian theories that had found their fullest application in the French Revolution. The state exists primarily to establish justice, not to maintain liberty. Above all, order is absolutely indispensable to progress of any sort.[43] There would be numerous echoes of this message, repeated warnings against popular excesses and doctrinaire socialism, along with emphases upon the need for order, obedience, and expediency in Wilson's addresses and writings all the way to 1908.

The *sturm und drang* of the mid-nineties also caused Wilson for the first time to search for personal roots in order to find his own identification with the American past. Perhaps the search was also an incidence of approaching middle age, a time when individuals often begin to look backward to family origins and boyhood associations in order to secure their personal identity. With Wilson, the search might, additionally, have grown out of his study of the sources of early American history that he began in 1893 in preparation for a general history of the United States. Whatever the cause, Wilson discovered that he was a southerner and a Virginian.

42. Expressed most eloquently in his lecture, "Democracy" (1891), printed in *Papers of Woodrow Wilson*, VII, 345–368.
43. See the Editorial Note, "Wilson's First Lecture on Burke," and Wilson's lecture, "Edmund Burke: The Man and His Times," *ibid.*, VIII, 313–343.

He announced his new identity and made clear the significance of his discovery in an address to the alumni of the University
of Virginia in Charlottesville on June 12, 1895. "It was from this
place that I set out, upon such a journey as I have made these
fifteen years; and hither I come again, as if to round out a stage
of my life, make report of the past, and take orders for the future,"
Wilson began. He continued· "It is thus a man assures himself
of his identity, and learns his spirit cannot grow old; by returning
to the places of his youth and inspiration—and recognizing his
home again." What made the South home for him, Wilson continued, was the power of steadfast conviction that dwelled in the
region. The South, alone among all the sections, had been left
with her English stock unspoiled by immigration. Southerners
were a people preserved apart "to recall the nation to its ideals,
and to its common purpose for the future." Southerners had been
called rebels for many years. Would it not be a happy revenge
if they should yet save the nation through their conservatism and
true understanding of liberty?[44]

Wilson later often reaffirmed his southernness, but at no time
more poignantly than in an address on Robert E. Lee at the University of North Carolina in 1909. "It is," he said,

all very well to talk of detachment of view, and of the effort to be
national in spirit and in purpose, but a boy never gets over his boyhood,
and never can change those subtle influences which have become a part
of him, that were bred in him when he was a child. So I am obliged
to say again and again that the only place in the country, the only place
in the world, where nothing has to be explained to me is the South.[45]

Self-discovery of his regional identity enabled Wilson henceforth to stand foursquare both as a southerner and an American,
indeed all the more confidently as an American now that he had
given up the struggle to adhere to an abstract nationalism and
accepted the truth—or so it seemed to him—that in a country as
large as the United States one can love his country only by first
loving the region and people with whom he identifies historically

44. University of Virginia *Alumni Bulletin,* II (July 1895), 53–55; Richmond *Dispatch,*
June 13, 1895.
45. *Robert E. Lee: An Interpretation* (Chapel Hill: University of North Carolina Press,
1924), p. v.

and emotionally. He adverted to the matter in a talk to the Southern Society of New York on December 9, 1903. The "real question, after all," he said, "is nationality." Southerners could make their greatest contribution to the country by retaining their unique individuality; and retention of certain prejudices and old habits of thought was not too large a price to pay for the preservation of regional identity.[46]

Given his activistic disposition, it was almost inevitable with Woodrow Wilson that the urge to action should follow new self-understanding. His role, as he now saw it, was nothing less than that of a publicist and historian who would help to reconcile the sections and unite the country by bringing the South back into the mainstream of American historical traditions on terms of honor.

For Wilson personally, this meant an ability to accept southern history without quarreling with it or feeling any shame about it whatsoever. As he told the American Historical Association in 1896, there was nothing, absolutely nothing, for which to apologize in the history of the South.[47] It was in this conviction that he ringingly affirmed in his *History of the American People* (1902), and most particularly in a chapter in the seventh volume of *The Cambridge Modern History,* the interpretation that he had advanced briefly in *Division and Reunion* in 1893—that southerners had seceded mainly to protect their fundamental right to self-government and because they sincerely believed that the Constitution was a dissoluble compact among the states. Going further, Wilson finally accepted the inevitability of the nation's great tragedy and could speak of his region's part in it with unalloyed pride. The southern people, he said in his address on Lee, had cherished the old conception of the Union. "Even a man who saw the end from the beginning," he went on,

should, in my conception as a Southerner, have voted for spending his people's blood and his own, rather than pursue the weak course of expediency. There is here no mere device, no regard to the immediate future. What has been the result?—ask yourself that. It has been that the South has retained her best asset, her self-respect.[48]

46. New York *Times,* December 10, 1903.
47. American Historical Association, *Annual Report, 1896* (Washington: Government Printing Office, 1897), p. 295.
48. *Robert E. Lee: An Interpretation,* pp. 28–29.

All the while, Wilson was earning what ought to be regarded as a secure position in the then burgeoning group of historians of the United States known later as the nationalist school. While interpreting and in one sense defending the generation of southerners who had attempted to destroy the Union, Wilson at the same time took his stand with other members of his school in hailing the victory of the North for preserving the Union and abolishing slavery.

For example, as early as 1898, in an address in the former capital of the Confederacy, Wilson said that the South in seceding had been right from her point of view. However, he went on, the North in resisting secession had been right from her own and the historical point of view. The conflict of ideas that resulted in the Civil War had to be fought out in the court of Mars; and after the conflict was ended and the bitterness of sectional strife had subsided, the country emerged with a stronger national life permeating all sections and all parties.[49] This was his consistent interpretation in all his historical writing. Nowhere did he state this interpretation more succinctly and eloquently than in the concluding paragraph of his chapter in *The Cambridge Modern History:*

For the whole country it [the Civil War] was to be the bitterest of all ordeals, an agony of struggle and a decision by blood; but for one party it was to be a war of hope. Should the South win, she must also lose—must lose her place in the great Union which she had loved and fostered, and must in gaining independence destroy a nation. Should the North win, she would confirm a great hope and expectation, establish the Union, unify it in institutions, free it from interior contradictions of life and principle, set it in the way of consistent growth and unembarrassed greatness. The South fought for a principle, as the North did: it was this that was to give the war dignity, and supply the tragedy with a double motive. But the principle for which the South fought meant standstill in the midst of change; it was conservative, not creative; it was against drift and destiny. . . . Overwhelming material superiority, it turned out, was with the North; but she had also another and greater

---

49. Address at Richmond College (now the University of Richmond), October 31, 1898, Richmond *Times*, November 1, 1898.

advantage: she was to fight for the Union and for the abiding peace, concord, and strength of a great nation.[50]

About slavery, Wilson could write as early as 1897 in the *Atlantic Monthly* that the peculiar institution had had to go, and by a heroic remedy; that the slavery controversy had been a mere episode in national development; and that the abolition of slavery had removed the chief barrier to homogeneous national life.[51] In the passage from *The Cambridge Modern History* just cited, Wilson added that the South, in fighting for slavery, was trying to protect "an impossible institution and a belated order of society; it withstood a creative and imperial idea, the idea of a united people and a single law of freedom."

To cite a final example, in his address on Lee, Wilson could proclaim, as he put it, "this delightful thing," that there were no sections in the United States any more and that the future lay with men who eschewed parochialism and devoted themselves to national thinking and the solution of the problems of national life.[52]

It would be risky indeed to try to establish any connection between Wilson's self-identification as a southerner with the development of his political thinking and policy. However, it says a great deal about him personally that, once he began to play something of a role in politics, Wilson spoke most often as a southerner to fellow southerners. He chose the occasion of an address to the third annual dinner of the Society of the Virginians of New York on November 29, 1904, to deliver his first public pronouncement as a potential political leader. The South, he said, had an opportunity to perform a great national service by demanding the expulsion of Populists and Bryanites, "contemptuous alike of principle and of experience," from the Democratic party. "The country, as it moves forward in its great material progress," Wilson concluded, "needs and will tolerate no party of discontent or radical experiment; but it does need a party of conservative reform, acting in the spirit of ancient institutions." [53] He would repeat the theme of the need for conservative reform in addresses to

50. A. W. Ward *et al.*, editors, *The Cambridge Modern History*, 13 vols. (New York and London: Cambridge University Press, 1903–1912), VII, 442.
51. "The Making of the Nation," *Atlantic Monthly*, LXXX (July 1897), 3–4, 9.
52. *Robert E. Lee: An Interpretation*, pp. 38–39.
53. New York *Sun*, November 30, 1904.

the Southern Society of New York in 1906 and to the South Carolina Society of New York in 1907.[54]

When in 1907 and 1908 Wilson began his metamorphosis from a conservative into a progressive, he signaled the change in addresses at the Jamestown Exposition on July 4, 1907,[55] and to the Southern Society of New York on December 9, 1908.[56] When he opened his campaign for the Democratic presidential nomination in 1911, he went first to the South and campaigned hardest for support in that region during the following year.[57] Finally, when Wilson enunciated most aggressively the rationale for his progressivism, he did so in an address before the General Assembly of Virginia and the City Council of Richmond on February 1, 1912. He had come home like a boy, he said, to talk to neighbors and take his stand on the Virginia Bill of Rights. In so doing, he added, he had "native soil" under his feet, "soil more fertile for the growth of liberty than any soil that can be compounded."[58]

This ends our account of Woodrow Wilson's odyssey to the watershed year of 1912. Ahead of him still lay the best-known and most constructive part of his career, when as President of the United States he would bring the South back completely into the mainstream of national politics and when, because of his background and regional self-identification, he would inaugurate national policies that were responsive to the aspirations and needs of all sections, not merely of the Northeast. The dramatic and stirring events of the presidential period are beyond the scope of this modest account. However, in thinking about them one is reminded of Ellen Axson Wilson's remarkable prophecy in her letter to her husband of May 22, 1886, to which we referred earlier. "I *do* believe," she wrote then, "you love the South, darling—that

54. Address before the Southern Society, December 14, 1906, MS in the Woodrow Wilson Collection, Princeton University Library, Princeton, N.J.; address before the South Carolina Society, March 18, 1907, New York *Times*, March 10, 1907.

55. "The Author and Signers of the Declaration of Independence," *North American Review*, CLXXXVI (September 1907), 22–33.

56. "Conservatism, True and False," *Princeton Alumni Weekly*, IX (December 16, 1908), 185–189.

57. Arthur S. Link, *Wilson: The Road to the White House, passim*; Link, "The South and the Democratic Campaign of 1910–1912" (Ph.D. dissertation, University of North Carolina, 1945).

58. Ray Stannard Baker and William E. Dodd, editors, *The Public Papers of Woodrow Wilson: College and State*, 2 vols. (New York: Harper & Brothers, 1925), II, 367, 386.

she hasn't a truer son, that you will be, and are, an infinitely better, more helpful son to her than any of those who cling so desperately to the past and the old prejudices. I believe you are her *greatest* son in this generation and also the one who will have the greatest claim on her gratitude." [59]

59. *Papers of Woodrow Wilson*, V, 251.

3

Woodrow Wilson and the Study
of Administration

DURING a scholarly career spanning a quarter of a century, Woodrow Wilson published only a single article specifically in the field of administration, "The Study of Administration," which appeared in the June 1887 issue of *The Political Science Quarterly.* This essay catapulted Wilson into the forefront of authorities in the field. Leonard D. White, the historian of administration in the United States, has observed that Wilson's "single contribution" was the "first recognition of the field of public administration as an object of study and a potential area of generalization." [1]

Wilson's *tour de force* of 1887 was, in fact, the culmination of the first stage in his thinking and writing on the subject, and, more important, only a harbinger of important work to come.

Wilson was introduced to the field of administration by Richard T. Ely at the Johns Hopkins University in the academic year 1884–1885. Ely's course, which he had begun about 1882, was the only formal work on general administration offered anywhere

This essay was an address to the American Philosophical Society in Philadelphia on April 18, 1968. It appeared in *Proceedings of the American Philosophical Society*, CXII (December 1968), 431–433, and is printed here by permission of George W. Corner, M.D., Executive Officer of the American Philosophical Society.

1. Leonard D. White, *The Republican Era: 1869–1901* (New York: Macmillan, 1958), p. 396.

at this time in the United States. However, Ely, lecturing only once a week during the second term, had merely surveyed administrative methods in Germany, France, and Great Britain. Wilson seems to have profited most of all from Ely's bibliographical references and commentaries, for we find Wilson returning again and again to his notes taken in Ely's lectures for bibliographical guidance.

It was a small beginning, to be sure, but it was enough to excite Wilson's interest. As he wrote on March 19, 1885, to Charles Kendall Adams, then of the University of Michigan, he was already so interested in administration that he had decided to specialize in it.[2] Not, however, until November of 1885 did he have the time even to set down his first thoughts upon the subject. The catalyst for this, Wilson's first effort, seems to have been his reading of Bluntschli's *Politik als Wissenschaft,* the third volume in the Heidelberg professor's great *Lehre vom Modernen Stat.,* which Ely had discussed extensively. Memoranda in the Wilson Papers[3] show how the *Gestalt* was working in Wilson's mind to pose what for him would be the central question: How could German and French administrative methods, devised for highly centralized and more or less authoritarian states, be assimilated in a democratic polity such as the United States possessed?

Wilson did not do much more than pose the question and call for the beginning of scientific study of administration in the first paper which he ever prepared on the subject—a brief piece entitled "The Art of Governing," which he wrote in about mid-November 1885 and never published.[4] Numerous other tasks—for example, the preparation of lectures for history courses at Bryn Mawr College and the beginning of a large general treatise on the modern democratic state—diverted Wilson's attention from administration during the next year. Then, in October 1886, C. K. Adams, now President of Cornell, invited Wilson to deliver a paper to the new Historical and Political Science Association of that university.[5] Wilson seized the opportunity afforded by this

2. Wilson to C. K. Adams, March 19, 1885, in Arthur S. Link *et al.,* editors, *The Papers of Woodrow Wilson,* 9 vols., (Princeton, N.J.: Princeton University Press, 1966-), III, 384.
3. See "Notes on Administration," *ibid.,* V, 49–50.
4. *Ibid.,* pp. 50–54.
5. C. K. Adams to Wilson, October 13, 1886, *ibid.,* p. 351.

invitation to expound the views on administration that had been crystallizing in his mind since early 1885. He read his speech, entitled "The Study of Administration," at Cornell on November 3.[6] With only one alteration—a revision of two paragraphs—the address constituted the text of the article that was published in *The Political Science Quarterly*. The speech-article was also "The Art of Governing" in expanded form. Not only did Wilson repeat the central question alluded to earlier; he also went on to define administration as the practical operation and functioning of government and to call for empirical study of the science in the United States and Britain, warning·

Old as democracy is, its organization on a basis of modern ideas and conditions is still an unaccomplished work. The democratic state has yet to be equipped for carrying those enormous burdens of administration which the needs of this industrial and trading age are so fast accumulating.

Wilson's speech-article made such an impact that Professor Herbert Baxter Adams of Johns Hopkins, on November 25, 1886, asked the young scholar to give an annual course in administration in Baltimore.[7] Moreover, Adams also began to plan for the establishment of what he called a "civil academy" in Washington, to be affiliated with Johns Hopkins and to train men for the public service, with Wilson and Elgin R. L. Gould as its heads. These discussions went so far that President Daniel C. Gilman, in the spring of 1888, requested Wilson to draw up plans for a Hopkins School of Public and International Affairs, and Wilson did draw up such plans even though they were never realized, at least not for many years.[8]

Meanwhile, Wilson had yielded to Herbert B. Adams's requests and had begun the course on administration at Johns Hopkins for which he would do his most important work in the field of administration. Before we go further, it might not be amiss to look briefly at the progress of academic work in administration in the United States at this time.

6. It is printed in *The Papers of Woodrow Wilson*, V, 359–380.

7. H. B. Adams to Wilson, November 25, 1886, *ibid.*, pp. 393–394.

8. See "A Plan for a School of Public Law," *ibid.*, p. 729, and Wilson to D. C. Gilman, May 22, 1888, *ibid.*, p. 730.

There was, actually, virtually no progress to recount. Surveying the catalogues of major American universities in the late 1880s, one can find only two institutions other than Johns Hopkins offering work more or less in the field of administration. Herbert Tuttle was offering a course in municipal government and what he called "comparative modern political methods" at Cornell. And Frank Johnson Goodnow had only recently begun to offer courses on municipal government and administrative law at Columbia, and had by 1888 published only several articles on municipal government, not his great work, *Comparative Administrative Law,* which did not appear until 1893. When Wilson began his course, there was not a single good book on administration or administrative law in the English language. Indeed, Wilson's "The Study of Administration" was the only good article on the subject in English.

Wilson's first course at Johns Hopkins consisted of three six-week series of lectures, twenty-five in each series, given in a three-year cycle from 1888 through 1890. In the first series, he concentrated on the functions of government and the structures and functions of central government in France, Prussia, Britain, Switzerland, the German Empire, and the United States. In his second series, Wilson focused on the methods and machinery of local government in Prussia, France, England, and the United States. In the third series, he discussed the place of municipal government in administration and then went on to try to define administration in terms of certain theories.[9]

Generally speaking, in the first course, Wilson—still following Bluntschli and, additionally, the German political scientist, Heinrich Rudolf von Gneist—ended with what was a thorough if descriptive comparative survey of the governments of most of the major European powers and the United States. For details on European governments, he mined the work of Gneist on England and certain volumes in the great series, *Handbuch des Oeffentlichen Rechts der Gegenwart,* then being edited by Heinrich von Marquardsen of the University of Erlangen: Paul Laband's mono-

9. For comments on this first course, with guides to the relevant documentary materials, see the Editorial Notes, "Wilson's Teaching at Bryn Mawr and the Johns Hopkins University, 1887–88," *ibid.,* pp. 600–602; and "Wilson's Teaching at Wesleyan and the Johns Hopkins University, 1888–89," "Wilson's Teaching at Wesleyan University and the Johns Hopkins University, 1890," all in *The Papers of Woodrow Wilson,* VI, 3–5, 397–398, 482–484.

graph on the German Empire, Heinrich Schulze's on Prussia, Alois von Orelli's on Switzerland, and André Lebon's on France. Virtually all of Wilson's notes found published form in his textbook on comparative government published in 1889 under the title of *The State.*

Wilson's first course and its published product were in fact very considerable achievements. *The State* was the first textbook of its kind in any language. Moreover, in his lectures and *The State,* Wilson had extended the boundaries of the field of administration to the hitherto uncharted terrain of the United States. However, Wilson—never content merely to describe anything—was feeling discontented and frustrated by the time that he gave the third series in his first course, in 1890. In inaugurating that course in 1888, he had announced that he thought that he could define and describe administration *"in a progressive order*—progressive from the existing machinery to the standing problems, the general tests, and the essential principles of Administration—*from form to meaning."* Yet, as he said in 1890, he was still working in the realm of description and was far from achieving his main objective of meaning.

The catalyst of Wilson's discontent was his reading, in late 1889 and early 1890, of three pioneering if recently published works on public law: Karl Gareis, *Allgemeines Staatsrecht;* Otto von Sarwey, *Allgemeines Verwaltungsrecht;* and Georg Jellinek, *Gesetz und Verordnung.* Once again, the *Gestalt* worked to produce a momentous mutation in Wilson's thought. For the first time, he understood that administration in general (not merely in particular, as, for example, administrative law) was a branch of public law.

He set forth this, for him, new interpretation in his lectures at Hopkins in 1890; indeed, he adumbrated the interpretation in his concluding lectures that year. Then, in early 1891, he began a new three-year course at Hopkins, rearranging his course and preparing new notes for lectures.[10]

In his first series, Wilson discussed the nature, scope, and method of study of administration, defining administration as a department of public law and illustrating his general interpretation

10. For a commentary and guide to the documentary materials, particularly Wilson's complete lecture notes, see the Editorial Note, "Wilson's Lectures on Administration at the Johns Hopkins University, 1891-93," *The Papers of Woodrow Wilson,* VII, 112–114.

by discussions of such matters as the relation of administrative acts to the laws. In his second series, Wilson concentrated upon central administrative organizations in England, France, Prussia, and the United States. In his third series, Wilson focused on local governments in the same countries. While discussing all these subjects within the context of public law, Wilson nonetheless ranged far and wide, giving, for example, extraordinary attention to the historical development of governmental institutions and practices, or, to cite a second example, the practical functioning of governments on various levels.

Realizing full well the dangers of generalizations, it is difficult to escape the conclusion that Wilson accomplished an important breakthrough in his second Hopkins course. To be sure, he had gained his indispensable understanding from his German masters. But he went beyond them and any other scholar of his time in the depth of his historical analysis, his attention to the mundane details, and the scope of his coverage. Above all, he was one of the first scholars to realize, in all its ramifications, the truth of the generalization that is now commonplace—that all government was destined to be administration.

Finally, one can only add, without going into details, that Wilson's research for this second course was nothing less than prodigious. He covered all significant literature and sources in English, French, and German, to say nothing of related work in economics, sociology, and general political science.

In a letter to Albert Bushnell Hart of Harvard in 1891, Wilson described his notes for his second course as mere skeletons.[11] Fortunately, this characterization is not entirely correct. The notes themselves are so full as to constitute the elaborate outline of a book which, if Wilson had published it, would have secured his reputation as the father of the study of administration in the United States and probably as the pre-eminent scholar in the entire field in his day.

Wilson continued to lecture on administration at Johns Hopkins until 1897. He had, before and after this time, a keen interest in practical problems of administration and government. For example, he laid out what was one of the first fully developed plans

11. Wilson to A. B. Hart, June 22, 1891, *ibid.*, p. 221.

for the commission form of city government in an address in Baltimore in February 1895.[12] However, not long after completing the third series in his second Hopkins course, Wilson embarked upon a radically different project—a history of the United States. Not long after completion of this work, Wilson was elected President of Princeton University. One thing followed another, including the governorship of New Jersey and the presidency of the United States. Hence Wilson's great scholarly work in the field of administration remained buried in his papers, lost for seventy years, actually, because badly scattered. Only now are we beginning to see the dimensions of his work in the field, and to understand why he is rightfully to be regarded as the pioneer in and father of the study of administration in the United States.

12. A report of Wilson's address is printed in *The Papers of Woodrow Wilson*, IX, 228–231.

4

Woodrow Wilson in New Jersey

THE annals of history are crowded with tales and sagas of heroes and wise men who, around camp fires, on battlefields, and in council chambers, have determined the destinies of tribes and nations. Our own American chronicle boasts of its warrior kings and statesmen who hewed out a continental empire and made it one nation. But we, like chroniclers since the beginning of recorded history, put blinders on our eyes and stare too much at the panorama of battlefields and events in Washington and other great capitals of the world. We forget that all history is local history, that communities make heroes and states make nations, and that we ourselves can be good and faithful citizens of the great Republic only insofar as we know, live in, and help to build the history of the communities where we are called to live. Herein, I take it, lies the indispensable value of using the three-hundredth anniversary of our life as a political community to review and remember that history without which we would be as babes if not babbling idiots.

Princeton University is proud to be privileged to play a part in this great state-wide enterprise. This university has done no small service to the state since provincial times. Its sons have

This essay was a public lecture delivered at Princeton University on May 5, 1964, as part of the university's celebration of the Tercentenary of the State of New Jersey.

helped to build communities as leaders in various walks of life, and in the state itself as legislators, governors, and administrators. I am personally proud to play a small part in this Tercentenary celebration and to talk to you tonight about the man who wrote a glorious chapter in the history of New Jersey.

Woodrow Wilson, as every Princetonian knows, was, to say the least, *primus inter pares* among the distinguished presidents of Princeton University. Indeed, it is no exaggeration to say that, in the relatively brief span of his eight-year presidency from 1902 to 1910, he stamped his thought and character indelibly on this institution. But I must forego comment on his part in the building of Princeton University and his indirect contributions through hundreds of students who went out under his spell to take leadership in various walks of life.

Wilson, as we all know, was also President of the United States and a world leader during one of the critical epochs of modern history. He, more than any other man, helped to lay the foundations for our contemporary political economy. He, more than any other world leader, deserves the title of father of the League of Nations and the United Nations, just as an earlier Princeton alumnus, James Madison, deserves the title of Father of the Constitution. Again, I must forego comment on Wilson's contributions to national and international history, important though these have been for the history of our own communities and state. My time is limited, and my single task is large: it is to tell how events in New Jersey strangely catapulted this man into politics and to show the contributions that he made in helping to lay the foundations of our modern state.

A historian of New Jersey, writing in 1909 or early 1910, could have truthfully recorded that the blood of citizens of his state had watered well the tree of liberty during the Revolution, that New Jersey men had played an important role in forming and later defending the Constitution and Union, and that New Jersey politicians, poets, ministers, and others had enriched the national life in numerous ways. But he would also have had to say that by some curious circumstance no *resident* of New Jersey had ever been elected to the presidency; indeed, that only one citizen of the state, Garet A. Hobart, had been elected Vice President—under McKinley—and that even Hobart had had the bad luck to die after two years in office. Three years later, the same historian could record that the long political drought had ended with Woodrow Wilson's election to the presidency in 1912. He would now have one of the most fascinating tales in American political history to tell. But if he was honest, he would also have to say that he was still dazed and more than a bit mystified about why and how it had all happened.

The opening of the year 1910 found Wilson deep in one of the great personal crises of his life. For more than a year he had been sparring with Andrew F. West, Dean of the Graduate School at Princeton, over construction of a new residential graduate college. The quarrel was ostensibly about the location of the college; underneath, it was a titantic personal battle between two stubborn Scots-Irishmen for control of important university policies, indeed, for leadership in the university itself. Faculty members and trustees had fallen in line on either side, and tension and bitterness mounted all through the late winter and early spring of 1910 as West and his friends pressed their attack relentlessly, and Wilson fought back clumsily. Then an old Princeton alumnus, Isaac Wyman, died at his home in Salem, Massachusetts, leaving his entire estate, estimated to be worth between $2,000,000 and $4,000,000, for construction and endowment of a graduate college and naming West as one of the executors of his estate. "We have beaten the living," Wilson told his wife, "but we cannot fight the dead. The game is up." It was indeed—or so it seemed. Wilson had no choice but to surrender or resign, and he could not in conscience desert his supporters among the faculty and trustees. But he was utterly discouraged and distraught and now willing to lend an ear to friends who were already saying that there was another road, a bright, inviting road to fame.

George Brinton McClellan Harvey, resident of Deal, New Jersey, and editor of *Harper's Weekly,* had known Wilson casually since 1901 through their mutual connection with the publishing house of Harper and Brothers. Harvey had begun the talk in 1906 by suggesting Wilson for the presidency of the United States. Harvey's proposal was almost as absurd as it sounded when he made it. It seemed nearly as absurd in 1910. Wilson, to be sure, had earned a national reputation as writer, scholar, and educational reformer; but he had been so totally absorbed in plans and programs for Princeton since the 1890s that he had taken little interest and played almost no part in the politics of his town, county, or state. He was a Democrat in a Republican state and country. Worst of all, his few public pronouncements, at least before 1909, had identified him squarely with the conservative, eastern wing of the Democratic party, while the majority of Democrats were southern and western agrarian radicals and progressives—followers of William Jennings Bryan, whom Wilson had publicly castigated.

Even so, Harvey was undaunted and, reading the political auguries shrewdly, set about to execute his plan. He invited his old friend, James Smith, Jr., of Newark, leader of the Democratic organization in Essex County, to lunch at Delmonico's in New York one day in January 1910 and suggested Wilson's nomination for the governorship as a stepping stone to the presidency in 1912. Smith was delighted. No doubt he thought, as has often been said, that Wilson would make a dignified and pliable front for the Democratic machine to head off a growing revolt among a group of young Democratic progressives in New Jersey. But Smith also genuinely admired Wilson and took keen pleasure in the thought that he, Smith, might also help to make a President of the United States. He would support Wilson, Smith told Harvey, if only Harvey could persuade the Princetonian to run.

That, as it turned out, was easier said than done. Harvey visited Wilson in Princeton in February and could obtain only Wilson's promise that he would give the gubernatorial nomination very serious consideration if it was offered with no strings. Harvey went to England and did not see Wilson again until he and Smith offered Wilson the gubernatorial nomination during a conference at Harvey's home at Deal on June 26. West had meanwhile won the battle over the graduate college, and Wilson must have welcomed this opportunity to escape from an intolerable personal situation. But he did not give a positive response until the first week in July, and then only after his friends among the trustees had all urged him to do so. He announced his decision in a statement published on July 15.

Wilson's announcement that he would accept the gubernatorial nomination was a crushing blow to Democratic progressives who had been fighting for the reformation of their party and state. They included Mayor H. Otto Wittpenn of Jersey City; Joseph P. Tumulty and Mark Sullivan, also from Jersey City; Matthew C. Ely, editor of the Hoboken *Hudson Observer;* George S. Silzer, of New Brunswick; James Kerney, editor of the Trenton *Evening*

Times; and Judge John W. Wescott, of Haddonfield. They were a small minority in their own party; but, it is fair to say, they now represented about the only hope for political reform in either camp.

The progressive movement in New Jersey, as in other states at this time, was an effort by various persons and groups to destroy the alliance between business enterprises and corporations, railroads, and public utility companies, on the one hand, and more or less corrupt politicians, on the other hand. This alliance gave businessmen immunity from fair taxation and effective public control and gave politicians financial rewards for favors rendered. This system of misgovernment had reached its apogee in New Jersey under the aegis of a Republican organization called the Board of Guardians, completely dominated by representatives of the major business interests. It was an almost perfect example of what Lincoln Steffens called "The System," and New Jersey was one of the last strongholds of an industrial-feudal order that was under violent attack by progressives throughout the country.

The progressive movement in New Jersey was, in its early stages, almost exclusively a Republican phenomenon. It began with the election of Mark M. Fagan as mayor of Jersey City in 1901 and his crusade to force railroads and the Public Service Corporation to pay their fair share of taxes for improvement of schools and city social services. It then spread to neighboring Essex County under the leadership of a wealthy young lawyer, Everett Colby, and his so-called New Idea movement. It seemed that Republican insurgency was irresistible in 1905, when Fagan was elected to a third term in Jersey City and New Idea men won control of the Republican party in Essex. But Republican regulars soon regained control in Newark, and Fagan lost his mayorship to Wittpenn in 1907. Not a single New Idea representative sat in the legislature in 1910. Republican insurgency was moribund if not altogether dead when Woodrow Wilson signaled his entrance into the New Jersey political arena. But these earlier campaigners for democracy, now forgotten, were the forerunners of Woodrow Wilson. Their battles against privilege, and their efforts to meet the problems raised by urbanization and industrialization, educated New Jersey voters in reform and laid solid foundations for the work that Wilson would do.

The Democratic progressives of whom we have spoken were

more hopeful but not much more numerous than their Republican counterparts in the summer of 1910. They had a broad-based platform that included demands for a public utilities commission with rate-making powers, an effective workmen's compensation system, direct primaries for selection of candidates, equal taxation of corporation property, and an end to the alliance of political machines and privileged business interests. They also had a spokesman, Frank S. Katzenbach, Jr., former Mayor of Trenton and Democratic gubernatorial candidate in 1907, around whom they were rallying. They greeted Wilson's announcement that he would accept the gubernatorial nomination with charges that he was a tool of Wall Street and corporate interests and a cat's-paw of bosses to defeat the burgeoning reform movement in the state.

Democratic progressives fought desperately during the summer to discredit the Princetonian and defeat his nomination. But Smith had won the firm support of Robert Davis, leader of the regular Democratic organization in Hudson County, and this alliance was decisive when Democrats met in state convention in the old Taylor Opera House in Trenton on September 15, 1910. Judge Wescott, seconding Katzenbach's nomination, nearly caused a riot by charging that a financial machine was attempting to foist Wilson upon the party by "bargain and sale and the double cross." But Smith's lines held, and Wilson was nominated on the first ballot.

Wilson spent the morning of September 15 on the golf course in Princeton. One of Harvey's assistants drove him to Trenton in the afternoon, and he appeared before the convention to accept the nomination dressed in what was then called a sack suit, with a knitted golf sweater under his jacket. Who among that motley crowd could have sensed the drama and significance of this historic moment as the man destined to play a momentous role in world history walked on the stage to deliver his first political address? The insurgents, feeling, as Tumulty later put it, "sullen, beaten, and hopelessly impotent against the mass attack of the machine forces," missed the significance of the occasion only briefly. They, along with many others, were soon electrified as Wilson proceeded to announce his political independence. "I did not seek this nomination," he declared. "It has come to me absolutely unsolicited, with the consequence that I shall enter upon the duties of the office of Governor, if elected, with absolutely no pledge of any kind to prevent me from serving the people of the State with singleness of purpose." Many former enemies were converted before Wilson had completed his speech. John Crandall of Atlantic County, a bitter opponent of Wilson's nomination before the convention, joined the demonstration at the end, for example, waving his hat and cane and yelling at the top of his voice, "I am sixty-five years old, and still a damn fool!"

It was clear after this performance that something important had happened in New Jersey. Here, obviously, was a new leader of great oratorical power and potential leadership. But exactly where he stood on many of the burning issues of the day, no one could yet tell. Nor did blinding light come during the first two weeks of the campaign. Wilson continued to avow his independence, but he was vague about measures, and he traveled in the company of James R. Nugent, Smith's nephew, chairman of the Democratic state committee, and the very personification of machine politics. Wilson was, we must assume, giving intense thought to the New Jersey situation preparatory to striking out upon his own course. Kerney, Ely, and other editors were saying that his only hope of victory lay in seizing leadership of all progressives, Republican and Democratic. Otherwise, they warned, his Republican opponent, Vivian M. Lewis of Paterson, former State Commissioner of Banking Insurance and a moderate progressive, would surely win. Wilson read their warnings, but his most important teacher at this time was Harry Eckert Alexander, editor of the Trenton *True American.* Alexander's letters, scribbled in pencil on rough copy paper, are still preserved in the Wilson Papers.

Wilson, following Alexander's advice almost to the letter, made his new departure in speeches in Newark on September 30 and Trenton on October 3. He came out for the progressive program, lock, stock, and barrel. He made an open bid for progressive Republican support, saying that the Democratic party now had new ideas, too. Most important, he promised, if elected, to be a new kind of Governor in New Jersey—not a part-time executive, a figurehead who presided amiably and ineffectively over affairs of state, as had been customary, but a tribune of the people who would fight their battles with the legislature and, as he put it, "take every important subject of debate in the Legislature out on the stump and discuss it with the people." The size and enthusiasm of the crowds immediately after this pronouncement proved that Wilson was striking fire. But some progressives still had doubts. As Kerney said in the Trenton *Evening Times* on October 22, "Thus far . . . Dr. Wilson has given no particular indications that, in the event of his election, the state will not be managed by the Democratic machine that nominated him." That was the one big remaining question. To find the answer, George L. Record, the Jersey City reformer, addressed a long public letter to the Democratic candidate demanding to know where he stood on every important issue and, more embarrassingly, how he proposed to free the Democratic party from control of an organization that was as reactionary as its Republican counterpart. Wilson replied audaciously on October 24. He approved every single measure for which progressives had been fighting for a decade. Then he went on to say that the Democratic bosses, Smith, Nugent, and Davis, were as bad as Republican bosses. The big difference between them, he added, was that the Republican bosses would continue to control the state if Lewis was elected, whereas the Democratic bosses would not and could not control affairs if he, Wilson, was elected.

"That letter," Record said truly after reading Wilson's reply, "will elect Wilson governor." It simply completed the conversion of most progressive Republicans and independents into enthusiastic Wilson supporters. Miraculously, it did not affect the loyalty of the Democratic regulars, who had no other place to go in any event. Announcement by the railroads of an increase in commuter fares just before the election also helped to swell the Democratic tide on election day, November 8, 1910. Wilson carried the state by a plurality of more than 49,000 votes and helped to carry a huge Democratic majority into the Assembly. The Republican, William Howard Taft, had carried New Jersey by a majority of more than 80,000 in the presidential contest only two years before.

New Jersey, as the independent Newark *Evening News* accurately said in assessing the significance of the returns, had recorded its political insurgency and discontent with the old order. Wilson's victory was no partisan triumph. The mass of voters had heretofore been voiceless. They had found a leader and spokesman who happened to be a Democrat. Now they expected him to redeem the political reputation of their state and to reconstruct the character of the forces that controlled the State House.

The Governor-elect had to begin his work of reconstruction even before he was inaugurated. It happened that the next legislature would elect a United States senator. James E. Martine, a nonentity from Plainfield whom no one, including himself, took seriously, had run unopposed in a non-binding Democratic senatorial preferential primary. Once election returns were in, Smith suddenly decided that he would like to return to the Senate, from which the voters had retired him in 1899 after he had served one term with very dubious distinction. Progressives in both parties demanded that Wilson support Martine, adding that his standing as a progressive would depend upon his decision. Wilson was in a dreadful dilemma. He thought that Martine's candidacy was a joke. He liked Smith and was grateful for his past support. But he knew that the contest between Martine and Smith was now in the popular mind a struggle between the old order and the new. He knew that his leadership and the fate of his legislative program, to say nothing of his future career, were at stake. Most important, Wilson knew that the vast majority did not want Smith as senator, and he felt under deep obligation to the people who had elected him. Hence, he went furiously to work rallying assemblymen-elect and, once he was certain that victory was in sight, he came out for Martine and against Smith in a public statement on December 8, 1910. Then he carried the fight directly to the people in brilliant addresses in Jersey City and Newark. His campaign was so dazzling that the old professionals were stunned and, for once, ineffective. The legislature elected Martine on January 25, 1911, and Wilson was undisputed leader of his party.

Meanwhile, Wilson had been inaugurated forty-third Governor of New Jersey on January 17 and had already turned to legislative tasks with the same vigor and skill that he had shown in the senatorial battle. Introduction of his first major measure, a bill drafted by George L. Record and sponsored by Wilson's old student, Elmer H. Geran from Monmouth County, set off a second battle with the Smith organization, one even more intense and crucial than the first. The Geran bill required the nomination of all party candidates in primary elections instead of county and state conventions and seemed to pose a dire threat to machine control. Wilson again went to the people in a series of electrifying speeches. Then, on March 6, he appeared in person before a caucus of Democratic assemblymen to plead for the Geran bill. It was the first time in the state's history that a governor had undertaken to assume personal leadership of members of his party in the legislature. The Assembly approved the Geran bill on March 21, and the Senate adopted a strengthened version on April 13.

Victory in the first, key struggle assured passage of the balance of the Governor's program. There followed in rapid succession enactment of measures that brought New Jersey abreast of the record of progressive reform in other states. One was a corrupt-practices law that attempted to prevent bribery, purchase of votes, and other flagrant frauds in elections. As later events proved, it was no guarantee of political purity, but it accomplished everything that could be done by legislation. Another measure created a board of public utility commissioners with sweeping control over the rates and services of railroads, street railways, telephone companies, and public utilities. It was as thoroughgoing as any public utilities statute in any state of the Union at the time. A workmen's compensation bill created a state-wide system of accident insurance, thus removing a heavy burden from the shoulders of workingmen and their families. Finally, the legislature approved, again under Wilson's spur, a measure permitting cities of a certain class to adopt the commission form of government as a substitute for the old system of government by mayors and councils and diffused authority.

The legislature adjourned on April 22 in a blaze of glory. "I think . . . [the time] will always be remembered as extraordinary in this," Wilson said in a public statement, "that it witnessed the fulfillment by the Legislature of every important campaign pledge."

"The present Legislature," Record agreed, "ends its session with the most remarkable record of progressive legislation ever known in the political history of this or any other State." Record did not exaggerate, and observers throughout New Jersey and the nation agreed that Wilson had been largely responsible. As the *Jersey Journal* of Jersey City put it, "The victory Governor Wilson has won is a revelation of the man's character and leadership and a marvel to the country. No Governor has ever achieved so much in so short a time. In less than four months he has turned New Jersey from one of the most conservative and machine-dominated States into a leader in the forefront of progressive commonwealths."

Wilson himself wrote the best and fairest epilogue to this chapter in his career in a letter to a friend:

The Legislature adjourned yesterday morning at three o'clock with its work done. I got absolutely everything I strove for,—and more besides. Everyone, the papers included, are saying that none of it could have been done, if it had not been for my influence and tact and hold upon the people. . . . As a matter of fact, it is just a bit of natural history. I came to the office in the fulness of time, when opinion was ripe on all these matters, when both parties were committed to these reforms, and by merely standing fast, and by never losing sight of the business for an hour, but keeping up all sorts of legitimate pressure *all the time,* kept the mighty forces from being diverted or blocked at any point. The strain has been immense, but the reward is great. I feel a great reaction to-day, for I am, of course, exceedingly tired, but I am quietly and deeply happy that I should have been of just the kind of service I wished to be to those who elected and trusted me. I can look them in the face, like a servant who has kept faith and done all that was in him, given every power he possessed, to them and their affairs. There could be no deeper source of satisfaction and contentment!

During the remaining months of 1911, Wilson was still head over heels in work in New Jersey, even though he was speaking frequently outside the state in a campaign for the Democratic presidential nomination in 1912. His main objective was now reorganization of the New Jersey Democratic party. He obtained Nugent's removal as state chairman easily enough, as it turned out, once Nugent made the mistake of publicly calling the Governor a liar and an ingrate. Wilson next placed his own followers in command of the party machinery and went back to the people during a long and grueling primary campaign in which he rallied popular support for Wilson progressives in every county. Wilson men were victorious in every county but Essex in the primary election held on September 25, 1911, and the Governor was now, at least momentarily, not only leader but also master of his party. He was also much engrossed in administrative problems and appointments and, in addition, conducted a one-man campaign for commission government, making speeches in Bayonne, Trenton, Hoboken, Jersey City, and Passaic. Finally, he took the stump again in the autumn in a whirlwind campaign for the Democratic legislative slate. Results of the general election on November 7 were discouraging. Republicans elected small majorities in both houses of the legislature, but this happened only because the Smith-Nugent machine knifed its own candidates in Essex County in order to assure a Republican victory. Actually, Wilson had succeeded in building enormous new Democratic strength in Republican strongholds in South Jersey.

Events of the following year—at least events in New Jersey—were anti-climactic in comparison to the dramatic happenings of 1911. Wilson was now deeply involved in a desperate campaign for the presidential nomination, and his enemies accused him of neglecting affairs and duties at home. There was some truth in the charge. The Governor did not lead the legislators in Trenton, and the session of 1912 was totally unproductive. But the spring of 1912 was not all pure loss, at least for Wilson. He won the nearly complete support of the New Jersey delegation to the Democratic national convention that met in Baltimore on June 25, and they played an important part in Wilson's victory there.

There was a dramatic dénouement to this story of Wilson in New Jersey. The split in the Republican party between Theodore Roosevelt and President Taft not only gave Wilson the presidency in the November elections but also gave Democrats control once again of the New Jersey legislature. Wilson consequently returned to the state political arena before he went to Washington to battle for two final reform objectives: antitrust legislation and reform of New Jersey's antiquated jury system that gave control to politically elected sheriffs. He won adoption of his antitrust laws, known collectively as the "Seven Sisters," easily enough, although it turned out that they were completely ineffective and later repealed. He failed to get jury reform, even though he returned to New Jersey as President of the United States to carry the battle to the people, mainly because a new political boss, Frank Hague, had emerged in Jersey City, and Wilson had lost control of the Hudson County delegation in the Assembly. Heretofore it had been the cornerstone of his legislative strength.

This ends our account of Wilson's career as Governor of New Jersey, one filled with enormous significance for Wilson, the nation and world, and, of course, for the people of this state. New Jersey, while contemplating her three hundred years of eventful history, can take rightful pride in the memory of her most distinguished statesman. The people of this state, by their suffrage in 1910 and again in 1912—in the presidential preferential primary—gave Woodrow Wilson his chance to become President of the United States and a maker of modern history. This ground on which we stand was the ground of his political apprenticeship. He had, it is true, studied politics and constitutional problems all his adult life. He had learned much about practical politics while fighting great battles at Princeton. Even so, it was during his governorship that he learned and used all the techniques of leadership that he would soon put into effective practice on a larger political stage.

Now, looking at the other side of the picture, we can also say that Woodrow Wilson gave much in return to the people of New Jersey, that he left a deep imprint on the politics and institutions of this state.

To begin with, he literally transformed the governorship. Governors before his time had been more or less constitutional figureheads, exercising little party leadership and having virtually no voice in legislation. The system of a weak executive and dif-fused responsibility and power might have sufficed for a largely agrarian society with simple problems. It had broken down by Wilson's day, and an intolerable situation could only have grown worse as problems of government and social welfare multiplied. Wilson's greatest contribution lay in proving conclusively, once for all, that the Governor of New Jersey, even under an unreformed constitution, could provide the responsible leadership that is indispensable in a modern democracy, mainly through leadership of his party and of public opinion.

It is also fair to say that Wilson and the men who worked with him from 1911 to 1913 literally transformed the governmental structure of this state. The constitution and, more important, the constitutional traditions and customs of New Jersey had been crystallized in the middle of the nineteenth century during the heyday of individualism and laissez faire, on the fundamental assumption that good governments were those that governed least. Private interests, uncontrolled and often irresponsible, had moved into the political vacuum created when the people abdicated their sovereignty over economic life. This, of course, is something of an exaggeration, but it is accurate to say that the state, by 1910, utterly lacked machinery to cope with and control private economic interests that served her daily life. Wilson and his co-workers in both parties at least laid the foundations of our modern regulatory structure by creating the Public Service Commission, instituting a workmen's compensation system, and permitting cities to streamline their governmental structures and to venture into new fields of regulation. They also amended the school laws to provide for larger state participation and support, instituted a state storage and food inspection system, and adopted new laws requiring stringent factory inspection and regulating the hours and kind of labor that women and children could perform. In brief, democracy in New Jersey learned to become efficient under Woodrow Wilson's tutelage.

It is interesting to speculate about what Wilson might have done further along these lines had he stayed longer in Trenton and the state. We know, actually, very little about his achievements as an administrator during his governorship because most of the essential documentary materials have been lost. What has been saved suggests that he took as keen an interest in appointments and in the administration and execution of statutes as in their enactment. He was also very much concerned about New Jersey's peculiar problems as a suburban state and its relation to the two great metropolitan centers of New York and Philadelphia. In one speech, for example, he described the necessity for and forecast the creation of what would become the Port of New York Authority.

One final contribution is difficult to measure. It was the new life, hope, and vision that Wilson brought to the politics of this state. He dispelled the despair of a people who had almost concluded that they could do nothing but endure corrupt rule and corporation control. He proved to the people of New Jersey that they were still a free people who could do great things under wise and forceful leaders. More specifically, he transformed the Democratic party by giving place and leadership to a large new group consisting mainly of young progressives who shared his vision. The pity was that he could not have stayed in New Jersey long enough to complete the work that he had begun. The character of the Democratic party in New Jersey was determined by the outcome of a crucial battle for control of Hudson County that had already begun before Wilson went to the White House.

He discovered, as all other Presidents before and since have discovered, even strong Presidents like the Roosevelts, that a President of the United States usually has to recognize local and state party organizations and then try to use them for constructive national purposes. Thus, instead of continuing to fight the rising Hague organization, he soon came to terms with it and in fact helped it to secure its hold on Hudson County. He even made his peace with the Smith-Nugent organization in Essex County. As a consequence, the young Wilson progressives were left rudderless and leaderless, and politics in New Jersey reverted to type in about 1914.

But this is like quarreling with history. On such an occasion as this, it is appropriate to remember that Woodrow Wilson was a Jerseyman who did mighty things with popular support. The people of New Jersey, as Wilson's successor James F. Fielder said, gave Woodrow Wilson "for the glory and uplift of the United States," and Wilson was deeply grateful for their trust. "I already loved the State of New Jersey when I became its Governor," Wilson said upon handing the seal of state to Fielder on March 1, 1913, "but that love has been deepened and intensified during these last two and a half years. I now feel a sense of identification with the people of this State and the interests of this State which have seemed to enlarge my own personality and which has been the greatest privilege of my life."

Wilson might have added, had not modesty forbade his saying it, that politics and government could never be the same in New Jersey because of what he had done. His spirit still hovers over the State House, and every governor knows that he can be a more effective leader of the people because Woodrow Wilson once sat in the gubernatorial chair.

5

Woodrow Wilson
and the Democratic Party

FEW presidents in American history established so complete and far-reaching a control over political parties as did Woodrow Wilson during the first years of his tenure in the White House. Indeed, before the end of his first term he had become almost the absolute master of his party, able to effect revolutionary changes in party policy without the previous knowledge and consent of Democratic leaders in Congress and the country. He attained this stature in part by his methods of public leadership—his bold representation of public opinion and his incomparable strategy in dealing with the legislative branch. He won this position of authority also through less obvious and more subtle means—a systematic use of the immense patronage at his command as an instrument by which to achieve effective and responsible party government. Confronted by no entrenched national party organization and no body of officeholders loyal to another man, he was able to build from the ground up and to weld the widely scattered and disparate Democratic forces into something approximating a national machine.

Reprinted from *The Review of Politics*, XVIII (April 1956), 146–156, by permission of the Editor.

Like its great opponent, the GOP, the Democratic party in 1913 was torn by fierce personal rivalries and by a conflict between machine and conservative politicians on the one hand and, on the other, a rising group of reformers, idealists, and professionals who called themselves progressives. This intraparty struggle for control, which was in progress on all levels of party organization, had most recently culminated during the pre-convention campaign of 1912 for the presidential nomination. Wilson, then Governor of New Jersey, had led the progressive forces in victory at the Baltimore convention over Speaker Champ Clark of Missouri and his coalition of conservatives and old-line politicians.

All Democratic eyes turned nervously toward Trenton, therefore, as the President-elect pondered the choice of a Cabinet and his patronage policies during the months following the election of 1912. Wilson soon made it clear that he meant to regenerate the Democratic party by giving initiative and control to its progressive element. Time and again in speeches and public statements during the preinaugural period he voiced this intention. "I have no liberty in the matter," he declared, for example, in an address before the New Jersey electors in Trenton on January 13, 1913. "I have given bonds. Therefore, I shall not be acting as a partisan when I pick out progressives, and only progressives. I shall be acting as a representative of the people of this great country." [1]

To Wilson, as to most progressives of his time, progressivism meant a general attitude and a method of approach more than a finely spun ideology. It meant, in brief, the combining of a fundamental democratic philosophy with a certain dynamic quality and a willingness to experiment. When Wilson, for example, talked about progressives, he meant men like Robert M. La Follette in Wisconsin and Newton D. Baker in Ohio, and the host of men and women all over the country who had been fighting to destroy political machines allied with corrupt businessmen. He meant men who stood for integrity and decency in politics and social and economic justice. He meant, insofar as his own party was concerned, the men who had fought for his nomination in 1912 and were eager to follow his leadership in the New Freedom.

These, then, were the kinds of men Wilson wanted to appoint

1. New York *Times,* January 14, 1913.

to office and to encourage in leadership of state and national Democratic politics. However, circumstances made it extraordinarily difficult for him to follow a policy dictated by principle alone.

To begin with, although Wilson gave an astonishing amount of attention to the minutiae of patronage and made perhaps several hundred personal appointments, the task of dispensing tens of thousands of jobs was simply more than he could comprehend or control. In one of his first statements after the inauguration, he announced his method: he would see no applicant except by invitation and would make appointments only through the Cabinet members. He then proceeded to lay down the general rules, to give each Cabinet member a list of Wilsonian progressives prepared by the Democratic National Committee, and to trust his Cabinet members and his unofficial adviser, Col. Edward M. House, and his secretary, Joseph P. Tumulty, to attend to the details. It was the only workable method, but he often did not know what his subordinates were doing; and as time passed he tended to care less and less.

The chief obstacles to the fulfillment of Wilson's intention to strengthen the progressive element, however, were the realities and necessities of practical politics. The most important of these was the fact that the so-called conservatives were firmly entrenched in many states and constituted a sizable minority of the Democratic congressmen and senators. A bold frontal assault by Wilson through patronage channels might, therefore, disrupt the party and insure the defeat of his legislative program even before it could be fully matured. Moreover, whether he liked it or not, Wilson as President was in fact the leader of the Democratic party, not merely of a faction; and the success of his administration would depend upon his ability to weld the Democrats into an effective national organization. Such an effort might require some compromise and a willingness to forgive and forget.

Even so, Wilson was apparently determined at the outset of his administration to defy the conservatives, even at the risk of endangering his legislative goals. Soon after his inauguration, perhaps in mid-March 1913, he called the Postmaster General, Albert S. Burleson of Texas, to the White House to discuss basic policy to govern the appointment of postmasters. "Now, Burleson," the President began, "I want to say to you that my administration is going to be a progressive administration. I am not going to advise with reactionary or stand-pat Senators or Representatives in making these appointments. I am going to appoint forward-looking men, and I am going to satisfy myself that they are honest and capable." Then he repeated, with emphasis: "I am not going to consult the old standpatters in our party."

Burleson was aghast. "Mr. President," he replied,

if you pursue this policy, it means that your administration is going to be a failure. It means the defeat of the measures of reform that you have next to your heart. These little offices don't amount to anything. They are inconsequential. It doesn't amount to a damn who is postmaster at Paducah, Kentucky. But these little offices mean a great deal to the Senators and Representatives in Congress. If it goes out that the President has turned down Representative So and So and Senator So and So, it means that that member has got bitter trouble at home. If you pursue the right policy, you can make the Democratic Party progressive.

"As your Postmaster General," Burleson continued,

I am going to make 56,000 appointments. I will see honest and capable men in every office. But I will consult with the men on the "Hill." I have been here a long time. I know these Congressmen and Senators. If they are turned down, they will hate you and will not vote for anything you want. It is human nature. On the other hand, if we work with them, and they recommend unsuitable men for the offices, I will keep on asking for other suggestions, until I get a good one. In the end we shall get as able men as we would in any other way, and we will keep the leaders of the party with us.

Burleson left the White House not knowing what impression he had made. A week later, Wilson called him to his study to discuss a mammoth list of names for postmasterships. Burleson began with a candidate hotly opposed by Wilson's friends in Tennessee. The President leaned back, threw up his arms, and said, "Burleson, I can't appoint a man like that!" The Postmaster General then explained why the appointment had been proposed and how important it was to a key Tennessee representative. "Well, I will appoint him," Wilson replied.[2]

2. R. S. Baker, interview with A. S. Burleson, March 17-29, 1927, the Ray Stannard Baker Collection of Wilsoniana, Library of Congress, Washington, D.C.

It was one of the early decisive turning points in Wilson's presidential career. Burleson's account is somewhat exaggerated, especially when he went on to relate how Wilson gave him complete control over all the postmasterships; but it is essentially correct. What the President did was to give to Burleson, Tumulty, and Thomas J. Pence, secretary of the National Committee, virtually complete control of the mass of petty jobs, reserving for himself and for Colonel House the right to advise and veto.

As Burleson and Tumulty preferred to control the Democratic party rather than to reform it, the result of Wilson's decision was the triumph of the professional politician over the idealist in the administration. Burleson and the professionals well knew that it made a tremendous difference to the rival factions in Kentucky who was postmaster in Paducah and a hundred other towns in that state. Imbued with the professional politician's conviction that control of the state organizations, party harmony, and support in Congress for administration measures were more to be desired than warfare and a risky regeneration of the Democracy, they used the patronage almost cynically for practical purposes. "I had the bait gourd," Burleson afterward boasted. "They had to come to me."

Generally speaking, the effect of Burleson's policy was to strengthen the factions already in control of the city and state organizations or, when the factions were evenly divided, to draw the rivals together in an agreement to cooperate and share the patronage. Thus Burleson and Tumulty tended to favor the Democratic organizations in New York, Boston, Chicago, and other large cities, although these so-called machines were often corrupt and had been among Wilson's most virulent enemies before the Baltimore convention. In many non-southern states, where progressive Democrats were dominant, Burleson's policy operated to strengthen Wilson's friends. In many states where conservatives prevailed, on the other hand, it worked to discourage and weaken the progressive factions.

This was particularly true in the South, where rising groups of anti-machine Democrats in nearly every state had joined the Wilson movement in 1911 and 1912 and launched a powerful campaign to destroy the old cliques allied with the railroads and corrupt courthouse rings. They were minorities in most of the southern states, but they were well organized and growing in strength; and they looked to their leader in Washington for the assistance they were sure would turn the tide of battle. They often looked in vain. The progressive minorities in the South found in Washington, not the sustenance and recognition that they, as the leaders of Wilsonian progressivism, had confidently expected, but aloofness and rejection.

In Kentucky, for example, Burleson gave control of the federal patronage to Senator Ollie M. James and the Democratic congressmen, most of whom were allied with the railroad and liquor interests and had bitterly fought Wilson's nomination. By the end of Wilson's first year as President, only one Wilson man had been named to federal office in the state. "The most vicious element in Kentucky politics has controlled the patronage. The men who fought for Wilson, not because of his personality only or chiefly, but because he stood for what they believed in, have been ostracized by him," the leader of the Wilson movement in Kentucky exclaimed in protest.[3]

There has never been, in the history of any state, a more glaring illustration of the use of patronage to build up a political machine to be used by a faction of the party; nor, in our judgment, a more deplorable illustration of the President permitting another to dictate his patronage so as to punish those who fought for, and reward those who fought against the President's nomination.[4]

Virginia was another testing ground of the administration's patronage policy. A large group of insurgents, led by Henry St. George Tucker, John Garland Pollard, and Allan D. Jones, had been fighting since the early 1900s to wrest control of the state Democratic organization from Senator Thomas S. Martin, Representative Henry D. Flood, and the machine closely identified with the railroad and business interests. They had fought hard to swing Virginia into the Wilson column in 1912, had nominated and elected a progressive governor in the same year, and had gone on to capture control in Norfolk, Roanoke, Petersburg, and other

---

3. Desha Breckinridge to William F. McCombs, March 7, 1914, the Papers of Woodrow Wilson, Library of Congress, Washington, D.C., hereinafter cited as Wilson Papers.

4. Desha Breckinridge, editorial in the Lexington (Ky.) *Herald*, March 7, 1914; see also W. G. McAdoo to Woodrow Wilson, September 29, 1913, Wilson Papers, enclosing a letter from Leigh Harris, editor of the Henderson (Ky.) *Daily Journal*.

cities. Thus it seemed that the progressive movement in the Old Dominion was on the verge of victory when Wilson, in an address at Staunton on December 28, 1912, attacked the Martin machine and inferentially promised to support the progressives.

And yet it did not work out that way. Tucker had a conference with the President on August 25, 1913, about the administration's patronage policies in the state. "I am much concerned about his attitude in Virginia affairs," Tucker wrote soon afterward. "He has a decided leaning to the recognition of the Senators with a view of holding them in line for the tariff and currency measures." [5] When Wilson justified these fears by giving practically all the important Virginia appointments to the Martin organization, the insurgents met in Richmond on January 5, 1914, and addressed a moving protest to the White House. By appointing only reactionaries in Virginia, they wrote, the President had violated his own principles and disheartened his friends in the state. "Can being proscribed because of their very allegiance to those principles have any other effect?" [6] It was a futile gesture.

There was, to cite a final example, the way in which the Wilson administration ignored the progressive minority and gave control of the patronage in Alabama to Senator John H. Bankhead, Representative Oscar W. Underwood, and the other politicians who had fought to prevent Wilson's nomination in 1912. [7]

The issue arose crucially first when Underwood asked the President to appoint Edward K. Campbell, a railroad and corporation lawyer of Birmingham, to the United States Court of Claims. "His appointment," a former governor and the Alabama member of the Democratic National Committee warned Wilson, "would put the teeth of your largest supporters in this state on edge." [8] "Please allow me to say that the appointment of this man would be the coldest chill you could give to your friends in this State," Wilson's most intimate friend in Alabama added. "No man was more extreme or resourceful in his opposition to any sort of

5. H. St. G. Tucker to Carter Glass, August 27, 1913, the Papers of Carter Glass, University of Virginia Library, Charlottesville, Va.

6. J. G. Pollard *et al.* to Woodrow Wilson, January 5, 1914, Wilson Papers.

7. For a general protest, see Horace Hood, editor of the Montgomery *Journal* and a leader of the progressive wing, to W. J. Bryan, October 11, 1913, the Papers of William Jennings Bryan, the National Archives, Washington, D.C.

8. W. D. Jelks to Woodrow Wilson, March 19, 1913, Wilson Papers.

recognition of the will of a large majority of the Democrats of this State. His promotion would be construed by all of your friends as a triumph of the active influence of your opponents in the State congressional delegation." [9] All that the President could say in reply was that he realized what Campbell's appointment would mean but that it was "inevitable in the circumstances." [10] He meant that he could not risk alienating Underwood, chairman of the ways and means committee, who had charge of the tariff bill then pending in the House.

It was embarrassing, this having to turn one's back on faithful friends; and time and again Wilson confessed his helplessness and chagrin. "As for the postmasterships you speak of," he wrote to Bryan in explanation of his policy, "it is extremely difficult, when we are convinced that the Congressmen in the several districts offer us good men, to turn away from their choice and take the choice of someone else." [11] "I am very much distressed that the friends in North Carolina, with whom you spoke, should have got the impression they have got," he explained again.

I do not blame them in the least, but there are many circumstances upon which I do not think they reflect. In the first place, I am bound by the old practice and expectation of everybody as opinion is organized here in Washington to respect and accept the recommendations of Congressmen and Senators, if they recommend men unobjectionable in character and ability. . . . It is a thorny and difficult matter altogether in which I have not satisfied myself and in which I am grieved to learn I have not satisfied my friends. [12]

He felt, he wrote to a friend, like putting up the sign that was nailed on the organ loft of a country church for the defense of the organist. It read, Wilson said, "Don't shoot. He is doing his damnedest."

There were, besides, a thousand minor vexations, most of which Burleson, Tumulty, and the Cabinet members absorbed but some of which found their way to the President. Whom could the administration trust in Wooster, Ohio, or Vermont, or Wash-

9. F. P. Glass to Woodrow Wilson, March 20, 1913, *ibid.*
10. Wilson to F. P. Glass, April 16, 1913, *ibid.*
11. Wilson to W. J. Bryan, June 25, 1913, *ibid.*
12. Wilson to S. S. Wise, June 4, 1914, *ibid.*

ington State?[13] Why had Burleson appointed Thomas Fox, a known lobbyist for the Southern Pacific Railroad, as postmaster at Sacramento?[14] Did Burleson know that he had appointed an alleged drunkard in Michigan; could he not give some favor to Representative "Alfalfa Bill" Murray of Oklahoma, "a very faithful and militant friend"; would Burleson please remember not to dismiss General Longstreet's widow, a Republican, as postmistress at Gainesville, Georgia?[15]

Or, again, there were embarrassments like the one Wilson related:

The Junior Senator from New York was in to see me yesterday and had this to say about the post office appointment at Buffalo: It seems that he recommended a German Lutheran and that upon some impression he gained at your office he permitted it to be announced in Buffalo that his candidate would be appointed, whereupon the said candidate was serenaded, etc., by various Lutheran societies and his not being appointed has caused him considerable mortification. I mean the candidate.[16]

The net effect of the administration's patronage policies, as executed by Burleson, Tumulty, and the other professionals in the Wilson circle, was, first, to undercut the progressives where they most needed support and, second, to win a host of new allies for the President among the city and state organizations and their representatives in the two houses of Congress. Indeed, it is not too much to say that the administration, after a few fitful attempts at supporting progressive groups in Illinois and New York, had come to terms with virtually every Democratic machine in the country by the autumn of 1914.

13. Wilson to A. S. Burleson, April 4, June 2, and July 28, 1913, *ibid.*
14. This appointment, incidentally, stirred up a controversy all over the West and drew protests from Thomas J. Pence, secretary of the National Committee, Sen. Key Pittman of Nevada, and many Californians. See T. J. Pence to Wilson, May 29, 1913, the Papers of Albert S. Burleson, Library of Congress, Washington, D.C.; Wilson to A. S. Burleson, May 29 and June 2, 1913, Wilson Papers. Burleson wrote at the bottom of the original of Wilson's letter of June 2, 1913, in the Burleson Papers, the following: "Stood by Fox and put him over. Sacramento went for Wilson in 1916 election and saved the state for Wilson."
15. Wilson to A. S. Burleson, October 7, September 26, and March 30, 1913, Wilson Papers.
16. Wilson to A. S. Burleson, November 25, 1913, *ibid.*

The way in which this was done and the consequences of this policy of reconciliation are most dramatically and ironically revealed by developments in the Democratic party of New Jersey after 1913. Wilson, it will be recalled, had won the governorship of that state in 1910 by defying the Democratic bosses of New Jersey, especially James Smith, Jr., and his nephew, James Nugent, who controlled the Democratic organization in Essex County. During the months following the election of 1910, Wilson and his friends had gone on to build a new organization and had pushed a number of reform bills through the legislature in 1911. The consequence was a violent rupture in the party which culminated in the expulsion of Nugent from the state committee and open warfare between the Wilson forces and the Essex machine.

Wilson had maintained his warfare against the "same old gang," as he called the Smith-Nugent organization, all during 1912 and during the legislative session of early 1913. Moreover, before he went to Washington, the President-elect promised the people of New Jersey that he would continue to stand behind the progressive forces of the state. "I have been surprised by numerous inquiries as to whether I would continue to 'take interest' in the political affairs of the state after assuming my duties as President," he declared in a public statement.

The people of the state need not fear that I will become indifferent so long as their confidence encourages me to believe that they wish my aid and counsel. I shall in the future use every proper and legitimate power I have and every influence at my disposal to support and assist the new forces which have regenerated our life during the past two years. I shall not go back in this business, for I understand my duty to be to stand back of the progressive forces in the Democratic party everywhere and at every juncture, and I feel that in those matters I am under particular obligations of conscience and gratitude to the people of New Jersey.[17]

The President did in fact return to his state a few months later to give his support to a movement for jury reform and the adoption of a bill for the convening of a constitutional convention. Moreover, he gave effective support to a progressive candidate

17. New York *World*, December 18, 1912.

for the Democratic gubernatorial nomination during the summer and autumn of 1913. But from this time forward, Wilson lost all personal interest in New Jersey affairs and gave charge of the federal patronage in the state to Tumulty and Burleson. More concerned with winning a Democratic majority in the congressional elections of 1914 than with building progressive strength, Tumulty and Burleson called off Wilson's war against the New Jersey bosses and applied the stratagem of supporting the strongest county factions, regardless of their political character. That this policy compelled recognition of men whom Wilson had once scourged and implied the betrayal of loyal Wilsonians did not cause Tumulty and Burleson to swerve from their course.

A case in point, important because it marked the beginning of the new policy of appeasement, was the appointment of J. J. O'Hanlon, a Nugent lieutenant who had been one of Wilson's bitterest foes in Essex County, as postmaster of South Orange in May 1914, in order to insure the re-election of Congressman Edward W. Townsend of Montclair. The progressive Democrats in Essex County, who had risked their political lives by trying to wrest control of the county organization from Nugent, were stunned.

The appointment "will have malevolent effects throughout the whole of Essex," the president of the Democratic Club of South Orange wrote in protest,

and is taken as a definite note of an understanding with the underworld of politics—a blow at the first causes for Wilson as a political power and a principle. It is virtually a Notice to Quit to those who have held principle and Wilsonism above Bossism and party manipulation for personal ends. It is a confession of surrender to the Old Gang . . . a statement that principles enunciated at Trenton find no echo at Washington.[18]

"Cases of this kind are developing every day in New Jersey," the Wilson leader in Jersey City added.[19]

But the Washington administration persevered in the new policy, although the Republicans captured the legislature in 1914 and the governorship in 1916. By 1916, the Wilson war against "the same old gang" was entirely over, and during the following

18. James F. McGrath to Sen. J. E. Martine, May 16, 1914, Wilson Papers.
19. H. O. Wittpenn to J. P. Tumulty, May 7, 1914, *ibid.*

years the President's feeling toward his former enemies mellowed. "Nugent is a strange fellow, and while we had some powerful disagreements I always had a sneaking feeling of regard for him," Wilson later told a friend. For his part, "Nugent, in the later years, had come to regard the Wilson leadership of the party as providential, although disagreeing with what he termed the surrender on woman-suffrage and other advanced ideas. It was the Nugent organization in Essex County that gave Wilson his best latter-day support in New Jersey." [20]

And thus it went all over the country. The vexations and embarrassments attendant upon this policy of "realism" were more than counterbalanced in Wilson's reckoning by the results of practical politics; the consequence was the establishment of the President's nearly absolute personal mastery over the Democratic party and the Democratic members of Congress. Without this mastery, Wilson most assuredly would not have succeeded either in accomplishing his broad reforms at home or in maintaining control of American foreign policy during the critical months before the entry of the United States into the First World War. "What you told me about the old standpatters is true," the President admitted to the Postmaster General in the summer of 1914. "They at least will stand by the party and the administration. I can.rely on them better than I can on some of my own crowd." [21]

20. James Kerney, *The Political Education of Woodrow Wilson* (New York: The Century Company, 1926) pp. 471–472.
21. R. S. Baker, interview with A. S. Burleson, March 17–19, 1927, Baker Collection.

"Wilson the Diplomatist" in Retrospect

I TRUST that you will permit me to say a personal word about the purpose of this lecture. As many of you no doubt know, in 1956 I delivered the Albert Shaw Lectures at Johns Hopkins University, which were published the following year under the title of *Wilson the Diplomatist: A Look at His Major Foreign Policies.* The first lecture, also called "Wilson the Diplomatist," attempted to explore Wilson's training and to review his thinking about foreign policy and his methods as a diplomatist. When Professor Oscar Handlin invited me to visit the Charles Warren Center and deliver a public lecture under its auspices, I decided to use the opportunity to take another general look at Wilson the diplomatist in the light of what I have learned during the past thirteen years. I also decided not to quarrel with myself in public, but rather to write a new general lecture in the knowledge that my listeners are themselves perfectly competent to see wherein my analyses and judgments have changed.

A gaunt man of serious mien walked to the stands outside the east front of the Capitol on March 4, 1913, to take the oath

This essay was an address delivered at Harvard University under the auspices of the Charles Warren Center for the Study of American History on December 3, 1969. Parts of this essay, which appeared in an earlier version in Arthur S. Link, *Wilson the Diplomatist: A Look at His Major Foreign Policies* (Baltimore: The Johns Hopkins Press, 1957), pp. 3–29, are printed by permission of the Editorial Director of the Johns Hopkins Press.

of office as twenty-eighth President of the United States. He was Woodrow Wilson, born in Staunton, Virginia, on December 29, 1856, educated at Davidson College and Princeton University, trained in law at the University of Virginia, and prepared for teaching and scholarship in history and political science at the Johns Hopkins University. He had taught successively from 1885 to 1902 at Bryn Mawr College, Wesleyan University, the Johns Hopkins University, and Princeton University. Elevated to the presidency of the last-named institution, he had helped to transform a venerable college into a modern university. Embroiled in a personal controversy with the Dean of the Graduate School, Andrew F. West, Wilson had escaped the troubled Princeton scene by accepting nomination for the governorship of New Jersey in 1910. Elected governor, he had gone on with irresistible power to capture the Democratic presidential nomination and the presidency of the United States itself in 1912.

The man inaugurated on that bright March morning in 1913 was privileged to guide the destinies of his country during eight of the most critical years of the modern epoch. For the American people, the period of his tenure in the White House, 1913 to 1921, was a time of far-reaching attempts to resolve the dilemma posed by the existence of private economic autocracy in a political and social democracy. Abroad, it was a time of revolutionary upheaval, cataclysmic world war, and shifts in the balance of power that threatened the very foundations of the international order.

As a domestic leader, articulating American democratic traditions and using the resources of party and presidential leadership to devise and achieve solutions for the problems raised by twentieth-century economic and social developments, Wilson succeeded so well that he earned an undisputed place among the first rank of presidents. As a leader in foreign affairs, guiding the American people from provincialism toward world leadership and responsibilities, Wilson's work was even more significant for the long future than were his immediate achievements in domestic affairs.

The sources of Wilson's strength and weakness as a maker of foreign policy will perhaps become evident as we proceed, but we might begin by saying that there is considerable revelation in the nature of his training as a diplomatist before 1913. Insofar as it went, that training was exclusively academic and theoretical. He had thorough training in international law, modern history, and comparative systems of government, and he taught all these subjects with increasing effectiveness and some distinction after 1885. His knowledge of these fields, and particularly his disciplined habit of looking at events with a self-conscious effort to take a detached, long view of them, would stand him in good stead when, as President, he had to confront momentous questions of policy. Over and over—for example, during crises with Mexico and Germany before 1917 and during the war and the Paris Peace Conference—we find Wilson trying to take the long historical view and to persuade others to follow his example. On numerous occasions he said that he was playing for the verdict of history. As he said to Ida Tarbell in 1916:

> In handling national affairs feeling must never take precedence of judgment. I used to tell my students long before I had an idea of going into politics that no case could ever be made up at the time it was developing. The final judgment on everything that happens in the world will be made up long years after the happening—that is, the student always has the last say. He interprets the letters, the documents. I have tried to look at this war ten years ahead, to be a historian at the same time I was an actor. A hundred years from now it will not be the bloody details that the world will think of in this war: it will be the causes behind it, the readjustments which it will force.

On the other hand, Wilson, as scholar and analyst, had been almost exclusively concerned with domestic politics in the Anglo-American tradition and only casually interested in the mechanisms and history of foreign relations. In his first and best-known book, *Congressional Government,* published in 1885, Wilson made only a passing reference to foreign affairs. Four years later, Wilson published *The State,* an excellent pioneer textbook in comparative government. Out of a total of more than one hundred pages devoted to the development of law and legal institutions, he gave a page and a half to international law. Moreover, in his summary chapters on the functions and objects of government, he put foreign relations at the bottom of his list of what he called the "constituent functions." He then went on to elaborate the functions and objects of government without even mentioning the conduct of external affairs!

Wilson began to evidence more than a casual interest in foreign affairs for the first time in the late 1890s and early 1900s.

In part, he was reacting to new shifts in international power then in process; in part, to changes in American thinking about the future role of the United States in world affairs as a consequence of the Venezuelan controversy with Great Britain, the War with Spain, the extension of American interests to the Far East, and the acquisition of an overseas empire. However, Wilson did more than merely react to these epochal developments; he also thought seriously about their future impact upon American policies and institutions. The War with Spain, he wrote in his *History of the American People* (1902), had been only one sign of a more important underlying development: the end of American isolation and the inevitable beginning of a new era in which the United States would have to play a widening role in world politics. It followed inexorably, Wilson added, at about the same time, in an essay in *Atlantic Monthly* called "Democracy and Efficiency," that Americans were living in a new and more perilous age in which changed circumstances had rendered meaningless and dangerous their time-encrusted traditions of self-sufficiency and security through isolation. The American people, he concluded, were now neighbors to the world, whether they liked it or not, and could not escape the coming challenges by ignoring them.

Wilson also saw clearly that the sudden emergence of the United States to world power would have a profound and enduring impact upon the location of authority and leadership in the federal government. "Much the most important change to be noticed," he wrote in the preface to the fifteenth edition of *Congressional Government* in 1900, "is the result of the war with Spain upon the lodgment and exercise of power within our federal system: the greatly increased power and opportunity for constructive statesmanship given the President, by the plunge into international politics and into the administration of distant dependencies, which has been that war's most striking and momentous consequence."

Finally, in the last scholarly lectures that he ever delivered outside a classroom—the Blumenthal Lectures at Columbia University in 1907, published the following year as *Constitutional Government in the United States*—Wilson once again noted as follows:

The war with Spain again changed the balance of parts. Foreign questions became leading questions again, as they had been in the first days of the government, and in them the President was of necessity leader. Our new place in the affairs of the world has since that year of transformation kept him at the front of our government, where our own thoughts and the attention of men everywhere is centred upon him. . . . Our President can never again be the mere domestic figure he has been throughout so large a part of our history. The nation has risen to the first rank in power and resources. . . . Our President must always, henceforth, be one of the great powers of the world, whether he act greatly and wisely or not. . . . We have but begun to see the presidential office in this light; but it is the light which will more and more beat upon it, and more and more determine its character and its effect upon the politics of the nation.

Regardless of the adequacy or inadequacy of his preparation, after 1912 Wilson faced foreign problems of greater magnitude than any President since the early years of the nineteenth century. Whether he responded wisely or unwisely to mounting international challenges, he carried out policies that were firmly grounded upon a consistent body of principles and assumptions that supplied motive power and shaped policy in the fields of action in diplomacy as, indeed, in domestic policy also. These principles and assumptions were deeply rooted in Wilson's general thinking about God, ethics, the nature and ends of government, and the role of his own country in the creative development of mankind. They were in turn enlarged and refined as Wilson sought to apply them in practical affairs after his inauguration.

The foundations of all of Wilson's political thinking were the values and beliefs that he inherited from the Christian tradition in general and from Presbyterianism in particular. Indeed, it is not too much to say that his every action and policy was ultimately informed and molded by his Christian faith. Regarding that faith, Wilson was like a little child, never doubting, always believing, and drawing power for life from Bible reading, church attendance, and prayer. Having derived his faith from his father, the Reverend Dr. Joseph Ruggles Wilson, the Westminster Confession, and the Shorter Catechism, Wilson was, inevitably, a Calvinist. He believed in a sovereign God, just and stern; in a moral universe, the laws of which ruled nations as well as men; in the supreme revelation of Jesus Christ; and in the Bible as the incomparable word of God and the rule of life. He believed that God controls history and uses men and nations in the unfolding of His plan according to His purpose.

A second main theme in Wilson's political thinking with large implications for his foreign policy was his belief in democracy as the most advanced, humane, and Christian form of government. From the beginning to the end of his adult career, he studied, wrote about, and put into practice the essential aspects of democratic government. We do not have the time to review his splendid synthesis of Anglo-American democratic theories and traditions. In any event, more important for our purposes is an understanding of the way in which these basic political beliefs helped to form his objectives and determine his policies in foreign affairs.

Much—everything—depended upon Wilson's view of the nature and capacities of man. He believed that all peoples were capable of self-government because all were endowed with inherent character and capacity for growth. It is important to say that he was too good a student of history to be visionary in these beliefs. He repudiated and condemned utopianism and taught that people learn democracy only by long years of disciplined experience. As early as 1885, we find him saying,

Democracy is, of course, wrongly conceived when treated as merely a body of doctrine. It is a stage of development. It is not created by aspirations or by new faith; it is built up by slow habit. Its process is experience, its basis old wont, its meaning national organic oneness and effectual life. It comes, like manhood, as the fruit of youth: immature peoples cannot have it, and the maturity to which it is vouchsafed is the maturity of freedom and self-control, and no other.

The fact remained, even so, that Wilson thought that all peoples, whether they be Mexican peons or Russian peasants, whites, blacks, or Orientals, were capable of being trained in the habits of democracy. "When properly directed," he said in 1914, "there is no people not fitted for self-government."

These assumptions inevitably had profound implications for Wilson's thought about the development and relationships of nations. His belief in the capacity of man, in progress as the law of organic life and the working out of the divine plan in history, and in democracy as the highest form of government fired in him the hope that democracy would some day be the universal rule of political life.

The final main assumptions of Wilson's thoughts about international relations grew out of his attempt to define America's role in world affairs within the context of American democratic traditions and his own political and religious faith. He believed that the American people had a peculiar role to play in history precisely because they were in so many ways unique among the peoples of the world. They were unique politically, he believed, not because they alone possessed democratic institutions, but because they had succeeded in organizing diverse sections and a hundred million people into a federal system such as one day (he at last conceived) might provide a model for a world organization. The American people were unique socially, first, because of their radical affirmation of equality and historic repudiation of everything for which the caste- and class-ridden societies of Europe and Asia stood, and, second, because they were in fact a new people, the product of the mixing of all races of the world. Finally, they were unique morally: the United States, Wilson believed, had been born that men might be free. Americans had done more than any other people to advance human welfare. Americans, above all other peoples, were, as he put it, "custodians of the spirit of righteousness, of the spirit of equal-handed justice, of the spirit of hope which believes in the perfectibility of the law with the perfectibility of human life itself."

Thus America's mission in the world was not to attain wealth and power, but to serve mankind through leadership in moral purposes and in advancing peace and world unity. One scholar has well summarized Wilson's view: America's "mission was to realize an ideal of liberty, provide a model of democracy, vindicate moral principles, give examples of action and ideals of government and righteousness to an interdependent world, uphold the rights of man, work for humanity and the happiness of men everywhere, lead the thinking of the world, promote peace—in sum, to serve mankind and progress."[1]

By emphasizing Wilson's concept of the American mission, I do not mean to suggest that he was oblivious to economic realities behind foreign policy, or even to the necessity of a nation having well-defined international economic policies and objectives. It is quite true, as N. Gordon Levin, Jr., has pointed out in his *Woodrow Wilson and World Politics* (New York: Oxford University Press,

---

1. Harley Notter, *The Origins of the Foreign Policy of Woodrow Wilson* (Baltimore: The Johns Hopkins Press, 1937), p. 653.

1968), that Wilson believed, as did numerous other thoughtful contemporaries, that, on account of the ending of the frontier, American prosperity in the twentieth century would in part depend upon the expansion of American overseas exports and investments. It is also true, as Carl P. Parrini has pointed out in his *Heir to Empire: United States Economic Diplomacy, 1916–1923* (Pittsburgh: University of Pittsburgh Press, 1969), that the foundations of modern American international economic policy were solidly laid by the Wilson administration, and that it worked quite knowingly to facilitate the transfer of financial hegemony from London to New York from about 1915 to 1920.

However, in devising international economic policy, Wilson and his advisers operated well within the boundaries that were firmly set by their conception of the historic mission of the United States, one which I think we might say was a national inheritance from the eighteenth and nineteenth centuries and was shared by the great majority of thoughtful Americans. This Wilsonian international economic policy, if such it may be called, included promotion of international trade through a general lowering of tariff walls, a destruction of all systems of monopoly and special privileges, and, above all, a fair field with no favors, as much for Americans as for the Japanese, British, or French. This was of course the historic conception of the Open Door, but it was an Open Door that was to be employed, not for the oppressive exploitation of underdeveloped areas, but for the slow and steady improvement of mankind through the spread of a reformed and socially responsible democratic capitalism. I do not recall a single instance when Wilson and his subordinates ever sought to obtain for any American citizen monopolistic concessions or preferential treatment in investment and trade.

The assumptions and ideals just enumerated bore so heavily upon the formation of Wilson's foreign policies that we cannot be content merely to describe them. We must also attempt to see the degree to which they equipped or unfitted President Wilson for the needs of practical diplomacy.

Only a confirmed cynic would fail to recognize that a large measure of Wilson's strength as a diplomatist and much of his contribution to the field of international relations stemmed in the first instance from his spiritual resources. There *were* certain practical advantages in idealism. By rejecting selfish, narrow nationalism and materialism as bases for foreign policy, and by articulating the noblest traditions of western culture, Wilson could and did speak as with universal authority. Ideals are a dynamic force in cultures that acknowledge their validity, and Wilson was a more effective war leader, a more fearful antagonist of German military leaders on the ideological battlefield, and a more indomitable fighter for a just peace settlement precisely because he stood for what most men in the western world (including his enemies) were willing to acknowledge were their own best ideals.

However, one cannot measure the significance of Wilson's idealism in practical terms alone. Without ideals to recall lost visions and give guidance for the present and future, societies degenerate into tyrannies of individuals, classes, or ideologies. It was Wilson's great contribution that he held high the traditions of humanity and the ideal of justice while hatreds and passions threatened to wreck western civilization. I refer specifically to his marvelous synthesis of humane international ideals embodied in his "Peace without Victory" speech to the Senate of January 22, 1917, his Fourteen Points address to Congress of January 8, 1918, and his subsequent war messages. By his rhetoric and moral power, he not only rallied men of good will in defense of these ideals but also helped to save them for future generations.

Wilson's assumptions and principles also to some degree impaired his leadership in the mundane affairs of state. His thinking, even more about foreign than about domestic matters, sometimes failed to take sufficient account of what specialists in international relations call "realities." The qualifying adjective *sufficient* is of vital significance. Wilson was never a fool or a visionary incapable of facing reality; on the contrary, he was keenly intelligent and often shrewd. And yet his faith in the goodness and rationality of men, the unbounded potentialities of democracy, and the inevitable triumph of righteousness sometimes caused him to make illusory appraisals and devise unworkable solutions.

Second, Wilson's uncommon concern with the fundamental principles of national and international life occasionally led him to oversimplify the complexities of international politics. He also had a tendency to invoke analogies between domestic and international politics without taking sufficient account of the enormous differences between the two.

A third point was the unreal quality of some of Wilson's thought and policy that resulted from his faith in the sufficiency of democratic solutions. This was revealed in his attempts to apply constitutional and democratic criteria to Central America and the Caribbean states, to the revolutionary upheaval in Mexico, and finally to the revolutionary situation in Russia between the fall of the czarist government and the triumph of the Bolsheviks. In all these situations, ordinary democratic concepts simply did not apply. Yet Wilson at least gave the impression of believing that solutions lay in the establishment of enlightened and responsible governments through free elections.

Having made these generalizations, I must also add that they apply largely to Wilson during his apprenticeship as a diplomatist. For example, in dealing with revolutionary situations in China, Mexico, and the Caribbean states during the first two years of his presidency, Wilson sought, among other things, to apply his assumptions about the mission of the United States to the world. He would teach the war-torn countries of northern Latin America how to elect good leaders. He would seek to protect the struggling Chinese Republic from avaricious imperialism. He would assist the Mexican people in their struggle for democratic institutions.

Wilson was a rapid learner, however. He soon discovered that a diplomacy of helpfulness can be immensely difficult, troublesome, and even dangerous because it often involves the power that tries to be helpful in the domestic quagmire of the country being helped. While trying to impose a democratic solution on Mexico, he also learned the realities of a revolutionary situation. Singlehanded, he turned the policy of his administration away from interference in Mexican affairs to acceptance of the Mexican Revolution on its own terms. After struggling vainly to help Dominicans and Haitians to achieve stability, he imposed military regimes on these peoples—surely a "realistic" solution. He soon recognized that noble intentions and moralisms did not suffice for complicated situations in the Far East. The Christian optimist had become very much of a realist in diplomacy at least by the middle of 1915.

From this point on, confronted by the challenges of war in Europe, Wilson grew in experience and stature as a diplomatist, one who was being forced by circumstances to move more and more on the stage of world affairs. He was able to thread his way through the Scylla and Charybdis of the British cruiser and the German submarine by increasingly deft steering of the ship of state, and to do so in the face of mounting challenges for more than two and a half years. At the same time, he began to try to use American diplomatic, economic, and military power for a rational and constructive purpose: the mediation of the European war. No one who has followed him from the autumn of 1916 through the spring of 1917, when he launched his mediation effort and then had to make his decision for war, can doubt, I think, that he had matured by this time into a seasoned diplomatist of superb technical ability and great flexibility.

Much light on Wilson is also shed by study of his techniques and methods as a diplomatist. These techniques and methods stemmed in an all-pervasive way from his temperament, and we have to begin by examining those aspects of his personality that bore directly upon his practice of leadership. In temperament, Wilson was an activist, endowed with an intensity that was never satisfied with mere speculation but had to find an outlet in action. Driving force, relentless energy, and striving for definitive solutions characterized most of his efforts in the field of foreign affairs. They were at once sources of power and of danger.

Mature conviction from scholarly study concerning the role that the President should play also helped to determine Wilson's methods as a maker of foreign policy. Even during that period in his scholarly writing when he emphasized congressional supremacy, Wilson recognized the President's latitude in the conduct of affairs abroad. That recognition had grown into a sweeping affirmation of presidential sovereignty by the time that Wilson had reached maturity in his thought about the American constitutional system.

"One of the greatest of the President's powers," he said in his Blumenthal lectures in 1907,

I have not yet spoken of at all: his control, which is very absolute, of the foreign relations of the nation. The initiative in foreign affairs, which the President possesses without any restriction whatever, is virtually the power to control them absolutely. The President cannot conclude a treaty with a foreign power without the consent of the Senate, but he may guide every step of diplomacy, and to guide diplomacy is to determine what treaties must be made, if the faith and prestige of the government are to be maintained. He need disclose no step of negotiation until it is complete, and when in any critical matter it is completed the government is virtually committed. Whatever its disinclination, the Senate may feel itself committed also.

It was a striking forecast of Wilson's own management of foreign affairs a few years later. In the areas that he considered vitally important—Mexico, relations with the European belligerents, wartime relations with the Allied powers, the problem of the Russian revolution, and the writing of a peace settlement—Wilson exercised almost absolute personal control. He wrote most of the important diplomatic correspondence on his own typewriter, sometimes bypassed the State Department by using his own private agents and advisers, occasionally conducted important negotiations behind the backs of his Secretaries of State, and in general acted like a divine-right monarch in the conduct of foreign relations.

No one who knows much about the Wilson era would quarrel with the foregoing generalizations. However, it is more important to understand why they were true than to state them.

Wilson took personal responsibility for the conduct of the important diplomacy of the United States chiefly because he believed that it was wise, right, and necessary for him to do so. Believing as he did that the people had temporarily vested their sovereignty in foreign affairs in him, he could not delegate responsibility in this field to any individual. His scholarly training and self-disciplined habits of work made him so much more efficient than his advisers that he must have thought that the most economical way of doing important diplomatic business was for him to do it himself. Experience in dealing with subordinates who sometimes tried to defeat his purposes also led him to conclude that it was the safest method, for he, and not his subordinates, bore the responsibility to the American people and to history for the consequences of his policies.

Second, Wilson had the bad luck to be President at a time when the structure of the Executive branch was woefully inadequate for the burdens imposed upon it. As President, Wilson had one assistant, Joseph P. Tumulty, a private secretary, and a few typists in the Executive Office to prepare his routine correspondence. In the conduct of foreign relations, Wilson was equally shorthanded. As compared to the Post Office, Treasury, and Interior Departments, the State Department was one of the smaller departments of the government. In size it was comparable to the foreign offices of Latin American and small European states. Morever, the State Department had no good system of intelligence. Yet, by 1913, the United States was a great power and having increasingly to act like one. Lack of adequate personnel meant that much of the increasing burden of conducting foreign relations fell upon Wilson himself.

Third, Wilson often felt obliged to take personal control because so many of his subordinates, from the Secretary of State down to division chiefs in the Department of State and including Ambassadors and Ministers in the field, were incompetent. Wilson's first Secretary of State, William Jennings Bryan, received his appointment, not because he had any particular qualifications for the post, but because the administration had to have his support for its domestic program. Unfortunately, Bryan was an avid spoilsman and dismissed most of the career men in the Foreign Service and replaced them with faithful and deserving Democrats. One of Bryan's appointees, James M. Sullivan, Minister to the Dominican Republic, was not only incompetent but also corrupt. In addition, it was difficult for Wilson to staff nonprofessional posts with experienced and able men simply because the Democratic party had been so long out of national power that it lacked a cadre of experienced personnel. For example, Wilson tried desperately to find what he called the best men for ambassadorships and to break the custom of using these offices as rewards for party service. Except in a few cases, the "best" men would not accept appointment, and Wilson had to yield to pressure and name party hacks to places like Berlin, St. Petersburg, Rome, and Madrid.

Wilson was also encumbered with his quota of disloyal advisers and agents, and this was a fourth reason for his conviction that it was necessary for him to keep close supervision over all details of foreign policy. I do not mean to distort this reason by exaggeration. Bryan was the soul of loyalty and resigned when he could not follow his superior's policy with complete sincerity. Most other officers in the State Department and Foreign Service were faithful servants. Col. Edward M. House, Wilson's most intimate adviser on foreign policy, usually managed to suppress his overweening egotism and to represent Wilson loyally before

1919. Wilson's greatest problem before that date was Robert Lansing, Secretary of State from 1915 to 1920. Lansing, who looked every inch the statesman, was brilliant while executing routine business and often bungling while conducting important negotiations. A very bad blunder by Lansing in the controversy over armed ships in January 1916 first revealed the Secretary of State's ineptness to the President and was one reason why Wilson increasingly refused to permit him to make any important decisions on his own. Worse still, the discussions over policy toward German submarine warfare in the spring of 1916 first made it apparent to Wilson that Lansing was trying to lead him into war, and Lansing revealed this purpose even more clearly in the following autumn and winter. Since Wilson did not want to go to war, his distrust of Lansing naturally increased. Finally, the President lost all confidence in his Secretary of State when Lansing tried to sabotage Wilson's efforts to end the war through mediation in December 1916 and January 1917. Unable to find a good replacement or to dismiss Lansing in the midst of various crises, Wilson thought that he had no recourse but to conduct all important negotiations himself.

Wilson's critics have suggested a final reason for his techniques as a diplomatist: his alleged personal egotism, jealousy of others, and inability ever to delegate authority. I am bound to say that a search of the record does not yield much evidence to support these charges. A fairer conclusion would be that Wilson was generous in dealing with subordinates, welcomed and took advice, and often changed his mind. However, he did insist upon recognition of the fact that he was the President of the United States, and that as such he bore the responsibility for decisions and had a right to expect his subordinates to accept and loyally support those decisions.

In the final reckoning, Wilson will be judged not so much by what he thought about foreign policy or his techniques as a diplomatist as by what he was able or unable to accomplish. No such pattern of almost unbroken success marked his record as a maker of foreign policy as it did his record in domestic affairs. He failed to achieve many of the foreign policy objectives nearest to his heart. During the first two and a half years of the First World War, he ardently desired to restore peace through his own mediation. He tried and failed. He sincerely hoped to keep his country from being sucked into the war's vortex. He tried and failed. He worked with incredible energy to construct a just and lasting peace settlement after the war. He did not succeed—at least, not completely. He destroyed his health in a supreme effort to persuade the Senate to consent to American membership in his creation, the League of Nations, and the American people to take leadership in rebuilding the international community. Again, finally, he failed.

It is interesting that the world honors Wilson most for his failures. It remembers the heroic, often lonely, figure standing foursquare at Paris against forces of hatred, greed, and imperialism. It remembers the dauntless fighter stumping the country in an incredible and nearly fatal forensic effort. It remembers the man broken in health but not in spirit, unyielding to what he thought was shameful compromise, confident that the sovereign Lord of history would turn all events into their appointed channels.

However, the passage of time—it is now more than half a century since the Paris Peace Conference—is enabling us to see Wilson and his contributions in the field of international relations with greater perspective than we once possessed. We have lost our innocence about foreign affairs and no longer expect either miracles or the millennium. And what once seemed like Wilson's failures do not look altogether like failures now.

We are beginning to see that Wilson's achievements in the realm of foreign affairs were larger than we once thought and that he accomplished much even in momentary failure. Indeed, we are able to see that the passage of time has crystallized these achievements into legacies for our own time.

One of these achievements was Wilson's strong reaffirmation of the old American tradition of disinterested helpfulness to nations struggling toward self-government and a more abundant life. Cynics will smile and say that no great power can ever be altruistic in dealing with other nations, particularly small and helpless nations. They are of course right to some degree. However, it was Wilson's accomplishment that he both showed the dangers of an excess of missionary diplomatic zeal and proved that it is possible for great nations to assist small ones with a varying degree of altruism and success.

A second achievement was Wilson's vindication of the tradition that all peoples have the right, qualified only by their capacity to exercise it responsibly and without doing injury to others, to self-determination and self-government. Wilson achieved notable immediate and long-term successes in fighting for this tradition. By defending the Mexican Revolution against European and American enemies, he made it possible for the Mexican people to hew out their own destiny. His utterances during the war and afterward helped to destroy ancient empires based upon the subjugation of minority peoples. His success in establishing the mandate system helped to spell an end to old-fashioned imperialism and colonialism.

A third achievement was Wilson's strengthening of the principle of peaceful settlement of international disputes and the avoidance of war if conceivably possible. Twice he personally prevented seemingly irresistible events from plunging the United States into war with Mexico. He fought long and hard to avoid participation in the First World War, enduring egregious violations of American neutral rights and taunts by his enemies that he was a moral coward, afraid, rather than too proud, to fight. His success in maintaining American neutrality for two and a half years in these circumstances was no mean achievement in itself. He accepted belligerency in 1917 because he was not able to find an alternative, but he took careful pains after the war to write into fundamental international law the principle that all international disputes had to be settled by arbitration or conciliation.

His final achievement was in laying strong foundations for the tradition that the American people can best serve mankind by committing their resources and power to the quest for peace through international co-operation. It is almost trite to say that Wilson, by his fight for American membership in and leadership of the League of Nations, did more than any other single man in our history to build this tradition. The fact that he failed momentarily is of minor significance in the long sweep of history.

This concludes my review of Wilson the diplomatist. It has necessarily been somewhat subjective. Opinions about Wilson will continue to vary, for he was not a small man, and he still evokes strong reactions one way or the other. On one point we can, I am sure, all agree: that it made considerable difference that he lived and played his role in world affairs.

7

Wilson and the
Ordeal of Neutrality

THE outbreak of war in Europe in August 1914 came, in its suddenness, to President Wilson like a bolt of lightning out of a clear sky. To be sure, Wilson had not been unaware of the possibility of a conflagration, for his confidential adviser and sometime agent, Col. Edward M. House, writing from Berlin in May 1914, had warned that Europe was a powder keg about to explode. However, House's talks with German and British leaders had raised the tantalizing possibility of an Anglo-American-German entente under Wilson's auspices. No one in Washington (or in European capitals, for that matter) saw that the fuse was burning rapidly after the murder of the heir to the Austrian and Hungarian thrones and his young wife by a Serbian nationalist in Sarajevo on June 28, 1914. Moreover, when the great European powers went over the brink in late July and early August, Wilson was mired in controversy with Congress and in deep despair over the fatal illness of his wife. He could only wait in fascinated horror as Sir Edward Grey, the British foreign minister, wept as he told the American ambassador in London, Walter Page, about the British ultimatum to Germany, and King George exclaimed, "My

Reprinted from *History of the 20th Century* (London: BPC Publishing Ltd., 1968), pp. 652–656, by permission of the Publishers.

God, Mr. Page, what else could we do?" One American well expressed what was surely Wilson's reaction when he wrote: "The horror of it all kept me awake for weeks, nor has the awfulness of it all deserted me, but at first it seemed a horrid dream."

But Armageddon *had* come. Wilson, as head of the greatest neutral power, whose interests would be vitally affected by belligerent measures, had perforce to work out his policies toward the warring powers.

Throughout the long months of American neutrality, from August 1914 to April 1917, Wilson, whatever his own predispositions, had to work within limits imposed by American public opinion. That opinion was so divided in its preferences for various belligerents during the first months of the war that any policy for the United States other than a strict neutrality would have been inconceivable. Wilson remarked to the German ambassador, Count Johann von Bernstorff, that "we definitely have to be neutral, since otherwise our mixed populations would wage war on each other." More important still, in spite of the attachments of various national and ethnic minorities, and of all the efforts of British, French, and German propagandists in the United States, the predominant American public opinion was consistently neutral before 1917. But Americans, even though they clung doggedly to their traditional isolationism and refused to believe that their vital interests were sufficiently involved in the outcome of the war to justify voluntary intervention, were nonetheless jealous of their sovereignty and international prestige. In other words, they would tolerate only a certain amount of provocation, and no more. To an extraordinary degree Wilson understood and shared the attitudes of the majority of his fellow-countrymen. Both expediency and conviction dictated policies that were agreeable to the great majority of Americans.

Although Wilson had strong emotional attachments to the Allies, particularly Great Britain, he profoundly admired German contributions to modern civilization. As a sophisticated student of modern history, he well understood that the causes of the war were complex and never imputed exclusive responsibility to either side. He was able to detach emotions from decisions and policies and, self-consciously, to make decisions on the basis of what he considered to be the best interests of America and Europe.

Wilson exercised greater personal control over foreign policy than any other chief of state among the great powers of the world. Constitutionally, as President, he was sovereign in the conduct of foreign relations, subject only to the Senate's veto on treaties. Weak Presidents have abdicated their responsibilities to strong secretaries of state or congressional leaders. But Wilson was a "strong" President. He believed that the people had invested their sovereignty in foreign affairs in him. He not only refused to delegate this responsibility, but insisted upon conducting foreign relations himself. Because he used his full constitutional powers to execute policies that the great majority desired, Wilson not only held the conduct of foreign affairs in his own hands, but was irresistible while doing so.

Wilson's whole world came tumbling down in the first week of August 1914. Ellen Axson Wilson, his beloved wife since 1885, died on August 6. Great Britain, which he loved, and Germany, which he admired, were already beginning to tear at each other's throats. Near hysteria reigned in Wall Street as a consequence of the disruption of international trade and exchange.

With his customary iron self-control, the President moved confidently and serenely to meet emergencies and establish American neutrality. The formalities were observed easily enough. Wilson proclaimed official neutrality on August 4 and, two weeks later, admonished his fellow-countrymen to be "impartial in thought as well as in action."

However, being neutral in the midst of a great war was easier said than done. For example, should the American government permit its citizens to sell vital raw materials and munitions to the Allies when British cruisers prevented the Germans from having access to such supplies? More difficult still, should the government permit American bankers to lend money, which the secretary of state, William Jennings Bryan, called the "worst of all contrabands," to the belligerents?

Having decided upon a policy of strict neutrality, Wilson, helped by Bryan and the counselor of the State Department, Robert Lansing, proceeded as systematically and as impartially as possible to be neutral in every circumstance. Hence he permitted the Allies to purchase as much contraband as they pleased, for to have denied them access to American markets and the benefits that flowed from dominant seapower would have been not only unneutral, but tantamount to undeclared war. For the same reason he permitted American bankers to lend money both to the Allied and German governments.

Wilson followed the rush of the German army through Belgium into northern France and was obviously relieved when the French and British were able to establish a secure defensive line by early autumn. At this point, at any rate, Germany seemed to threaten neither America's vital interests nor her neutral rights. Wilson's main problem in late 1914 was defending American trading rights against British seapower, or, to put the matter more realistically, coming to terms with the British maritime system.

Acting as neutrals always have during wartime, Wilson wanted to keep the channels of commerce to all of Europe open as widely as possible to American ships and goods. Acting as dominant seapowers always have, the British set about to cut off the flow of life-giving supplies from the United States to Germany and Austria-Hungary. Consequently, dispatches about these matters passed frequently between Washington and London, not only during the first months of the war, but as late as 1916. There was much talk of "freedom of the seas" on the one side and of legitimate belligerent rights on the other. Actually, what sounded like the rhetoric of developing crisis masked the fact that there was substantial goodwill and accommodation on both sides. For their part, the British instituted maritime measures that were not only largely legitimate, but also were based upon precedents established by the United States government itself during the American Civil War of 1861–65. For his part, Wilson, understanding these facts, rejected demands of highly partisan German Americans and American economic interests with a large stake in free trade with Germany for measures to break the British blockade or prevent the Anglo-American trade in contraband.

Having passed through troubles that might have burgeoned into serious Anglo-American crisis, Wilson, at the end of 1914, could view the general state of American relations with the belligerents with some equanimity. There seemed to be no chance of serious conflict with Germany: there were simply no points of contact between the two nations. By Wilson's reckoning, the war would end either in stalemate or, more likely, in an Allied victory. He told a reporter for the New York *Times*, in an off-the-record interview on December 14, 1914, that he hoped ardently for a peace of reconciliation based upon negotiation. But, Wilson added, he did not think that it would "greatly hurt" the interests of the United States if the Allies won a decisive victory and dictated the settlement.

The German decision, announced on February 4, 1915, to use an untried weapon, the submarine, in a war against merchant shipping in the English Channel and a broad zone around the British Isles, created an entirely new situation, fraught with peril for the United States. Actually, at this time, the German navy did not possess enough submarines to prosecute an effective campaign, even against Allied merchant ships. But the Germans had compounded the blunder of acting prematurely, largely in bluff, by adding that *neutral* ships might be torpedoed because of the Allied use of neutral flags. It was only the first of a series of blunders by the German admiralty and the high command that would drive the United States into the war.

President Wilson replied to Berlin on February 10 with a stern warning that the United States would hold the German government to a "strict accountability" and probably go to war if German submarines indiscriminately and illegally attacked American vessels on the high seas.

As it turned out, the gravest German blunder was to provide the British and French governments with a good excuse for doing what they had already planned to do—severely to tighten their blockade measures. Now they need fear no serious American reprisal. Invoking the ancient right of reprisal, the London and Paris authorities announced on March 1 that, in retaliation against the illegal and ruthless German submarine campaign, they would stop *all* commerce of whatever character to the Central powers, even commerce through neutral ports.

Wilson and Bryan worked hard to arrange an Anglo-American agreement that would provide some protection for American shipping against the cruisers and submarines. Their efforts foundered upon the shoals of the German refusal to give up the submarine campaign except at the price of virtual abandonment by the British of an effective blockade. Wilson was in fact now helpless; he could only acquiesce in the new Anglo-French blockade so long as the sword of the submarine hung over his head.

The President waited in uncertainty all through the early spring of 1915 to see what the Germans would do. There were several attacks against American ships that might have set off a crisis. However, the submarine issue was brought to a head suddenly and dramatically when *U20*, Kapitänleutnant Walther Schwieger, without warning torpedoed the pride of the Cunard Line, the unarmed *Lusitania*, in the Irish Sea on May 7, 1915, killing 128 American citizens among many others.

It was impossible for Wilson to temporize, so violent was the reaction in the United States. Yet what could he do? It was evident after the first shock that a majority of Americans wanted their President to be firm and yet avoid war if possible. This, actually, was Wilson's own intention. In three notes between May and early July, Wilson eloquently appealed to the imperial German government to abandon what was obviously a campaign of sheer terror against *unarmed Allied passenger ships.* In the last note he warned that he would probably break diplomatic relations if the Germans did not abandon that campaign. To each of Wilson's pleas, the German foreign office replied by truculently refusing to admit the illegality of the destruction of *Lusitania.* The impasse was broken by a second incident that came hard on the heels of the *Lusitania* affair—the torpedoing without warning of the White Star liner, *Arabic,* outward bound from Liverpool, on August 19. Only when they saw that Wilson was on the brink did the Germans yield and promise not to sink unarmed Allied passenger liners without warning. Indeed, Wilson's firmness, and the lack of enough submarines to prosecute a decisive underseas campaign, paid even larger dividends in the form of guarantees that the German navy would sink American ships only after making full provision for the safety of human life, and that compensation would be made for all ships and cargoes captured or destroyed.

The subsequent German-American *détente* (encouraged by a temporary abandonment of the submarine campaign in general) set off demands in the United States, primarily by southern cotton producers in deep depression on account of the closing of their central European markets, for action against the total Allied blockade as firm as that taken against the German submarine campaign. Bryan had resigned in the middle of the *Lusitania* crisis, because he feared that Wilson's notes might lead the Germans to declare war against the United States. The new Secretary of State, Robert Lansing, did prepare a formidable indictment of the British maritime measure, and Wilson permitted it to go to London on November 5. But the President had no intention of enforcing the note's demands until German-American differences were clarified.

On the face of it, American relations with Great Britain and Germany had reached a state of tolerable equilibrium by the end of 1915. The Germans had quietly abandoned their submarine campaign in the North Atlantic, hence there were no incidents in that area to exacerbate German-American relations. For their part, the British had gone to extraordinary (and successful) lengths to support American cotton prices and to come to terms with other American producers who had been hard hit by the Allied blockade. But Wilson and his two principal diplomatic advisers, Colonel House and Lansing, were not reassured as they contemplated potential dangers in the months immediately ahead. The Allies were beginning to arm not only passenger liners but ordinary merchantmen as well, and, apparently, were ordering these ships to attack submarines upon sight. Second, reports from Berlin made it unmistakably clear that there had been only a respite in the submarine campaign, and that the Germans were preparing to use the arming of Allied ships as an excuse for an all-out campaign. So far, *ad hoc* solutions had sufficed to preserve the peace, but it now seemed that events might develop which would remove all options. For example, a really ruthless submarine campaign might drive the United States, willy-nilly, into war, without any other purpose than sheer defense of national rights.

Wilson and House pondered long about the situation in the hope of gaining some initiative and of giving some purpose to American belligerency if it had to come. Sir Edward Grey had said only two months before that his government might be willing to consider a negotiated settlement if the United States would promise to join a postwar league of nations and guarantee to help maintain future peace. Seizing the seeming opportunity offered by Grey's suggestion, Wilson sent House to London in late December 1915 with instructions to work for Anglo-American agreement to co-operate in a drive for peace under Wilson's auspices. If that *démarche* should fail on account of German obduracy, Wilson said, the United States would probably enter the war on the Allied side.

While House was in London opening negotiations, Lansing and Wilson launched their own campaign to get the United States off the submarine hook. The Secretary of State, on January 18,

1916, urged the Allies to disarm their merchantmen if the Germans would agree to warn such vessels and evacuate their crews before sinking them. Lansing added that his government was contemplating treating armed merchantmen as warships, which would mean that they could not engage in commerce at American ports. The Germans, gleefully agreeing with the Secretary of State, announced that submarines would sink all armed merchantmen without warning after February 28.

Reaction in London to what was called Lansing's *modus vivendi* was so violent that it threatened to wreck House's negotiations. Wilson thereupon hastily withdrew the *modus vivendi.* This action in turn set off a panic in Congress that the United States would go to war to protect the right of citizens to travel on armed ships. Wilson beat back a congressional resolution warning Americans against travelling on armed ships, but he made it clear that only lightly armed merchantmen would be permitted to use American ports, and, more important, that he did not intend to make a great issue with the German government over armed ships in any event.

There was considerable relief both on Capitol Hill and in Whitehall. In London, Sir Edward Grey and House initialled, on February 22, 1916, what is known as the House-Grey Memorandum embodying Wilson's plan of mediation.

Colonel House returned to Washington on March 5 in high excitement to tell the President that the British and French were eager to move as rapidly as possible for peace under Wilson's aegis. While Wilson and House were in the midst of planning for the great venture, a German submarine torpedoed a French packet steamer, *Sussex,* in the English Channel on March 24 with heavy loss of life. Reports of ruthless attacks against unarmed merchantmen followed in rapid succession.

After much backing and filling, and mainly in order to pave the way for his mediation, Wilson sent an ultimatum to Berlin on April 18, warning that he would break relations with Germany if she did not agree hereafter to require her submarine commanders to observe the rules of visit and search before sinking all unarmed ships, whether passenger liners or merchantmen. The German admiralty lacked enough U-boats to justify the risk of war with the United States and European neutrals like Holland and Denmark. Consequently, the imperial chancellor, Theobald von Bethmann Hollweg, won the Kaiser's support for submission to Wilson's demand. However, while yielding, the Germans reserved the "right" to resume freedom of decision on the use of submarines if the American government failed to compel the Allies to respect international law in the conduct of their blockade.

The happy settlement of the *Sussex* crisis, coupled with intimations that the Germans were eager for peace talks, spurred Wilson to action to put the House-Grey Memorandum into operation. His first public move was to announce, in an address in Washington on May 27, that the United States was prepared to abandon its traditional isolationism and join a postwar league of nations. Privately, through Colonel House, he exerted heavy pressure on Grey to put the memorandum's machinery into motion by signalling his government's readiness for Wilson's mediation. Grey responded evasively at first; but Wilson would not be diverted, and then Grey had to tell him frankly that neither the British nor the French governments would consent to peace talks at this time or in the foreseeable future.

Grey's refusal to execute the House-Grey Memorandum, a crushing blow to the President's hopes for an early peace in itself, combined with other developments to cause Wilson to effect what would turn out to be an almost radical change in his policies toward the European belligerents.

First, the British government not only refused to relax its controls over American commerce, but, on the contrary, intensified its maritime and economic warfare in the spring and summer of 1916. In retrospect, the new British measures (including search and seizure of American mail on neutral ships and publication in the United States of a "blacklist" of American firms still doing business with the Central powers) seem trivial when compared with policies in which the Washington administration had already acquiesced. However, Wilson and a majority of Americans resented the new measures as direct affronts to their national sovereignty. Second, the British army's severe repression of the Easter Rising in Dublin in April not only inflamed Irish Americans, but also caused a tremendous diminution in Great Britain's moral standing throughout the United States. Finally, the German-American *détente,* following the *Sussex* crisis, sent a wave of neutralism across the country, one so strong that it engulfed the

Democratic national convention that re-nominated Wilson for the presidency.

These developments, of course, had their most important impact upon the man in the White House. They convinced him that the American people did not want to go to war over the alleged right of Americans to travel and work on belligerent ships. They forced Wilson to stand as the "peace" candidate and to accuse his Republican opponent, Charles Evans Hughes, of wanting war. More important, they caused a very considerable hardening of Wilson's attitudes against the Allies, particularly the British. By the early autumn, Wilson believed that the Allies were fighting for victory and spoils, not for a just peace.

Wilson could do nothing, of course, while the presidential campaign was in progress. However, once the voters, on November 7, 1916, invested him with their sovereignty for another four years, Wilson was free to act. And action of some kind seemed to be imperative, for it was growing increasingly evident that both sides were preparing to use desperate measures to break the stalemate that was consuming human life and resources at a prodigious rate. For the British, this would mean further intensification of economic warfare; for the Germans, it would mean revoking the *Sussex* pledge and launching a wholesale campaign against maritime commerce. The only way to peace and safety, Wilson concluded, was to bring the war to an end through his independent mediation.

Diverted briefly by domestic developments and Germany's own offer to negotiate, Wilson launched his peace bolt on December 18, 1916, by asking the belligerents to state the terms upon which they would be willing to end the fighting. The British and French were stunned and furious. But they were helpless to resist, so dependent had they become upon American credit and supplies for continuation of their war efforts. Then Lansing intervened. Committed emotionally to the Allied cause, he set out to sabotage the President's peace move by encouraging the British and French governments to state such terms as could be won only by a decisive military victory. The Germans, who very much wanted Wilson to force the Allies to the peace table but did not want him meddling once the conference had begun, returned an evasive reply.

Wilson was undisturbed. In mid-January 1917 he launched the second and decisive move in his campaign for peace—high-level, direct, and secret negotiations with the British and German governments to obtain their consent to his mediation. While waiting for their replies, the President went before the Senate on January 22 to tell the world what kind of settlement he had in mind and the American people would support by membership in a league of nations. The peace to be made, Wilson said, had to be a peace of reconciliation, a "peace without victory," for a victor's peace would leave "a sting, a resentment, a bitter memory upon which terms of peace would rest, not permanently, but only as upon quicksand."

For reasons that are still obscure, the new British cabinet, headed by David Lloyd George, sent word on January 26 to Wilson that it was prepared to accept the President's mediation. The Austro-Hungarians were desperately eager for peace. But on January 31, Wilson was informed of the German decision to adopt unrestricted submarine warfare.

Woodrow Wilson and Peace Moves

SIR Winston Churchill, commenting upon the role that Woodrow Wilson played during the era of the First World War, said:

Writing with every sense of respect, it seems no exaggeration to pronounce that the action of the United States with its repercussions on the history of the world depended, during the awful period of Armageddon, upon the workings of this man's mind and spirit to the exclusion of almost every other factor; and that he played a part in the fate of nations incomparably more direct and personal than any other man.

Churchill did not exaggerate the significance of President Wilson's role. Indeed, even before the war had ended, Wilson had become the principal exponent of a new world order and the chief hope of liberals throughout the world. But this did not happen all at once or at any given moment; and in this brief narrative I will try to relate how and why the American President moved to the center of the world stage.

No sooner had war begun in August 1914 than men began to talk of peace. Wilson had been too dazed by the swirl of events immediately preceding the declarations of war to take any forceful measures to avert hostilities. And he was going through a time-

Reprinted from *The Listener*, LXXV (June 16, 1966), 868–871, by permission of the Editor.

honored ritual when he offered American good offices of mediation to the belligerents in early August. He had to devote a great portion of his time during the autumn of 1914 to coping with problems raised by the British blockade of Germany and other threats to American neutral rights. By the end of 1914, American public opinion, while more friendly to the Allies than to Germany, was also clearly determined to avoid involvement if at all possible. This, too, was Wilson's own firm determination. Moreover, he had recovered his balance after the first shock of the war's outbreak and concluded that both alliances were fighting for what he thought were unworthy motives—revenge, military mastery, and selfish economic interests. So strong were American traditions of isolation, so massive was American neutralism, and so eager was the President himself to avoid entanglement that it seemed altogether improbable that the American government or its spokesman would play any decisive role in the outcome of Armageddon.

But events, as they often do to statesmen, slowly but inexorably took control out of Wilson's hands and led him into uncharted international waters. In early 1915, the American government was caught between the cross fire of a German submarine campaign that threatened American ships and lives and a greatly intensified British blockade that imperiled the interests of American producers and merchants. Wilson responded with a firmness tempered by flexibility, trying to find a *modus vivendi* with both Britain and Germany. In the midst of these efforts came the German torpedoing of the *Lusitania* on May 7, 1915, and of another British liner, *Arabic,* later in the summer, with heavy loss of American life. These incidents forced Wilson to a showdown encounter with the Germans over the safety of passenger liners. He won out in this struggle mainly because the Germans did not have enough submarines to justify risking war with the United States.

It was the great submarine crisis of 1915 that first caused Wilson to take a serious initiative for peace. To be sure, he coveted the role of peacemaker for humanitarian reasons. And he had sent his principal adviser on foreign policy, Col. Edward M. House, to Europe in the early months of 1915 to explore the possibilities of American mediation. But the grave dangers of being drawn into war on account of German submarine policies made a necessity out of virtue and impelled Wilson into his first aggressive action for peace.

Remarks by the British Foreign Secretary, Sir Edward Grey, in letters to Colonel House on August 10 and 26, 1915, seemed to suggest that American mediation might be possible. Grey hinted broadly that Britain, at least, might welcome American mediation if it were accompanied by guarantees that the United States would join a postwar league of nations and help to enforce the peace settlement to be made. Wilson responded eagerly with a positive commitment. Then, when Grey began to backtrack under increasing pressure from Washington, the President dispatched House to London in January 1916 to press for firm Anglo-American understanding.

House went also to Berlin, where he told the Germans nothing about his plans, and to Paris, where he tried to pave the way for French co-operation. But he stayed longest and worked hardest in London, trying to persuade Grey and the rest of the Cabinet to accept the plan that his fertile brain had matured. Under its provisions, Britain and France would request the American President to call a peace conference. The United States would not only issue the invitation but also probably enter the war if Germany refused the call. If the peace conference met, the United States would co-operate with the Allies in demanding a reasonable settlement and establishment of a league of nations. If the Germans were again obdurate, then the United States would probably enter the war on the side of the Allies.

House, in his discussions in London, made it crystal clear that Wilson, when he talked about a reasonable settlement, had in mind a peace of reconciliation, virtually the status quo ante bellum, accompanied by disarmament and establishment of a league of nations. The United States would support the restoration of Belgium, France's claim to Alsace-Lorraine, and certain other Allied war aims. But House insisted that Germany would have to be compensated also, and he at no time promised that the United States would go to war to achieve any particular Allied war objective, except, perhaps, restoration of Belgium. This, precisely, was the rub insofar as the British leaders were concerned. Grey, on February 22, 1916, initialled a memorandum embodying House's plan. But the Foreign Secretary was careful to stipulate that the Allies retained the right to decide when the plan was to be implemented.

In one of the most startling instances of self-delusion in history, House returned to Washington to inform the President that the British and French were eager for his mediation under the terms of the so-called House-Grey memorandum. Wilson thereupon reoriented his foreign policy, even running the risk of war with Germany during the crisis set off by the torpedoing of the Channel packet, *Sussex*. Wilson's next step was to announce to the world, in a speech in Washington on May 27, 1916, that the United States was prepared to join a postwar league of nations. "We are," he said, in announcing the end of America's century-old policy of isolation, "participants, whether we would or not, in the life of the world. The interests of all nations are our own also. We are partners with the rest. What affects mankind is inevitably our affair as well as the affair of the nations of Europe and of Asia."

All this in Wilson's mind was mere prelude. The culmination would be an irresistible drive for peace through Anglo-American co-operation. Hence the President, using House as his intermediary, began to apply heavy pressure on Grey to set the machinery of the House-Grey memorandum in motion. Unfortunately for Wilson's hopes, Grey had never taken that memorandum seriously, any more than he had made any legal or moral commitments in its provisions. To the end of his tenure in the Foreign Office, he thought of American mediation under its terms as a last resort to be used only as an alternative to defeat, and never to be invoked so long as the Allies had any reasonable hope of military victory. Grey, in his refusal to consider American mediation, reflected the positions of all leading belligerents at this time. The French and Germans, still locked in death grapple at Verdun, were in no mood for peace talks. The British were about to launch the great offensive on the Somme that they were sure would smash the German lines. Moreover, none of the belligerent leaders trusted Wilson. He was, they believed, unreliable, indecisive, and naive. Worse still, he seemed to face certain defeat in the presidential election in November 1916.

It was clear before summer had reached its midway mark that Grey would not co-operate. It was also clear that the American people were in no warlike mood. Neutralism and antiwar feeling surged through the country following the peaceful settlement of the *Sussex* crisis. It engulfed the Democratic party, particularly, and made it possible for the President to make peace the leading issue of his campaign. American opinion had, moreover, turned sharply against the British on account of their intensification of the blockade and, more important, their severe suppression of the Easter Rebellion.

Wilson inevitably reacted to these upheavals in public opinion. But he was also undergoing profound changes in his own thinking about the war and his role as possible mediator. Grey's refusal to co-operate, along with other British actions, had convinced him that the Allies were fighting not for a just peace but to destroy Germany for selfish economic and military reasons. Hence, in his own mind, Anglo-American co-operation for peace through the House-Grey memorandum was no longer desirable. His mediation, if the opportunity for it should come, would have to be an independent, truly neutral mediation.

That opportunity seemed to arrive in October 1916, when the German government asked the President to move for peace and warned that it might have to resume unlimited submarine warfare if the President's efforts failed. Wilson was surprised but excited, and he at once began discussions about plans for independent mediation with his principal advisers on foreign policy, Colonel House and Secretary of State Robert Lansing. These discussions were protracted, bitter, and revealing. Lansing was by this time emotionally committed to the cause of the Allies. He argued that American co-operation with Germany might well lead to a German-American sympathetic alliance if the Allies refused to come to the peace table. House supported Lansing, partly because he actually seems to have feared rupture and war with Britain.

Wilson rebuffed his advisers, saying that he was prepared to run these risks. But he could do nothing until the election was over. And even after his narrow re-election, he was diverted by domestic events and by certain German military measures in Belgium and several new submarine incidents. Meanwhile, the situation in Europe had changed, to Wilson's advantage and disadvantage. The Germans had invited Wilson's intervention in panic after Rumania's entry into the war, and while a strong Russian offensive in Galicia seemed to imperil the eastern front. By the end of November, the Germans and the Austro-Hungarians had not only turned back the Russians but had also virtually knocked Rumania out of the war. Even so, the German high command believed that they would lose the war if they could not gain victory by 1917. They thought that their only hope of winning lay in an all-out submarine campaign. Not certain about its outcome, they permitted the Imperial German Chancellor, Bethmann Hollweg, to issue his own call for a peace conference on December 12.

The Allies were in an equally deep gloom on account of the failure of the Somme offensive and reverses in the east. A suggestion that the British should move at once for peace, made by Lord Lansdowne on November 13—not to be confused with Lansdowne's letter to the *Daily Telegraph* a year later—set off a bitter debate in the Cabinet. Lloyd George, soon to become Prime Minister, believed that the war was lost. Worse still, from the British point of view, was the knowledge that the Allies were now so dependent upon the United States for munitions and supplies that the President held them in his hands.

To the President it was obvious that both the necessity and opportunity for his own independent action had come. He well knew that the Germans might launch a desperate submarine campaign, and that it might force the United States into the war. He also understood, at least partially, his absolute power over the Allies. Thus, still contrary to Lansing's advice, he launched his own peace bolt on December 18 by asking the belligerents to state the terms upon which they would be willing to end the war. This was the first public intervention in European affairs by a President since the founding of the United States. More important in our own context is the fact that it marked Wilson's emergence as a leading world figure.

Everything now depended upon the replies from Europe. The British and French leaders were stunned and outraged, but they well understood their helplessness and were in great disarray. Then Lansing intervened. Convinced that Wilson's course was disastrous, the Secretary of State set out to sabotage his peace effort. This Lansing did in several ways, but most importantly by intimating to the British and French ambassadors that the Washington administration expected their governments to say that their peace terms included, among other things, the return of Alsace-Lorraine to France, an indemnity for France, Belgium, and

Serbia, and establishment of an autonomous Poland under Russian sovereignty. Lansing knew that an announcement of such terms would be tantamount to a second declaration of war and drive the Germans over the brink in submarine policy. And he almost certainly knew that the latter would lead to American military involvement.

Receipt of Lansing's advice in London and Paris on December 20, 21, and 22 dispelled all gloom and apprehension. An Anglo-French conference to frame replies both to Bethmann's and Wilson's peace bids opened in London on December 26. The conferees quickly agreed to announce precisely the terms that Lansing had suggested. The Germans, too, reacted exactly as the Secretary of State had anticipated. The Berlin government had earlier returned an evasive reply to Wilson because it wanted only his help in forcing the Allies to the peace table, not his participation in the conference. Publication of the Anglo-French replies convinced many German leaders that the war had to be fought to the finish and upset the precarious balance of power between the generals and admirals on the one side and the Imperial Chancellor on the other. An Imperial Conference at Pless, on January 9, approved the navy's demand for an all-out submarine campaign against all merchant shipping, including American ships, to be inaugurated on February 1, 1917.

Wilson, unaware of the full degree of Lansing's disloyalty, had been undisturbed by the Anglo-French replies. They were, he told the German government, pure bluff and not to be taken seriously. Nor was he discouraged by the German reply. His peace note of December 18 had been merely the first, public step. In mid-January he launched the second and decisive stage of his campaign: secret negotiations with the British and German governments with a view to his immediate mediation. While waiting for their replies, he went before the Senate on January 22 to tell the world what kind of settlement he had in mind and the American people would support. The peace to be made, Wilson said, had to be a peace of reconciliation—as he put it, "a peace without victory." "Victory," he went on,

would mean peace forced upon the loser, a victor's terms imposed upon the vanquished. It would be accepted in humiliation, under duress, at an intolerable sacrifice, and would leave a sting, a resentment, a bitter memory upon which terms of peace would rest, not permanently, but only as upon quicksand. Only a peace between equals can last.

Moreover, the peace had to be built upon respect for self-determination for minority peoples and had to include measures for disarmament. The American people, he concluded, would be eager to join a league of nations to help enforce this kind of peace.

If Wilson's peace note of December 18 had made him a leading world figure for the first time, the "peace without victory" speech made him indubitably the commanding figure in the world. What Wilson did, in brief, was to marry the concept of a liberal settlement to the plan for a league of nations. By so doing, he at once became the hero, leader, and spokesman of the various liberal, labor, and socialistic groups throughout the western world who had themselves long since worked out the programme that the President now proposed.

It seemed for a moment that Wilson's bold stroke and secret negotiations might succeed. The British government, for reasons still unknown, returned a favorable response to Wilson's overtures on January 26. The Austro-Hungarian government soon sent secret feelers to the White House. Everything now depended upon the reply from Berlin. Bethmann was so excited by Wilson's secret appeal that he rushed to Pless to plead for a friendly response. It was too late to postpone the submarine campaign, for U-boats were already on the way to their stations. But the Imperial Chancellor did obtain permission to send a statement of moderate peace aims and an appeal to Wilson to persevere in his efforts for peace.

Events immediately afterwards led to an intensification rather than to an end to the war. But they need not have turned out that way. Wilson, to be sure, broke diplomatic relations with Germany on February 3, soon after the announcement of the new submarine campaign. But he was still as dead set against belligerency as ever. He clearly would have accepted a severe intensification of the submarine war, and he yielded to the growing American demand for war only after the Germans began to sink passenger liners and American merchantmen without warning, and only after the bungling Zimmermann telegram, proposing a military alliance between Mexico and Germany, had caused him to lose all faith in German good intentions. But in the end, when he made his final decision, it was the conviction that the war was in its last stages, and American participation would hasten its end, that most powerfully influenced the President to decide for belligerency.

Wilson's posture and policies inevitably changed somewhat after American entry on April 6, 1917. He did of course set full-scale mobilization on foot, and he was eager for Americans to do their share of the fighting as soon as possible. But his long-range objective—a peace of reconciliation—and his short-range goal—a negotiated peace as soon as possible—did not change, at least not before the spring of 1918. Carefully dissociating himself from Allied war aims, he waited for some moves from Germany and Austria-Hungary to resume peace negotiations. He failed to respond to two such moves in the summer—adoption by the German Reichstag on July 19 of a resolution favoring a peace of reconciliation, and a peace appeal issued by Pope Benedict XV on August 1. But he was sorely tempted to respond more affirmatively than he did to the Pope's appeal, and was restrained only by warnings both at home and from the Allies that discussion of peace terms was premature. Wilson's eagerness to avow American peace aims in specific detail mounted all through the autumn of 1917. He did not miss the opportunity to speak out, once the Bolsheviks had seized power in Russia, published Allied secret treaties, and called upon workers and soldiers in the west to convert the war into a proletarian revolution.

Wilson went to work with the guidance of a group of young American liberals and experts whom House had assembled to make tentative plans for a peace settlement. The President embodied his programme in his Fourteen Points Address to Congress of January 8, 1918. It was high time, he said, for peace-loving nations to avow their ideals and objectives. These Wilson proceeded to describe in a series of general points, including an end to secret diplomacy, freedom of the seas, general disarmament, the removal of artificial barriers to international trade, an impartial settlement of colonial claims, and establishment of a league of nations. Two points—the restoration of Belgium and self-determination for Russia—were, Wilson said, indispensable to a just settlement. Other points, including return of Alsace-Lorraine to France, an independent Poland with access to the sea, and autonomy for the subject peoples of the Austro-Hungarian Empire, were desirable but presumably negotiable, as Wilson said that they "should" rather than "must" be achieved. There was, finally, an implied fifteenth point—that the United States had no quarrel with the German people and no desire to continue the war for punitive or selfish ends.

It seems almost gratuitous to comment upon the significance of this address, so well known is it as the moral standard to which many peoples, including liberal Germans, rallied. But the Fourteen Points Address was much more than an avowal of peace aims. It was democracy's answer in its first full-dress debate with international communism. Lenin and Trotsky had appealed to the peace hunger of the world in order to begin a universal class war to destroy western civilization in its democratic and Christian forms. In contrast, Wilson had appealed for peace in the name of all that was high and holy in the Christian democratic tradition in order to give western civilization a second chance.

Wilson had also hoped to begin a dialogue with leaders of the Central Powers, and he did in fact succeed. But the discussion was cut short by the decision of the German high command to risk everything upon one great final offensive to knock France out of the war before substantial American reinforcements could arrive. Ludendorff's great offensive of March 1918, and the imposition by the Germans of the punitive Treaty of Brest-Litovsk upon the Russians in the same month, convinced Wilson that the war had to be fought to the bitter end, that, as he put it, only "righteous and triumphant Force" could make "Right the law of the world, and cast every selfish dominion down in the dust."

But even while he and his ever-growing armies waged war with increasing ferocity, Wilson refused to permit himself to be captured, much less enslaved, by the demons of total war. On the contrary, in the Four Additional Points of July 4 and the Five Additional Points of September 27, 1918, he made American peace aims even more explicit than ever before and continued to hope that a new German government would respond.

It is well known how the German government appealed to the American President in October 1918 for an armistice based upon Wilsonian terms and principles, and how Wilson through deft negotiation prepared the way for the armistice signed on November 11, 1918. Two facts about this momentous affair are, however, still not widely known. The first is that Wilson, by insisting on a negotiated peace, resisted a powerful movement, in his own country and among some of his own generals, for a march to Berlin. The second is that the President was eager to maintain sufficient German military power as a counterweight to French and British power once a conference had assembled. That, of course, it was not possible to do once the entire German imperial structure collapsed unexpectedly in November.

Wilson had lost other trumps by the time that the Paris peace conference opened on January 18, 1919; but he was still the commanding figure in the world as he faced the great challenges of peace-making. By rhetoric rivalled in the modern era only by Churchill's, Wilson had given liberals and war-weary peoples everywhere hope for a new future based on justice and free from the terrors of war. He had forced the Allies (with certain reservations) as well as the Germans to agree to make peace upon a basis of liberal principles. The greater and more difficult task of converting hope into reality, and the greatest challenges to Wilson's leadership, now lay ahead.

President Wilson
and His English Critics:
Survey and Interpretation

I VENTURE upon this subject with considerable misgiving for
several reasons, but not because I have any doubt about its relevance or its inherent interest to my listeners today.[1] Thoughtful
people in this country have always paid Woodrow Wilson the
tribute—and it is, I suppose, the highest kind of tribute that can
be paid a historical figure—of never ignoring him. English opinions
of Wilson's character and of the way in which he played the
role assigned to him by Providence have of course ranged from
one extreme to the other. To a group of English leaders who shared
his ideals and dreams for a brief period during his lifetime, he
was a mighty champion come out of the West to redeem an Old
World on the brink of ruin. To a still larger group, he was to
a varying degree the author of much of the mischief that beset
their world. As a don at one of the Oxford colleges, echoing a
view that was common a generation ago, said to me, "President

This essay was an Inaugural Lecture as Harmsworth Professor of American History
delivered at Oxford University on May 13, 1959. It is reprinted by permission of the
Clarendon Press, which published the lecture in 1959.

1. The author wishes to take this opportunity to express his gratitude to the Rockefeller
Foundation of New York, whose assistance made possible much of the research for this
paper.

Wilson has done more harm with his good intentions than any other leader of the twentieth century." But English admirers and hostile critics alike have never ceased to be intrigued by this man who for good or ill presided over the destinies of the American people during their emergence, full grown, to world power and momentary leadership, who issued the first clarion call to the English-speaking peoples to unite in a great alliance for the vindication of their best ideals, and whose downfall signified the refusal of this call and, worse still, the death of the new world order for which he had been struggling.

One of the reasons for my hesitancy to embark upon this theme is the fact that I should prefer to tell a happier story. In this inaugural lecture, which in the circumstances must be as much a farewell as a greeting, one would like to reflect his happy memories of association with this venerable and hospitable institution. I have, however, felt myself being almost irresistibly impelled to this subject because of its poignancy, tragic character, and enormous consequence. I have been impelled, above all, by the conviction that we historians of this period are under obligation to try harder than we have in the past to understand the reasons for the portentous failure of the first great drive for an Atlantic alliance—why it was, in brief, that the union of the English-speaking peoples, which apparently functioned so well under the stress of war, should have disintegrated under the stress of peace.

To be sure, we cannot see the answer in all its vast complexity here today. Not the least important reason for the failure of the first Anglo-American alliance, however, was the fact that no solid foundations in mutual trust and common objectives were laid during the years 1914 to 1919, when they had to be built if they were to endure. This, I daresay, is a rather obvious statement. What is not so obvious are the reasons why this was true. The most important of these, in my opinion, was the failure of the leaders of British thought and politics, and leaders of every important party and class, either to understand the purposes of the American President, or to accept his leadership when they did.

This English misunderstanding of President Wilson can be seen most clearly in the changing images that English critics formed of the man from 1913 to 1920, and it is my purpose today to describe these images and to show how decisively they affected the formation of British policy toward the United States during this period. I should hasten to add that many American critics—and, for that matter, European critics—formed the same images, and that there was nothing unique about the English views. There was, however, this considerable difference, that the hostile English images directly affected official policies to a much greater degree in this country than in the United States. Indeed, as I hope to demonstrate, English policies and attitudes based to a large extent upon a distorted view of President Wilson and his purposes contributed not a little to the unfolding tragedy of Anglo-American relations between 1914 and 1920.

During the first year and a half of President Wilson's tenure in the White House, however, there was nothing to indicate that the following years would witness any untoward or even unusual developments in Anglo-American relations. English observers watched the inauguration of this new leader of the Democratic Party, who seemed to be so much like their own political leaders, with keen interest in 1913. They, like many Americans, were thrilled by his eloquence, his bold leadership, and his obvious success as a parliamentary leader in obtaining the adoption of a comprehensive and far-reaching programme of liberal reform legislation. They were, to be sure, mystified and even frightened at times by his and Secretary of State W. J. Bryan's novel methods of diplomacy, particularly in dealing with revolution and civil war in Mexico and in attempting to teach the peoples of Central America and the Caribbean region how to elect good rulers and practice constitutional democracy. On the other hand, the leaders and people of Great Britain responded warmly when the Washington government offered a treaty aimed at preventing diplomatic difficulties between the two countries, and particularly when the President yielded generously in a minor but exacerbating dispute over free passage through the Panama Canal for American coastal shipping. On balance, then, the verdict of English critics during the first eighteen months of Wilson's presidency was an emphatically favorable one; there were few signs on this side of the Atlantic of any disposition to regard the President as being other than what he then seemed to be—a resourceful and realistic political strategist who was at the same time an eloquent spokesman of triumphant Anglo-American liberalism.

This estimate did not change all at once at the outset of the period that would see the first really serious Anglo-American alienation since the American Civil War, that is, the two and a half years of American neutrality after the outbreak of the First World War. No responsible English leader at the outset expected the American government to do anything other than establish and maintain a rigid neutrality; few English spokesmen actually desired American participation in the beginning; and most English critics watched President Wilson's determined fight against a German-American movement for the adoption of an arms embargo and his acceptance of British control of neutral trade roughly within the rules of international law with some admiration and under-standing of the enormous difficulties and pressures that he faced at home in his struggle for neutrality.

This was the general English view at least until the spring of 1915, if not a bit beyond. And yet within less than two years this widespread popular admiration for the American President had in many quarters turned into scorn and contempt; friendship and understanding had given way to hostility, or at least to strong aversion. The same metamorphosis had occurred for the most part at Whitehall, and in such a way as to involve a positive repudiation of the Wilsonian hand of fellowship. The conse-quences for official Anglo-American relations were, one hardly need say, dire: by early 1917, the two nations stood, it seemed, in actual danger of rupture. At the very moment when they were finally about to join forces on the battlefield in defense of common interests and ideals their estrangement could hardly have been more complete.

The causes of this state of affairs are, to be sure, to be found in developments on both sides of the Atlantic, developments over which leaders in both countries had little control. They are to be found, also, in the growth in this country of a wartime mentality that was as understandable as it was inevitable. But they are also to be found in the emergence in Great Britain of a view of President Wilson and his policies that affected the formation of English policies in a critical way. It was misunderstanding and hence divergence on a transatlantic scale, and it grew out of three major sources of tension and alienation.

The first of these was the spread in Great Britain during the period of American neutrality of the conviction that the President, for all his fine talk about international ideals, was really a parochial

American who did not begin to understand what the war was all about. This, in turn, was a reaction to two of Wilson's policies, namely, his continued insistence upon the full observance of American neutral trading rights by the British Admiralty, and his refusal ever to affirm that he and the American people preferred the Allies to the Central Powers in the struggle for mastery of Europe, or even saw much difference between the methods and objectives of the rival alliances.

Actually, the two policies were very much connected in the minds of English critics and to them reflected a cold and sometimes calculating unconcern that became all the more infuriating as the savagery of the war increased. If we may believe their professions in correspondence and the printed word at the time, and there is no good reason not to believe them, the fact is that to the vast majority of liberal-minded Englishmen the war *was* an authentic crusade—a life-and-death contest to determine whether treaties were sacred, whether small nations could survive in a world dominated by superstates, and whether a brutal military despotism should dominate Europe in the future. These convictions, one might almost say, were the spiritual food that fortified the bulk of English intellectuals and a good part of the governing class, to say nothing of the rank and file of the people and the sailors and soldiers directly engaged on the fronts.

What the English people wanted most desperately was encouragement and cheer from the Great Republic of the West and a large measure of assistance by a benevolent neutrality, that is, by American acquiescence in all British and Allied measures for the defeat of Germany. They expected this because they believed that they were fighting America's battles as much as their own. As one editor said:

We would put two propositions to the American people who can think impartially. Is it not true that we are fighting not only for the future security of ourselves and of our Allies, but of the New World as well? Is it not according to American ideals of humanity that this war should be as short as circumstances can make it? Neither proposition needs much demonstration. . . . The war can be ended in two ways: by the slaughter of hundreds of thousands of vigorous lives, or by an economical pressure which will deny the enemy sufficient of the essential sinews of war. To help bring about the more merciful consummation is Great Britain's present object. And we hold that it is the duty of the United

States, as a civilising Power, to assist us, even if the obligation entails material losses and bars the way to great profits.[2]

What the English people received from President Wilson was what appeared to them to be moral condemnation and interference, the only result of which could be to increase the likelihood of a German victory, or at best a prolongation of the war. The President not only refused to align himself and his people morally on the side of the Allies; instead, he appealed to the American people to be impartial in thought as well as in action and declared over and over in public statements either that the causes and issues of the war were obscure, or that the chief cause of the conflict had been the *European* system of alliances and power politics. Except for a brief period during the spring of 1915, moreover, the President not only refused to favor the Allies with a benevolent neutrality; on the contrary, he waged a grim and increasingly relentless struggle to prevent the British navy from enforcing a full-fledged blockade of the Central Powers—and all, so many English critics believed, in order that American producers and shippers might profit even more than they were already doing from the war.

This view of President Wilson's policies was not entirely fanciful. He did believe, for example, that the causes of the war were complex and that it would be futile to attempt to apportion guilt. He was never wholeheartedly committed to the Allied cause or persuaded that British war objectives were altogether pure. Part of his defense of American neutral trading rights was a response to important economic and political pressures at home. On the other hand, it must also be said that the essential reality of Wilson's thoughts and purposes was never very clear to his English critics (or, for that matter, to many of his American critics) during the period of American neutrality, and that what understanding did exist became increasingly obscured by the consequent Anglo-American stress. He refused to become engaged in the ideological warfare and international name-calling of the time, not because he did not care about the issues or outcome of the war, but because he hoped desperately and prayed fervently that the nations of Europe would finally turn to him as mediator and peacemaker.

2. *The* (London) *Outlook*, XXV (January 2, 1915), 5.

He practiced a strict neutrality because he believed that the international law upon which neutrality was based was the world's best political heritage and had to be preserved, and above all because he believed that America could perform her healing task of reconciliation only by remaining neutral.

Some of these things—that, for example, he of course detested German militarism and feared its triumph—Wilson could not say publicly without compromising his integrity as a potential neutral mediator. Other things—his remarks, for example, about the American mission to the world—he said somewhat maladroitly, so as to give the impression of an assumption of moral superiority. The result, in any event, was the same—the emergence among English critics of the picture of an essentially provincial American, ignorant of European problems, and so morally callous as to be unable to see the difference between right and wrong. As one London editor who usually tried to see the American point of view put it, after reading Wilson's Annual Message of 1915, in which the President had reaffirmed his public position on the question of war guilt:

Shall we appear to overstate our feelings if we say that we are shocked, and that our blood freezes at the deliberation and detachment of those words? "No part or interest in the policies which seem to have brought the conflict on"! No part or interest in the tyrannical suppression of the tiny State of Serbia, no part or interest in the violation of the solemn pledge to respect the integrity of Belgium! . . . These things were not worth even a protest. Here was an issue between right and wrong if ever there was one, even before the horrors of Belgium were committed. We should be grieved indeed to think that the day will ever come when Americans cannot be found passionately to take the side of right against wrong even at the cost of disturbing the "self-possession" of a State Department at Washington.[3]

The British Ambassador in Paris expressed the same point of view more brutally when he confided to his diary that President Wilson and his government were "a rotten lot of psalm-singing, profit-mongering humbug."[4] And the British Ambassador in

---

3. *The Spectator*, CXV (December 11, 1915), 817.
4. Lady Algernon Gordon Lennox, editor, *The Diary of Lord Bertie of Thame, 1914–1918*, 2 vols. (London: Hodder & Stoughton, 1924), I, 267.

Washington summarized it poetically in a warning to his friend Lord Bryce to expect no help from America in the struggle, as follows:

> Trust not for freedom to the Franks.
> They have a King who buys and sells.
> In native swords and native ranks
> Tis there alone that freedom dwells.[5]

English critics saw a second Wilson during this period of American neutrality—a man who was at best a weakling or man of indecision, at worst, a coward who preferred safety to national honor and would accept almost any insult before he would fight. This picture began to form in the English mind first during the *Lusitania* crisis, when Wilson, in a moment of mental anguish, said,

The example of America must be a special example. The example of America must be the example not merely of peace because it will not fight, but of peace because peace is the healing and elevating influence of the world and strife is not. There is such a thing as a man being too proud to fight. There is such a thing as a nation being so right that it does not need to convince others by force that it is right.[6]

This remark, which flowed from the President's subconscious mind and by no means represented his whole thought, did more to damage his reputation for strength of character among the people of this country than anything he ever said or did. And the suspicion that it raised was seemingly confirmed during the following months as Wilson went to extraordinary lengths to avert hostilities and to find agreement with Germany over the issue of the latter's submarine war against maritime commerce.

Evidences of this violent turn in English opinion abound in all the sources of the time. Wilson was jeered at in pubs and mocked in *Punch;* even so staunch a friend as Lord Bryce had to admit that English critics regarded the President as "pusillanimous" for his delay in breaking relations with Germany.[7] As the

5. Sir Cecil Spring Rice to Lord Bryce, January 5, 1914 [1915], the Papers of James, Viscount Bryce, Bodleian Library, Oxford University, Oxford, England.

6. New York *Times,* May 11, 1915.

7. The Diary of Walter H. Page, September 15, 1915, Houghton Library, Harvard University, Cambridge, Mass.

American Ambassador in London, Walter Page, summarized the feeling in one of his many confidential reports on the subject to Washington:

[This will be a disagreeable letter,] but I conceive I sh ^{d} fall short of my duty if I didn't faithfully report to you such a swift and violent change in public feeling here towards the United States as fairly takes one's breath away.

[Cabinet leaders, Bonar Law among them, are saying] with sorrow that the U.S. had shown that she w ^{d} submit to any indignity or insult. . . . They all agreed that the slowness of our Gov't to act had taken away all fear of it and respect for it, and that its protests henceforth w ^{d} count for nothing. . . .

[I have heard such expressions every day.] The press is full of criticism and innuendo. I can describe the change of feeling in no other way than by calling it a complete revulsion. . . . Unless some explanation be made or some action taken, I am sorry to report that we shall be regarded with slight respect by English opinion for a long time to come. I spare you the insulting remarks that go about London, but the genuine grief expressed by our best friends is oppressing—grief, to use a common phrase, "that a democracy lacks courage and character." [8]

We have seen two images of Wilson formed by his English critics—of the provincial American morally obtuse about the issues of the war, and of the weak and timid statesman. There was a third image constructed during the period before American entrance into the war, one that was perhaps the most important because it was the most enduring. It was the image of a well-intentioned idealist so naïve as to be almost completely visionary, a kind of American Don Quixote tilting at European windmills.

This view of Wilson emerged during the early months of the war among the leaders of the British government and spread rapidly among thoughtful critics during late 1916 and early 1917 primarily as a consequence of the President's recurrent efforts to bring the war to an end. Those efforts began, actually, during the late summer and early autumn of 1914. They took serious form in the two peace missions by Col. Edward M. House, the President's intimate adviser, to Europe in the early months of

---

8. W. H. Page to Woodrow Wilson, September 9, 1915, the Papers of Woodrow Wilson, Library of Congress, Washington, D.C.

1915 and 1916. They reached their climax in the President's public appeal to the belligerents of December 18, 1916, asking them to state the terms upon which they would be willing to conclude the fighting, and in his secret negotiations with the British and German governments soon afterward looking toward finding some ground of accommodation.

The image of Wilson the visionary knight-errant took shape among the leaders at Whitehall first, because the President's efforts for peace were known only on the official level before the autumn of 1916. It, along with the other images that I have described and events that lie beyond the scope of this discussion, was responsible for what was one of the most important decisions that the London authorities made during the entire course of the war, a decision that blasted the first best hope of an Anglo-American *entente.* Hereon hangs a tale that reveals how powerfully the images of Wilson that were formed in this country affected the formation of policies for good or ill.

In the autumn of 1915, President Wilson and Colonel House conceived a plan of mediation envisaging peace mainly through Anglo-German agreement on the restoration of Belgium and disarmament on land and sea. They sounded the British Foreign Secretary, Sir Edward Grey, who, not wishing to give the appearance of being uninterested, replied that his government might indeed welcome such a move, provided, however, that the United States was willing to join a postwar league of nations to help underwrite such a settlement. The culmination of the subsequent negotiations was the initialling by Grey and House of a memorandum commonly known as the House-Grey Agreement in London on February 22, 1916. It declared simply that President Wilson was ready, on hearing from France and England, to call a peace conference to end the war, and that the United States would probably enter the war on the side of the Allies if Germany rejected this call or refused to make terms "not unfavorable to the Allies."

In spite of the memorandum's calculated vagueness, President Wilson thought that it signified British willingness to follow his lead in a drive for peace. Mediation was by this time his grand and overriding objective. He consequently risked war with Germany over the issue of submarine attacks against armed merchant ships and began a speaking campaign to prepare the American people for the great events ahead. At the same time, he applied increasingly heavy and, in the end, threatening pressure upon the authorities in London for their consent to the execution of the House-Grey Agreement. He was, assuredly, prepared and eager to go all the way.

In response to these appeals, which, as he later observed in his memoirs, might well have led to the most promising kind of Anglo-American co-operation if not alliance, Grey returned at first a polite refusal and in the end a rather brutally firm one. There were many reasons why such a *démarche* would have been a risky one from the London government's point of view, but they were not seriously explored because Grey did no more than inform his colleagues in the War Cabinet that he had signed the memorandum with House and, later, of the President's insistent demand for the implementation of the document. Never at any time during the remaining months of his tenure at the Foreign Office did Grey advocate co-operation with the United States along these lines; indeed, the weight of his advice was strongly against any such policy. And not the least important reason for Grey's failure to grasp the President's hand of friendship was the fact that even he, along with most other members of the Government, had formed the images of Wilson of which I have already spoken. So distorted were his own views of Wilson's character, thought, and purposes by this time, and so much had he been seized by the neuroses of the war, that co-operation with the American President seemed too risky and profitless an enterprise to be ventured upon.

What had been largely an official British image of Wilson the visionary would-be peacemaker became a public one in consequence of the President's peace appeal of December 18, 1916, and even more of an epochal address that he delivered before the United States Senate on January 22, 1917. In this pronouncement, he outlined the kind of peace settlement that he thought the American people would be willing to help enforce through a league of nations. It must be, he declared, a peace of reconciliation, without forcible annexations and transfers of sovereignty and punitive provisions. It must be, he said, a "peace without victory," because only a peace among equals could stand.

In the eyes of English critics, it was all extraordinarily offensive, or nearly incredible to the ears—offensive in that the President had no business interfering, incredible in that any allegedly sane man should think that any kind of lasting peace could be achieved until the Germans had been decisively beaten on the battlefield. As a distinguished English historian put it,

The feelings of honest, true Americans must be touched by Bonar Law's noble, and perhaps immortal, phrase, "What Mr. Wilson is longing for we are fighting for." The man is surely the quintessence of a prig. What a notion that the nations of Europe, after this terrible effort, will join him in putting down international encroachments by arms, at some future time, if he is afraid to denounce such encroachments even in words now![9]

Before I give too much the impression that English opinion of Wilson was altogether monolithic in composition, I should hasten to add that there was one group in this country who formed quite a different image of the President during these years of Anglo-American stress. They were the so-called radicals—certain leaders of the Labour faction, young idealists, and pacifists—who banded together in the Union for Democratic Control, an organization devoted to the advancement of what might be called liberal internationalism. Struggling unsuccessfully at home against the rising tide of war passions, by the end of 1916 they were looking to the American President as the one last hope for an early end to the carnage and a peace of reconciliation. Their image of Wilson was in a sense as distorted as were the images of the hostile critics: they understood the President's thoughts and purposes but overestimated the possibilities of his leadership.

And now we come to that part of our survey which is at once culmination and tragedy: the way in which the English images of President Wilson helped to shape and almost to control the response that the British government made to the President's second great appeal for Anglo-American *entente* and alliance in the building of a new international order.

The second opportunity for such co-operation of course came when the United States was driven to belligerency in April 1917 by the German bid for total victory through an unrestricted submarine campaign against all maritime commerce. Anglo-American

9. Sir G. O. Trevelyan to Lord Bryce, January 26, 1917, Bryce Papers.

co-operation, intimate and successful, there was in all matters connected with the prosecution of the war. But there was none at all in the business that weighed most heavily upon the President's mind and conscience, that is, the necessity of planning constructively (as he saw it) for agreement on common war aims. Over and again during the summer and autumn of 1917, Wilson pressed the British and French leaders for discussions that might lead to a statement of common war objectives. Over and over he was rebuffed by the cold warning from London that this was no time to bring the matter up. The consequence was that the President, since he was under unbearable pressure from public opinion at home and from his own conscience, felt compelled to undertake the task himself in 1918—by proclaiming in his Fourteen Points address and subsequent pronouncements what the *American* people were fighting for, and, incidentally, what he thought the majority of English people were fighting for as well.

There were, to be sure, many reasons why the London government refused to grasp the opportunity for a frank confrontation with the leader in Washington. The British Cabinet knew, for example, that acute embarrassment would ensue when Wilsonian objectives clashed with the programme to which they were by now considerably committed. But the basic reason for the refusal, I am inclined to believe, was the image that the men now in control of the British Government had formed of the man across the sea.

The revolution of December 1916, resulting in the downfall of the Asquith Coalition and the elevation of a new, largely conservative coalition under Lloyd George, had brought a harsher and a more so-called realistic group of men to power at Whitehall. Their methods, character, and political and international ideals, if such they may be called, are too well known to require any description here. They were not, actually, incapable of speaking the same language as the American President, or of understanding what he was talking about or attempting to achieve. They simply did not have either the desire or the ability to take the President seriously. And this was true in large measure because their image of Wilson as an obstinate visionary was even more distorted than the image that their more rational predecessors had held, and because cynicism and strident nationalism as well as sheer misunderstanding played a large role in the distortion. Given their preconceptions, how else could President Wilson—this man who prattled so about a peace of reconciliation and disarmament as much on sea as on land—how else could he seem to Lloyd George and most of his colleagues but irrelevant and absurd? And thus they went their own way toward their own solution.

The climactic confrontation did finally occur, of course, in the weeks before the Armistice and during the months that followed. There is neither time nor the necessity here for any detailed discussion of the tumultuous events of late 1918 and the first half of 1919. In any event, such a discussion would obscure the deeper tragedy that underlay the obvious one of the Versailles settlement and made the ensuing American repudiation of the peace treaty well-nigh inevitable. What I mean was the final playing out of the tragedy of Anglo-American misunderstanding and lost opportunities that occurred during these months.

It is obvious at this late date that Wilson's only hope for the realization of most of his peace aims lay in the possibility of a firm and generally unshakable Anglo-American common front against the French and Italians, but particularly the French. This is what the President in fact sought to achieve during the conferences that he held with leaders in London before the Peace Conference opened. It is what he kept on seeking all through the discussions at Paris from January through June of 1919. It is what he in part achieved on several vital aspects of the settlement, for on the three key issues of the dismemberment of Germany in the West, the necessity for an Anglo-American guarantee of French security, and the creation of a League of Nations, there was striking Anglo-American accord and successful co-operation.

In the short range, and the long range, too, as the consequences worked out, the most important fact of the Paris Peace Conference was the refusal of the British Prime Minister and his colleagues to follow Wilson's lead when it meant yielding what seemed to be a British or Commonwealth advantage. This was true, obviously, on general disarmament, on the disposition of German oversea territories, on reparations and punitive damages, and on the proper way in which to deal with Italian and Japanese territorial claims. Anglo-American co-operation on each of these questions might well have—indeed, surely would have—produced a different result. It might well have meant, for example, a peace settlement that would have been acceptable to the British conscience in the long run and the cementing of a firm Anglo-American alliance for years to come by the nearly immediate ratification of the Versailles Treaty by the United States Senate. I am inclined to believe that this would have been the result.

If my hypothesis that Wilson would have been irresistible had he returned to the United States with a peace settlement that vindicated humane and liberal ideals, if this *is* true, then the decision of the British leaders to co-operate more often with Wilson's antagonists than with the President at Paris must take its place among the most fateful decisions made by the leaders of any great nation during the modern epoch.

Why did Lloyd George and his associates reject the Wilsonian hand of friendship extended to the British government for this third time and, as events would soon prove, throw away the chance of realizing what even they regarded as being the major long-range objective of British foreign policy? Fundamentally, I believe, because they simply were not able to perform the great act of faith of following Wilson in adopting policies that seemed to require a sacrifice or to imperil their own political interests. I am not suggesting here that the matter can be put thus simply. I know the hostages that the Coalition Government had given to momentary war passions at home, to the Commonwealth, and to Italy and Japan. I understand the genuine doubts that racked the minds of the members of the British delegation. But I would still maintain that the gamble could have been taken, or largely so, and in such a way as to have meant a vastly different treaty from the one that was signed at Versailles on June 28, 1919.

The point to which I am leading is why events turned out so dismally when they might have led to the beginning of a new and brighter international era. I cannot escape the conclusion that the chief cause was the fact that the British leaders did not take Wilson seriously at Paris and could not do so because the image of the man that they saw at the Peace Conference was the same distorted image that they had formed earlier. I should emphasize that the records show clearly enough that it was the old image and not any new one formed at Paris that really counted. However, to the old image of the obstinate and essentially ignorant visionary had been added the new features of an incompetent leader who had been discredited and repudiated at home. Surely this latter new impression (which, actually, was an extremely doubtful interpretation of the meaning of the recent American congressional elections of November 1918) weighed heavily upon the members of the British delegation. It goes a long way toward explaining Lloyd George's policy, which was to have his cake and eat it too—by making the minimum concessions that he thought were necessary to assure American guarantee of the new international system at the same time that he was trying to ensure future British security in the event of President Wilson's failing to obtain ratification of the Versailles Treaty.

There was a final image of President Wilson that would in the end be nearly as damaging to Anglo-American relations and more damaging to Wilson's reputation than the images that the leaders of the British government had formed. It was the one constructed by the men who had heretofore been the President's staunchest friends in this country, that is, the so-called radicals. They had hitched their wagon to the star of Wilsonian idealism. They had hailed the President on his coming to Europe as a new Messiah. Then, at Versailles, they had discovered that their hero had not merely feet but also arms and a head of clay. He was merely a Presbyterian fanatic facile with words, a visionary without a plan, a naïve and ignorant man easily "bamboozled" by cunning adversaries. This, of course, was the image of *The Economic Consequences of the Peace,* to a lesser degree of Harold Nicolson, and of a whole generation of the disillusioned on the British Left.

It mattered not that the men who formed this image, which was more a confirmation of old images than a new one, knew little of the President's titanic struggles and refused to see the really splendid foundations that he had laid. It mattered not that they misunderstood the President's character and the role that he had to play at Paris. It mattered not that they found a convenient scapegoat for their own frustrations and failures in the broken and helpless man in the White House. The damage on both sides of the Atlantic was done. The image that they constructed in the aftermath of disillusionment and despair is the one that has largely survived in this country. It is the one that the American counterparts of the English so-called radicals adopted, and adopted in part from their English friends. It played a decisive role in preventing the very thing that both groups ardently desired: Anglo-American co-operation in the service of mankind during the very period when such service might have been most constructive.

The historian need add no final anticlimactic words. The story is doleful enough without embellishment; the dimensions of the tragedy need no exaggeration. The lessons, if any there are to be learned, must be plain enough without further exegesis. Perhaps it can all be summarized by pointing to the fact that no statue of this first great American champion of Anglo-American alliance stands in Grosvenor Square or, for that matter, in any marble temple in Washington. And in the thought that peacemakers are only the children of God, not of men.

10

The Higher Realism
of Woodrow Wilson

ON March 4, 1913, a gaunt man walked to the stands outside the east front of the Capitol in Washington to take the oath of office as twenty-eighth President of the United States. Although his face was somber with a sense of high seriousness, it radiated strength and determination, and there was thrilling power in his voice as he summoned the American people to the tasks of national reconstruction. Eight years later, in 1921, he assisted in the rituals inaugurating his successor, Warren G. Harding. Now he was broken in body, and his drawn face reflected the pain that had come from his recent repudiation at the hands of the people during the election of 1920.

He was Woodrow Wilson, born in Staunton, Virginia, on December 29, 1856, reared in Presbyterian manses in Georgia and the Carolinas, educated at Davidson College in North Carolina and Princeton University, trained in the study of law at the University of Virginia, and prepared for a career in teaching and scholarship at the Johns Hopkins University. He had taught successively

This essay was the Founder's Day Address to the Presbyterian Historical Society in Philadelphia on October 12, 1962. It appeared in *Journal of Presbyterian History*, XLI (March 1963), 1–13, and is reprinted by permission of the Manager of the Presbyterian Historical Society.

from 1885 to 1902 at Bryn Mawr College in Pennsylvania, Wesleyan University in Connecticut, and Princeton, and had served as president of the latter institution from 1902 to 1910. Plunging into the troubled sea of politics in 1910, he had won the governorship of New Jersey and had gone on with almost irresistible power to capture the presidency in 1912. Then he had guided the destinies of the American people from 1913 to 1921 and helped to direct the destinies of the world during eight of the most critical years of the modern epoch.

I am happy to come before this particular audience in this venerable city to talk about the man who has been the subject of my main thought and work for twenty years. I must confess at the outset that I have prepared this paper with a definite purpose in mind. It is neither to praise Woodrow Wilson nor to bury him. The record of his contribution has its own integrity, and what little I could say would neither add to or detract from it. It is not to bring you any new view of President Wilson, for I doubt that I could say anything really new about him at this point. My purpose is, rather, to attempt to pull together a number of thoughts and convictions that have been coursing through my mind during the past few years, in brief, to clarify my own conclusions about the subject of my life's work.

I have felt impelled to this undertaking in part by many conversations with English and German historians which have challenged my own emerging view of President Wilson. My experiences during a year abroad in 1958–59 have brought home the fact that Europeans on the whole still view Wilson very much as many of them viewed him forty years ago at the end of the Paris Peace Conference and the great struggle in the United States over ratification of the Treaty of Versailles. This European image is, I think it is fair to say, one of a well-intentioned idealist, a a man good by ordinary Christian standards, but essentially a destructive force in modern history because he was visionary, unrealistic, provincial, and ignorant of European problems, and zealous and messianic in conceit but devoid of either practical knowledge or the humility to follow others better informed than he. I do not think that this is an essentially unfair statement of the European point of view. It was, of course, the image held by John Maynard Keynes, Georges Clemenceau, and most of the thoughtful European public at the end of the Peace Conference.

It is the view still largely held by English, French, and German scholars alike, if for different reasons.

I have felt impelled to my subject not only by recent forceful reminders of the strong survival of the old European image of President Wilson, but also by the emergence in our own country during the past few years of a new school of historical critics, and by their work in constructing an image of President Wilson that is remarkably like the older European one. Calling themselves realists, and drawing their inspiration from the distinguished diplomat-historian, George Kennan, and the Austrian-trained authority in international relations, Hans J. Morgenthau, now at the University of Chicago, these new American critics have found Wilson wanting because he did not think in terms of strategy, bases, and armed power, but dwelt too much in ethereal realms.

Are the old European and new American critics right, I have asked myself over and over during the past few years: is this the image that I also see, the Wilson that I know? Were the Austrians right in thinking that his irresponsible preaching of a slogan, "self-determination," was primarily responsible for the destruction of the Hapsburg Empire? Were the Germans right in holding him responsible for what they regarded as the monstrous betrayal of Versailles? Were the French right in thinking that he prevented the imposition of the only kind of peace settlement upon Germany that could endure? Were the English and new American critics near the truth when they portrayed him as a tragic figure irrelevant in the modern world?

I must confess that I have sometimes been tempted to agree. No one who has ever given any serious attention to President Wilson's life could fail to agree that he was *primarily* a Christian idealist. By this I mean a man who almost always tended to judge policies on a basis of whether they were right by Christian standards, not whether they brought immediate material or strategic advantage. I mean also a man whose foreign policies were motivated by the assumption that a nation as much as an individual should live according to the law of Christian love, and by a positive repudiation of the assumptions of the classical "realists" about international behavior.

No one who has given serious study to Wilson's career, moreover, could fail to agree that there is at least an appearance of reality about the old European and new American image. Wilson was not merely an idealist, but a crusading idealist. An orator of enormous eloquence and power, he was also a phrasemaker who more than once fell victim to the magic of his own words. In international relations, he did not give undue weight to material forces or base his policies upon the assumption that nations must always act selfishly. At times, he did seem to give the appearance of believing that he was a kind of messiah divinely appointed to deliver Europe from the cruel tyranny of history.

I have myself made all these criticisms and others more elaborately in my own writings. But they have never really satisfied me and do not satisfy me now. I do not think that they add up to a historical image that is accurate. Indeed, I cannot escape the conclusion that they altogether miss the main point and meaning of President Wilson's career.

The point, in my opinion, and the theme of this paper, is that among all the major statesmen and thoughtful critics of his age, President Wilson was in fact the supreme realist, and that because this is true, what he stood for and fought to accomplish has large meaning for our own generation.

This is, to be sure, a very broad, perhaps even an audacious, statement, one that does not mean very much unless we are careful to define our terms. A realist, I take it, is one who faces life and its situations without illusions, in short, one who can see realities or truth through the fog of delusion that normally shrouds the earth-bound individual. If the European and American critics of President Wilson who thought mainly in strategic and material terms, who measured national power by army divisions and naval bases, and the like, if *they* were realists, then President Wilson was a realist of a different sort. Sheerly for purposes of convenience, let us call his view of the national and international situations with which he had to cope a "higher realism," higher because more perceptive, more in accord with ultimate reality, more likely to win the long-run moral approval of societies professing allegiance to the common western, humane, Christian traditions.

We still have not passed beyond the statement of a thesis and a definition of elementary terminology. There now remains the much more important task of seeing to what degree the evidence of Wilson's career supports my generalization. We obviously do not have time to review all the important events of Wilson's long and active career here tonight. On the other hand, we cannot concentrate our attention on one aspect without running the risks of distortion. President Wilson actually had three separate public careers: as university president and educational statesman, as a domestic leader concerned almost exclusively with problems of political and economic reconstruction in the United States, and, finally, as a world statesman who attempted to give leadership in a movement for the reconstruction of the international community. He made large and seemingly different contributions in each field. And yet we must try to view his career and labors as a whole, for he was fundamentally the same man throughout. His "higher realism" was no less a force in his leadership at home than abroad.

It was evident in a striking way in the first contributions that he made as a public leader, as president of Princeton University from 1902 to 1910. There were, first, the things that he did and tried to do for Princeton: his introduction of a systematic and meaningful course of undergraduate study, and his positive repudiation of a chaotic free-elective system; his creation of the preceptorial, or conference, method of instruction to supplement the lecture system; and his proposal for the reorganization of undergraduate social life in order to elevate the intellectual climate of the University. By such plans and by his own inspiration, he not only transformed Princeton, but also helped to transform higher education in the United States.

And yet Wilson made his greatest contributions in the field of education more by the things that he fought for than by what he did. For one thing, he stood for standards and academic integrity. For another, he had an exalted concept of the university and college and the role that they should play in preparing men and women for the nation's service because they were dedicated to the cause of truth and the intellectual enrichment of mankind. Finally, during an era of increasing specialization and degradation of undergraduate curricula by the introduction of all sorts of so-called useful programs of study, Wilson never ceased to remind fellow teachers and administrators that their first job was to help perpetuate the cultural traditions upon which western civilization rested, not to teach students how to make money.

Who, we are entitled to ask, were the true "realists" in educational policy? Were they the alleged realists of Wilson's time, the sincere devotees of the new so-called progressive concepts and faddists, who were then beginning their long attack upon traditional studies and destroying the unity of university curricula? To ask the question is almost to answer it. The entire drive in American higher education during the past twenty years toward recovery of standards and unity in curricula and against the vulgarization that followed the widespread introduction of so-called useful courses of study—this entire movement, so full of promise, is testimony to the higher realism of Wilson's leadership in the academic world.

It was the same, I would suggest, with Wilson's leadership during his second career as governor of New Jersey from 1911 to 1913 and President of the United States afterward. He came to political leadership at one of the most critical junctures in American history, at the high tide of what American historians call the progressive movement. For more than a quarter of a century, the American people had been in revolt in city, state, and nation against corruption and venality among officeholders, irresponsibility on all levels of government, and, above all, the emergence and spread of great aggregations of economic power among railroads, banks, corporations, and so on, which were uncontrolled and often repudiated any responsibility to the people as a whole. This revolt was at the point of culmination at the very time that Wilson was catapulted into political life in 1910, and because this was true the American people were now confronted with certain choices that would determine their future political system and the role that government would hereafter play in making fundamental economic decisions.

There was, first, the choice concerning the reconstruction of the American political system. Some so-called realists of the time argued cogently from the facts that the very concept and structure of representative government were fatally defective, and that the answer lay either in direct democracy or in concentration of political power in fewer hands. "Realists" on the other side, eager to preserve a status quo that benefited their own economic interests, argued just as convincingly that the American constitutional system, with its diffusion and separation of powers, was the most nearly perfect form of government on earth.

There was, second, the choice concerning the role that government should play in economic life. At the one extreme were the "realists" who, talking in terms of immutable economic law, defended traditional American policies of laissez-faire in an effort to protect their privileged position. At the other extreme were "realists" with a greater popular appeal—men who demanded a sweeping extension of the power of government to bridle all hitherto uncontrolled economic interests. Some of these were socialists, ready to abandon capitalism in the major sectors of the economy altogether. Others were progressives who believed in capitalism but argued that it had reached a permanent phase of semi-monopolistic maturity in the United States and could be saved only by instituting sweeping and rigorous public controls over all important areas of national economic life.

It was Woodrow Wilson's privilege to play a decisive role in the determination of these choices. To the "realists" who had despaired of representative government in the cities and states he replied more by example than by precept—by giving a spectacular example of responsible leadership in action as governor of New Jersey. By making representative government work on the local level he, along with a company of other leaders at the time, guaranteed its survival. To the "realists" (and he had earlier been among them) who had proclaimed the incapacity of the presidential-congressional system to cope with the great problems of national administration, Wilson responded, both by reasoned word and striking deed, by transforming that system and demonstrating that it had immensely greater capacities than the so-called realists had thought. He did this by transforming the office of President from that of an aloof presiding official into incomparably the most powerful force in the American constitutional system—the force that gave unity and direction not only to the other branches of the federal government but to public opinion as well. This, we can now see, was the "higher realism" of a man who well understood the weaknesses of the American institutional structure but who knew the fundamental strength of the American democracy far better than most so-called realists of his time.

I think that it is also fair to say that President Wilson demonstrated the same kind of long-run wisdom, or "higher realism," in leading the American people to adoption of new policies for the regulation of economic life. He rejected the arguments both of defenders of the status quo and of proponents of violent change as being unsound in principle and unacceptable to the majority of the people. And he (along with his supporters in Congress) instituted a series of measures to impose increased public direction and control, but also to balance private initiative with public regulation in order to stimulate the enormous latent competitive energies of the people. In short, he laid the solid foundations of the present mixed American system of political economy, which, to the amazement and bafflement of many Europeans, works so curiously and so well. Viewing the subsequent development of the American economy within the framework erected by President Wilson and his colleagues, I think that we would have to conclude that Wilson's solution was the only "realistic" one that could have been adopted. It saved American capitalism by making it socially responsible and hence acceptable to the people, without, however, impeding the forces that are essential for growth in the capitalistic system.

I am sure that in talking about Wilson's "higher realism" in meeting domestic challenges, I have simply been saying things and making judgments with which virtually every historian of the United States would readily agree. It is precisely this "higher realism" that has entitled Wilson to rank, by the agreement of American historians, among the four or five most successful Presidents in our history. In talking about Wilson's policies and contributions in the realm of foreign affairs, I am, I know, on more controversial ground. Wilson was magnificently prepared for leadership in internal affairs by long study of American history and institutions. He had little if any preparation for leadership in the world at large; indeed, at the outset of his tenure in the White House he had no serious interest in foreign affairs. At the outset and later he made mistakes that still seriously impair his record. Even so, I cannot but conclude that President Wilson on the whole showed the same kind of wisdom and long-range vision and understanding—in short, "higher realism"—in his third career as international statesman as he had already revealed in his first two careers at home.

This, I know, is a big statement, and I would like to preface it with a few generalizations about Wilson's thought and character as a diplomat in order to lay foundations for some later observations.

The first is the most obvious and the one with which most historians would agree, namely, that President Wilson was, as I have already said, above all an idealist in the conduct of foreign affairs, one who subordinated immediate goals and material interests to what he considered to be superior ethical standards and moral purposes. His idealism was perhaps best revealed in his thinking about the purposes that the United States should serve in the world. The mission of America, he said over and over and sincerely believed, was not a mission of aggrandizement of material power but one of service to mankind. It was a mission of peace, of sacrifice, of leading the nations into a new international community organized to achieve right ends.

Second, all of Wilson's thinking about international relations was conditioned, in general, by a loathing for war and, in particular, by a conviction that physical force should never be used to achieve selfish and material aims.

Third, Wilson was actually in many ways "realistic," even by conventional standards, in his thinking about and methods in the conduct of foreign relations. For example, he used armed force in the classic way to achieve certain diplomatic objectives in Mexico and the Caribbean. He understood the meaning of the term "balance of power." He was keenly aware of the relevance of material interests and had few illusions about the fundamental bases of international behavior. It is, one must say, the sheerest nonsense to talk about him as an impractical idealist and visionary.

Fourth, while admitting that there were times when a nation had no recourse but to use armed force in international disputes, and while using force himself on behalf of the American government on certain occasions, President Wilson never permitted war's neuroses and fascinations either to derange his reason or to obscure the political objectives for which force was being used. Hence he was never the victim of that greatest twentieth-century delusion, that it is necessary to win wars even at the risk of losing everything for which wars are fought.

This is a very imperfect characterization of the thought and character of Wilson the diplomatist, but it may help us to understand his policies during the greatest tragedy of the modern epoch and the event that raised the gravest challenges to his leadership—the First World War. It was for Wilson a period with three distinct stages: the period of American neutrality, from August 1914 to April 1917; the period of American belligerency, from April 1917 to November 1918; and the period of peacemaking, from November 1918 to June 1919. The challenges of each period were different, but he met them all, on the whole, with the same "higher realism" that had characterized his leadership at home.

His policies during the first period can best be briefly described by saying that from the outbreak of the war in Europe to the beginning of the German unlimited submarine campaign in early 1917, President Wilson tried as hard as any man could have done to be neutral, to make the necessary accommodations to the exercise of belligerent power, and to engage in stern defense of American rights only when they could not, because fundamental human principles were involved, be compromised.

Some of the recent American "realists" have joined the older English and French critics in charging Wilson with impractical idealism precisely because he did follow such a course—because he did not rally the American people to preparation for what they have said was an inevitable participation; because he conducted long and patient negotiations to avoid a break with Germany; because he did not undertake large and early measures of assistance to the Allies and thus help to shorten the duration of Europe's agony; because he refused throughout the period of American neutrality even to align the American people and their government morally on the Allied side.

Looking back upon the final outcome, as we are entitled to do, we well might wonder who the true realists were during this period: so-called realists, or President Wilson, who in an almost uncanny way kept himself immune from the emotional hysterias and passions that seized other men; who believed that the causes of the war were so complex and remote that it was impossible to assess the blame; who, overborne by the tragedy of the event, fought desperately to preserve American neutrality so that he could perform the healing task of reconciliation once the nations of Europe had come to some sense; who believed that an enduring peace could come only through a "peace without victory," a "peace between equals"? Who were the deluded men who had lost sight of reality? The European leaders who thought that they could win decisive victories on the battlefields and on or under the seas, and who thought that they could impose their nations' wills upon other great peoples? Or Wilson, who thought that they were momentarily mad?

The climactic confrontation, the supreme reckoning between so-called realists and the alleged impractical idealist, came, once the United States had been forced into the conflict and Germany was defeated. It did not occur earlier, because the British and French leaders had refused to permit it to occur before the Armistice was safely signed. But it could not then be long postponed, for the Allied leaders had matured their plans, and President Wilson had meanwhile formed a peace program of his own and announced it to the world in the Fourteen Points address and other speeches.

There is no need to review the turbulent events of the Paris Peace Conference here. They are familiar enough, to begin with; but a detailed account of them now would obscure my larger purpose—to look back upon the Paris settlement and, while looking back, to attempt to see who the true realists were.

The supreme task of the victors at Paris in 1919 was, obviously, to work out a peace settlement and reconstruct an international order that could endure. It had to be a peace that could survive the ebbing of passions and hatreds that consumed Europe in 1919. It had to be a peace that could survive because it could command the approval of the German people. Above all, it had to be the kind of settlement that would endure because it could retain the long-run support of the American and English peoples, even of the French people. The necessity of constructing this kind of settlement was, as we can now see clearly, the supreme reality of peacemaking in 1919. We must, therefore, judge men and measures at the Paris Conference according to whether they met this test or not.

By this criterion I do not see how any fair historian can but conclude that the so-called realists at Paris—the dedicated if cynical Clemenceau, concerned only about the destruction of the ancient foe and the future security of France; the well-intentioned Lloyd George, who had given so many hostages to war passions at home and to the Commonwealths that he was no longer a free man; and the Italians, Sonnino and Orlando, eager only for spoils—how could they be called anything other than sublime irrationalists and dreamers? Theirs was a dream, a nightmare, of unreality. Given the task of reconstructing Europe and preventing a future war, they would have responded by attempting to perpetuate the division of Europe and by making a new war almost inevitable.

On the other side and standing usually in solitary if splendid isolation was the alleged impractical idealist fighting for the only kind of settlement that had any chance of survival—for a peace of reconciliation, for disarmament by victors as well as vanquished, against annexations and indemnities, and for a new international organization that would include former enemy states as active members from the beginning. Over and over he warned that this was the only kind of peace that would prove acceptable to the American people in the short run and to the moral opinion of the world in the long run, in short, the only kind of settlement that could endure. It should require little reference to events that followed the Paris Conference to demonstrate the "higher realism" of President Wilson's views.

If proof is needed on specific points, one could cite, for example, Wilson's point of view on the problem of reparations. Over and over he insisted, and with a steadfast consistency, that reparations should be compensation for specific willful damage only, not indemnity; that the Germans should not be saddled with a debt that was heavier than they could carry; and that there should be a time limit to the obligation that the German nation should be forced to assume. What the Allied leaders demanded and finally obtained is well known to this audience. What the realistic solution of this problem was is now too obvious for comment. Or, as a second example, one might cite Wilson's attitude toward the Russian Revolution—how he saw the deeply rooted causes of that cataclysm and the futility of any western effort to suppress it by military force; and how the realism of his attitude contrasted with the egregious folly of so-called realists who thought that it lay within their power to change the course of Russian history.

The result of the clash between European so-called realism and Wilsonian so-called idealism was of course the Treaty of Versailles, that compromise that violated the terms of the agreement by which the Germans had stopped fighting and made a mockery of some of the principal planks in the American President's peace program. Why, it is fair to ask, did President Wilson permit such a peace to be made and sign the treaty embodying it? The answer, I submit, is that it was "higher realism" that drove him to this difficult decision. Having won, at least partially, many of the things for which he had been fighting, he had to give as well as to take, for he could not impose his will entirely upon his colleagues. He signed the Versailles Treaty in the conviction that the passage of time and the Treaty's new creation, the League of Nations, would almost certainly operate to rectify what he knew were the grievous mistakes of the Peace Conference. He signed the Versailles Treaty, in short, because he believed that it was the best settlement possible in the circumstances of 1919.

What President Wilson hoped would occur did of course in large part take place during the 1920s and early 1930s, even though alleged realists in the United States combined with authentic visionaries to repudiate Wilson's work and prevent their government from playing the role of mediating leadership within the League of Nations of which Wilson had dreamed. The great tragedy of the postwar period was not that the Versailles Treaty was imperfect. It was that the forces of reconciliation could not operate rapidly enough without American leadership in the League, that France and Great Britain had neither the will nor the strength to defend the Treaty alone during the 1930s and, above all, that the German people submitted to demonic forces that promised a speedy rectification of all the injustices of Versailles. But this is precisely what President Wilson, in another flash of "higher realism," predicted would occur if the so-called realists, both in the United States and in Europe, continued to have their way.

That is the age-old question, whether the so-called realists or the higher realists shall have their way in determination of national and international policies. President Wilson survives as a more powerful force in history than when he lived because he gave us the supreme demonstration in the twentieth century of higher realism in statesmanship.

This, obviously, was no accident. Woodrow Wilson's "higher realism" was the product of insight and wisdom informed by active Christian faith. He was not, fundamentally, a moralist, as he so often seemed to be, but a man who lived in faith, trying to be guided by the Holy Spirit in meeting the complex problems of a changing nation and world. Using one of his own metaphors, we can say that the light of Heaven gleamed upon his sword. His precepts and ideals will be relevant so long as democracy endures, so long as men seek after a new international community organized for peace and the advancement of mankind.

11

The Case for
Woodrow Wilson

IN his Foreword to *Thomas Woodrow Wilson*, by Sigmund Freud
and William C. Bullitt, Mr. Bullitt, former U. S. Ambassador to
the Soviet Union and France, explains how he and the founder
of psychoanalysis collaborated in the early 1930s to write this
book.[1] Bullitt assumed responsibility for gathering the biographical
data (his notes, he says, ran to more than 1,500 typewritten pages),
and he wrote a digest of data pertaining to Wilson's childhood
and youth. Freud contributed a brief introduction explaining his
system of psychoanalysis and his own involvement in the project.
Then the two men—at least so they both testify—worked together
on the body of the book. Each author apparently wrote sections
of these main chapters and then later, in conference, reconciled
and amalgamated them.

A number of profoundly disturbing questions have been
raised about the integrity of this book—whether the analytical parts
of the text were in fact written by Freud. Since I am not qualified
to engage in this kind of textual detective work, I will concentrate

Reprinted from *Harper's Magazine*, CCXXXIV (April 1967), 85–93; copyright 1967,
Arthur S. Link.
1. Boston: Houghton Mifflin, 1967. Bullitt died in Paris on February 15, 1967, at
the age of 76.

on an equally important issue: whether this study is based upon sound biographical and historical evidence.

Wilson, the authors tell us, was a weak and sickly boy who found reasonably satisfactory outlets for his sexual libido in his relations with his mother, sisters, cousins, and, later, his two wives. However, he vacillated between passivity and hostility to his stern and demanding father, the Reverend Dr. Joseph Ruggles Wilson, who set impossible objectives for Woodrow's superego to achieve. Like most boys, Woodrow suffered from the Oedipus complex caused by this internal tug-of-war. But Woodrow never resolved the Oedipus complex, and this failure prevented him from ever having a normal, independent, and integrated personality.

For one thing, Wilson was incapable of healthy masculine relationships, in part because his passivity to his father found one outlet in identification with his mother, in part also because he invariably regarded male friends as substitutes for his younger brother, Joseph R. Wilson, Jr. Failure to resolve the Oedipus complex also caused Woodrow Wilson to identify his minister-father as God and himself as the only begotten Son, Jesus Christ. And, more's the pity, once Joseph Ruggles Wilson died, Woodrow became in his own mind the Trinity—Father, Son, and Holy Spirit. Needless to say, this caused monumental troubles. One was the compulsion that Woodrow felt, as Jesus Christ, to have a Judas Iscariot, or betrayer, among his close friends. This paranoia forced Wilson to break with all his male intimates.

However, there were two more fateful consequences of Wilson's failure to resolve the Oedipus complex. Ridden by unconscious hatred of his father, Woodrow focused this hatred like a laser beam on men who challenged his leadership and authority, most particularly Dean Andrew F. West at Princeton and Senator Henry Cabot Lodge. Driven at other times by feminine passivity to his father, Wilson craved domination by and submission to other men, for example, the Allied leaders at the Paris Peace Conference of 1919.

All these inner conflicts, the book suggests, made it difficult enough for Woodrow Wilson to function normally while his father was alive. Once Joseph Ruggles Wilson died, Woodrow went around the bend. At least by 1907 he was an extreme neurotic, if not a psychotic, living in a world of illusion and delusion, unable to distinguish between fact and fancy: "Distortion of fact thereafter became a pronounced trait of Wilson's character. Thousands of distorted, ignored or forgotten facts mark the remainder of his life" (p. 125). Since circumstances catapulted him into positions of immense influence and power, he wreaked incalculable damage damage upon his own nation and the world.

This is not the first highly critical study of Woodrow Wilson, nor even the first attempt to use Freudian psychoanalysis to understand his personality. William Bayard Hale published a semi-Freudian analysis of Wilson's use of language, *The Story of a Style* (New York: B. W. Huebsch, 1920), in 1920. Alexander L. and Juliette L. George emphasized Wilson's alleged father fixation (his tendency to concentrate his hatred of his father on men who opposed him) in their *Woodrow Wilson and Colonel House* (New York: John Day Company, 1956), published in 1956. But neither Hale nor the Georges, nor any other serious writers, insofar as I know, have ever contended that Wilson was nearly a psychotic. Thus *Thomas Woodrow Wilson* posits a very new and radical interpretation.

Is this portrait of Woodrow Wilson true and faithful to the evidence? Some of the biographical and historical data in the Bullitt-Freud book are accurate. For example, the authors relate with reasonable accuracy and even some understanding Wilson's very un-psychotic efforts to mediate the European war and achieve a peace of reconciliation in 1916–1917. In addition, they recognize certain well-known contours of Wilson's personality. However, Bullitt and Freud are not to be trusted on most details, particularly details marshaled to prove that Wilson was neurotic. I am talking not only about their numerous factual errors, but also about their distortion and abuse of evidence and, worse still, their bold and uninhibited invention of evidence when necessary to support their psychological analysis.

Perhaps it was inevitable that *Thomas Woodrow Wilson* had to turn into the shambles that it is.

For one reason, it is obviously very difficult and dangerous to try to psychoanalyze a dead man. Freud's earlier attempt to analyze Leonardo da Vinci had already pointed up these dangers (see the searching review by Meyer Schapiro in the *Journal of the History of Ideas*, April 1956). I do not mean to imply that psychiatrists and psychologists cannot help the biographer to see things that would otherwise escape his notice, or that they should not attempt to do their own independent work upon a careful examination of the evidence. But no biographical study, and particularly no "psychological study," can be better than its evidence. Most of the evidence that Bullitt gathered and fed to Freud would not stand up in any court of law or pass any sound test of scholarship. This is true in part because the materials for a sound biography of Wilson or a study of his personality were not available when Bullitt and Freud wrote their book.

Incidentally, there is no great mystery about the sources that Bullitt used and did not use. He had no access whatever to what was thought in the 1930s to be the complete corpus of the Wilson Papers. Ray Stannard Baker, Wilson's official biographer, had these papers under lock and key until 1939. But Bullitt could not have gathered evidence sufficient for a sound study of Wilson's early life even if he had seen all the papers in Mr. Baker's possession. The main body of the Wilson Papers for the first forty years of Wilson's life was not discovered until 1963, in the Wilson house on S Street in Washington.

The documents in this great addition are absolutely indispensable to an understanding, among many other subjects, of Wilson's relationship to his father. Bullitt's and Freud's analysis of that relationship—and of its impact upon Woodrow's personality and psyche—was based mainly on Baker's brief description of it. Baker, they said, had seen all the letters between Woodrow and Dr. Wilson. Actually, Baker never saw more than a handful of these letters; and the statement to the contrary was not his, but Bullitt's and Freud's.

If Bullitt did not see more than a tiny portion of the Wilsonian documentary record, where, then, did he obtain his so-called evidence? He picked and chose from the few biographies in print by the early 1930s, principally the first three volumes of Baker's *Woodrow Wilson: Life and Letters.* He also relied heavily, among other books, on Robert E. Annin's hostile biography, published in 1924, and on the memoirs of the even more hostile William F. McCombs, published in 1921. Bullitt also interviewed every critic, foe, or *former* friend of Wilson whom he could find. Dean Andrew F. West not only told Bullitt about Wilson's supposed double-dealings during the Graduate College controversy at Princeton but seems also to have permitted Bullitt to read his manuscript history of this controversy. Colonel House, apparently a mine of so-called information, also permitted Bullitt to read his massive diary. Bullitt paraphrases sections of this diary that were totally unknown to scholars until the document was opened to researchers in the 1940s. We are entitled to wonder whether Bullitt interviewed a single one of Wilson's friends and admirers who survived in large numbers in the 1930s. In any event, there is no evidence in the book that Bullitt did so.

Third, it does not seem likely that *Thomas Woodrow Wilson* would have turned out much differently even if Bullitt had had access to the entire body of the Wilson Papers and had taken the trouble to try to obtain a reasonably fair cross section of contemporary opinion about Woodrow Wilson. Both authors admit that they undertook their study with strong feelings against their subject, but they assure us that their original hostility turned into sympathy and pity for a very sick man the more they studied Wilson's career.

The latter statement strains credulity far beyond the breaking point. Bullitt was one of that small group of so-called liberals, which included John Maynard Keynes and Walter Lippmann, who turned savagely against Wilson when he failed to achieve an international millennium at Paris in 1919. Bullitt's animus against Wilson is not only old but well-known. Freud shared the pathological hatred of his fellow-Viennese against the man whom they blamed for destroying the Austro-Hungarian Empire. In addition, Freud never liked Americans, and it was natural for him to react against the man who embodied so many American traits and gave voice to so many American traditions.

That the authors were not moved by pity only is revealed among other things by the dozens of snide and contemptuous remarks that they interspersed quite irrelevantly throughout the text of their book. Here are a few notable examples:

Joseph Ruggles Wilson "talked too much" and "incidentally is not to be recommended as a model for fathers" (pp. 3, 113). While Dr. Wilson was strong and handsome, young Tommy was sickly and ugly; and Mrs. Joseph R. Wilson had no existence beyond the wishes of her husband and no influence over her son (pp. 7, 54). Woodrow Wilson "always did badly in studies unless they were connected with speech"; "his pleasures were all connected with the use of his mouth" (pp. 13, 30). Woodrow Wilson "could never admit that he had done wrong" (p. 62). He "was, in fact, ill at ease with men of any distinction" and "could never permit any friend to meet him on terms of mental and moral equality" (pp. 30, 124). "He seems to have thought about political or economic problems only when he was preparing to make a speech about them either on paper or from the rostrum. His memory was undoubtedly of the vaso-motor type. The use of his vocal chords was to him inseparable from thinking" (p. 73). "In all his recorded words there is no sign that he understood French, German or Italian civilization, to say nothing of the classic Greek" (p. 107). Wilson was ignorant of European languages (p. 107). When he was fifty-one, he was "an ugly, unhealthy, 'intense' Presbyterian, who had little interest in women and none in food, wine, music, art or sport, but enormous interest in speaking, in himself, in his career, and in God" (p. 132). As President of the United States, Wilson rarely worked hard and "saw little or nothing of the members of his Cabinet or of the leaders of his party in the Congress." He entertained in a niggardly fashion, offering his guests neither "wine, cigarettes nor cigars" (pp. 150–151). With few exceptions, Wilson shunned or hated everyone (p. 152). His "notable legislative program of the years 1912 to 1914 was largely the program of House's book, *Philip Dru: Administrator*" (p. 152).

As it turns out, every one of the statements just quoted or paraphrased (and they are only a few among many such) is demonstrably false, silly, or only very partially correct. I do not know how Bullitt discovered the fact that Joseph Ruggles Wilson talked too much. Actually, he had a reputation for being very reserved. Whether he was a model for fathers is of course a matter of opinion, but it would have been helpful if Bullitt had seen Dr. Wilson's letters to his son. Woodrow Wilson did very well in studies unconnected with speech, and he enjoyed a few pleasures other than those connected with the use of his mouth. Wilson was an accomplished student of the Greek and Latin languages (he resumed the study of Greek after his retirement from the White House), and he read French and German with considerable facility. He taught courses in Greek and Roman history, as well as in Italian, German, and French history. Incidentally, he gave much attention to art in his course on the Italian Renaissance. One of Wilson's best essays was a long piece on French history. Entitled "Self-Government in France," it is published in the first volume of *The Papers of Woodrow Wilson* and is easily available to anyone interested in reading it. To say that Wilson did not work hard (as Bullitt does several times in the book) is on the same order as saying that the earth is flat. Wilson's papers, spanning the years between 1873 and 1924, provide abundant evidence that he was highly disciplined and worked with an almost furious intensity from his youth onward. For example, as a youth he taught himself a complicated shorthand system. To cite another example, while President he wrote virtually all the important diplomatic correspondence of the United States on his own typewriter.

It is of course not insignificant that Bullitt was obviously immensely ignorant of Wilson's biography. It is even more significant that many of Bullitt's errors are not careless mistakes—a fact which says something about Bullitt's deep hostility to his subject.

Freud revealed his own hostility by throwing in irrelevant observations that could have been included only for the purpose of besmirching Wilson's character.

Consider, for example, Freud's strong inference that Woodrow Wilson, at the age of sixteen, had a homosexual attraction to Francis J. Brooke in Columbia, South Carolina (p. 73). There is not an iota of evidence that Wilson "began to love Brooke deeply," and a great deal of evidence that Wilson and Brooke were never close friends. This imagined love affair was thrown in, not because it shed any light on Wilson's personality (after all, some tendency toward homosexuality is not uncommon among boys of sixteen), but in order to shock the naïve reader.

It would require as many pages as Bullitt and Freud have written to expose all the factual errors, fabrications, and irrelevancies in *Thomas Woodrow Wilson,* and there is no point in boring the reader by going on about them ad nauseam. I prefer to use this space to comment on Bullitt's and Freud's important hypotheses about the causes and manifestations of Wilson's alleged neuroses.

1. The authors put such emphasis on Wilson's Oedipus complex that their entire argument hangs or falls on the validity of this hypothesis.

I am aware of Freud's theory about the universality of the Oedipus complex. All that I can say is that if Woodrow Wilson did have an Oedipus complex, he resolved it as unconsciously as he had experienced it. To be more specific, there is no good evidence of any unusual passivity by Woodrow toward his father.

The relationship in the beginning was of course that of father and son and teacher and pupil. The relationship had become one of comradeship by the time that Wilson matured; and Woodrow was the dominant partner at least from the mid-1880s onward. Throughout, however, the relationship was one of mutual love, not of domination or submission, and it was extraordinarily creative and liberating for both partners.

Freud argues at great length that one outlet for Wilson's passivity to his father was a mother identification. A clear and unquestionable example of this occurred, Freud says, when Wilson dropped Thomas from his name. He did so in about June 1881, according to Freud, because Hattie Woodrow of Chillicothe, Ohio, daughter of his Uncle Thomas Woodrow, rejected his proposal of marriage. (The rejection actually occurred in September 1881.) Thomas Woodrow Wilson at this point dropped his first name. He had gone to Chillicothe to marry his mother. Hattie's rejection made him dreadfully unhappy. By dropping Thomas from his name he was in fact satisfying his need for a mother representative "by becoming himself his mother" (pp. 90–91).

This is a marvelous example of an exercise that Freud engages in many times in this book, that of constructing an elaborate psychological interpretation on a solid foundation of nonfact. Now, it is perhaps true that Wilson was looking for a wife who was something like his mother in his courtship of Hattie, although it would be easy to overdo this point. But Freud's analysis is pure nonsense. Wilson began to drop Thomas or Tommy in November 1879 and had largely gone over to plain Woodrow Wilson by April 1880. However, he continued to sign himself Tommy in letters to old friends for years after Hattie refused his hand. The demonstrable fact is that Hattie's rejection had nothing to do with his shortening of his name.

There is not a shred of reliable evidence of Woodrow's hostility to his father. I have to add that I regard as nothing less than arcane the theory that Wilson's father fixation was responsible for his difficulties with Dean West and Senator Lodge. There is really no mystery why Wilson's controversies with these two men occurred. Wilson and West were old rivals at Princeton. They fell out primarily over the location and character of a Graduate College. But this was only the surface manifestation of their increasingly bitter struggle for control of the Board of Trustees and of the university itself. Wilson's quarrel with Lodge was over the very posture that the United States should assume in world affairs. These two titanic struggles would undoubtedly have occurred and proceeded to their tragic conclusions whether or not Wilson had a father fixation.

2. *After admitting that they had limited evidence on the subject, Bullitt and Freud mention repeatedly Wilson's psychosomatic illnesses as evidence of his psychic disturbances. The authors even provide a table of fourteen "breakdowns" (p. 80).*

There is no evidence that Wilson was weak and sickly as a boy. His health did not "break down" at Davidson in the spring of 1874, and he did not go home to be "nursed for fifteen unhappy months" (pp. 79–80). Wilson finished his freshman year at Davidson, and the college records reveal that his health was as good as if not better than that of his fellow students. Wilson did not have a "breakdown" at the University of Virginia. He simply had severe digestive troubles from bad food and probably bad water and went home to complete his legal studies. "It is not surprising that the year and a half which followed were the most unhappy of his life," the authors tell us. "Not only was his activity toward his mother without outlet but also his activity toward his father. His dyspepsia and headaches barred him from the path he hoped would lead him to a career as a statesman until the spring of 1882" (p. 91). This is pure fiction. Between January 1881 and May 1882, when he went to Atlanta to begin his legal career, Wilson was in good health and spirits. He not only completed his legal studies but also wrote several articles and made good progress on his first book. It is equally fanciful to talk about Wilson having "breakdowns" in 1883–1884 and 1887–1888. The cause of Wilson's later attacks, particularly the serious ones in 1906 and in the autumn of 1919, is well known—arteriosclerosis. These two major attacks, along with other minor ones, were probably caused by overwork and sheer nervous exhaustion. It is really only slightly accurate to say that Wilson's "neurasthenic symptom complex invariably reappeared as a reaction to difficult situations" (p. 81).

3. *Bullitt and Freud permitted their imaginations to run riot when they described the various manifestations of Wilson's passivity to his father, which, Freud asserts, accentuated his femininity.*

Contrary to what Bullitt and Freud say, all evidence indicates that Wilson had a normal boyhood, at least as normal as was possible for boys growing up in the South during the Civil War and Reconstruction. His playmates were boys. He had a strong temper and was by nature combative (not merely as a boy but throughout his life). He dreamed of being a soldier and of going to sea. He played baseball avidly. At Davidson, he was on the freshman nine; at Princeton, he played baseball nearly every day and was elected president of the Base Ball Association. His interest in sports continued throughout his life. For example, he was an adviser to the football team at Wesleyan University, 1889–1890.

Bullitt and Freud miss the mark most widely in portraying Wilson as being so undersexed as to be almost a neuter. (Such a description was, of course, essential to their theory that feminine passivity predominated in Wilson's psyche.) Statements to this effect, repeated over and over, would be enough to make Bullitt's and Freud's personality analysis ridiculous. Wilson was in fact extremely virile. His letters to his fiancée and wife, Ellen Louise Axson, to be published in forthcoming volumes of *The Papers of Woodrow Wilson,* provide abundant evidence of this fact. Wilson's sexual drive was probably primarily responsible for his tremendous inner drive and burning intensity. His masculinity made him attractive to women as well as a leader of men.

4. *Bullitt's and Freud's description of the nature of Wilson's friendships, particularly their assertion that he had to have little-brother substitutes as male friends, is also so much balderdash.*

Bullitt and Freud very conveniently ignore the most important facts about Wilson's male friendships—first, that from his youth onward he had and retained a host of male friends; second, that most of these friends were strong, independent, and highly successful in their own careers. While Wilson was at Princeton—to select only one period of his life—his friends among the faculty included Henry B. Fine, Edward S. Corwin, Edwin Grant Conklin, Christian Gauss, Robert K. Root, George McLean Harper, Luther P. Eisenhart, Bliss Perry, and William Berryman Scott. In the larger academic world at the same time they included A. Lawrence Lowell, Charles W. Eliot, Frederick Jackson Turner, Munroe Smith, J. Franklin Jameson, E. R. L. Gould, and Herbert B. Adams. All these men were distinguished scholars and administrators, leaders in their own right, and formidable characters. They would have been the first indignantly to repudiate Bullitt's and Freud's statement that Wilson "was ill at ease with men of any distinction" and "could never permit any friend to meet him on terms of mental and moral equality." It was, actually, the other way around. Wilson had very little patience with stupidity. It was one of his faults that he too obviously did not suffer fools gladly.

Every strong innovating leader in history has fallen out with friends and associates, or they have fallen out with him for various reasons. Wilson was not unique in having his share of broken friendships. But Bullitt and Freud tell us that these ruptures occurred, indeed had to occur in the case of every intimate friendship, because of Wilson's delusion that he was Jesus Christ and required a betrayer like Judas Iscariot (pp. 122 ff. and *passim*). This generalization, like many others in *Thomas Woodrow Wilson*, can be believed only if one keeps saying to himself that it is true because it is true because it is true.

I have space to discuss only one of the better-known ruptures. Since the authors correctly note that in fact there never was an open break between Wilson and Colonel House (however, they completely misunderstand or misrepresent the reasons for Wilson's loss of confidence in House), we can turn to the other most notorious rupture, that between Wilson and John Grier Hibben.

As is well known, Hibben was Wilson's closest friend at Princeton. Hibben opposed Wilson's plan to abolish the eating clubs at the university and build quadrangles, or colleges, in which undergraduates and unmarried faculty members would live. The estrangement between Wilson and Hibben eventually became complete; at least Wilson cast out Hibben altogether at a certain point.

Bullitt and Freud (following Baker largely) say that it was Hibben's seconding, in faculty meeting in 1907, of Henry van Dyke's motion opposing the quadrangle plan that shattered the Wilson-Hibben friendship. "To protect himself from the dammed flood of his passivity [to his father], Wilson at once converted Hibben into a betrayer: a man to be hated. The conversion of Hibben into a Judas was doubtless made easy for Wilson by his unconscious identification of himself with Christ" (p. 123).

This is all very interesting and arresting. The main defect of this analysis is that it is not true. Hibben did indeed oppose the quadrangle plan. During the summer of 1907, more than two months before the faculty meeting referred to, Hibben wrote Wilson a long letter telling him that he would have to oppose the quadrangle plan. Wilson replied on July 10, saying that he believed that the plan was right and necessary and concluding as follows:

This, my dear Jack, is the whole matter, as I would speak it to my own heart. You have done your duty, and I love and honour you for [it]; I shall try to do mine, and so win your love and respect. You would not wish me to do otherwise. And our friendship, by which I have lived, in which I have drawn some of the most refreshing, most renewing breath of my life, is to be as little affected by our difference of opinion as is everything permanent and of the law of our hearts. Do not, I beg of you, torture yourself in any way about it all. A struggle is ahead of me,—it may be a heartbreaking struggle,—and you cannot stand with me in it; but we can see past all that to the essence of things and shall at every step know each other's love. Will not that suffice?
. . . Bless you for the letter and believe the truth,—that everything is all right and as it should be.

Your devoted friend, Woodrow

Hibben did second van Dyke's resolution at the faculty meeting on September 26, 1907. But the Wilson-Hibben friendship survived. As late as 1909, we find Wilson addressing Hibben as "My dear Jack" and signing himself "Affectionately yours." The causes of the breach were (1) Hibben's gradual alignment with West in the Graduate College controversy and, more important, (2) Hibben's acceptance of the presidency of the university from the hands of the very men who had forced Wilson to resign from that office. Hereafter, Wilson had to shut Hibben out of his mind altogether in order to protect himself against the pain that Hibben's actions had caused him.

5. *Bullitt's and Freud's description of Wilson's passivity and femininity reaches its climax in their account of the President's activities during the Paris Peace Conference.*

To state their thesis briefly, Wilson, after venting his aggressions and showing some masculine tendency to stand and fight, was overcome by the stronger compulsion to submit to Clemenceau, Orlando, Lloyd George, and other Allied leaders. In thus yielding to the greedy demands of these leaders, Wilson violated his liberal principles and betrayed the hopes of mankind.

It must suffice for me to say (1) that we have a large and rich historical literature on the Paris Peace Conference (to cite only one recent example, John M. Thompson's *Russia, Bolshevism, and the Versailles Peace*[Princeton: Princeton University Press, 1966], which sheds much light, incidentally, on Bullitt's own activities at the conference), and (2) that there is a growing and fairly solid consensus among historians that Wilson fought for his principles and program as hard as any man could have done and made certain concessions only in order to avoid worse evils. I think that it is also accurate to say that a great majority of historians agree that Wilson was not only the best-informed leader at Paris but also the wisest, the most disinterested, and the most farsighted. I myself believe that Paris was Wilson's finest hour.

6. *Bullitt and Freud go into orbit when they dilate upon Wilson's so-called religious delusions.*

They go too far too fast for me. I cannot grapple with their absurdities without writing an essay on the development of Wilson's religious thought and faith. Since I have already published such an essay (in George L. Hunt, editor, *Calvinism and the Political Order* [Philadelphia: Westminster Press, 1965]), I must respectfully enter my dissent against the Bullitt-Freud view and refer readers who are interested in this subject to my article.

7. *The authors point to Wilson's speeches (and to one alleged sentence in one particular speech) in defense of the Versailles Treaty on his Western tour of 1919 as final, conclusive proof that the President was virtually a psychotic.*

Bullitt and Frued write that Wilson's Western tour in September 1919 was "the supreme expression of the neurosis which controlled his life" (p. 285). They arrive at this very new conclusion apparently because Wilson, then engaged in a desperate effort to defend the League of Nations, put the best face possible on the Versailles Treaty and did not give his opponents additional ammunition by enumerating the treaty's deficiencies, which he knew better than anyone else.

Nowhere do Bullitt and Freud even mention Wilson's great central theme in his speeches—the necessity for America's reconciling leadership in the League of Nations if another war was to be prevented in the next generation. On the contrary, the best that Bullitt and Freud can do is to quote passages out of context and to point ominously to what was either a slip of Wilson's tongue or of the reporter's pencil. This occurred in a sentence in Wilson's speech at Columbus, Ohio, on September 4, 1919, which the reporter for the New York *Times* rendered as follows: "I have been bred, and am proud to have been bred, in the old revolutionary stock which set this government up." Wilson, the authors assert, had forgotten that his mother was an immigrant from England and his father's parents immigrants from Ulster. He had "left fact and reality behind for the land in which facts are the mere embodiment of wishes" (p. 285). In the official published text the sentence reads: "I have been bred, and am proud to have been bred, in the old revolutionary school which set this government up." Either this is the way Wilson's stenographer, Charles L. Swem, took the sentence down, or else Wilson changed it to read this way before final copy went to the Government Printing Office. In any event, it is difficult to see how this molehill can be made into much of a mountain. The authors will have to find better evidence than this to prove that Wilson was insane.

To be sure, Woodrow Wilson had his quota of faults, which he was the first to admit and exaggerate. He was proud, sensitive, ambitious, possessive with friends, sometimes stubborn, opinionated, etc. But he was also warm and winning, full of life and fun, generous to a fault with friends, acutely self-critical, and a man of deep Christian faith.

As for his rationality, it is obvious that the acid test of this characteristic is the individual's ability to function effectively in the world of men and affairs. For a mentally unbalanced person, Wilson had a remarkable career. Somehow he managed to make distinguished contributions to the four separate fields of scholarship, higher education, domestic politics, and diplomacy. He was spectacularly successful in leadership as president of Princeton, as governor in Trenton, and in Washington. He had the principal hand in laying the foundations of the modern American political economy. Among the major leaders of the world, he alone was able to keep his head during the first world war; that is, he never permitted himself to be captured by the demons of total war. He helped to construct the first international organization dedicated to prevention of war, the League of Nations. Almost single-handed, he defended the Mexican Revolution and gave it a chance to begin the long process of reconstructing Mexican society. He enjoyed the love and devotion of a host of friends and members of his family. Considering the variety and dimensions of Wilson's achievements, one is entitled to wonder whether *Thomas Woodrow Wilson* does not tell us a great deal more about its authors than about its subject.

12

The Wilson Movement in
Texas, 1910–1912

FOR more than half a century after the Civil War, Texas was the "dark and bloody battle ground" of progressive and conservative Democratic factional struggles. Although the state was traditionally and historically southern, it was too much a frontier to be politically conservative.[1] The Farmers' Alliance, from which Populism grew, had its beginnings within the wide borders of Texas, and the agrarian-progressive movement swept throughout the state. The last decade of the nineteenth century was the heyday of agrarian reform in Texas.[2] And Texas was a pioneer in successful progressive legislation. Many significant reforms were enacted during Gov. James Stephen Hogg's administration,[3] but a succes-

Reprinted from *Southwestern Historical Quarterly*, XLVIII (October 1944), 169–185, by permission of the Assistant Director of the Texas State Historical Association.

1. Research on this article was made possible by a grant from the Julius Rosenwald Fund.

2. Roscoe C. Martin, *The People's Party in Texas* (Austin: The University, 1933), is a splendid treatment of this subject.

3. Among the numerous progressive reforms of Hogg's administration were the following: establishment of a railroad commission with power to set freight and passenger rates; passage of a law regulating the issuance of railroad stocks and bonds; important land reforms; insurance and monetary regulatory laws; labor legislation, a mechanics' lien law, and an antitrust law. See Paul L. Wakefield, "James Stephen Hogg, the Great Democrat," in Frank Carter Adams, editor, *Texas Democracy* (Austin: Democratic Historical Association, 1937), especially pp. 312–314.

sion of progressive governors—Charles Allen Culberson, Joseph
D. Sayers, Samuel W.T. Lanham, and Thomas M. Campbell—carried on Hogg's liberal tradition.

By 1910, however, Texas was in a state of conservative reaction. The rise to power of Joseph Weldon Bailey, called by his
biographer the "last Democrat," had served as an effective check
to the progressive movement. This young politician, brilliant of
intellect and charming of personality, was a vigorous champion
of the status quo. By means of the superb political organization
he had erected, Bailey's influence was so widespread that he was
one of the dominant forces in Texas politics. In 1910, Bailey was
the junior United States Senator from Texas. The "last Democrat's" control in Texas politics was apparently secured when his
candidate, Oscar Branch Colquitt, was elected governor, while
the state Democratic executive committee completely dominated
by Bailey lieutenants held the reins of Democratic power in Texas.[4]

It was altogether natural, then, that a large body of Texas
progressive Democrats should have looked to Woodrow Wilson
as their political deliverer. Wilson, in the fall of 1910, had left
the cloistered halls of Princeton to accept from the hands of the
New Jersey Democratic bosses the gubernatorial nomination of
his party. Before the gubernatorial campaign was ended, Wilson
had repudiated the bosses who nominated him, had assumed
leadership of the progressive Democrats in New Jersey, and by
his spectacular campaign had definitely established himself as
one of the leaders of the progressive wing of the national Democratic party. Even before he was inaugurated governor, Wilson
was forced to break openly with James Smith, Jr., leader of the
New Jersey Democratic machine, when the Boss attempted to get
himself elected to the United States Senate. Wilson dealt Smith
a resounding defeat and during the early months of 1911 pushed
through the New Jersey legislature a series of progressive reforms.
Within the space of seven brief months after his entrance into
the political field Wilson was perhaps the chief contender for
the Democratic presidential nomination in 1912.

Wilson's political and economic philosophy, later known as
the "New Freedom," was progressive in that it envisaged greater

4. Sam Hanna Acheson, *Joe Bailey, the Last Democrat* (New York: Macmillan, 1932),
is an entertaining and authoritative study.

popular control of the state and national governments, destruction of financial and industrial monopolies in the interests of the people, and a low tariff; and in no section of the country did it have a more powerful appeal than in the South. During 1911 and 1912, the movement to make Wilson the Democratic presidential nominee swept over the South, and the progressive character of this movement was emphasized by the fact that, in practically every southern state, the progressive faction of the party rallied wholeheartedly to his support, while the conservatives and reactionaries consistently opposed him.[5]

It was logical that Texas progressives, who were themselves struggling against the dominant Bailey faction in power, should espouse the cause of a new political leader who had already demonstrated his ability as a smasher of political machines. Their earnest advocacy of Wilson's political ideals and their antagonism to Bailey and his organization generated the enthusiasm that produced the most effective state Wilson organization in the nation.

Immediately after Wilson's election as governor of New Jersey in November 1910, several Texas politicians hastened to proclaim him their standard-bearer for 1912. These men—Thomas B. Love,[6] Otis B. Holt,[7] Thomas Watt Gregory,[8] and Albert S. Burleson[9]—like so many other men, had been drawn to Wilson because of his distinguished service in the educational and political fields. But it was Thomas B. Love who forged ahead and assumed leadership of the Wilson movement in Texas. Soon after Wilson's smashing victory in New Jersey in 1910, Love wrote the Governor that he was already heartily advocating his nomination for the

5. For a discussion of the Democratic pre-nomination campaign in the several southern states, see Arthur S. Link, "The South and the Democratic Campaign of 1910–1912" (Ph.D. dissertation, University of North Carolina, 1945).

6. Love was a prominent lawyer of Dallas and one of the prohibition leaders in Texas. He had represented Dallas in the legislature in 1903 and 1905 and was Speaker of the House of Representatives in 1907. He became Commissioner of Insurance and Banking for Texas in 1907 and held that position for several years. Love to Woodrow Wilson, December 1, 1910, copy in Ray Stannard Baker Papers, manuscripts in the Library of Congress, Washington, D.C.; hereinafter cited as Baker Papers.

7. Holt was a Houston banker. See his letter published in Houston *Post,* November 24, 1910, in which he pledged his support to Wilson.

8. Gregory was a noted "trust-buster" of Austin, an intimate friend of Col. Edward M. House, and later Attorney General of the United States.

9. Burleson was a Representative in Congress from Texas and was later Postmaster General during Wilson's administration.

presidency.[10] An exceedingly friendly correspondence between the Texan and Wilson resulted, and Love set to work to organize the state for Wilson. Love was, for a time, compelled to give his energies to the cause of Prohibition, whose forces he championed; but after that battle had been fought and lost,[11] he turned his attention to the details of political organization.

After conferring with Wilson sympathizers throughout the state, Love decided that the hour for formal organization had arrived, and he issued a call to all Texas Wilson men to meet at Austin on August 7, 1911, to inaugurate formally the Texas Wilson movement. His organizational meeting was a decided success, for more than two hundred prominent Texas Democrats met at Austin, declared their allegiance to the Wilson cause, and resolved to fight Wilson's battle in their state. Love and his colleagues conscientiously endeavored to create an organization unencumbered by the Prohibition or the anti-Bailey label. Although they were in part successful, it was apparent to most observers that in large measure they had failed, for Love, president of the Texas Wilson organization, Cato Sells, chairman of the executive committee, and Thomas W. Gregory, vice-president, were all evangelical Prohibitionists and bitter enemies of Bailey.[12]

The opening gun of the Wilson campaign in Texas was sounded in an address written by Gregory and published in the state press. The address, "To the Democrats of Texas," as it was called, narrated the history of Governor Wilson's career and proclaimed the magnificence of his victory for democracy in New Jersey. The South, wrote Gregory, had long awaited the day when she could present one of her own sons to the nation. The hour and the man had met! It was manifestly incumbent upon the

10. Love to Wilson, November [1]5, 1910, Baker Papers.

11. Though the Texas prohibitionists lost their fight for a state-wide prohibition amendment, they were confident that the power of the "liquor machine" had been destroyed. And Love was sure that the undoing of the liquor interest made certain a Wilson victory in Texas. Love to Wilson, July 26, 1911, Baker Papers.

12. George D. Armistead, a correspondent for the San Antonia *Express*, was named secretary, and R. C. Roberdeau of Austin was elected treasurer of the organization. O. T. Holt of Houston was chosen a vice-president. Other initial organizers included M. T. Barret and M. L. Buckner of Dallas, R. M. Wynn of Fort Worth, W. T. Bartholomew of San Angelo, C. E. Gilmore of Wills Point, A. R. McCollum and Bert Moore of Waco, A. D. Rogers of Decatur, Guy M. Gibson of Coriscana, S. A. Tinsey of Tyler, T. F. Harwood of Gonzales, and T. W. Davidson of Marshall. From letterhead of the "Woodrow Wilson for President of the United States in 1912" organization, in Baker Papers.

citizens of Texas, Gregory wrote, to lead the southern states in the cause of making Wilson president. The letter ended with a vigorous appeal to Texans to organize Wilson clubs in their individual communities and to give their whole-hearted support to the well-deserving cause.[13]

The response to this call for organization was encouraging, for within one month after the Austin meeting, Wilson clubs had been organized in strategic points throughout the state. The mayor of Houston led in the organization of a Wilson club in his city,[14] while Love's former law partner joined with hundreds of enthusiastic Democrats in Dallas to form a club there.[15] Naturally the two hundred Democrats who began the movement at Austin took the lead in organizing Wilson clubs in their communities. The spontaneity of the enthusiasm for the Wilson movement was something of a surprise to even the most ardent supporters, and several prominent politicians who had not attended the Austin conference hastened to declare their allegiance to Wilson's candidacy.[16]

As early as April 1911, Thomas B. Love and his co-laborers had urged that Wilson come to Texas and deliver a decisive blow in his own behalf in that state. Wilson willingly agreed to speak at the state fair in Dallas in the latter part of October,[17] and the representatives of Wilson clubs in Texas formed a reception committee for the New Jersey governor, who arrived in Dallas at ten o'clock on the morning of October 28, 1911.[18] The reception given Governor Wilson was exceedingly cordial. As he stepped from

13. Houston *Post,* August 13, 1911.

14. The mayor of Houston was H. B. Rice. Dallas *Morning News,* August 11, 1911.

15. John C. Robertson was the leader at Dallas. Dallas *Morning News,* August 18, 1911. The Dallas Wilson Club had over a thousand members within two weeks after it had been organized. See Dallas *Morning News,* August 25, September 17, and October 28, 1911, for details of other organizations.

16. Among them were Thomas H. Ball, state chairman of the prohibition forces, former Gov. Thomas M. Campbell, Railroad Commissioner W. D. Williams, and Rep. Rufus Hardy of Coriscana. Dallas *Morning News,* September 27, 1911; San Antonio *Express,* September 8 and October 20, 1911.

17. Love to Wilson, April 18, August 5, 1911; Wilson to Love, April 24, July 31, August 8, 1911, Baker Papers.

18. The list of Wilson men on the reception committee revealed that the lines of the campaign had already been tightly drawn.

For the names of the members of the committee, see the Dallas *Morning News,* October 22, 1911. The membership of the committee reveals also the widespread growth of the Wilson clubs within less than a year after Wilson had achieved national prominence.

the train, the raucous noise of a brass band, the cheers of a large crowd, and the concerted yells of a small group of Princeton and Virginia alumni generated a welcome of amiable confusion.[19] Wilson immediately climbed into a carriage filled with prominent Texas politicians, including Gov. Oscar B. Colquitt, Sen. Charles A. Culberson, Mayor W. M. Holland of Dallas, Thomas B. Love, John C. Robertson, and the city commissioners. This group rode slowly through the streets of the city lined with cheering mobs, while a solid mass of people filled the lobby of Wilson's hotel and crowded the sidewalks and streets nearby. The curiosity and enthusiasm of the crowds were boundless. It was an altogether auspicious beginning for a great campaign in Texas!

At the Baptist church at Dallas, on the morning of October 28, bishops, preachers, politicians, and laymen united in paying spiritual homage to Wilson, the Christian statesman. Five thousand men and women gathered to hear Wilson express the need of an intimacy between human life and the Divine Word. The occasion was the celebration of the three-hundredth anniversary of the translation of the Bible into the English language. Before the program began, Wilson was introduced to the ministers of Dallas, members of various religious organizations, and the American Bible executive committee. It was not strange that Christian ministers were often in the vanguard of the Wilson movement!

Bishop E. R. Hendrix of Kansas City,[20] who presided, gave Wilson a hearty welcome. "It gives me great pleasure to welcome to this state our great Christian statesman and scholar," he said. "In his daily life he has done much to exemplify the teachings of the Great Book." Dr. Samuel P. Brooks, president of Baylor University, introduced Wilson as the people's candidate for the presidency. Politics and religion were bedfellows on that occasion! Wilson's speech was definitely second-rate, and on reading it today one is hardly impressed by it, but he seemed to enthrall his audience by his sincerity and the felicity of his phrases.[21]

At the conclusion of the Bible celebration, Wilson went immediately to the Oriental Hotel, where he was the guest at a

19. Dallas *Morning News*, October 29, 1911.

20. Bishop Hendrix was a member of the College of Bishops of the Methodist Episcopal Church, South, and president of the Federal Council of the Churches of Christ in America, 1908–1912.

21. Dallas *Morning News*, October 29, 1911.

luncheon given in his honor. Perhaps the most significant feature of the occasion was the presence at the luncheon of notable representatives of every faction in the state Democratic party. Bourbon Governor Colquitt sat on one side of Wilson, while Progressive Judge William F. Ramsay sat on the other. Most conspicuous, however, were the Texas Wilson leaders: Ramsay, Cone Johnson, T. M. Campbell, Thomas B. Love, Morris Sheppard, Robert L. Henry, Cato Sells, and John C. Robertson. Sells presented Wilson as the man "whom we all hope will be the next President of the United States," while Henry, Campbell, and Johnson pledged to Wilson their enthusiastic support.[22] The superficial harmony which reigned at the affair led several observers to suppose that harmony of the progressive stripe had been restored within the party.[23] They mistook, however, hospitality for harmony, for Governor Colquitt contented himself with the utterance of a few meaningless platitudes, and said nothing at all about supporting Wilson for the presidency. Neither did Senator Bailey give his blessing to the occasion.

From the Oriental Hotel, Governor Wilson and the luncheon party went directly to the Coliseum at the Texas State Fair grounds. Before an audience of some 7,500 persons, Sen. Charles A. Culberson introduced Wilson, and for the first time publicly declared his faith in the New Jersey governor.[24] Culberson's introduction was a truly eloquent encomium. He declared that Wilson was imbued with the fundamental principles of Jefferson and George Mason, that the Declaration of Independence, the Bill of Rights, and the Statute of Virginia for Religious Freedom were precious inheritances to him. Wilson achieved national fame, Culberson

22. Representative Henry nearly caused a riot in the crowd. In the morning papers, a prominent Democrat had been quoted as saying that since Texas Democrats had been instructed for Joseph W. Bailey for President the year before, the party should hold to its pledge and give the "last Democrat" its vote in the Democratic convention in 1912. Henry shouted that the expression of a "Bailey convention" was not the wish of the "sovereign Democrats of Texas," who would pay no attention to Bailey's demands. Texas Democrats, Henry declared, would instruct their delegates to vote for Woodrow Wilson for President. San Antonio *Express*, October 29, 1911.

23. *Ibid.*

24. Born in Dadeville, Alabama, in 1855, Culberson was graduated from the Virginia Military Institute in 1874 and studied law at the University of Virginia. A lieutenant of Gov. James S. Hogg, Culberson was elected Attorney General of Texas in 1890 and 1892, and governor in 1894 and 1896. In 1899, he was chosen United States senator to succeed Roger Q. Mills, and was re-elected in 1905, 1911, and 1916.

declared, because he led his party against the forces of entrenched privilege and political corruption. The Senator clearly met the issue of Wilson's progressive doctrines. Wilson was, Culberson admitted, somewhat in advance of the Democratic party regarding the vital issues of the day—issues of the perfection of representative government, the destruction of privilege and private graft in government, and the complete dissolution of the partnership between the Republican party and the nation's industrial leaders.[25]

Wilson turned to the immense audience and poured forth his message to the people of Texas. By way of introduction, he immediately ingratiated himself with the Texas progressives by giving fulsome praise to the significant reforms in which Texas had pioneered under the great liberal triumvirate, Sen. John H. Reagan, Governor Hogg, and Judge A. W. Terrell.[26] He declared that it was "a particular and vital thing" for him to speak in Texas, because there was some progressive language he wanted to use that would not be understood anywhere else.

Wilson's theme concerned the rights and responsibilities of the state governments within the federal framework. The liberty of the people, he insisted, had to be expressed first within the community, then within the nation. But if Wilson's hearers had expected an academic lecture on a theoretical subject, they were disappointed. For, once again, the former professor talked politics. Only recently, he declared, had the people realized that there was something standing between them and their state governments—some concealed power with which they could not reckon. And now the American people were changing their political methods at the very time that they were changing their lives. There was never an era, therefore, when thoughtful and moderate statesmanship was more desperately needed; the problems facing Americans were enormous, but the political leaders had only imperfect instruments with which to solve them.

---

25. Dallas *Morning News*, October 29, 1911. Culberson's endorsement of Wilson marked the entrance of a powerful ally—powerful both in the state and in the nation—into the Wilson camp. It further accentuated the anti-Bailey character of the Wilson movement in Texas, for Culberson was one of Bailey's bitterest antagonists.

26. Thomas W. Gregory had carefully tutored Wilson on the political history of Texas and had emphasized that Wilson should mention favorably the powerful political leaders who were heroes to the masses of the people. Gregory to Wilson, October 7, 1911, copy in Baker Papers.

Industrial tyros, Wilson declared, were not the servants of the people; they were instead the masters of the people. And that which gave the appearance of radicalism to modern politics was the insistence of the people upon stating the very extraordinary, ungarnished facts. Remedies were undoubtedly necessary, Wilson asserted, but they need not be radical. "We can not afford to do anything less than what we should have done all along," he declared, "namely, to draw all of the hearts of the American people into the enterprise of reform." Though she had kept her eyes closed for a season, America had again opened them to gaze upon the visions of a day when the government should appear fair and pleasant to all men, "because all men should know that under her banners there march those that are free, resourceful and full of confident hope; those who have seen and shall accomplish the freedom of the human race." [27]

The response to Wilson's speech was not entirely favorable. Although several editors insisted that he had done great service in emphasizing the imperative necessity of a restoration of popular government,[28] Wilson's critics hastened to point out that his address contained no concrete measures of reform, no commitments as to governmental policy, but only "a mass of platitudinous philosophy." [29] Preceding Wilson's arrival in Texas, the Fort Worth *Record* had propounded to him a series of searching questions: Would he apply the principles of the initiative, referendum, and recall to federal laws? Did he favor the Bryan doctrine of free raw materials? Did he favor the principles set forth in a monograph on the short ballot written by the executive secretary of the Short Ballot Association, of which Wilson was president?[30] Wilson failed to answer specifically a single one of these questions. Then, as before, Wilson was loath to commit himself to any definite program of reform.

But Wilson's visit to Texas did give tremendous encour-

27. Dallas *Morning News*, October 29, 1911. Wilson went from Dallas to Fort Worth on the evening of October 28 and addressed an audience there. The burden of his speech was practically the same as that of his Dallas address.

28. Dallas *Morning News*, October 31, 1911; *ibid.*, November 8, 1911, quoting Denton *Record-Chronicle*; San Antonio *Express*, December 1, 1911, quoting San Marcos *Times*.

29. Houston *Post*, November 1, 1911.

30. *Ibid.*, October 26, 1911, quoting Fort Worth *Record*.

agement to his followers in that state.[31] The leaders in the Wilson camp, faced with a hostile state Democratic executive committee which refused to allow the party to hold a preferential presidential primary, redoubled their efforts and carried on embittered agitation to force the hand of the executive committee. On August 1, 1911, the state legislature endorsed the presidential primary proposal, while the Dallas *Morning News* and other Wilson journals continually clamored for its adoption. Rep. Robert L. Henry and Senator Culberson urged the Democrats of Texas to demand a primary.[32]

On March 2, 1912—Texas Independence Day—the executive committee of the Wilson state organization met at Waco and struck a mighty blow for the cause of a presidential primary and for Wilson. The Waco conference marked the real beginning of the presidential campaign in Texas. The committee sent to the state Democratic executive committee a petition, emphasizing the necessity of holding a primary, and insisting that the committee adopt the measure.[33] The conferees at Waco, however, concerned themselves more specifically with the details of campaign management and promotion. The attendance was representative of every section of Texas; unanimity of opinion was manifest to a remarkable degree, and enthusiasm for the cause was at a high pitch.[34] The Waco conference, perhaps the most notable gathering of Texas Democrats which had assembled in a decade, was attended by more than one hundred prominent political leaders. Added to the original Wilson men were such notables as A. W. Terrell, Thomas W. Ball, Samuel P. Brooks, M. M. Crane, and Cullen F. Thomas.[35]

One week after the Waco meeting, on March 11, Cato Sells [36] established Wilson campaign headquarters at the Hotel Southland in Dallas. The work of organizing Wilson clubs was carried for-

31. Ray Stannard Baker asserts that Wilson's addresses at Dallas and Fort Worth were the reasons for his victory in Texas. *Woodrow Wilson, Life and Letters,* 8 vols. (Garden City, New York: Doubleday, Doran & Co., 1927–1939), III, 299. But this statement completely ignores the almost perfect organization built up by the labors of the loyal Wilson followers, which was the basic and important reason for Wilson's victory in Texas.

32. Dallas *Morning News,* January 13, February 15, 1912.

33. Written by T. W. Gregory, copy in Baker Papers.

34. Dallas *Morning News,* March 3, 1912.

35. *Ibid.*

36. Chairman of the executive committee of the Texas Wilson organization.

ward with renewed enthusiasm, and by the end of the campaign there was scarcely a county or town that did not have one or more thriving organizations. The action of the Democratic executive committee in denying the petition for a preferential primary increased the necessity for thorough organization, for it was necessary that the Wilson men capture the city and county conventions controlled in large measure by the Bailey-Colquitt organization.

Col. Edward M. House, a Texas politician of some repute, in the fall of 1911 entered the Wilson campaign in a sort of advisory capacity. House returned to Austin in December 1911, and lent his energies to the task of organization. His contributions to the Wilson campaign consisted of a small financial donation and intermittent advice to the Wilson leaders on the management of the campaign.[37] But the burden of the tremendous task of promotion fell to Cato Sells, Gregory, and Love, who labored indefatigably for three months to perfect and reinforce the organization. Of course, the Wilson managers experienced moments of despondency. At times it appeared that their labors would come to naught.[38] But their job was excellently executed. Their extreme care that trustworthy lieutenants in city and county would "bring out the votes" and capture the local conventions paid rich dividends when the issue was finally decided. In short, the Texas

37. After a thorough examination of the House Papers, the Burleson Papers, and the Woodrow Wilson Papers, in addition to the outstanding Texas newspapers, this writer desires to add his opinion as to the importance of House's work in Texas. Charles Seymour, *The Intimate Papers of Colonel House,* 4 vols. (New York and Boston: Houghton Mifflin Co., 1926–1928), I, 57 ff., states that House was almost entirely responsible for the success of the Texas Wilson movement. The myth of Colonel House was considerably exaggerated by Arthur D. Howden Smith's *Mr. House of Texas* (New York and London: Funk & Wagnalls Co., 1940), which attributed all good things of the Wilson administration to House's influence. Colonel House played a minor, almost inconsequential, rôle in the Texas campaign. I cannot see but that the results would have been exactly the same regardless of whether House aided Wilson. This is the position shared by several of the chief campaigners. Love, for example, wrote that "It is the simple truth to say that Colonel House's influence and contribution were in no way decisive of the result. It is certain that Texas would have gone as it did if Colonel House had never supported Woodrow Wilson." (Love to Ray S. Baker, June 7, 1928, Baker Papers.) Burleson once remarked that although he had a tender affection for House, the egotism of his book paralyzed him. (Burleson to Baker, interview, March 17–19, 1927, Baker Papers.)

38. This apprehension is expressed by Gregory in a letter to Burleson of May 4, 1912, Albert S. Burleson Papers, Library of Congress, Washington, D.C.

Wilson men organized the most enthusiastic and successful Wilson state campaign in the country.[39]

The support that Governor Wilson received from several Texans in Congress greatly enhanced his chances of success in the Lone Star State. On the day that Gov. Judson Harmon of Ohio invaded Texas for a whirlwind campaign of the state, four members of the Texas delegation in the House of Representatives—Rufus Hardy, W. R. Smith, Robert L. Henry, and Albert S. Burleson—issued an address to the Democrats of their state, explaining the reasons for their faith in Woodrow Wilson.[40] Senator Culberson, however, three days later, struck the most effective blow for Wilson. Culberson, the legatee of the Hogg tradition, had a great influence over Texas Democrats. He had received at their hands every political honor he had desired, and his opinions dominated the thinking of thousands of his fellow citizens. House had written Culberson several alarming letters, pleading with him to travel to Texas and campaign for Wilson. If he could not do that, House wrote, would he not write a vigorous letter endorsing the Governor? [41] Senator Culberson willingly responded on April 27 with a long address to the Democrats of Texas in which he declared that Wilson's moral fiber, his scholarly attainments, his intellectual genius, and his comprehension of the serious issues of the day placed him in the very front rank of the nation's public figures.[42]

As far as the newspapers of Texas were concerned, Wilson had only fair support.[43] The Dallas *Morning News* and Galveston

---

39. The Wilson leaders in Texas spent less than $2,000—probably $1,500—all of which was contributed by Texas Democrats. Thomas B. Love to Edward M. House, May 5, 1912, Edward M. House Papers, the Library of Yale University, New Haven, Conn.; hereinafter cited as House Papers.

40. Dallas *Morning News*, April 25, 1912.

41. House to Culberson, April 19 and 23, 1912, House Papers.

42. Culberson declared that Wilson had cleaned the Augean stables in New Jersey, had rid the state of the pernicious influences of the trusts and the political bosses, and had achieved a notable victory in legislative reform. Culberson agreed with his candidate that the overshadowing issue facing the people was the restoration of the government to the people. "This is the broad basis of the candidacy of Gov. Wilson for the Presidency," Culberson wrote, "and this is what makes him a candidate." (Dallas *Morning News*, April 28, 1912.)

43. For Wilson editorials in the Texas press, see: *Harper's Weekly*, November 18, 1911, quoting Cleburne *Review*, Victoria *Fact*, and Houston ·*Chronicle*; of the editorials in the

Daily News led the vanguard of newspapers supporting the Wilson movement,[44] while the Houston *Chronicle,* the Fort Worth *Star,* the Beaumont *Journal,* and the Waco *Times-Herald* were other important newspapers adhering to the Wilson cause. Numerous county weeklies also lent their influence to the movement. Generally speaking, these newspapers spoke for the progressive wing of the Democratic party in Texas. And what was true of them was essentially true of the Wilson movement in Texas;[45] not only did it represent a revolt against the domination of the party by Senator Bailey, but it also represented the progressive spirit in the state.[46]

In Texas, the lines of battle were tightly drawn between Wilson and Gov. Judson Harmon of Ohio. Harmon, like Underwood, represented the conservative element of the party; he was the stolid, old-fashioned, prosaic governor of Ohio. Since Harmon developed little actual strength within the nation except in Texas and Ohio, the support he received in Texas is of great significance. In the summer of 1911, the Harmon supporters in Texas formed a loose organization,[47] and Harmon-for-President clubs appeared in the latter part of 1911 and during the winter and spring of

---

Dallas-Galveston *News,* the editorial of May 3, 1912, is the best. Both of these papers were among the most important Wilson journals in the nation, and an examination of them for 1911 and 1912 brings fruitful rewards. See also the San Antonio *Express,* January 5, 1912, quoting Waxahachie *Light; ibid.,* March 8, 1912, quoting Beaumont *Journal;* Houston *Post,* September 21, 1911, quoting Abilene *Reporter; ibid.,* September 26, 1911, quoting Wichita *Times; ibid.,* September 28, 1911, quoting Athens *Daily Review; ibid.,* October 29, 1911, quoting Bryan *Eagle; ibid.,* December 21, 1911, quoting Paris *Advocate.*

44. These two newspapers had a joint editorial policy and printed the same editorials.

45. Ralph W. Steen writes that the Wilson leaders made but one demand upon Wilson—that should he be elected President, he should not give a single office to Bailey men. Wilson willingly agreed, Steen declares. (Ralph W. Steen, "A Political History of Texas," in F. C. Adams, editor, *Texas Democracy,* p. 369.)

46. An editorial from the Houston *Chronicle,* cited in W. J. Bryan's *Commoner,* March 15, 1912, illustrates this point. It follows·

The progressive wing of the Texas democracy has rallied under Wilson's banner, the stand-pat wing under the banner of Harmon.

Now, in all candor, the Chronicle feels that the democrats of Texas are fortunate in having the opportunity to choose between two such men as Wilson and Harmon, in a campaign where the main issues are so clearly drawn that no man can mistake them. . . .

They are to say whether they wish the party to stand for class government, advocated by the Harmon men, or genuinely democratic government, advanced by the Wilson men.

47. Dallas *Morning News,* August 8, 1911.

1912.[48] Harmon headquarters were established in Dallas in March 1912, under the direction of Rice Maxey of Sherman.[49]

At a conference of prominent Harmon Democrats at Dallas in March, the conservatives sounded their call to the Democrats of Texas. They lauded Governor Harmon for his conservatism and pleaded with their fellow citizens to preserve the fundamental and conservative principles of the Democratic party and to destroy forever the Populistic and Socialistic "heresies" which were again gaining ascendancy in the candidacy of Woodrow Wilson. Progressive Democrats they labeled radicals, Populists, and Socialists. The president of the Harmon organization "showed the cloven hoof" by declaring that if the Democratic party adopted the principles of "this so-called progressivism," he would turn Republican.[50]

Col. Reinze M. Johnston, publisher of the Houston *Post* and Democratic national committeeman from Texas, was perhaps the most prominent and resourceful Harmon supporter in Texas and, along with many editorial colleagues, he waged a bitter campaign against Wilson. He and other Harmon editors endeavored to prove that Wilson was an advocate of the doctrine of free raw materials and that he desired to enrich the manufacturers and trusts of the North at the expense of the raw-material-producing South. Johnston declared that this was the real issue of the presidential campaign.[51] The Harmon press in Texas was widespread and was successful in creating sentiment favorable to its candidate.[52]

48. Harmon clubs were organized at Dallas, Houston, Fort Worth, San Antonio, Greenville, McKinney, Decatur, Grand Saline, Kentucky Town, Goree, Mansfield, Sherman, Grapevine, Arlington, Smithfield, Tuxedo, and Lexington.

49. Dallas *Morning News*, March 10, 1912.

50. *Ibid.*, March 5, 1912; Houston *Post*, March 5, 1912.

51. Houston *Post*, May 2, 1912. See also *ibid.*, March 18, 1912, and *ibid.*, March 21, 1912, quoting Fort Worth *Record*.

52. See editorials in the Houston *Post, passim,* quoting Wortham *Journal,* Port Lavaca *Wave,* Pettey *Enterprise,* Fayette County *Record,* Navasota *Examiner Review,* Eagle Pass *News Guide,* Dallas *Times-Herald,* Shiner *Gazette,* Gainesville *Register,* Dallas *Beau Monde,* El Dorado *Success,* Corpus Christi *Caller,* Hamilton *Herald,* Greenville *Herald,* Baird *Star,* Corsicana *Democrat and Truth,* Gilmer *Mirror,* McAllen *Monitor,* Mexia *News,* Trenton *Tribune,* El Paso *News Guide,* Teague *Herald,* Venus *Times,* Childress County *Post,* Commerce *Commercial,* Richardson *Journal,* Victoria County *Advocate,* Dawson *Herald,* Kaufman *Herald,* Decatur *News,* Bellvian *News,* Newton *News,* and Nocona *News,* for expressions of opinion favorable to Governor Harmon.

At the very conclusion of the pre-convention campaign in Texas, Governor Harmon visited the state, speaking at Denison, Sherman, Dallas, Howe, Van Alstyne, McKinney,

The Bailey issue, which the Wilson leaders had tried assiduously to avoid, reached the boiling point when the "last Democrat" announced his intention of coming to Texas to carry on a personal campaign against Wilson.[53] Bailey was resentful of Wilson's treatment of his intimate friend, James Smith, the former boss of the New Jersey Democracy, while his prejudices against Wilson were increased by Smith himself.[54] So great was Bailey's anger at Governor Wilson that the Texan told President William H. Taft that he would support him for re-election should Wilson be the Democratic nominee.[55] Bailey was, moreover, outraged at a story Champ Clark told in Washington on his return from a visit to Texas. Clark declared that he had asked Thomas B. Love, a former Missourian, why he was supporting Wilson instead of the Speaker himself. To which question Love allegedly answered, "Well, you see, we have to act quickly in order to keep Bailey from dominating things down here." [56]

Bailey was stirred by this remark into going to Texas to throw the weight of his personal influence against the New Jersey governor. It was a fatal mistake, for the Wilson forces were firmly entrenched, and the local conventions and primaries were less than two weeks off. At Paris, Texas, on April 27, where he opened his campaign, Bailey revealed the personal bitterness that he

---

Plano, Hillsboro, Waco, San Antonio, Austin, and Houston. The burden of his appeal to the people of Texas concerned his past record of accomplishment in Ohio, an arraignment of the protective tariff, and a depreciation of the initiative, referendum, and recall as national issues. Dallas *Morning News*, April 25, 26, and 27, 1912; Houston *Post*, April 28, 1912.

The Dallas *Morning News*, Wilson's chief spokesman in Texas, declared on April 28:

Texas patriotism and Texas heroes, ancient and modern, need no eulogisms when delivered by one who, ostensibly, is in this state to tell the people why he is better fitted than anyone of several others to be the democratic party's nominee for the presidency. Governor Harmon's speeches during his three days in Texas have been a flagrant waste of brief and fleeting time, to say nothing of the tax they have put on the patience of the people.

53. Fort Worth *Record*, February 15, 1912.
54. Sam H. Acheson, *Joe Bailey*, p. 302.
55. Archie Butt, *Taft and Roosevelt: The Intimate Letters of Archie Butt, Military Aide*, 2 vols (Garden City, N.Y.: Doubleday, Page & Co., 1930), II, 610.
56. Clark, in a letter to Bailey, amplified his statement. He declared that Love had told him that the presidential campaign was "largely a Bailey and anti-Bailey fight in Texas." Clark to Bailey, April 17, 1912, published in Dallas *Morning News*, April 26, 1912. Love indignantly denied Clark's statement. Regardless of the authenticity of Clark's statement, it clearly demonstrates that the Speaker had no qualms about betraying a personal confidence if he thought it would inure to his benefit.

harbored against Wilson. For over ninety minutes, he spoke to a crowd of two thousand persons, arraigning Wilson for his advocacy of free raw materials, the recall of judges, and the initiative, referendum, and recall. It made little difference to Bailey that Wilson was not definitely committed to free raw materials, that he was in favor of using the initiative, referendum, and recall only as a last-ditch method to restore representative government, and that he was unalterably opposed to the recall of judges. Bailey closed his speech with a malediction against Wilson, in which he prophesied that Wilson's success would spell the triumph of Socialism within the Democratic party within a single decade.[57] Again, several days later at Waxahachie, Bailey predicted the destruction of American civilization should Wilson be elected President. Obviously excited by his own verbosity, Bailey prophesied that historians five hundred years in the future would rescue his name from oblivion should the republic be destroyed by the initiative, referendum, and recall. "Five hundred years is a long time to wait for a vindication," he declared, "but the vindication I will receive then will be worth waiting for." Bailey spoke also at Greenville, Daingerfield, and McKinney.[58] His vituperations against Wilson and his phantasmagorical illusions concerning Wilson's "revolutionary policy" failed either to influence or to frighten the voters. Of the seven counties in which Bailey campaigned, Wilson carried six.[59]

The results of the Democratic county primaries and conventions fulfilled the most optimistic hopes of the Wilson leaders. The outcome was an overwhelming victory for Wilson. By May 8, with some sixty counties yet unreported, he had already secured votes sufficient to give his supporters absolute control of the state convention.[60]

At the state Democratic convention which met at Houston May 28 and 29, the Wilson men were in complete control. They rewarded Cato Sells for his labors by discharging Johnston as national committeeman and electing Sells in his stead. They elected a solid delegation of forty Wilson men to the national

57. Dallas *Morning News*, April 28, 1912.
58. *Ibid.*, May 2 and 3, 1912; Houston *Post*, May 4, 1912.
59. Dallas *Morning News*, May 8, 1912.
60. The division in the convention vote stood: Wilson 346 5/6, Harmon 130 2/3, Clark 46 1/2. *Ibid.*, May 9, 1912.

Democratic convention at Baltimore, instructed them to vote for Wilson, and joyfully proclaimed: "We commend to the Baltimore convention as our party's candidate for President that great Democrat, bright scholar, profound student of economics, Christian gentleman, capable executive . . . —Woodrow Wilson."[61]

The anti-Wilson journals laconically lamented the Wilson victory. They declared that the zealous Prohibitionists, Populists, and Socialists had combined to snatch the victory from the true Democrats.[62] But the woe of the anti-Wilson men was the joy of his followers. One Texas editor declared that Wilson's victory proved that Texas Democrats were not awed by the personality of Bailey and that they would not be the pawns of a small group of reactionary politicians.[63]

The Wilson victory in Texas had a psychological value of incalculable importance to Wilson's candidacy in the nation.The Wilson movement had, in the rest of the country, failed to make any considerable headway; and had Wilson lost Texas it is entirely probable that his candidacy would have failed altogether. But the sweeping victory gave the Wilson movement a new lease on life. Furthermore, it spelled the complete overthrow of Bailey's domination of politics in the state. Bailey himself had made his position in Texas politics a chief issue of the campaign, and the rebuke he received at the hands of Texas Democrats was heartening to progressives throughout the nation. One editor not usually favorably inclined to Wilson voiced the feeling of numerous Democrats when he declared that "The waning of that brilliant but erratic star is cause for congratulation to democrats all over the country"; it removed a reactionary influence from the party's councils, and served warning upon public officials "that genius and learning will not be permanently accepted by the people . . . as a substitute for honesty of conviction and fidelity to public trust."[64]

61. *Ibid.*, May 28, 29, and 30, 1912.
62. Houston *Post*, May 6, 1912; *ibid.*, May 12, 1912, quoting Fort Worth *Record.*
63. Dallas *Morning News*, May 9, 1912.
64. Norfolk *Virginian-Pilot*, June 3, 1912.

13

Democratic Politics and the Presidential Campaign of 1912 in Tennessee

"IF an exact account should be written of important events in this State during the past year, no novel of the season could compare with it in sensational features," wrote a Nashville woman during the early spring of 1909. "The one element lacking," she added, "is erotic decadence." [1] Even if one makes a charitable allowance for literary license to our Nashville observer, the fact remains that the Democratic party in Tennessee during the years from 1908-1912 was the victim of nearly every imaginable political hysteria. "To the outside world," commented an influential political journal, "Tennessee doubtless seems a State gone mad." [2] Families and churches were disrupted by political disagreements; to a degree, business and social life was disorganized; and certainly it was evident to political observers outside the state that government had become a mockery, while the executive, legislature, and

Reprinted from *The East Tennessee Historical Society's Publications*, No. 18 (1946), 107–130, by permission of the Managing Editor.

Research on this article was financed by grants from the Julius Rosenwald Fund.

1. Mrs. L. H. Harris, "The Willipus-Wallipus in Tennessee Politics," *Independent*, LXVI (March 25, 1909), 622.

2. "Political Hysteria in Tennessee," *Independent*, LXIX (September 22, 1910), 663.

judiciary had, on one occasion or another, been prostituted to the vagaries of partisan politics.

So complex and manifold were the causes for the chaotic state of Democratic politics in Tennessee during the period 1908–1912 that the historian is hard put to it to unravel the tangled web of confused issues and bitter personal controversies, or to distinguish among them. Basically the chief bone of contention was the prohibition issue; it was upon this rock that the Democratic party foundered in 1910 and 1912. Prohibition sentiment in Tennessee antedates the Civil War, but it was not until the early 1870s that any really organized antiwhiskey movement got under way. In 1887, a proposed state-wide prohibition amendment to the constitution was decisively defeated at the polls; but the large vote cast in favor of the amendment (117,504 for; 145,234 against)[3] was an early indication of the widespread antiliquor sentiment. In 1899, the legislature enacted a local-option law for towns of less than 2,000 population, and by subsequent amendments the law was extended to all cities and towns in the state by 1907. In the meantime the prohibition crusaders, chief among whom were such powerful organizations as the Women's Christian Temperance Union, the Anti-Saloon League, and the evangelical churches, had been assiduously at work. By 1908, only Nashville, Memphis, Chattanooga, and La Follette were outside the prohibition pale.[4]

State-wide prohibition was, in fact, about the only issue in the Democratic gubernatorial contest in 1908, when former Sen. Edward W. Carmack attempted to defeat Gov. Malcolm R. Patterson for renomination. Patterson was a resourceful foe of state-wide prohibition and an advocate of local option; he was conservative on economic issues and—compared with Carmack—had a colorless personality. His political strength lay in the support he received from the powerful Democratic city machines, the liquor interests, and the bulk of the Negro voters, whose good will he assiduously cultivated.

3. William H. Combs and William E. Cole, *Tennessee: A Political Study* (Knoxville: University of Tennessee Press, 1940), p. 40.

4. Philip M. Hamer, *Tennessee; A History, 1673–1932,* 4 vols. (New York: American Historical Society, Inc., 1933), II, 704.

Few politicians in the history of Tennessee have had as stormy a career, or so commanded the devotion of a large following of voters, as Edward Ward Carmack. Born in 1858, the son of a Campbellite minister, Carmack was educated at the Webb School, afterwards read law, and entered the state legislature in 1884. As editor of the Nashville *American* from 1888 to 1892 and the Memphis *Commercial Appeal* from 1892 to 1896, he fought throughout for prohibition, free silver, and Bryan; and he resigned from the editorship of the *Commercial Appeal* during the campaign of 1896 because of a disagreement with the "Gold Democratic" owners of the newspaper.[5] In 1896, he was elected to Congress on a free-silver ticket from Memphis, and was re-elected for a second term in 1898. In 1901, he was elected to the United States Senate, where he served until 1907, when he was defeated for re-election by former Gov. Robert L. Taylor.

The Democratic gubernatorial nomination contest of 1908 was bitterly fought between Carmack and Patterson. Carmack of course had the support of the church groups, the prohibitionists, and the progressive Bryan Democrats; Patterson was the candidate of the state machine, the antiprohibitionists, the liquor interests, and conservatives in general. The result was one of the most memorable campaigns in the history of Tennessee. The Democratic party was split wide open on the liquor question and Patterson defeated his rival by a majority of some seven thousand votes.[6]

Shortly after his defeat in the primary contest, Carmack became editor of the Nashville *Tennessean*, which Luke Lea, an enterprising and ambitious young man of Nashville, had recently established. Throughout the summer and fall of 1908, Carmack carried on a veritable crusade for prohibition in the editorial columns of the *Tennessean*. He also carried his fight to the Democratic state convention. In the determination of disputed elections, many of his followers were unseated, and he failed to secure approval of a prohibition platform commitment. But he did succeed in helping to nominate and elect a legislature, a majority of the members of which were pledged to vote for a state-wide prohibition law.

5. Kenneth McKellar, *Tennessee Senators as Seen by One of Their Successors* (Kingsport, Tenn.: Southern Publishers, Inc., 1942), pp. 464–465.
6. *Ibid.*, 474–475; William L. Frierson, "Edward Ward Carmack," *Dictionary of American Biography*, 21 vols. (New York: Scribner, 1928–1944), III, 496–497.

During Carmack's editorial campaign against Patterson, he took occasion to ridicule one of Patterson's chief political advisers, Duncan B. Cooper.[7] On the day the editorial was published, November 9, 1908, Carmack met Cooper and his son Robin on one of Nashville's main streets; gun play resulted, in which the Coopers shot and killed Carmack and Robin Cooper was wounded. Thus ended the career of one of Tennessee's most turbulent figures. After a prolonged trial, the Coopers were convicted of murder and were sentenced to twenty years in prison. The state supreme court upheld Duncan B. Cooper's conviction and ordered that his son's case be remanded for retrial, whereupon Patterson, on April 13, 1910, promptly pardoned the older man.

For some time after 1908, Edward W. Carmack was a more powerful factor in Tennessee politics in death than he had ever been in life. He was immediately canonized as the martyr of the prohibition cause by the church and prohibition press, and the political character of his assassination gave the prohibition movement exactly the impetus that it needed for successful achievement. The legislature, in January 1909, passed the prohibition law that was a memorial to Carmack's name and, when Patterson promptly vetoed it, just as promptly passed the measure over the governor's veto. Officially, at least, Tennessee became "dry" on July 1, 1909.[8]

In the meantime, the prohibition Democrats had organized their faction into the so-called Independent Democratic party, of which Richard M. Barton of Memphis was the chairman and Luke Lea of the Nashville *Tennessean* (soon to become the Nashville *Tennessean and American)* and E. B. Stahlman of the Nashville *Banner* were the chief editorial spokesmen. The Independents carried their fight into the judicial election during the summer of 1910 and, with the support of the Republicans, who nominated no candidates, succeeded in defeating the regular Democratic nominees. The judicial campaign was just as bitterly contested as the gubernatorial campaign of 1908 had been; and Governor Patterson, who had entered the fight, now suffered his second serious defeat at the hands of the Independents. The prohibition Democrats refused to participate in the regular Democratic convention, which reno-

7. Nashville *Tennessean,* November 9, 1908.
8. Hamer, *Tennessee; A History,* II, 705.

minated Patterson for the governorship, and they held a state convention of their own in Nashville on September 14. As a sort of last-ditch effort at reconciliation, Patterson withdrew from the gubernatorial contest three days before the Independent convention; but the Independents were by now in no mood for compromise and they endorsed the Republican candidate, Ben W. Hooper, an outspoken advocate of prohibition enforcement and a leading "dry."[9]

It was one of the most amazing political conventions in the history of Tennessee, this meeting of the Independent Democrats, and the similarities between it and the national Progressive convention at Chicago in August 1912 are striking. For there was, first of all, an almost perfect union of political and religious fervor on both occasions. "The impression upon a comparative stranger," wrote one astonished onlooker at the Nashville convention, "was that it was a great company [there were some 1,500 delegates] of three or four thousand men filled with deep earnestness, which was of high moral quality. . . . The atmosphere was heavy with aroused spirit of righteous indignation."[10] In the second place, both the Tennessee Independents and the Roosevelt insurgents were revolting against what they conceived to be machine, reactionary control of their respective parties.

The efforts of the Regulars to save their party from disruption and defeat were utterly fruitless. The regular Democratic state committee also resigned and a new convention met on October 6 and elected a new state committee, and nominated Robert L. Taylor for governor. But even Taylor, who had for years been the idol of the Democratic masses and a great conciliator, could neither win the election nor draw the warring factions together. The Independents stayed outside the party and elected Hooper governor; it was the first Republican administration in Tennessee since 1880.

Lea's newspaper, in its analysis of the election returns, declared:

The Democrats of Tennessee elected Hooper not because of, but despite,

9. George A. Gates, "Democratic Insurgency in Tennessee," *Independent*, LXIX (October 20, 1910), 866–867.
    10. *Ibid.*, p. 868.

the fact that he is a Republican. They elected him as the only way
left open for them to destroy a corrupt political machine and to drive
from power those men who have taken over the Democratic organization
as a personal asset for their own base uses and defiled and despoiled
the public service.

In making a fight for the destruction of the corrupt political machine
the loyal and patriotic Democrats here in Tennessee have in no way
impaired the National Democracy, for while they were purging the party
of Pattersonism, they gave the full measure of their strength to the
Democratic candidates for Congress, returning to the national house the
eight Democratic members.[11]

Hooper's victory, the Independents declared, and the election
of an anti-Patterson legislature marked a new turn of affairs in
Tennessee history. The Patterson machine had been dealt a heavy
blow, it is true, but it is doubtful that its power had been utterly
destroyed as the Independents imagined. Certainly it was true
that the Independent revolt had been an uprising of the progressive
elements in the state Democratic party against ring rule, domination of the party by the liquor interests, and venality in the public
service. It was in every respect a reflection of a general progressive
revolt against the old order of things that was convulsing the South
and the nation at the time. Needless to say, the ghost of Edward
W. Carmack must have enjoyed the election postmortems that
filled the Tennessee newspapers on November 10, 1910.

Without an understanding of the causes for and events leading
to the disruption of the party in Tennessee in 1910, it would be
impossible to comprehend the alignment of the Democratic factions in the presidential preconvention campaign that followed
during the next eighteen months.

On the same first Tuesday after the first Monday in November in 1910 when Ben Hooper rode easily to victory over Bob
Taylor, a new political figure rose to prominence in the East. He
was Woodrow Wilson, former president of Princeton University,
who had left the university to accept the Democratic gubernatorial
nomination at the hands of James Smith, Jr., and Robert Davis,
bosses of Newark and Jersey City, respectively. Wilson had begun

---

11. *Nashville Tennessean and American,* November 10, 1910. There were, at this time,
ten congressmen from Tennessee, two of whom were usually Republican.

his campaign timidly because he thought he was a conservative but really was not sure of his political opinions; yet the impelling force of circumstances and the obviously corrupt domination of his party by a political ring forced him quickly to change his mind with regard to the leading issues. Before the campaign ended, he emphatically endorsed a sweeping reform program and repudiated publicly the very bosses who had gone to considerable effort to nominate him. All of which won him the support of the independent voters, most of whom were nominally Republicans, and the governorship of New Jersey by the thumping majority of some 50,000 votes. And that, in a state which only two years before had given the Republican presidential candidate an 80,000 majority, was an accomplishment that made political observers sit up and take notice.[12]

In many respects it might be said that the congressional and gubernatorial elections of November 1910 resulted in the creation of a new Democratic party in the country at large. In the first place, the Democratic landslide signalled the end of Bryan's domination of the party and brought to the fore a new group of Democratic leaders within the states and in Congress: Woodrow Wilson, whose victory in New Jersey was perhaps the most spectacular of all; Judson Harmon, elected governor of Ohio for the second time by a tremendous majority; Champ Clark of Missouri, the next speaker of the House of Representatives; and Oscar W. Underwood of Alabama, the ranking Democratic member of the House Ways and Means Committee and the leading proponent of tariff reduction and reform. Bryan, actually, had bolted the Democratic ticket in Nebraska; his power and influence in party councils would decline precipitously during the preconvention campaign. In the second place, the Democratic victory brought to the forefront a new set of issues, pre-eminent among which was tariff reform, and laid to rest, at least temporarily, Bryan's favorite issues of free silver, anti-imperialism, and government ownership of the railroads (which he had broached in 1908).

Before the 1910 campaign had ended, it was obvious also that Wilson would have the support of progressive Democrats for the presidential nomination in 1912. It was a tentative offer

12. All material in this article relating to Wilson is taken from Arthur S. Link, *Woodrow Wilson: The Road to the White House* (Princeton, N.J.: Princeton University Press, 1947).

of support that they made, to be sure, predicated upon Wilson's successful administration of the governorship; but it was plain by election day that progressives preferred him to Judson Harmon, the conservative, respectable governor of Ohio. Throughout the southern states, where the Democratic party was divided into conservative and progressive factions that to all intents and purposes constituted separate parties in political contests, the progressive Democratic leaders looked to Wilson to provide a new liberal leadership for the party, devoid of the stigma of Bryanism, yet squarely advanced on the issues.[13] As the Nashville *Tennessean and American* put it, "The anti-machine Democrats in Tennessee who aided in the election of Ben W. Hooper on a Democratic platform would have voted for that splendid type of leadership, Woodrow Wilson, in New Jersey."[14]

The reaction of the Democratic press in Tennessee to Wilson's entrance upon the political stage was typical of the remarks of pleasant surprise and enthusiastic comment one finds in most southern newspapers of the time. To begin with, Wilson was practically without a political past, and because of the general nature of his campaign appeals, southern observers saw him as both a progressive and a conservative—depending upon the point of view. The militantly progressive Nashville *Tennessean and American*,[15] for example, was elated by Wilson's victory in New Jersey and immediately began to boom him for the presidency. "It was a happy day," it declared, "when the scholar arrived in politics."[16] On the other hand, the conservative prohibitionist Nashville *Banner* and the conservative regular Democratic Chattanooga *Daily Times* were just as enthusiastic. Wilson, declared the *Banner*, was "the

13. For a general treatment of the reaction of southern progressives to Wilson's rise to political power, see Arthur S. Link, "The South and the Democratic Campaign of 1910–1912" (Ph.D. dissertation, University of North Carolina, 1945), *passim;* for specific treatments, see "The Wilson Movement in Texas, 1910–1912," in this volume, pp. 155–171; see also Arthur S. Link, "The Democratic Pre-Convention Campaign of 1912 in Georgia," *Georgia Historical Quarterly*, XXIX (September 1945), 143–158.

14. Nashville *Tennessean and American*, November 10, 1910.

15. The *Tennessean and American* was easily the leading progressive newspaper in the state; it was also the chief Bryan spokesman among Tennessee Democrats. See issues dated December 20, 21, 1910, and February 12, 1911, for discussions of the direct election of senators and the initiative, referendum, and recall; see especially the editorial of December 19, 1910, "The Democratic Party Must Be Progressive," for a discussion of the general issues.

16. Nashville *Tennessean and American*, November 21, 1910.

type of man whose success in the political field promises a return to the statesmanship of the old days,"[17] and the *Daily Times* confidently predicted that Wilson's wise, patriotic, and "conservatively radical" administration in New Jersey would win the support of an overwhelming majority of Democrats in the presidential nomination campaign.[18]

Events that followed in the course of Wilson's career in New Jersey from December 1910 through April 1911 moved so rapidly and were so spectacular in character that they must have left the average observer in Tennessee gasping for breath. When Boss James Smith attempted to win the senatorship in New Jersey (during December 1910 and January 1911), Wilson led the progressive revolt that succeeded in smashing Smith's senatorial ambitions and was largely responsible for the election of James E. Martine, who had been endorsed at a rump party primary. Actually, the fight in New Jersey developed into a struggle for control of the Democratic party, and Wilson's success in breaking the hold of the Smith machine over the state party was his most significant accomplishment. To Tennessee Democrats who followed the controversy day by day in the newspapers, Wilson appeared as the defender of popular rights, political faith, and good government.[19] The senatorial controversy was really of profound importance in shaping the future course of Wilson's political career and of the Wilson presidential movement, for he was immediately thrust forward as the foremost Democratic progressive champion. "It requires the unselfish devotion to principle and the splendid powers of such men as Dr. Wilson," declared one Tennessee editor, "to wrest the reins of government from the hands of men who would prostitute it to the base service of greedy and corrupt interests."[20] The Chattanooga *Daily Times* observed that Wilson was revealing the "fearless and sterling qualities for large leadership that impress most emphatically his

17. Nashville *Banner*, November 9, 1910.
18. Chattanooga *Daily Times*, November 10 and 13, 1910.
19. There was full reporting of the controversy in the Tennessee press. For typical editorial comments, see Nashville *Banner*, December 13 and 21, 1910, January 25, 1911; Chattanooga *Daily Times*, December 10, 1910, January 25, 1911; Nashville *Tennessean and American*, January 8 and 26, 1911; Knoxville *Journal and Tribune*, December 17, 1910, January 27, 1911.
20. Nashville *Tennessean and American*, January 8, 1911.

fitness for the leadership of the party in the nation."[21] The *Tennessean and American,* always anxious to lambast the Patterson machine, sought to point the moral and adorn the tale by comparing the political situations in New Jersey and Tennessee:

The similarity of the conflicting forces in New Jersey and in Tennessee is so marked, and Dr. Wilson's position is so clearly and distinctly on the side of the people as against ring rule, official venality, force and fraud, that we need no committee to tell us where he would stand if he were in Tennessee. He would be fighting the James Smiths who have sought and are now seeking to convert both parties into servile and slavish agencies of greedy interests. He would be fighting those men who are serving insolent political machines instead of the great political parties.[22]

No sooner had Wilson won his victory over Smith than he set about to redeem his party's platform by securing the enactment by an unwilling legislature of a reform program which included a sweeping primary election law, a new public utilities commission empowered to set rates, a workmen's compensation law, and a stringent corrupt practices act, [23] as well as a number of other minor reform laws. The significance of Wilson's reform administration, coming so close upon his victory in the senatorial controversy, can best be understood when it is realized that it inevitably made him the leading and apparently the strongest contender for the Democratic presidential nomination. By the time the New Jersey legislature convened, Wilson had priority on the front pages of almost every Democratic newspaper in Tennessee. Tennessee Democrats applauded when Wilson almost literally kicked an obnoxious Democratic boss out of his office;[24] they followed his earnest appeals to the legislators for the redemption of party pledges; and they congratulated themselves when he succeeded in securing the enactment of all of his reform program. "He absolutely refuses to be gauged by the measure of ordinary politics," declared the leading Chattanooga newspaper. "If we do not

21. Chattanooga *Daily Times,* December 10, 1910.

22. Nashville *Tennessean and American,* January 8, 1911.

23. *Acts of the One Hundred and Thirty-Fifth Legislature of the State of New Jersey, Session of 1911* (Paterson, N.J.: News Printing Co., 1911), Chapter 183, pp. 276–325; Chapter 195, pp. 374–389; Chapter 96, pp. 134–145; Chapter 188, pp. 329–349.

24. See e.g., Chattanooga *Daily Times,* March 26, 1911.

take such a man, we will be the losers, not he." [25] The Nashville *Banner* gave what was probably the most accurate summary of Democratic opinion in the state in the spring of 1911, at a time when Wilson's preconvention popularity was at its peak:

No man in the late years of American politics has come more suddenly into national view or made a stronger impression on the American public than this erstwhile college president. His coming into public life has been unique, but even if he lacked experience in what has been called practical politics, he has given full proof that he did not lack study and knowledge of such matters. He has proved himself more than a match for the practical politicians with whom he has had to cope. He has succeeded in all he has undertaken, and he has undertaken things from which most governors shrink as being no part of their official duty and unnecessarily complicating their chances in politics. . . .
The thoroughly educated man, free from any objectionable influences, one of clear common sense and strong character, is the ideal man in American public life and Woodrow Wilson approaches that ideal nearer than any man now prominent in the country's politics. [26]

During the early part of May 1911, Wilson embarked upon a speaking tour of the West, during the course of which he made over thirty speeches in seven states. It was, in effect, his first important bid for the Democratic nomination in 1912, and he used his western audiences as sounding boards for his campaign appeals. Actually he said nothing new or startling, except that he believed in Christianity and in popular government—in the initiative, referendum, and recall (except the recall of judges), commission city government, and the like[27]—but he said enough to frighten fearful conservatives into believing that he was well on the way to becoming another Bryan. [28] Practically all the Democratic newspapers in Tennessee published Wilson's most important western addresses, and for the first time Democrats in the

25. *Ibid.*, May 28, 1911.
26. Nashville *Banner*, April 25, 1911.
27. For Wilson's western speeches, see the Kansas City *Journal*, May 6, 1911; Kansas City *Times*, May 6, 1911; Denver *Rocky Mountain News*, May 8, 10, 1911; Los Angeles *Times*, May 14, 1911; Pasadena *Star*, May 13, 1911; San Francisco *Bulletin*, May 16, 1911; San Francisco *Chronicle*, May 17, 1911; Portland *Oregon Daily Journal*, May 19-20, 1911; Portland *Evening Telegram*, May 19, 1911; Seattle *Times*, May 21, 1911; St. Paul *Pioneer Press*, May 25, 1911; Lincoln *Nebraska State Journal*, May 27, 1911.
28. See e.g., New York *Sun*, May 13, 1911.

state could see what stand he took on national issues. Editorial reaction in Tennessee, on the whole, was overwhelmingly favorable to Wilson's new progressive departure. "Gov. Wilson is touching a responsive chord when he points out the prevailing evils and calls for their correction," commented the Nashville *Tennessean and American*. "He is representing the great progressive movement, not of one party, but of all parties. He is reflecting the views of the mass of American people."[29] Conservative editors, on the other hand, were pleased by the absence of demagoguery in Wilson's appeal and the sober temper and rationality of his speeches. They compared him with Bryan and observed that the Commoner suffered by the comparison.[30]

Interest in the course of the Wilson campaign did not, however, overshadow or diminish the struggle between the Independents and regular Democrats that was in progress in Tennessee during 1911. The legislature of that year was about as turbulent as any, and the two factions were, if anything, farther apart than they had been a year before. The Independents and Republicans in the legislature united into a solid bloc to prevent any weakening of the prohibition laws. This the Fusionists, as they were called, succeeded in doing; after a bitter and protracted struggle, they also elected Luke Lea, the prohibitionist leader upon whom Carmack's mantle had fallen, to the United States Senate.

While it was true that the prohibitionists had written their moral opinions into the Tennessee statutes in 1909, they had not come anywhere near assaulting the remaining strongholds (as they thought) of wickedness and sin: the cities of Memphis, Chattanooga, and Nashville, where the prohibition laws were openly flouted both by the saloon-keepers and the municipal authorities. Especially notorious was Nashville, where Mayor Hilary E. Howse made no effort to conceal his contempt for prohibitionists and their laws. In July 1911, the Nashville *Banner* began a campaign to drive Howse from power in the municipal election in the fall. It charged that Howse's refusal to enforce the liquor laws was responsible for the rapid growth of liquor dens, gambling dives, and houses of prostituion; that the underworld and the city administration were working hand in glove; that there was no doubt

29. Nashville *Tennessean and American*, May 9, 1911.
30. Chattanooga *Daily Times*, May 21, 1911.

that Howse was protecting the lawless elements in the city.[31] The presidents of twelve colleges and seminaries in Nashville, led by Chancellor James H. Kirkland of Vanderbilt University, entered their emphatic protest against "The conditions of lawlessness and vice . . . unparalleled in the history of Nashville."[32] The Baptist ministers of the city, a week later, published a fervent appeal for a clean sweep,[33] but the struggle to dislodge the boss was unsuccessful; Howse was triumphantly re-elected and was mayor of Nashville six months hence when he led the fight against Woodrow Wilson.

The organization in Tennessee of the movement to make Wilson the Democratic presidential nominee in 1912 followed a pattern typical of the movements in most other states. First came the spontaneous organization of Wilson-for-President clubs, such as the club organized at Columbia, Tennessee, in September 1911.[34] The beginnings of the organized Wilson movement in the state, however, were auspicious and altogether encouraging to the New Jersey governor's friends. A group of Democrats gathered at the Maxwell House in Nashville on October 14, formed a preliminary state organization headed by five men strategically selected from four of the cities in the state, and sounded a call to the Wilson followers in Tennessee to take the lead in organizing Wilson clubs in their communities.[35] In the organization of the campaign which followed as a result of the Nashville conference, University of Virginia and Princeton alumni played a prominent role. Lewis M. Coleman, Wilson's fellow student at Virginia, for example, led in organizing the Hamilton County Wilson Club in Chattanooga in November.[36] Robert F. Fisher, prominent Memphis attorney and Princeton alumnus, joined with Judge R. M. Barton and David Fentress to initiate a Wilson organization in Memphis.[37]

31. Nashville *Banner*, September 30, 1911.
32. *Ibid.*
33. *Ibid.*, October 4, 1911.
34. Atlanta *Georgian*, September 8, 1911.
35. Judge John E. Richardson of Murfreesboro was chairman of the state organization. The other members of the executive committee were William L. Talley and Judge Robert Ewing of Nashville, Judge R. M. Barton of Memphis, and Lewis M. Coleman of Chattanooga. Nashville *Banner*, October 14, 1911; Chattanooga *Daily Times*, October 15, 1911.
36. T. S. McCallie of the McCallie School was also a leader in the Chattanooga organization. Chattanooga *Daily Times*, November 7, 1911.
37. Nashville *Banner*, December 2, 1911.

The Reverend Dr. Josiah Sibley and D. C. Webb organized a group of Wilson enthusiasts in Knoxville in November.[38] After this flurry of activity, the organization of Wilson clubs came to an end with the formation of a club in Nashville in January 1912.[39]

At the outset of the movement, the Wilson leaders made an assiduous effort to disassociate their cause from the internal political squabbles that had disrupted the Democratic party in Tennessee. One is reminded of an identical situation in Texas, where the Wilson leaders, who were generally prohibitionists and progressives and opponents of Sen. Joseph W. Bailey, protested that the Wilson movement was above factional quarrels. This simply was not true—either in Texas or Tennessee, or in any other state in the union, where the opposing Democratic factions invariably lined up behind different candidates. Actually the Independent-prohibitionist character of the Wilson movement in Tennessee was evident from the very outset. With a few exceptions, all of the Wilson leaders were prominent Independents; the leading Independent and prohibitionist newspapers in the state—the Nashville *Tennessean and American*, the Nashville *Banner*, and the Knoxville *Sentinel*, to mention only the leaders—were the leading Wilson journals.[40] In the rural counties, where the prohibition sentiment was strongest, thirty-five out of fifty-four newspapers supported the Wilson cause.[41]

Under these circumstances, the regular Democrats did what they would probably have done had there been no split in the Tennessee Democratic ranks: they came out solidly against Wilson and supported either Harmon, Underwood, or Clark. Even the Chattanooga *Times*, which had been the most enthusiastic supporter of Wilson's candidacy in the state, turned its back on the New Jersey man. It declared in February 1912 that Democrats were suspicious of any movement led and fostered by the Independents,[42] and by April was declaring that Wilson was "laboring under an erratic obsession" in his campaign appeals.[43] The

38. Chattanooga *Daily Times*, November 10, 1911.

39. Wilmington (N.C.) *Morning Star*, January 7, 1912.

40. Other Tennessee Wilson newspapers were the Tipton *Record*, Pulaski *Citizen*, Lawrence *Democrat*, Manchester *Times*, Morristown *Gazette*, and Lewisburg *Tribune*.

41. Columbia (S.C.) *State*, February 21, 1912.

42. Chattanooga *Daily Times*, February 28, 1912.

43. *Ibid.*, April 21, 1912.

Harmon, Underwood, and Clark supporters came largely from
the ranks of the Regulars. Harmon, who spoke in Knoxville and
Nashville during the campaign,[44] made a desultory campaign and
had the support of the conservative Memphis *Commercial Appeal.*[45]
Underwood's campaign in Tennessee was managed by none other
than the notorious mayor of Nashville, Hilary E. Howse, and H.
H. Mayberry of Franklin.[46] It made little headway among the
people. Senator Bob Taylor set out in the fall of 1911 to lead
the Clark forces and to secure Tennessee's votes in the national
convention for the Speaker, but he, too, worked largely among
the politicians and made no popular campaign.

After all, the situation in the Democratic party was such as
to dampen the ardor of the most enthusiastic promoters of presidential candidates. What constituted the Democratic party—the
Regular or the Independent faction? What if the Independents
carried out their threat to hold a separate state convention, nominate their own delegates, and carry the fight to the floor of the
national convention itself? How best could the two factions be
brought together again, even temporarily, for the purpose of se-
lecting the delegates? All these questions were infinitely more
important than the question of whom Tennessee should support
at the Baltimore convention and consequently so subordinated
the national campaign to the considerations of local politics that
for a time it appeared that no one really cared whom Tennessee
supported.

Such was the chaos of Tennessee Democratic politics when
Woodrow Wilson came to Nashville in February 1912, to speak
at the dedication of a new Young Men's Christian Association
and, incidentally, to do a little campaigning on the side. Wilson's
little-known brother, Joseph R. Wilson, Jr., city editor of the
Nashville *Banner,* was among the group of Nashville citizens who
greeted him on his arrival in the city on February 24.[47]

44. At Knoxville on September 16, 1911; at Nashville on April 9, 1912. See Knoxville
Journal and Tribune, September 16–17, 1911; Nashville *Banner,* April 9–10, 1912.

45. For a leading editorial, see Memphis *Commercial Appeal,* March 7, 1912.

46. Nashville *Tennessean and American,* February 5, 1912; Chattanooga *Daily Times,*
February 7, 1912; Atlanta *Constitution,* March 20, 1912.

47. The other members of the reception committee of the Nashville Wilson Club
were Judge Thomas E. Matthews, Gen. W. H. Washington, Lee Douglas, I. I. Pendleton,
James T. Miller, Chancellor James H. Kirkland, and Frank A. Berry.

During the afternoon, two hundred Democrats from Tennessee, Kentucky, and Alabama gathered at the Hotel Hermitage at
a luncheon given in Wilson's honor by the local Wilson organization. Judge T. E. Matthews presided and introduced Wilson with
a felicitiously phrased encomium. Wilson was in high spirits; he
had just returned from a successful speaking tour in the Midwest,
and he proceeded to discuss again the general issues of the preconvention campaign: the tariff, control of monopolies, and the
necessity for federal banking reform—all of which was very general
and exceedingly vague. He concluded with one of his perorations
(for which he was famous) which usually succeeded in ignoring
the issues:

What thrills my imagination is this—we are at the threshold of a great
enterprise, the retranslation of American liberties in terms of our
present-day life. The party that first takes up this great programme will
govern the country for the next generation. . . .
Now, what should we do? We ought above all things to get together.
This is a national enterprise. It is too big for any man or any set of
men to declare that it shall be done in their way or not at all. The
cost of failure is too big. We shall be judged for a generation as we
act in 1912, for to fail now means that democracy in American will
be denied fresh fruitage, that America has become a nation dominated
by self-interests, and has joined the ranks of nations which go down
because they have forgotten the destiny of men.[48]

It would perhaps be difficult to find a more general statement
of rather vague idealistic objectives; but it stirred Wilson's listeners
immensely. Hardly had he completed his concluding sentence
when they were standing in their chairs, shouting at the tops of
their voices.

On the following evening, February 25, Wilson spoke at the
dedication of the YMCA building. It was a thoroughly Fusionist
affair; Republican Gov. Ben Hooper gracefully commented that
if the Republican candidate for the presidency had to be defeated,
he hoped "the southern man who comes from New Jersey" would
be elected. Independent Sen. Luke Lea set off a riotous Wilson
demonstration by declaring that Wilson was "The man whom

48. Nashville *Banner*, February 24, 1912.

the majority of the people of the United States want for their next President."[49]

The political character of the noisy demonstration, however, was in marked contrast to Wilson's speech on the occasion. He had come before the association, not as a presidential candidate, but rather as a lay preacher, striving to interpret the meaning of Christianity to his audience. The chief success of the YMCA, he declared, had been its advancement of the spirit of Christ. Political liberty had been Christianity's unique discovery, he continued; America therefore ought not to have to be taught that greatness was spiritual, that it was the vision of goodness and the spirit of self-sacrifice that made a nation great.[50] The address drew from the Nashville *Christian Advocate* the observation that Wilson "places first things first, believing that there is liberty for the individual and for the nation only through surrender to Jesus Christ."[51]

Aside from the unpredictable number of new recruits his Nashville speaking tour brought him, and a sizable amount of friendly publicity, the results of Wilson's visit were barren. When he left Nashville, the political situation was in exactly the same condition as when he arrived and the preconvention campaign picture was so confused by the Democratic rupture that no man could confidently predict the future. The problem of reorganizing the party was rendered highly critical when a subcommittee of the Independent state committee called a state convention to meet in Nashville on June 18 to select delegates to the Baltimore convention and to nominate candidates for presidential electors.[52] Should two Democratic state conventions meet and nominate different electors, the result might easily be the defeat of the Democratic ticket in the state. In order to forestall any such catastrophe, the Democratic editors of the state, sixty in number, met in Nashville on March 22, 1912, to formulate some compromise that would be acceptable to both factions. By a unanimous vote the editors adopted a plan whereby a state Democratic convention, in which both factions would be represented, should meet, elect delegates to the Baltimore convention, nominate candidates

49. From an account in the Nashville *Tennessean and American,* July 3, 1912.
50. *Ibid.,* February 26, 1912.
51. Nashville *Christian Advocate,* LXXIII (March 1, 1912), 5.
52. Chattanooga *Daily Times,* March 19, 1912.

for the state supreme court and the court of civil appeals, and elect a new Democratic state committee. The reconciliation plan would become effective when a majority of both the Independent and Regular state committees had signed an agreement to accept the proposal as that of the Democratic party and had entered into full party fellowship with the leaders in the movement.[53]

The acceptance of the editors' plan by both Democratic factions ended the confusion which had discouraged the spokesmen of the several presidential candidates and was the signal for the beginning of a brief and intense struggle for control of the Tennessee delegation to the national convention.[54] Early in May, the Wilson leaders opened headquarters in the Maxwell House, where G. Bibb Jacobs was in charge of operations. The prospect of controlling the state convention seemed at least within the realm of possibility, and the Wilson managers thought there was an even chance that some such miracle would happen. The Clark men, too, were active and had set up headquarters a few doors away from the Wilson office in the Maxwell House. Senator Taylor had died in April, and in his passing the Clark men had lost a powerful leader; former Governor John I. Cox had assumed leadership of the Clark organization.[55]

Around May 12, Democratic politicians of all factions and groups began to gather in Nashville for the state convention, which was to meet on May 15. Luke Lea came down from Washington; Mayor Ed Crump and former Governor Patterson arrived from Memphis.[56] The managers for Wilson, Clark, Underwood, and Harmon hovered around the Maxwell House, and all seemed confident that their candidate would secure the support of the Tennessee delegation. On the eve of the convention, some 150 Wilson delegates gathered at the hotel for a last-minute caucus and soon afterwards published an optimistic prediction that Wilson's friends would control the state convention.[57] The opposition leaders, be it noted, simulated an equal amount of confidence. Actually, the situation was still incredibly confused. No one

53. Nashville *Tennessean and American*, March 23, 1912.
54. Chattanooga *Daily Times*, May 3, 1912.
55. Nashville *Tennessean and American*, May 9, 1912.
56. Chattanooga *Daily Times*, May 13, 1912. Even Republican Sen. Newell Sanders happened to be on the scene.
57. Nashville *Tennessean and American*, May 15, 1912.

seemed to know whether there would be a fight by either of the groups to secure instructions for their candidate, but the likelihood of such a struggle was made highly improbable when it was discovered that no candidate had a majority of the convention vote.[58]

The chief task before the convention, of course, was to re-create the Democratic party as an integral unit; and since tempers were already dangerously short, a fight in the convention over instructions would hardly be calculated to restore harmony, or even to preserve the semblance of it. When the convention met on May 15, therefore, the leaders agreed to divide the delegates-at-large equally among the four candidates. S. M. Young and George Fort Milton were chosen by the Wilson men; William A. Percy and Luke Lea by Underwood's supporters;[59] John A. Tipton and H. C. Adler by the Clark managers; and Nat Baxter and M. M. Allison by the Harmon men.[60]

Divided among themselves, without unity or singleness of purpose, the twenty-four Tennessee delegates at the Baltimore convention exercised practically no influence, certainly no important influence at all, in the deliberations of that body. They divided their votes equally among the four leading candidates on the first ballot; and although there were fluctuations in their voting,[61] they persisted in this division until the last ballot was taken.[62] With the exception of Luke Lea, there were also no leaders of any importance among the Tennesseans. Lea, however, was one of the most resourceful and influential Wilson managers at Baltimore; he it was who succeeded in effecting an alliance early in the convention between the Wilson managers and Roger Sullivan, Democratic boss of Illinois, an agreement that was as much re-

58. *Ibid.*, May 14, 1912.
59. Senator Lea was an avowed Wilson supporter, although he had refused to take an active part in the Wilson campaign organization in Tennessee. He was elected by the Underwood men, who were aware of his personal preference in the matter, and agreed to vote for Underwood as long as Underwood's name was before the convention. See Luke Lea to Frank Dibrell, published in the Nashville *Tennessean and 'American,* October 22, 1912.
60. Pulaski (Tenn.) *Citizen,* May 23, 1912.
61. Harmon was eliminated as a candidate early in the balloting. On the tenth ballot, the Harmon men in the Tennessee delegation went over to Clark and generally voted for him thereafter.
62. *Official Report of the Proceedings of the Democratic National Convention . . . 1912* (Chicago: Peterson Linotyping Co., 1912), *passim.*

sponsible as any other single factor in Wilson's nomination.[63]

After the long and gruelling struggle in the convention had culminated in Wilson's nomination on the forty-sixth ballot, the progressive Wilson newspapers in Tennessee were naturally highly elated by the unexpected turn of events. "No braver or better men ever went to battle than those who led this conflict, and no greater victory for a righteous cause was ever achieved," declared Lea's newspaper. "The struggle was one against the combined forces of pelf and plunder, and to say the rights of the people were successfully defended against the assaults of such powerful interests is to say that those who waged and won this battle fully demonstrated their courage."[64] The Nashville *Banner,* which had never been overfriendly to Bryan, admitted that the Nebraskan had "flushed an ambuscade into which Wilson might have fallen," and proceeded to declare that "In Woodrow Wilson the Democratic party may find at once its Moses and its Joshua; the great leader who, properly supported, will deliver it from the long thraldom of defeat and the great ruler to give it permanent establishment in the promised land."[65] Significant, too, was the reaction of the conservative newspapers which had opposed Wilson's nomination and which, with amazing felicity and ease, became overnight the most ardent champions of progressive Democracy, ready now to defend Wilson against any charges the Republicans might make.[66]

Just as the Tennessee Democracy had done little to cause Wilson's nomination, it did little to secure his election. The root of the difficulty, of course, was the Independent-Regular controversy; and any hope that Democratic leaders might have had that Wilson's nomination would draw the factions together was soon disappointed by the continuation of the controversy during the summer and fall of 1912. Actually, the acceptance of the editors' plan for Democratic reorganization turned out to be noth-

63. I have discussed Lea's activities in "The Baltimore Convention of 1912," pp. 224, 226, this volume. There is also an excellent contemporary account of the convention, in which Lea figures prominently, in Arthur S. Link, "A Letter from One of Wilson's Managers," *American Historical Review,* L (July 1945), 768–775.

64. Nashville *Tennessean and American,* July 3, 1912.

65. Nashville *Banner,* July 3, 1912.

66. See especially the Memphis *Commercial Appeal,* July 3, 1912, in this connection; also Knoxville *Journal and Tribune,* July 3, 1912, for the reaction of a Tennessee Republican newspaper.

ing more than an uneasy truce which was openly broken when the Regulars nominated for the governorship Benton McMillin, an antiprohibition leader in the Patterson organization. There occurred during the early fall an amusing tug-of-war between the two groups, each bidding for the approval and support of Wilson and the national Democratic organization. From all outward appearances, it would seem that the Independents, since they had been the leaders in the Wilson movement in Tennessee before the Baltimore convention, would secure Wilson's support. Then the Nashville *Democrat,* which had been established in 1911 as the newspaper spokesman of the Regulars, began a pressure campaign to force Wilson and the national committee to support the Regular Democratic ticket. It published demands that Wilson come to Tennessee and speak in McMillin's behalf, and warned Wilson that failure on his part to do so might result in the defeat of the national ticket in the state. The state Democratic executive committee soon afterward followed up the Nashville *Democrat's* demands with a similar resolution of its own.[67]

The upshot of the matter was that Wilson found himself in an embarrassing dilemma. There are unfortunately no letters or memoranda in the Wilson Papers that reveal his thoughts on the Tennessee situation, but he was an exceedingly busy person with more serious problems to settle during the hectic days of October; and it is a safe assumption that he let William G. McAdoo, acting national chairman, and the national committee make the decision for him. In mid-October, therefore, McAdoo finally wrote Rice A. Pierce, chairman of the Regular Democratic state committee, that Wilson and the national committee were "not opposed to Gov. McMillin and the other Regular Democratic nominees for state offices in Tennessee," and that they were "warmly in favor of, and are supporting with all their power, the Regular Democratic nominees in every state in the Union."[68] It was about as noncommittal an endorsement as McAdoo could possibly have made.

The publication of the McAdoo telegram set off again the fireworks of political controversy in Tennessee. Especially vociferous was the Nashville *Banner,* which rushed to the attack as soon

67. Nashville *Banner,* October 19, 1912.

68. McAdoo to R. A. Pierce, October --, 1912, published in the Nashville *Banner,* October 19, 1912.

as the telegram was published. It charged, first of all, that the Regular state committee had demanded from the Democratic national committee a sum of money sufficient to print the Democratic ballots and had threatened to leave the names of the electors off the Democratic ticket unless the money was forthcoming.[69] Pierce replied that he had made no such demands or threats,[70] yet the chairman of the Democratic state executive committee admitted that he had asked Wilson's "friends" to furnish money to print the ballots.[71] The *Banner* next charged the Regular Democratic leaders with trafficking with the enemy; Chairman Pierce, it asserted, had concluded an agreement with Theodore Roosevelt, when the Bull Moose leader was in Jackson, Tennessee, whereby the Progressives in the state would support McMillin for the governorship and the Regulars would support Roosevelt for the presidency.[72] When Pierce vehemently denied this charge of political treason, the *Banner* flung back the charges at him and pointed to the fact that he had not denied being in Jackson while Roosevelt was there. It was a malodorous affair, to say the least. The truth of the matter apparently was that Chairman Morton of the state executive committee visited national Democratic headquarters around September 1 and asked the national committee for money with which to run the campaign in Tennessee; and that after his return from New York, he asked the national committee for $15,000 to aid in carrying the state for Wilson and in electing a legislature that would send a Democrat to the United States Senate.[73] All of which was rather ridiculous, the Independents charged, in a state traditionally Democratic, and which proved, furthermore, that the Patterson machine was supported by "the liquor trust, the saloons . . . the gamblers, bummers, loafers, and vagabonds."[74]

Despite the factional quarrels which precluded any united Democratic action in Tennessee during the presidential campaign, the mass of Democratic voters seem to have been genuinely stirred

69. Nashville *Banner*, October 19, 1912.

70. *Ibid.*, October 22, 1912.

71. *Ibid.*, October 23, 1912.

72. *Ibid.*, October 19, 1912.

73. *Ibid.*, October 23, 1912.

74. *Ibid.*, October 19, 1912; see also Nashville *Tennessean and American*, November 2, 1912.

by Wilson's campaign appeals and desirous of his election. Wilson-Marshall [75] clubs were organized in every county and town in the state, and a woman's Wilson-Marshall movement was organized a week and a half before election day.[76] Needless to say, the Democratic newspapers, Regular or Independent, published Wilson's important campaign speeches and approved them (publicly, at least) enthusiastically. The New Freedom thus became official Democratic doctrine in Tennessee, and Regulars and Independents vied with one another in praising Wilson and berating Theodore Roosevelt and Taft.[77] Reviewing the presidential campaign a few days before the election, the Chattanooga *Daily Times* published an editorial which summarized most of what the Tennessee newspapers had already said:

In no campaign in recent years has a Democratic leader so clearly and so courageously stated and advocated the basic principles of his party as Woodrow Wilson. He has driven straight ahead for tariff reform along right lines; for the destruction of monopoly through the reinstatement of regulated competition, and for the dethronement of bosses and the restoration of the powers of government into the hands of the people. He has not been diverted from his definite course in pursuit of these underlying principles by non-essentials, nor has he introduced fads and questionable isms to confuse the minds of the people. He has followed a direct path back to democratic simplicity and the rule of the people and their emancipation from the burdens of privilege and caste. The people believe in him because in the two distinguished administrative positions he has held—president of Princeton University and governor of New Jersey—his conduct and record square with his democratic professions. These qualities of his have stood unassailable during a campaign that has brought out every conceivable objection active, alert, and experienced opponents could muster against him. Sympathetic in every fiber of his being with the people, he has been able to impress them with his honesty, his courage, and his sincerity and they are for him. His attitudes are sound because they are taken upon the immutable rock of human liberty and equality, and he is safe because the intelligence of the American people expressed in his favor will stand to and abide by the salutary policies he proposes.[78]

75. Gov. Thomas R. Marshall of Indiana, Democratic vice-presidential candidate.

76. Nashville *Tennessean and American,* October 30, 1912.

77. For typical campaign editorials from the Independent and Regular press, see Nashville *Tennessean and American,* September 8 and October 13, 1912; Nashville *Banner,* September 3, 1912; Chattanooga *Daily Times,* August 31, 1912.

78. Chattanooga *Daily Times,* November 3, 1912.

Although the Tennessee Democracy contributed nothing by way of leadership in the national councils of the party during the campaign, yet there remained one task—the matter of raising campaign funds for the Wilson cause—in which all the people could participate. And it was this issue, quite naturally, that figured most prominently during the summer and fall of 1912 in Tennessee. When the Regular state committee showed an amazing reluctance to take the initiative in the matter, the Regular and Independent editors took the lead and carried through a successful drive for funds to support the national ticket. Two days after Wilson was nominated, the Nashville *Tennessean and American* got under way a campaign fund drive by contributing $25. "If the people do not respond and themselves run their elections, as they hope to run their government," the newspaper warned two weeks later, "the professional campaign contributors will respond for them, and endeavor to control the elections as they have endeavored to do in the past." [79] By November 1, the *Tennessean and American* had collected $889 in its campaign for dollar contributions.

Although the Nashville newspaper was the first in the field, the Memphis *Commercial Appeal,* which began a drive for campaign funds on August 11, was much more active and successful. At first, it appealed to the enthusiasm and goodwill of the Democratic voters by reminding them that, since Wilson was the people's candidate, they, and not the monied interests which dominated the party in 1904, would have to support the ticket in 1912. "This is not a funeral procession," it declared. "It is a fight, and we had better get on our fighting clothes." [80] Yet, despite the badgering of the Democratic press, the people gave reluctantly and parsimoniously, if at all, and by the middle of October the *Commercial Appeal* was predicting that the Democratic campaign would collapse if sizable financial reinforcements were not forthcoming. "Gov. Wilson's inherent popularity may carry him through," it declared, "but we doubt it. A victorious army can not move without rations." [81] This newspaper spurred a great burst of giving during the last two weeks of the campaign and managed to collect over $6,000 for the Wilson cause—and that was a remarkable achievement indeed.

79. Nashville *Tennessean and American,* July 19, 1912.
80. Memphis *Commercial Appeal,* September 15, 1912.

Since the Democratic organizations in Tennessee could not stop fighting each other long enough to pull together for Wilson, McAdoo at the national headquarters in New York intervened and appointed a campaign contributions committee for Tennessee in late September.[82] While the newspapers solicited contributions from the people directly, the state committee concentrated their efforts on "frying the lard out of the politicians."

When one considers the condition of the party in Tennessee, the achievement of the newspapers and the state committee in raising $15,390.63 during the presidential campaign [83] seems indeed remarkable. Tennessee was the thirteenth state in rank, measured in terms of total contributions, and contributed more than either Michigan, Wisconsin, Ohio, California, or Indiana, whose governor was the vice-presidential nominee. Interestingly enough, Tennessee could boast of none of the 153 men who contributed $1,000 or more to the Wilson-Marshall fund.

It would be almost historical sacrilege to discuss the presidential campaign of 1912 in Tennessee without mentioning Theodore Roosevelt and his Progressive, or Bull Moose, party. Roosevelt, it will be recalled, had campaigned for the Republican presidential nomination; and when President Taft was nominated instead, Roosevelt organized a new third party and went before the country on a platform that embodied a queer mixture of advanced social democracy and big business paternalism. Democratic newspapers in Tennessee completely ignored Taft, who made hardly any campaign at all, and concentrated their attacks against Roosevelt. They scored especially Roosevelt's inconsistencies—his refusal to allow southern Negroes in the Progressive party while admitting them to full party fellowship in the northern states; his charges that the Democratic party was boss-ridden and boss-controlled and his own striking similarity to the popular conception of a political boss; the commendable program of social reform which

81. *Ibid.*, October 11, 1912.
82. K. T. McConnico was appointed chairman of the Middle Tennessee area; William H. Carroll of Memphis, chairman of the West Tennessee district; and Lewis R. Coleman of Chattanooga was made chairman of the East Tennessee district. Mayor Hilary E. Howse and Judge Thomas E. Matthews, president of the Nashville Wilson Club, were named to direct the campaign fund drive in the capital. Nashville *Tennessean and American,* September 25, 1912.
83. Rolla Wells, *Report of the Treasurer, Democratic National Committee* (St. Louis: Allied Printing, 1913), 174.

he advocated, contrasted with his suggestions for legalizing and establishing permanently the trusts.[84]

A vigorous and enthusiastic Progressive party was organized in Tennessee during the summer; yet, as Edith Snyder Evans points out, its members consisted largely of former Republicans, who broke away from the regular party organization, not because they were truly progressive, but simply because of factional differences within the Republican party organization.[85] Only one newspaper of importance in the state, the Memphis *News Scimitar,* supported the Progressive ticket. Nevertheless, the fact that Roosevelt polled in Tennessee almost as many votes as Taft—and that in its first test of strength—revealed that the foundations for a permanent third party had been well laid.

Roosevelt was almost pathetically anxious to win the electoral votes of at least one southern state. "Really, if I could carry one of the eleven ex-Confederate States," he wrote his southern manager, "I should feel as though I could die happy." [86] Consequently, he decided to carry the campaign through the heart of the South. His "swing around the circle" through the region in late September and early October took him to Little Rock, Memphis, New Orleans, Birmingham, Montgomery, Atlanta, Chattanooga, Knoxville, and Raleigh. He appealed to the southerners to throw off political tradition and lethargy, which had bound them to one party, and to join with the Progressives in their crusade for the social, political, and moral regeneration of the nation.

Roosevelt opened his Tennessee campaign at Memphis on September 26, when he spoke before the Inter-State Levee Association.[87] His address on that occasion, however, was non-partisan, and it was not until he spoke at Jackson on the following day that he began his political campaign in the state in earnest. He spoke next in Chattanooga, on September 29; on September 30, he made two addresses at Knoxville, in the Republican stronghold

---

84. See, e.g., Nashville *Banner,* August 6, 8, 1912; Memphis *Commercial Appeal,* August 8, 25, September 18, 1912; Chattanooga *Daily Times,* June 4, September 10, 1912; Nashville *Tennessean and American,* August 10, October 15, 1912.

85. Edith Snyder Evans, "The Progressive Party in Tennessee in 1912" (M.A. thesis, University of Tennessee, 1933).

86. T. Roosevelt to J. M. Parker, July 15, 1912, Theodore Roosevelt Papers, Library of Congress, Washington, D.C.

87. Memphis *Commercial Appeal,* September 27, 1912.

of East Tennessee. Needless to say, the Bull Moose leader spoke always before huge audiences and received one tumultuous reception after another in his tour through Tennessee. Yet his appeal fell largely upon deaf ears and he was soon to learn that people often shout one way and vote another. He did not carry a single electoral vote in any of the southern states in the election of 1912. Southern and Tennessee progressives, who might have been expected to support Roosevelt, had helped to nominate the Democratic candidate of their own choosing; many of them had risked their political lives in making the prenomination fight for Wilson. It was futile, therefore, for Roosevelt to hope that he could draw progressive support away from Wilson in the South. Southern conservatives, on the other hand, were not likely to vote for a man who advocated the adoption of judicial recall, woman suffrage, or a number of other reforms.

During the campaign there was at least some semblance of Democratic unity in Tennessee with regard to the presidential contest; but insofar as the state election was concerned, there was as much discord and bad feeling as there had been in 1910. When the regular Democrats nominated Gov. Benton McMillin for the governorship, the Independents again supported Governor Hooper, who had been renominated by the Republicans. The result was McMillin's defeat, by a vote of 123,828 to 114,369.[88]

On Tuesday, November 5, the people of Tennessee also cast a majority of their votes for Woodrow Wilson. Few persons had doubted that the result would be otherwise, for the Republican rupture had resulted in guaranteeing Wilson's election. In Tennessee, Wilson received 130,335 votes (52.59% of the popular vote), Taft 59,444 (23.89% of the popular vote), and Roosevelt 53,725 (21% of the popular vote).[89] The enthusiasm of Tennessee Democrats over Wilson's victory was considerably dampened by the Republican success in the gubernatorial contest; and the Regular spokesmen warned their Independent foes that "The time will come when truth will win and the treacherous betrayers of their fellow Democrats in Tennessee will get their just deserts."[90]

Needless to say, the cup of the Independents ran over. Wilson's victory was in a very real sense their own; it was the

88. *World Almanac, 1913* (New York, 1912), 761.
89. *Ibid.*
90. Chattanooga *Daily Times*, November 6, 1912.

fulfillment of a dream they had dared to dream in 1910 and of their own considerable efforts to give substance and reality to their hopes. In the state contest, also, they had triumphed for a second time. By standing immovable against the Democratic machine, they established definitely the principle that an antiprohibition Democrat could not be elected governor; and they forced finally the reorganization of the state party in 1914 on an antiliquor platform, with a prohibitionist candidate. "The people have shown their faith in Democratic principles," exulted Luke Lea's newspaper,[91] while the Nashville *Banner*, on the afternoon after election day, published perhaps the most fitting epilogue to this story:

The Democratic party comes again into complete control of the nation under happy auspices that should give it continued hold on power. It has chosen for the next President a man of great scholarly attainment, but wide awake in the ways of the practical world; of unusual force of character, but mild and restrained of manner. Very firm, quite aggressive, indeed, but thoroughly self-controlled; of marked conservative temperament yet fully abreast of the times and thoroughly progressive on those lines of progress that come of intelligent thought and a judgment based on accurate knowledge of the science of government drawn from both the past and present; an open enemy of the machine and defiant of bosses, yet withal a consummate politician who has made no blunders, but has astounded some pastmasters of the craft with the boldness and success of his movements. . . .

The old order has changed. The parties no longer reflect the crystalized sectional sentiment that attached to them so long after all sectional issues were dead. The Democratic party is now thoroughly national.[92]

---

91. Nashville *Tennessean and American*, November 6, 1912.
92. Nashville *Banner*, November 6, 1912.

14

The Underwood Presidential Movement of 1912

DURING the presidential campaign of 1912, for the first time since 1860, a southerner living in the South was an active candidate for the Democratic presidential nomination. He was Oscar Wilder Underwood, born in Louisville, Kentucky, on May 6, 1862. His grandfather, Joseph R. Underwood, had been Henry Clay's Whig colleague from Kentucky in the United States Senate; his father, a distinghished lawyer, was the first attorney for the Louisville and Nashville Railroad. In early childhood, Underwood moved with his family to St. Paul, Minnesota, where he lost much of his southern accent and learned something of the spirit of the frontier West. When he was thirteen, his family returned to Louisville. At the University of Virginia, Oscar W. Underwood studied law and drank deeply from the wells of Jeffersonian democracy. Thenceforth, he though of himself as a Jeffersonian Democrat.[1]

Reprinted from *The Journal of Southern History,* XI (May 1945), 230–245, by permission of the Managing Editor.

1. Research for this article was made possible by a grant-in-aid from the Julius Rosenwald Fund.

There is no full-length biography of Underwood. An appreciative sketch, by Claude G. Bowers, appears as the Foreword of Oscar W. Underwood, *Drifting Sands of Party Politics* (New York: The Century Co., 1931), pp. vii–xxiv. For a contemporary appraisal, see Burton J. Hendrick, "Oscar W. Underwood, a New Leader from the New South," in *McClure's Magazine,* XXXVIII (1912), 405–420.

Upon graduation, Underwood turned westward and again went to St. Paul to begin his legal practice. Soon he was drawn by his brother to the rapidly growing town of Birmingham, Alabama. In this iron and steel center of the New South, Underwood built up a prosperous legal practice and married Bertha Woodward, daughter of a pioneer iron manufacturer. At thirty, he was chairman of the executive committee of his congressional district; at thirty-three, he was elected to Congress. He moved slowly forward in the House of Representatives. Beginning his congressional career as an inconspicuous member of the House Committee on Public Lands, Underwood steadily advanced until, in 1909, he was the ranking Democrat on the Ways and Means Committee.

During the congressional session of 1910–1911, insurgent Republicans aided by the Democrats revolted against the dictatorship of Speaker Joseph G. Cannon and deprived him of his plenary powers over the House of Representatives. The power to appoint members of congressional committees was taken from the speaker and vested in the Ways and Means Committee, thus establishing that committee as the dominant body of the House. The chairman of the Ways and Means Committee not only exercised decisive influence in framing money bills and in appointing the members to the House committees, but he also became the recognized leader of the House majority.

When President William H. Taft called Congress into special session in the spring of 1911 to ratify his reciprocity agreement with Canada, it was the Democratic House of Representatives elected in the Democratic landslide of November 1910 that was organized. Underwood advanced to the chairmanship of the Ways and Means Committee and to the position of Democratic leader of the House, and the American people soon began to learn what manner of man was guiding the destinies of the Democratic party in Congress. Of commanding presence, Underwood was strong-framed and sturdily built. His round, clean-shaven face was serene and his blue eyes had a friendly twinkle in them. In 1911, Underwood was only forty-nine. There was little about him that suggested the old-fashioned southern politician. So conventional was his dress that he might have been mistaken for a banker, manufacturer, or prosperous merchant.[2] His consummate tact, modesty,

2. Hendrick, "Oscar W. Underwood," *loc. cit.,* 405.

even temperament, and perfect self-control made him an ideal party leader. His years of assiduous study of tariff legislation and his clarity and conciseness in expressing his tariff opinions marked him as the outstanding Democratic authority on the important question. His associates in Congress knew him as a sound thinker, a student of the intricate facts and figures of tariff legislation, and a friendly compromiser and conciliator.[3]

In one respect, Underwood was an old-fashioned Democrat. He believed firmly in what were then called the fundamentals of Jeffersonian Democracy: tariff legislation for revenue only, opposition to the concentration of government authority, strong local government, and state sovereignty.[4] He was not a progressive, then, in the conventional sense of the word. He stood, for example, unalterably opposed to the initiative, referendum, and recall.[5] Though a conservative by conviction, he supported a number of progressive reforms, particularly the reduction of the Republican protective tariff. He was honest and courageous and, as one commentator wrote in 1912, progressives who did not agree with him could at least respect him.[6]

William J. Bryan, thrice leader of the Democrats, immediately challenged the rising leadership of the Alabamian. He regarded Underwood as a reactionary and a pawn of Wall Street.[7] The personal issue between the two men came to the boiling point during the summer of 1911. Because the Democrats were undertaking a revision of the tariff laws, Bryan hurried to the capital to take a hand in the management of the details of legislation. Rebuffed by the Democrats, who refused to heed his demands for an open party caucus, the Nebraskan withdrew from the scene and waged a campaign of prejudiced criticism against the Democratic leader from the South.

At the beginning of the extra session, Underwood told his colleagues on the Ways and Means Committee that he believed the steel and iron schedules should be the first to undergo revision

3. Robert W. Woolley, "Underwood of Alabama, Democracy's New Chieftain," in *Review of Reviews*, XLIV (1911), 296.

4. Bowers's Foreword, in Underwood, *Drifting Sands of Party Politics*, p. xxi.

5. See, for example, Underwood's speech on these reforms, quoted in *La Follette's Magazine*, February 3, 1912, p. 4.

6. Ray Stannard Baker, "Our Next President and Some Others," in *American Magazine*, LXXIV (1912), 134–136.

7. *Commoner*, November 17, 1911, p. 1.

and that he did not want them to feel any embarrassment because steel-making was the chief industry of his district. The committee, however, thought the woolen, cotton goods, and agricultural implements schedules demanded their immediate attention, and Underwood acquiesced in the opinion of the majority.[8]

Immediately Bryan began a loud demand from Lincoln for a tariff bill embodying a free wool schedule. The bill, as reported by the Ways and Means Committee and unanimously approved by a Democratic caucus, levied a 20 percent tax on wool. The Nebraskan hastened to attack Underwood. "Many honest men have been misled by Mr. Underwood's specious argument, but The Commoner asks these democrats to watch the chairman of the ways and means committee," Bryan warned.[9] The Democratic wool bill passed the House despite Bryan's objections and he became more irascible. He recklessly attacked Underwood, charging that he had opposed an immediate effort to revise the iron and steel schedules, and thus had shown favoritism to the steel and iron interests of his own district. Underwood's action, Bryan declared, had revealed him as an opponent of tariff reform. "The unmasking of Chairman Underwood will serve a useful purpose," Bryan added, "if it arouses the democrats to an understanding of the mistake made in putting Mr. Underwood at the head of the committee." [10]

On August 2, 1911, Underwood rose in the House of Representatives to defend his personal integrity against Bryan's assaults. For the first time, it appeared that the Alabamian lost control of himself. He bitterly excoriated and denounced the Commoner and openly declared that his statements were without any basis of truth. In defense of his attitude on the revision of the iron and steel schedules, Underwood called upon his Democratic colleagues on the Ways and Means Committee to corroborate his statement that he had desired to attack first the iron and steel schedules. This they gladly did. Claude Kitchin, a devoted friend of Bryan's, believed that the Commoner had been "misin-

8. Based on Underwood's speech in the House of Representatives on August 2, 1911. The truth of the facts in the case was attested to by the other members of the Ways and Means Committee. *Congressional Record,* 62d Cong., 1st sess., August 2, 1911, p. 3511.

9. *Commoner,* June 9, 1911, p. 1.

10. *Ibid.,* August 4, 1911, p. 1. This editorial had been given to the press previous to its publication in the *Commoner,* and appeared in many newspapers on August 2, 1911. See, for example, the Washington *Herald,* August 2, 1911.

formed." [11] Underwood's arraignment of Bryan aroused the intense enthusiasm of his colleagues in the House. They stood on their chairs and yelled at the tops of their voices when he fired his broadsides. It was a remarkable endorsement of the Alabamian's leadership.[12]

Undoubtedly, Bryan realized that he was losing his position as spokesman for and leader of the Democrats, for he fought a lone fight against Underwood. Woodrow Wilson, striving to steer a middle course between conservatism and Bryanism, announced in June 1911 his approval of the course of the Democratic House.[13] Practically none of the old Bryan editors rose up in the Commoner's defense. Most of them agreed with one sincere Bryan man who wrote that the Nebraskan had "lost more friends through his attack upon the honesty and sincerity of Representative Underwood than as a result of anything he had said or done in his career."[14] Manifestly, the Commoner was rapidly being relegated to a position of doubtful leadership.[15]

Perhaps unwittingly, Underwood, by his controversy with Bryan and because of his successful leadership in tariff reform, was catapulted into the presidential campaign. The Underwood movement began as a very definite "favorite son" movement in Alabama. Tyler Goodwin, chairman of the Democratic executive committee in that state, initiated Underwood's campaign by declaring in July 1911 his intention to support Underwood for the presidency.[16] Sen. John H. Bankhead immediately assumed the leadership of Underwood's campaign and after a conference with Alabama Democrats declared that the state would stand by her representative.[17]

During the following month, however, when Senator Bankhead endeavored to secure the endorsement of Alabama for her

11. Underwood's speech and the testimony of the Democratic members of the Ways and Means Committee are printed in *Congressional Record,* 62d Cong., 1st sess., August 2, 1911, pp. 3511–3513.

12. Petersburg *Daily Index-Appeal,* August 4, 1911.

13. Charleston *News and Courier,* June 6, 1911.

14. Petersburg *Daily Index-Appeal,* August 4, 1911.

15. For the first time since Bryan's nomination in 1896, his name was not applauded when it was spoken in a legislative body in Arkansas. Little Rock *Arkansas Democrat,* April 6, 1911.

16. Montgomery *Advertiser,* July 28, 1911.

17. *Ibid.,* October 1, 1911.

son, he encountered considerable difficulty, for many Alabamians spoke lightly of Underwood's candidacy and praised Woodrow Wilson.[18] Frank P. Glass, editor of the Birmingham *News*, who feared that Underwood's candidacy was being used in Alabama as a front for Judson Harmon, conservative governor of Ohio, forced Bankhead and Underwood to deny that the state's delegation would be turned over to the Ohio governor.[19] But there was no doubt that the rank and file of Alabama Democrats were overwhelmingly disposed to support Underwood's candidacy,[20] while Alabama's representatives in Congress gave a ringing notice of their unanimous approval.[21]

The Wilson men in Alabama bowed to the inevitable. One by one, the Wilson newspapers [22] joined in the hue and cry for Underwood. In January 1912, a number of prominent Wilson Democrats conferred at Montgomery and agreed that there should be no campaign for Wilson in Underwood's state. Wilson supporters in Alabama should attempt, rather, to secure second-choice representation for their candidate.[23] Consequently, Alabama experienced no preconvention presidential campaign. At a Democratic presidential primary in April 1912, one hundred thousand Alabama Democrats gave their unanimous endorsement to Underwood, while the state Democratic convention instructed its delegation to vote "first, last, and all the time" for Alabama's favorite son.[24]

National Underwood headquarters were established in Washington in February 1912. Bankhead installed Thomas M. Owen of Montgomery in charge at Washington and designated him as the publicity director of the headquarters.[25] The Underwood campaign committee played shrewd politics. Inasmuch as the straightforward Underwood appeal of tariff reform would make a deep impression upon southern farmers who thought they were

18. Atlanta *Georgian*, November 14, 1911, quoting Birmingham *News;* Atlanta *Journal*, March 29, 1912, quoting Huntsville (Ala.) *Times.*

19. Pensacola *Journal*, March 10, 1912; Mobile *Register*, November 25, 1911.

20. Birmingham *Age-Herald*, December 21, 1911.

21. Mobile *Register*, December 8, 1911.

22. The most prominent of these were the Birmingham *News*, Birmingham *Age-Herald*, Mobile *Register*, Montgomery *Times.*

23. Charlotte *Daily Observer*, March 11, 1912, quoting Birmingham *News.*

24. Montgomery *Advertiser*, April 2 and 18, 1912; Birmingham *Age-Herald*, April 20, 1912.

25. Birmingham *Age-Herald*, February 20, 1912.

the chief victims of the Republican protective tariff, the Underwood campaign committee prepared a four-page supplement for distribution by southern newspapers. This supplement, containing a brief history of Underwood's career and voluminous endorsements of him by newspapers and politicians, was spread, especially by the country newspapers, throughout the Southeast. It was a capital stroke, for thousands of southern farmers who got most of their information from their county newspapers were told for the first time of what Underwood was attempting to do, and what he would do for them if elected president.

The publication and distribution of the supplement entailed some expenditures by the Underwood managers.[26] The report given out by the Wilson headquarters at Washington that Thomas Fortune Ryan, notorious Wall Street financier, was financing the Underwood campaign evoked a spirited, if evasive, denial from Bankhead, who declared that the campaign was being financed entirely by contributions from Underwood clubs in Alabama.[27] The Underwood manager, months later, admitted before a Senate investigating committee that the New York financier had contributed $35,000 to the Underwood coffers.[28]

The Underwood movement gained tremendous momentum in the first half of 1912 and swept through the Southeast. Alabama, Georgia, Florida, and Mississippi were captured by enthusiastic Underwood campaigners, while inroads were made in Virginia, North Carolina, and Tennessee. Underwood leaders realized, however, that even should their candidate sweep the entire South into his ranks, his nomination would still be far from probable. What was needed was the support of some powerful northern delegation at the Baltimore convention. This, unfortunately for his candidacy, Underwood never received. Many northern news-

26. Newspapers which circulated the Underwood supplement were given financial compensation by the campaign committee at the following rate: $10.00 to newspapers whose circulation did not exceed 1,000; $12.50 to papers with a circulation of from 1,000 to 1,500; $15.00 to papers with a circulation of 2,000 and upward. "The use of the supplement would not be intended to in any way commit you to Mr. Underwood's claim for the nomination. The whole transaction is purely a business one, and is allowable in every way, by the ethics of good journalism," Bankhead wrote. John H. Bankhead to southern weekly newspaper editors, published in Nashville *Tennessean and American,* February 9, 1912. The letter was sent to more than one thousand editors.

27. Birmingham *Age-Herald,* February 12, 1912.

28. Testimony of John H. Bankhead before the Clapp Senatorial Committee, in United

papers praised his leadership of the party and commended his candidacy, but none advocated his nomination.[29]

The appeal of the Underwood leaders to the southern people was made fundamentally upon the issues of sectional pride and tariff reform. The appeal to sectional loyalty was so greatly emphasized that at times it obscured the real issues of the campaign. It was taken for granted that Underwood was southern until a journalist, writing in an influential magazine, stated that the Alabamian had barely escaped being both a northerner and a tariff protectionist.[30] Underwood countered with the statement that his father had been imprisoned by federal authorities during the Civil War because of his sympathy for the southern cause and that three uncles had fought in the Confederate army.[31]

The Underwood press in the South reiterated again and again that the sacred honor of the region was involved in the Alabamian's candidacy. The North was ready to accept Underwood, these editors declared, if the South would rally to his support. For half a century southerners had constituted the backbone of the Democratic party, had "hewn the wood and drawn the water," and eaten "the husks that fell from the table." "The South for a Southerner" became the Underwood battle cry. Should southerners refuse to support a southerner, Underwood journals insisted, they would bequeath to their children the birthright of "perpetual serfdom" and deny to them the privilege of national political equality which would be their lot should Underwood become president.[32] Southerners could, by voting for Underwood,

---

States Senate, *Campaign Contributions: Testimony before a Subcommittee of the Committee on Privileges and Elections, United States Senate, Sixty-Second Congress, Second Session* (Washington: Government Printing Office, 1912), p. 938. In all, the Underwood managers expended $52,000.

29. See editorials in New York *World,* August 6, 1911; Cincinnati *Enquirer,* October 23, 1911; New York *American,* September 25, 1911; Albany (N.Y.) *Argus,* November 23, 1911; New York *Times,* November 26, 1911; Chicago *Inter-Ocean,* September 26, 1911; New York *Evening Post,* August 2, 1911; Atlanta *Constitution,* April 4, 1911, quoting New York *Herald; ibid.,* May 28, 1912, quoting Washington *Times;* Mobile *Register,* August 7, 1911, quoting Brooklyn *Eagle;* Jacksonville *Florida Times-Union,* February 28 and 29, 1912, quoting New York *Sun; ibid.,* March 4, 1912, quoting Providence *Journal,* Butte (Mont.) *Miner,* and New York *Evening Post; ibid.,* March 7, 1912, quoting St. Louis *Republic; ibid.,* March 19, 1912, quoting Jersey City *Jersey Journal; ibid.,* March 23, 1912, quoting Springfield *Republican; ibid.,* April 11, 1912, quoting Chicago *Journal;* Birmingham *Age-Herald,* July 28, 1911, quoting Baltimore *Sun.*

30. Hendrick, "Oscar W. Underwood," *loc. cit.,* 405.

31. Atlanta *Constitution,* March 24, 1912.

32. *Ibid.,* May 1, 1912.

break the unwritten law which decreed that no southerner should aspire to the presidency; they could substitute political manhood for misgiving and timidity; they could tear loose political shackles that "scorched and festered." [33] In other words, southerners should "Vote for the South!" [34]

The "southern" issue was a two-edged sword which might be used against the South by northern Republicans; but Underwood supporters were on surer ground when they advocated his nomination because of his constructive statesmanship. In fact, Underwood's pre-eminent leadership in tariff reform constituted his strongest claim upon the Democratic masses. "Tariff for revenue only" had been the traditional battle cry of the southern Democratic party for many decades, and southern agrarians in 1912 were convinced that the discriminatory protective tariff policy of the Republican party was the chief cause of their economic difficulties. It was therefore natural that thousands of southern Democrats should regard tariff reform as the most important issue of the campaign and that they should look askance at Woodrow Wilson's statements that the details of tariff legislation were relatively unimportant.

When President Taft vetoed the tariff bills enacted by Congress in 1911, many southerners were confident that he had set the stage for the coming political battle. The Democratic party, these southerners declared, was unfaithful to true Democratic principles when it went the way of the Great Commoner. Since tariff reform was the only issue upon which the Democratic party had ever achieved success, since it constituted the outstanding issue of the 1912 campaign, was it not logical that Oscar W. Underwood should lead the Democratic hosts? His enemies could not deny, Underwood supporters asserted, that he was the greatest Democratic exponent of tariff reform and that his consummate and masterful leadership had been an important factor in defining

33. *Ibid.*, May 12, 1912.
34. On this theme, see also editorials in Memphis *Commercial Appeal*, April 18, 1912; *ibid.*, March 14, 1912, quoting Columbus (Ga.) *Ledger; ibid.*, March 17, 1912, quoting Savannah *Morning News;* Jacksonville *Florida Times-Union*, February 16, April 30, 1912; *ibid.*, February 3, 1912, quoting Gainesville (Fla.) *Sun; ibid.*, March 1, 1912, quoting Live Oak (Fla.) *Democrat; ibid.*, March 15, 1912, quoting Suwanee (Fla.) *Democrat;* Montgomery *Advertiser*, January 1, 1912, quoting Shreveport *Times; ibid.*, April 15, 1912, quoting Macon *Telegraph;* Mobile *Register*, January 2, 1912; Birmingham *Age-Herald*, February 3, May 1, 1912; Charlotte *Daily Observer*, April 19, 1912, quoting Thomasville (N.C.) *Davidsonian.*

the very issue of the campaign. The party could not afford to forfeit its only claim to existence, Underwood men declared; Democrats must not leave their ancient moorings again to follow another Bryan.[35]

At the same time, Thomas E. Watson, whom few would have classified as a conservative in 1912, aroused many southern farmers to the support of Underwood by his constant praise of the Alabamian. The following editorial is typical of his appeal:

For 30 years, I have dreamed of *a union of the South and West, against the Money Power of the East and North. . . .*
At this time, I again see a chance to weld together the agricultural sections, both of which are bled white by tariff taxation. And, again, it is Bryan who is balking the strategy.
Oscar Underwood succeeded in passing through Congress a bill which virtually carried into effect the demand which the Farmers' Alliance put into the Ocala platform of 1891. HIS FARMERS' FREE-LIST BILL PROPOSED TO REMOVE THE TARIFF-TAX, FROM THE ARTICLES "WHICH THE POOR MUST HAVE TO LIVE."
Underwood's bill was the most sweeping measure of free trade that Congress has passed since John C. Calhoun won his magnificent battle over Daniel Webster, Henry Clay, and Andrew Jackson.[36]

Underwood's skill in uniting the divergent elements of the party in Congress into a solid, working group undisturbed by party rebellion and antagonisms was a fundamental reason for the success of the Democratic House in 1911 and 1912. He had demonstrated that he could lead. Manifestly, here was a reasonable argument for his nomination. He had proved that Democrats did not have to gratify their Republican opponents by "doing the wrong thing at the right time." Underwood's leadership was desperately needed, his advocates insisted, to weld the discordant elements of the party into a harmoniously functioning organism.[37]

35. Some of the more significant editorials concerning Underwood and his achievements in tariff reform are found in the following: Jacksonville *Florida Times-Union*, July 29, 1911, January 25, February 2, 1912; Mobile *Register*, June 11, November 30, December 24, 1911; Norfolk *Virginian-Pilot*, May 26, 1912; Charlotte *Daily Observer*, February 9, 1912; Atlanta *Constitution*, February 6, March 14, and 30, 1912; Birmingham *Age-Herald*, July 17, October 28, December 17, 1911; Charleston *News and Courier*, January 30, 1912; Vicksburg *Herald*, February 25, April 25, 1912; Montgomery *Advertiser*, April 5, 1912.
36. *Jeffersonian* (Thomson, Ga.), February 8, 1912.
37. Jacksonville *Florida Times-Union*, February 10, 1912; *ibid.*, March 21, 1912, quoting

The Underwood campaign, generally speaking, united conservative southern Democrats into a counter movement against the flood tide of Wilsonian progressivism which was sweeping the South. The truth of this generalization is revealed by the nature of the support the Alabamian received. In every state in which the contest was fought between Underwood and Wilson men, the conservative state organization was the body and substance of the Underwood movement. In Virginia, the Martin-Swanson organization, in North Carolina the Simmons organization,[38] in Georgia the Joseph M. Brown–Clark Howell–Tom Watson coalition, and in Florida the conservative faction led by Gov. Albert W. Gilchrist and the Jacksonville *Florida Times-Union* were arrayed in the vanguard of the movement to make Underwood president. The same general conservatism was apparent in Underwood's newspaper support, for the pre-eminent conservative journals of the Southeast—the Charlotte *Daily Observer*, the Atlanta *Constitution*, the Augusta *Chronicle*, the Savannah *Morning News*, the Macon *Telegraph*, the Montgomery *Advertiser*, the Vicksburg *Herald*, and the Memphis *Commercial Appeal*—were the spokesmen for the Underwood cause. Moreover, this identical conservative faction quite naturally was in opposition to William J. Bryan and his brand of progressive Democracy. It was not uncommon in the South, therefore, to read that Underwood was the "safe and sane candidate," that he stood in opposition to destructive Socialism, that he was the man destined to safeguard American institutions from the violent ravages of the mob.[39]

On the other hand, there were numerous southerners—largely in the Wilson ranks—who, despite their high regard for Underwood's personal character and for his services to party and to country, honestly believed that he had no possible chance to win the nomination. His record had been one of clear, sane, constructive legislation, they said, but he had had no executive experience. He was a fearless leader, but he had neither prestige nor popularity

Raleigh *Times; ibid.,* April 4, 1912, quoting Birmingham *News;* Pensacola *Evening News,* April 5, 1912; Birmingham *Age-Herald,* March 19, 1912, quoting Columbus *Enquirer-Sun;* Charlotte *Daily Observer,* May 16, 1912, quoting Danville (Va.) *Register.*

38. Sen. Furnifold M. Simmons, however, did not take an active part in the campaign.

39. Jacksonville *Florida Times-Union,* April 4, 1912, quoting Birmingham *News;* Charlotte *Daily Observer,* November 26, 1911; Atlanta *Constitution,* March 14, 1912, quoting Savannah *Morning News.*

with the mass of the American people, both of which were prere-
quisites of national leadership. The appeal to the South's pride
and "manhood," the battle cry, "The South for a Southerner,"
were not only meaningless sentimentality, thought these southerners; they were pernicious slogans which would result only in
magnifying sectional antagonisms.

Why then did not the entire South immediately rally in
support of Underwood? The reasons, of course, were complex,
but perhaps the most important factor was the understanding by
scores of influential party leaders of the realistic fact that the
South alone could not nominate the presidential candidate. These
leaders were extremely reluctant, moreover, to test public opinion
on the sectional issue, which might be used by the Republicans
to fan into a burning fire the prejudice which had so long constituted an unwritten ban on the Democratic party. Even the most
irrational Underwood advocates could not escape the inevitable
conclusion that their candidate was, politically speaking, unavail-
able. There was little probability that he could, in a straightforward
Republican and Democratic campaign, carry a single state outside
the South. A conservative, he would encounter the opposition
of northern independents and western insurgents. It was also
conceded that Bryan would not support him. But the most irrevo-
cable conclusion undermining the strength of the Underwood
movement was the inescapable fact that he was from a solidly
Democratic state within the Solid South and was therefore "un-
available" as a presidential candidate.[40]

40. For a general discussion of the factors operating against the Underwood movement,
see: Mobile *Register,* August 6, 1911, quoting Birmingham *News;* Atlanta *Journal,* March
28, 1912, quoting Tampa *Tribune;* Richmond *Virginian,* April 5, 1912; Nashville *Banner,*
October 26, November 27, 1911; Richmond *Times-Dispatch,* June 12, 1912; Raleigh *News
and Observer,* May 26, 1912, quoting Monroe *Carolina Democrat;* Norfolk *Virginian-Pilot,*
October 28, 1911, March 5, 1912; Dallas *Morning News,* March 4, 1912; Pensacola *Journal,*
October 29, 1911.

Bryan's attitude toward Underwood's candidacy had been indicated in a statement
in his *Commoner* that

The Harmon strength shows signs of shifting to Congressman Underwood. This was
to be expected. The Wall street crowd does not lack intelligence and it would be
very dull if it did not see in Mr. Underwood a more efficient representative than
Governor Harmon could possibly be. . . . If Mr. Underwood is nominated, it will
increase his prestige and he will be in a position to lead the reactionary element
of the party against progressive measures. . . . Mr. Underwood has youth, ability
and courage—just the combination that Wall Street needs. Watch him grow—in the
subsidized press of both parties *(Commoner,* November 17, 1911, p. 1).

Wilson leaders suspected, also, that Underwood's candidacy was insincere, and that it was an underhand trick to draw away from Wilson the support he would likely have received in the Lower South. Since the Underwood movement was essentially a southern conservative cause, many Wilson advocates predicted that the Underwood delegations would be delivered to Harmon or some other northern conservative at the Democratic national convention at Baltimore. After thirty years, the doubts of the sincerity of the Underwood movement still rise to plague us. There can be little doubt, however, that Underwood's managers entered the presidential adventure firmly convinced that their candidate had a good chance to win the nomination. They fought, therefore, not for Harmon nor for any candidate except their own. The Democratic outlook, furthermore, appeared to favor Underwood's candidacy. To all appearances, the rising tides of the Champ Clark and Wilson movements might, when they clashed in the convention, neutralize the strength of each other. Under such circumstances, a deadlock would create an impasse in which it would be impossible for either Clark or Wilson to secure the nomination. They believed, therefore, that the swing of several powerful northern delegations to Underwood at the propitious moment could easily result in an irresistible landslide to their candidate. Thus, with a solid block of southern votes, Underwood possibly might, as the compromise candidate, win the nomination.

The Underwood forces went to the Baltimore convention with instructed delegations from Alabama, Florida, Georgia, and Mississippi—a total of eighty-four votes; and these four delegations remained faithful to him throughout the forty-five ballots which had to be taken before the deadlock between Clark and Wilson was broken. His name was placed before the convention by William B. Bankhead of Alabama, a son of the Senator, and on the first ballot he received 117½ votes, including fourteen from Virginia and scattered support from members of the North Carolina and Tennessee delegations. Ahead of him were Clark, with 440½ votes; Wilson, with 324; and Harmon, with 148, all of them, of course, far short of the two-thirds majority necessary for nomination. As the balloting proceeded, Underwood received a few occasional votes from Connecticut, Maine, Maryland, Massachusetts, and Michigan; and on the nineteenth ballot, his highest total of 130 votes was reached. At no time was there a serious possibility of his being accepted as a compromise candidate, and as the tide slowly turned toward Wilson after the tenth ballot, when Clark received the support of the Tammany-controlled 90 votes from New York, some of the Underwood delegates began to urge that they be released from their pledge to support the Alabamian. Senator Bankhead held on stubbornly, however, until the forty-fifth ballot showed that his support had dropped to 97 votes; and when he withdrew his candidate's name at the beginning of the next roll-call, the Underwood delegates immediately joined in the landslide which gave Wilson the nomination.[41]

Although there was never any considerable chance that Underwood would receive the nomination, his delegates nevertheless played a significant role in the convention. By refusing to go over to Clark on the tenth ballot, for example, when the Missourian received 556 votes—a majority of the convention vote—the Underwood men co-operated with the Wilson managers in creating a solid block of more than one-third of the convention votes and successfully prevented a Clark landslide. The formation of the Wilson-Underwood alliance was the result of skillful bargaining on the part of Wilson's managers, who saw early in the convention that the Underwood managers held the balance of power at Baltimore. Thomas W. Gregory, William F. McCombs, and other Wilson leaders conferred with the Underwood managers before the tenth ballot and both groups agreed that the Underwood delegates should stand by their candidate during the threatened Clark landslide; and, in return, the Wilson managers agreed to throw the weight of their influence to the Underwood candidacy if "Wilson should be put out of the race at any stage of the game." [42] Thus, a vote for Underwood during the crucial tenth, eleventh, and twelfth ballots was as good as a vote for Wilson.[43]

41. *Official Report of the Proceedings of the Democratic National Convention, Held in Baltimore, June 25, 26, 27, 28, and 29, and July 1 and 2, 1912* (Chicago: Peterson Linotyping Co., 1912), passim.

42. Thomas W. Gregory to Edward M. House, July 9, 1912, in Edward M. House Papers, Yale University, New Haven, Conn.

43. It is interesting to speculate why the Underwood managers, who had the power to decide the contest in Clark's favor, refused to effect the Missourian's nomination. The vice-presidency must certainly have been offered to them by the Clark managers; but Underwood and Bankhead were not at all interested in the vice-presidency (Underwood refused to accept the nomination when Wilson later offered it to him). They were after nothing less than the presidential nomination. The truth of the matter was that Wilson really was the second choice of a good majority of the Underwood delegates, most of whom disliked Clark intensely.

During the course of the voting in the convention from the tenth to the forty-fifth ballots, Wilson steadily gained strength. His greatest gain came on the forty-third ballot, when Illinois, Virginia, and West Virginia went over solidly to him and boosted his total vote to over 600. The forty-fifth ballot marked the major crisis for Woodrow Wilson at Baltimore, for, despite his considerable gains, the New Jersey governor was still 97 votes short of a two-thirds majority. There were rumors that Roger Sullivan, Illinois Democratic boss, would take his delegation back to Clark on the forty-sixth ballot, and the Wilson managers were convinced that if their candidate could not secure the support of the Underwood delegations, he would surely be defeated. After hurried conferences between the Wilson and Underwood managers, the Alabama men immediately decided to withdraw Underwood's name. This, they believed, would break the convention deadlock and result in Wilson's nomination.[44] On the forty-sixth ballot, consequently, when Senator Bankhead withdrew Underwood's name, there was a wild scramble of delegates to the Wilson standard and the New Jersey governor was immediately nominated.

When the Underwood movement is considered in the setting of the conflict between conservative and progressive forces within the Democratic party in 1912, it can hardly be said to have had any great significance in itself. If it was intended as a conservative movement, it lost its sense of direction in the swing to Wilson; if, on the other hand, it was designed primarily to break down the barrier against southern aspirants for the presidency, as Senator Bankhead claimed in withdrawing Underwood's name, it had merely emphasized the fact that, under existing circumstances in the Democratic party, a southerner was still not to be considered as an available candidate. It began, in the last analysis, as a "favorite son" movement in Alabama and developed subsequently into a regional "favorite son" campaign; but it also heralded the approach of the day when southerners were to dominate the national government during the Wilson administration. Although the movement failed in its immediate objective—the presidential nomination—it played a role of tremendous importance at Bal-

44. This story is told in interesting detail in the Birmingham *Age-Herald,* July 4, 5, 7, 1912.

timore. It is perhaps a bit ironic that the Underwood campaigners, who, along with Champ Clark, provided the only real opposition to Wilson in the South during the preconvention campaign, should have become one of the few really important forces that secured his nomination at Baltimore in July 1912.

15

The Baltimore Convention of 1912

THE movement to make Woodrow Wilson the Democratic presidential nominee in 1912, fathered by George Harvey and carried forward by a group of young progressive Democrats, stood in a fair way of foundering on the rocks of factional politics by the spring of 1912.[1] Wilson had campaigned vigorously for the nomination during the early months of 1912, but in few states in which he campaigned did the New Jersey governor win support. It was Champ Clark of Missouri, speaker of the House of Representatives, who loomed up as the man most likely to win the nomination. Following his smashing victory over Wilson in the Illinois primaries in April 1912, Clark swept through Missouri, Kansas, Iowa, Kentucky, New Hampshire, Maryland, Nebraska, West Virginia, Washington, Arkansas, Rhode Island, California, and several of the less populous western states.[2]

Early in April, Wilson made an extended "swing around the

Reprinted from the *American Historical Review*, L (July 1945), 691–731; copyright 1970, Arthur S. Link.

1. The author's research in this field, made possible by a grant from the Julius Rosenwald Fund, has been embodied in "The South and the Democratic Campaign of 1910–1912" (Ph.D. dissertation, University of North Carolina, 1945).

2. For the Democratic prenomination campaign, see Ray Stannard Baker, *Woodrow Wilson, Life and Letters*, 8 vols. (Garden City, New York: Doubleday, Doran & Co., 1927–1939), III, 175–321, and Arthur S. Link, "The South and the Democratic Campaign of 1910–1912."

circle" in his wife's native state of Georgia, only to see it fall to Oscar W. Underwood of Alabama.³ Florida and Mississippi soon afterward followed Georgia into the Underwood ranks. Wilson himself fell ill. William F. McCombs, his campaign manager, was disheartened, and his office and the headquarters at 42 Broadway were deserted.⁴ Col. Edward M. House, who had played a minor role in the Wilson prenomination campaign, began to doubt that Wilson could be nominated. He thought that the opposing candidates in November might again be Bryan and Roosevelt,⁵ and wrote to Mary Baird Bryan, pledging his support to the Commoner if he were again the Democratic nominee.⁶ House also turned to his old friend, Sen. Charles A. Culberson of Texas. "Do you feel that your health would permit you to accept the nomination if it were tendered to you?" he wrote. "In the event of a deadlock, which seems likely to occur, I can think of no one excepting you that would be satisfactory to all factions."⁷

There were, however, a few signs of encouragement. Texas, on May 28, went overwhelmingly for Wilson, and his friends in Pennsylvania carried that state solidly for him. Moreover, in Wisconsin, Oregon, Delaware, Minnesota, North Carolina, and South Carolina, the Wilson leaders were successful. The greatest encouragement came when the New Jersey primaries gave Wilson twenty-four out of the state's twenty-eight delegates. It furthermore appeared that the Wilson forces were strongly represented in the Michigan, Ohio, Louisiana, Oklahoma, Maine, Virginia, North Dakota, and South Dakota delegations. Of the total convention vote of 1,088, some 248 were instructed for Wilson, and the additional support of the Wilson men in the uninstructed delegations would hardly give him control of one third of the convention vote.

3. For the identification of Underwood, McCombs, and many others, see the preceding essay in this volume, "The Underwood Presidential Movement of 1912," pp. 200-215. See also biographical footnotes to the Gregory letter in the *American Historical Review,* L (July 1945), pp. 768-775.

4. Maurice F. Lyons, *William F. McCombs, the President-Maker* (Cincinnati· the Bancroft Co., 1922), pp. 75-76.

5. House to Charles A. Culberson, May 1, 1912, Edward M. House Papers, Yale University, New Haven, Conn.; hereinafter cited as House Papers.

6. House to Mary B. Bryan, June 22, 1912, *ibid.*

7. House to Culberson, April 23, 1912, *ibid.*

Clark, on the other hand, would enter the convention with over 400 votes; Underwood was assured of over 100 votes from the South; Gov. Judson Harmon of Ohio, Gov. Thomas R. Marshall of Indiana, and other "favorite sons" controlled over 100 votes, while some 224 votes were uncertainly controlled by political bosses who scented a Clark victory and were eager to use their delegations as weapons for bargains and trades with the Missourian's managers.

The results of the Republican convention, which met in Chicago two weeks before the Democratic convention, further weakened Wilson's chances for the Democratic nomination, for the great schism between the Taft and Roosevelt forces led many Democrats to conclude that it really made no essential difference whom they nominated. Certainly the argument of Wilson's supporters that only he could win the presidency because only he among the Democrats could divide the Independents from the Republican party was completely vitiated now that Roosevelt had accomplished the division for them.

The hectic and confused week preceding the Democratic convention at Baltimore saw the occurrence of events of tremendous import for the outcome of the presidential struggle. Wilson, resting peacefully with his family at Sea Girt, New Jersey, could write that "deep down, my soul is quiet" [8]—but not for long, for William J. Bryan disturbed the peaceful scene at Sea Girt by his concern over the Democratic national committee's decision to select Alton B. Parker, Democratic standard-bearer in 1904, as the temporary chairman at Baltimore. The committee on arrangements of the national committee, meeting at Baltimore on June 20, supported Chairman Norman E. Mack in his campaign to make Parker temporary chairman. [9] Bryan was convinced that the same conservative forces that controlled the Republican convention were

8. Wilson to Mary A. Hulbert, June 17, 1912, Baker, III, 333.

9. *Official Report of the Proceedings of the Democratic National Convention* (Chicago: Peterson Linotyping Co., 1912), p. 473; hereinafter cited as *Proceedings of the Convention.* See also Josephus Daniels, "Wilson and Bryan," *Saturday Evening Post,* CXCVIII (September 5, 1925), 48. Four months prior to the convention, Mack had given Bryan assurance that, should he desire to be temporary chairman, Mack and most of the members of the committee on arrangements would gladly support him. Bryan refused to be a candidate for the position and suggested that Wilson and Clark be asked to agree upon a candidate. Norman E. Mack, "Wilson and Marshall—Mr. Bryan and New York," *National Monthly Magazine,* IV (August 1912), 65.

preparing to move to Baltimore. He protested in vain against Parker's selection, stating that he could not believe such "criminal folly" was possible. Undismayed by the rebuff he received from the committee on arrangements, the Nebraskan determined to carry his fight against Parker into the national convention itself. Ignoring Harmon and Underwood, whom he considered "reactionaries," he immediately sent identical telegrams to Wilson, Clark, and several "favorite son" candidates, asking if they would stand by him in his fight against Parker.[10]

William F. McCombs, at the Wilson headquarters in Hotel Emerson in Baltimore, was terror-stricken by Bryan's move. He feared that an unequivocal answer from Wilson supporting Bryan's stand would alienate Charles F. Murphy and his Tammany cohorts and thereby forestall any chance Wilson might have of securing the New York delegation.[11] McCombs therefore immediately forwarded to Wilson a suggested reply to Bryan's query which embodied the essence of a statement Wilson had already made to the Baltimore *Evening Sun.*[12]

But Wilson, at the insistence of Joseph P. Tumulty, his secretary, William G. McAdoo, and his wife, gave a straightforward answer to the Commoner. "You are quite right," he asserted. "The Baltimore convention is to be a convention of progressives—of men who are progressive in principle and by conviction," which must, moreover, "express its convictions in its organization and in its choice of the men who are to speak for it."[13] Wilson's statement was a masterful move, for it marked him at the very

10. Mary B. Bryan, editor, *Memoirs of William Jennings Bryan* (Philadelphia and Chicago: John C. Winston Co., 1925), pp. 161–166, has an interesting discussion of Bryan's activities during this period.

11. William Gibbs McAdoo, *Crowded Years* (Boston and New York: Houghton Mifflin Co., 1931), pp. 137–141, gives a good account of McCombs's attitude.

12. Before Bryan sent his appeal to the candidates, the *Evening Sun* had requested that Wilson give his views regarding the temporary chairmanship contest. Wilson replied instantly that

My friends in Baltimore, who are on the ground, will know how to act in the interest of the people's cause in everything that affects the organization of the convention. They are certain not to forget their standards as they have already shown. It is not necessary that I should remind them of those standards from Sea Girt; and I have neither the right nor the desire to direct the organization of a convention of which I am not even a member." (Undated letter in Woodrow Wilson Papers, Library of Congress, Washington, D.C.; hereinafter cited as Wilson Papers.)

13. Original draft in *ibid.;* see also New York *World,* June 23, 1912.

outset of the convention as one of the progressive leaders with backbone. Champ Clark, on the other hand, attempted to hedge by a noncommittal appeal for party harmony.[14]

On Sunday and Monday, June 23 and 24, the Democratic hosts descended upon Baltimore, traditional scene of Democratic gatherings. "It is of good augury that once more we meet in the glorious metropolis of Maryland," old "Marse Henry" Watterson wrote. "Noble city! In deep reflection the spirit of democracy walks thy streets this day; broods amid thy solitudes." [15] But the solitude within the historic city was rudely shattered by the incoming Democrats. Tammany Hall, led by Murphy and August Belmont, came in a special train. Thomas Fortune Ryan arrived under cover of the night and quietly slipped into his rooms.

The arrival of the Democrats was the signal for the traditional bargaining among the presidential managers to begin, or rather to become intensified. The temporary chairmanship became the outstanding issue of the day when, in a plenary meeting of the national committee, the Clark representatives combined with Tammany Hall and the conservatives to defeat the nomination of Ollie M. James of Kentucky [16] in favor of Parker for the temporary chairmanship.[17] This seemingly unnatural and, to many progressives, immoral alliance between Clark's managers and Tammany fomented suspicions that the Speaker's managers had concluded a bargain with Murphy by which the Clark delegations would support Parker for the temporary chairmanship and New York's ninety votes would come to the Missourian at a propitious moment in the balloting.[18] Probably this was the truth of the matter, for the Clark forces held the key to the temporary chairmanship. Clark's managers could either defeat Bryan or they could aid him in smashing the plan of the few conservatives to control the convention. But these conservatives controlled enough votes to give Clark a majority of the delegates in the convention while Bryan did not. Moreover, the Clark men had a very real dread that, should the Commoner win his fight against Parker by an

14. *Commoner* (Lincoln, Neb.), XII (June 28, 1912), 1.
15. Louisville *Courier-Journal,* cited in Pensacola *Journal,* July 4, 1912.
16. James was an ardent Clark supporter.
17. *Proceedings of the Convention,* p. 490.
18. Dallas *Morning News,* June 25, 1912; Robert Latham in Charleston *News and Courier,* June 25, 1912; W. E. Gonzales in Columbia *State,* June 25, 1912; Alexander Forward in Richmond *Times-Dispatch,* June 25, 1912; St. Louis *Republic,* June 25, 26, 1912.

overwhelming vote, he would be unbeatable as a presidential candidate himself.[19]

The tremendous crowd in Convention Hall, gathered for the first session of the convention on the afternoon of June 25, became hushed as the venerable Cardinal Gibbons invoked the blessing of God upon the deliberations of the body. The prayer was the lull before the storm. Chairman Mack rapped his gavel vigorously for order. He had been instructed by the national committee, he said, to nominate Alton B. Parker for temporary chairman.[20] Bryan was immediately on his feet. Standing on the convention platform, "His heavy black brows . . . contracted over his piercing eyes,"[21] the Nebraskan nominated Sen. John W. Kern of Indiana, his running mate in 1908, as the man most worthy of the confidence of the convention. Bryan declared that now the hour of Democratic triumph had arrived, a true progressive should lead the convention in the keynote address. The Democrats were announcing to the country, he insisted, whether they would take up the challenge thrown down at Chicago by a convention controlled by "predatory wealth," or answer it by giving themselves over to the same sinister forces. The dramatic climax in Bryan's speech came suddenly. "The Democratic party is true to the people," he declared. "You cannot frighten it with your Ryans nor buy it with your Belmonts." This palpable defiance electrified the convention and at this point Bryan should have sat down; but he went on in a sort of anticlimactic excoriation of Parker.[22]

Senator Kern rose gravely and made a dramatic appeal to Parker to withdraw from the contest and declared that if the New York delegation would agree to support either Sen. James A.

19. Arthur Krock in Louisville *Times*, June 25, 1912. Senator-elect James K. Vardaman of Mississippi was selected by the Parker forces to offer the olive branch of compromise to Bryan. It was a wise selection, for Vardaman had for years been an intimate friend and loyal follower of the Nebraskan. He offered Bryan the permanent chairmanship of the convention if the Commoner would accept Parker as temporary chairman. Bryan became so "frigid," according to one report, that Vardaman picked up his hat and started to leave the room. Turning again to the Commoner, he said, "I thought our personal and political relations were intimate enough to permit me to talk about the matter to you." Bryan smiled sadly, put his hand on the Mississippian's shoulder and told him that he had not meant to hurt him, but that he could not possibly consent to such an agreement. (Birmingham *Age-Herald*, June 24, 1912.)

20. *Proceedings of the Convention*, pp. 2–3.

21. New York *World*, June 26, 1912.

22. *Proceedings of the Convention*, pp. 3–7.

O'Gorman, Senator Culberson, Henry D. Clayton, Luke Lea, or Joseph W. Folk, all discord would cease. When there was no answer to Kern's proffered compromise, the Indiana senator withdrew from the contest and nominated Bryan himself.[23] The convention was in an uproar. Theodore Bell of California, who rose to answer Kern, was overwhelmed by a torrent of noise from the Wilson delegates. Rep. John J. Fitzgerald of New York seemed to have arrested the confusion and was delivering some telling blows for Parker when Cullen F. Thomas of Texas climbed into his chair and yelled, "Are you the distinguished New York Congressman who supported Joe Cannon?" This pointed interruption ended Fitzgerald's speech.[24] The convention was anxious to vote, but Bryan pleaded for five additional minutes of discussion before the roll call. Cone Johnson of Texas pushed to the front of the speaker's platform and, with a voice as loud as a "human fog horn," quieted the mob. The contest was not between men, he declared, and he did not pause to inquire who caused the fight, for "This one thing I know—the fight is on, and Bryan is on one side and Wall street is on the other." [25]

The convention then proceeded to endorse the national committee and elected Parker temporary chairman by a vote of 579 to 508. The Clark managers were able to deliver enough of their delegates to insure Bryan's defeat, although practically all of the Clark men on the western delegations refused to deal what they considered a treacherous blow against their old leader.[26] They accordingly stood by the Nebraskan, and the Wilson delegates almost to a man voted for the Commoner. Champ Clark himself had remained neutral during the fight but, as Bryan noted, the Speaker's managers were "working like beavers for Judge Parker." [27]

The dramatic conflict between Bryan and Parker was a fitting introduction to the struggles at the Baltimore convention. In the first place, it convinced thousands of progressive Democrats that the fight was on between Wilson and Bryan on the one hand,

---

23. *Ibid.,* pp. 7–9.
24. Dallas *Morning News,* June 26, 1912.
25. *Proceedings of the Convention,* p. 13.
26. *Ibid.,* pp. 17–19.
27. William J. Bryan, *A Tale of Two Conventions* (New York and London: Funk & Wagnalls Co., 1912), p. 192.

and Clark, Wall Street, and Tammany on the other. It furthermore convinced Bryan that his old friend Champ Clark would without hesitation desert him for the support of New York.

But the victory of the Tammany-Clark alliance was a Pyrrhic one. A move by the Murphy organization to retain Parker as permanent chairman was quickly detected and blocked by former Gov. Thomas M. Campbell of Texas. At the insistence of the Wilson men, Ollie M. James was chosen permanent chairman by the committee on arrangements, and Bryan was delighted.[28] Urey Woodson was ousted as secretary of the convention and Edward E. Britton, city editor of the Raleigh *News and Observer*, was chosen in his stead.[29]

Progressive sentiment was rising in the convention; and the first important progressive victory occurred in the abrogation of the ironclad unit rule in the voting of certain state delegations. The occasion for the fight arose when the committee on rules decreed that nineteen Wilson delegates from Ohio had to vote for Governor Harmon because the state Democratic convention had thus instructed. The chairman of the rules committee, J. Harry Covington of Maryland, argued that the traditional Democratic usage should not be changed, that the national convention had no right to interfere in the internal party affairs of the states.[30]

Robert L. Henry presented the minority report of the committee,[31] but the foremost champion of the abrogation of the unit rule was Newton D. Baker, mayor of Cleveland. In an impassioned appeal to the convention, Baker declared that the law of Ohio had taken from the state convention the authority to select delegates to a national convention and had vested it in the people. He had given a sacred pledge to his constitutents that he would vote for Wilson. Would the convention force him to betray the trust the people had confided in him?[32] Sen. John Sharp Williams of Mississippi lost his temper. If the convention adopted the majority report, he declared, it would do "the most dangerous and most damnable thing" in its power. And "when you get

28. *Ibid.*, p. 153.
29. *Proceedings of the Convention, p. 120; Dallas Morning News*, June 27, 1912.
30. *Proceedings of the Convention, pp. 59-60.*
31. *Ibid.*
32. *Ibid.*, pp. 65-68.

through with it you can quit your talk about 'popular govern-ment,' " he shouted.[33]

When John W. Peck of Ohio attempted to defend the majority report, he mentioned Wilson's name and set off a wild demon-stration by the Wilson delegates.[34] Robert L. Henry, Wilson floor leader, sensed the rising Wilson enthusiasm and after the demon-stration had subsided, he announced that Virginia, "the mother of the doctrine of state sovereignty," had signed the minority report.[35] Largely because of the support the Wilson men received from Mississippi, Virginia, Florida, and Alabama—the Underwood delegations—they succeeded in turning the tables on the Clark men. The convention, by a vote of 565½ to 492⅓, adopted the minority report.[36] This decided Wilson victory was an effective antidote to the growing belief that Clark was certain to be nomin-ated. It demonstrated to the convention and to the country at large that the Wilson delegates, although in a decided minority, were united and fired with something like an evangelical zeal for the Wilson cause.

A minor episode in the struggle at Baltimore concerned the disposition of the South Dakota delegation. Two delegations from that state, one representing Wilson, the other Clark, presented their claims as the rightful delegation to the credentials committee on June 26. Clark supporters, who controlled the committee, voted to seat the Clark delegation. In the meantime another contest had come before the credentials committee. Two delegations from Cook County, Illinois—one group representing Roger Sullivan, the Illinois Democratic boss, the other representing the Hearst-Carter Harrison Chicago organization—claimed to be the lawful repre-sentatives from Chicago. Luke Lea, spokesman for the Wilson forces in the committee, made a bargain with Sullivan whereby the Wilson delegates would support Sullivan and the Illinois boss would vote to seat the Wilson delegation from South Dakota.[37] Consequently, the Sullivan delegates were seated by the creden-tials committee and when the South Dakota issue was considered

33. *Ibid.,* p. 72.
34. Montgomery *Advertiser,* June 27, 1912.
35. *Proceedings of the Convention,* p. 75; see also Richmond *Times-Dispatch,* June 27, 1912.
36. *Proceedings of the Convention,* p. 77.
37. Charlotte Daily *Observer,* June 27, 1912; Houston *Post,* June 28, 1912.

by the convention, Sullivan threw the weight of Illinois's fifty-eight votes to the Wilson men and they were seated.[38]

As a result of the Wilson successes in the struggle for the abrogation of the unit rule and for the South Dakota delegation, there followed a decided reaction in the convention against the Clark-Tammany alliance. It was apparent that the progressives had taken a new lease on life. But Bryan suspected that the conservatives were only biding their time and waiting for the propitious moment to strike. "I found that the representatives of Morgan, Belmont, and Ryan were at work," he later recorded.[39]

The fact that Thomas Fortune Ryan, one of the financial czars of Wall Street, was sitting as a delegate from Virginia was a matter of severe embarrassment to Sen. Claude A. Swanson and other leaders in the Virginia organization.[40] In the first place, Ryan had secured membership in the Virginia delegation through trickery.[41] Moreover, Ryan's activities were of a suspicious character. One reporter charged that the Virginia financier was the "captain-general of the plutocrats" who were in Baltimore to depose Bryan as Democratic leader and to prevent Wilson's nomination.[42]

At three o'clock on Thursday morning, June 27, Charles W. Bryan told his brother that Clark's managers had concluded an agreement with Tammany whereby New York's ninety votes would be delivered to Clark at some time early in the balloting. This agreement, Charles W. Bryan insisted, would place the party

38. *Proceedings of the Convention,* pp. 93–94. The importance of the Sullivan-Lea bargain has not been generally recognized. First of all, it added ten votes to the growing number of Wilson delegates, but more important, it assured Sullivan's dominance in the Illinois delegation and enabled him later to cast the fifty-eight Illinois votes for Wilson at a very crucial moment in the balloting.

39. Mary B. Bryan, p. 173.

40. Richmond *News Leader,* June 28, 1912.

41. At a meeting of the Tenth District committee at the Democratic state convention at Norfolk in May, the anti-Wilson men, led by Hal D. Flood, greatly outnumbered the Wilson supporters. Flood, who was regarded as Ryan's chief lieutenant, made an agreement with the Wilson men to divide evenly between the two groups the district's delegates to the national convention. There would be no election, as the offer went, but each group would choose its own man. Astonished at this seeming liberality, the Wilson men gladly accepted the offer. The organization faction then announced that they had selected Ryan to represent them. At the time, Ryan's son was present, and the Wilson men supposed it was he who had been chosen as delegate. The secret was well kept, and it was no little surprise to the Wilson delegates from Virginia to discover that the financier was a member of their delegation. (Carter W. Wormley in Richmond *News Leader,* June 27, 1912.)

42. Samuel G. Blythe, in the New Orleans *Times-Democrat,* June 27, 1912.

under obligation to Wall Street and would prevent Clark from carrying out a progressive program were he elected president. In order to see if the Clark organization would stand by Wall Street instead of the Commoner, he would have one of the progressive leaders introduce a resolution to expel Ryan and August Belmont from the convention. Charles W. Bryan told his brother that he would call together the Wilson leaders and endeavor to persuade one of them to introduce the resolution. William J. Bryan approved of the plan.[43]

Charles W. Bryan soon afterward called together Thomas P. Gore, Luke Lea, Cone Johnson, Jerry B. Sullivan, Harvey Garber, and Henderson Martin. These Wilson leaders unanimously agreed that the proposed resolution demanding Ryan's and Belmont's expulsion from the convention was too harsh and, furthermore, unwise. None volunteered to introduce it.[44] Charles W. was consequently discouraged when he saw his brother at his hotel Thursday evening. At Charles W.'s suggestion, the Commoner wrote out a resolution which specifically named Belmont, Morgan, and Ryan as conspirators of Wall Street. W. J. Bryan was not certain that he would introduce the resolution when he started to the evening session of the convention, but on the way he decided to take the fateful step.[45]

In the convention on the evening of June 27, therefore, Bryan arose and asked unanimous consent to introduce a resolution. When there was no objection, Bryan read the following words:

Resolved, That in this crisis in our party's career and in our country's history this convention sends greeting to the people of the United States, and assures them that the party of Jefferson and of Jackson is still the champion of popular government and equality before the law. As proof of our fidelity to the people, we hereby declare ourselves opposed to the nomination of any candidate for president who is the representative of or under obligation to J. Pierpont Morgan, Thomas F. Ryan, August Belmont, or any other member of the privilege-hunting and favor-seeking class.

Be it further resolved, That we demand the withdrawal from this convention of any delegate or delegates constituting or representing the above-named interests.[46]

43. Charles W. Bryan in the New York *Times,* March 6, 1921.
44. *Ibid.*
45. Mary B. Bryan, pp. 175–176.
46. *Proceedings of the Convention, p. 129.*

It seemed as if all the furies of hell had broken loose on the convention floor. Scores of delegates leaped to their feet, demanding recognition.[47] When the uproar finally subsided, Bryan defended his resolution:

There is not a delegate in this convention who does not know that an effort is being made right now to sell the Democratic party into bondage to the predatory interests of the nation. It is the most brazen, the most insolent, the most impudent attempt that has been made in the history of American politics . . . to make the nominee the bond-slave of the men who exploit the people of this country.

Bryan was now quite red in the face. If the New York and Virginia delegates would take an "honest poll" of their delegations, and if a majority of both states did not ask for Ryan's and Belmont's withdrawal, Bryan promised that he would expunge the latter part of his resolution.

As Bryan concluded, Hal Flood of Virginia forced his way up to the speaker's platform. As he came up to Bryan's side, the Commoner turned and held out his hand. Flood looked squarely at Bryan, made an angry rejoinder with a vigorous shake of his head, and rejected the proffered hand. He stepped nearer to Bryan and shouted that Virginia accepted "the insolent proposition made by the only man who wants to destroy the prospect of Democratic success."[49] Bryan then declared that Virginia had notified him that she wanted the expulsion resolution withdrawn. He asked that a delegate from New York speak for his delegation.[50] Former Gov. W. A. McCorkle of West Virginia shouted from the platform, "This is a senseless and foolish resolution." Bryan tried to speak, but his voice was drowned in a roar of hisses and catcalls. Flood was back on the platform. The Virginia delegation asked nothing of Bryan, he declared. If the Commoner withdrew the second part of his resolution, it was not at Virginia's request.[51]

Bryan was in a difficult position. Obviously he wished to withdraw the expulsion resolution, for if it remained, the entire

47. Josephus Daniels to the author, January 24, 1942; McAdoo, p. 149; Mary B. Bryan, pp. 176–177.
48. *Proceedings of the Convention*, pp. 131–132.
49. *Ibid.*, p. 132; New York *World*, June 28, 1912.
50. *Proceedings of the Convention*, p. 133.
51. *Ibid.*, p. 135.

resolution would probably be defeated, and when James K. Vardaman suggested that he withdraw the latter part, Bryan gladly did so.[52] The Commoner hastily demanded a roll call. While the vote was being recorded, Vardaman hurried over to Boss Murphy and urged him to vote for the resolution. "If you do, Murphy, we will make Bryan look like a fool," he urged. After consulting with Sullivan and Thomas Taggart, Democratic boss of Indiana, Murphy cast New York's vote for the resolution.[53] The Tammany leader, with a sly grin on his face, turned to August Belmont and said, "August, listen and hear yourself vote yourself out of the convention."[54] The emasculated anti-Morgan-Belmont-Ryan resolution was overwhelmingly endorsed by the convention.[55]

Back of the scenes at Baltimore, the Wilson and Clark men were working furiously. The Wilson leaders realized that only by shrewd strategy could they overcome the power of the forces arrayed against them and nominate their candidate. The general outline of the strategy was clear. The Wilson men had to hold at least a loyal third of the delegates in order to block the first major threat—Champ Clark's nomination. Several weeks before the Baltimore convention assembled, Wilson had designated McCombs as leader of his forces at Baltimore and A. Mitchell Palmer and Albert S. Burleson as official floor leaders in the convention.[56] At a meeting of the "General Staff" in McCombs's apartment in the Emerson Hotel immediately preceding the balloting for the nomination, the Wilson managers counseled together and pledged to one another their loyalty. Immediately afterward, Thomas Watt Gregory and Thomas B. Love of Texas went to the Hotel Stafford and sought out the members of the Pennsylvania delegation. The Texans and Pennsylvanians agreed that the two delegations should work hand in hand in the convention and that the individual delegates would immediately set to work to persuade the Clark delegates to swing over to Wilson.[57]

During the night and early morning of June 27 and 28, the

52. *Ibid.*

53. New York *World*, June 28, 1912.

54. Mary B. Bryan, p. 178.

55. By a vote of 883 to 201½. *Proceedings of the Convention,* pp. 137–138.

56. R. S. Baker, "Memorandum of a Conversation with Albert S. Burleson, March 17–19, 1927," in the Ray Stannard Baker Papers, Library of Congress, Washington, D.C.; hereinafter cited as Baker Papers.

57. Thomas W. Gregory to Edward M. House, July 9, 1912, in Arthur S. Link, editor, "A Letter from One of Wilson's Managers," *American Historical Review,* L (July 1945), 768–775.

nominations for President were made. It was nearly midnight and the teeming auditorium was sultry and hot; the riotous disturbance over Bryan's inflammable anti-Morgan-Belmont-Ryan resolution had scarcely been quieted when Chairman Ollie M. James called for nominations for President. Alabama was the first state to be called and made the first nomination. William B. Bankhead presented Alabama's "favorite son" and the Deep South's representative, Oscar W. Underwood, as the chief exponent of tariff reform and attempted to convince the convention that since there was no North, no South, the Alabamian was ideally available as a presidential candidate.[58] When Arkansas was called, she yielded to Missouri. Sen. James A. Reed, in a flamboyant nominating speech, presented Champ Clark's claims to the Democratic nomination.[59] The Clark forces, at the end of Reed's address, staged an enthusiastic demonstration which lasted for one hour and five minutes.[60] After the nomination of Gov. Simeon E. Baldwin of Connecticut by Henry Wade Rogers, dean of the Yale Law School, the call of the states was resumed. At eight minutes after two, Delaware yielded to New Jersey and Judge John Wescott came forward to nominate Woodrow Wilson. The lateness of the hour and the weariness of the delegates did not dampen the enthusiasm of the Wilson men. In fact, they did not give Wescott a chance to speak before they began a wild, uncontrolled demonstration which lasted at least one hour and fifteen minutes.[61] Wescott, in a magnificent tribute to Wilson, nominated the New Jersey governor for President as "the ultimate Democrat, the genius of liberty and the very incarnation of progress."[62] There was quite a volley of seconding speeches, and day was breaking when Governor Marshall of Indiana and Governor Harmon of Ohio were nominated. It was about seven o'clock in the morning when the first ballot was taken. The ballot stood:[63]

Clark	440½	Marshall	31
Wilson	324	Baldwin	22
Harmon	148	Bryan	1
Underwood	117½	Sulzer	2

58. *Proceedings of the Convention,* p. 143. See also Birmingham *Age-Herald,* June 28, 1912.
59. *Proceedings of the Convention,* pp. 144–151.
60. Montgomery *Advertiser,* June 28, 1912; New York *Times,* June 28, 1912.
61. Trenton *True American,* June 28, 1912; Trenton *Evening Times,* June 28, 1912.
62. *Proceedings of the Convention,* pp. 157–161.
63. *Ibid.,* p. 196.

The convention, having set the stage for the great struggle, then adjourned.

When the delegates assembled in the afternoon, the lines were tightly drawn for the coming battle. McCombs, nervous and excited, was in charge of the Wilson forces. On the speaker's platform, A. Mitchell Palmer stood by the chairman's side and bespoke Wilson's interests. On the convention floor, Burleson was in command of the Wilson delegates. Blind Senator Gore and McAdoo were constantly at Burleson's side, while Rep. William Hughes of New Jersey and Thomas J. Pence of North Carolina gave aid to Palmer.[64]

During the first nine ballots, little change in the voting occurred. Clark gained some fourteen votes and Wilson's strength increased by twenty-eight votes, but the managers were only sparring. The Wilson men knew that the knockout blow was yet to come. They expected that New York's ninety votes would be delivered to Clark on the third or fourth ballot but were forewarned by their friends in the New York delegation when Murphy decided to transfer the votes to the Missourian at a later time.[65] The expected transfer came on the tenth ballot, when the Tammany leader electrified the convention by casting his state's ninety votes for the Speaker.[66] It was the signal for a Clark landslide, for New York's vote gave Clark 556 votes—well over a majority of the convention. It was now or never for Clark. Not since 1844 had a Democrat obtained a majority in a national convention and not been nominated by the then necessary two thirds.

Clark's managers fully expected that this powerful tradition, in addition to the irresistible momentum generated by New York's action, would bring about the Speaker's nomination on the tenth

64. Otto Praeger, "How Winning Fight for Wilson Was Made," Dallas *Morning News*, July 3, 1912.

65. W. G. McAdoo to R. S. Baker, October 15, 1928, Baker Papers. One of the leaders of the New York delegation afterward wrote that

New York, after the ninth ballot, turned to Clark in preference to Wilson because many of the friends of the Missouri statesman had given their support to New York's candidate for temporary chairman in the meeting of the subcommittee, again in the National Committee and on the floor of the convention, and had put the New York delegation under an obligation to him which New York—in full recognition of the highest party welfare—could honorably repay. (Mack in *National Monthly Magazine*, IV, 65.)

66. *Proceedings of the Convention*, 221. New York voted for Harmon on the first nine ballots.

or eleventh ballot and the Clark delegates naturally were beside themselves with joy. They shouted, sang, and marched for almost an hour. It was a discouraging hour for Woodrow Wilson. His managers scurried over the convention hall, pleading with the Underwood delegations not to go over to Clark. What would the states following New York do? As soon as the Clark demonstration had subsided, North Dakota was called. An expectant silence fell over the great crowd. When the steady response, "Ten for Wilson," followed, the Wilson delegates let out a wild yell. Chairman James then called Oklahoma. One Oklahoman was on his feet. He had voted for Wilson, he declared, but since it seemed that Clark was the convention's choice he demanded a poll of his delegation. "Alfalfa Bill" Murray—collarless and wiping his face with a red bandana handkerchief—roared out that he did not object to a poll of the delegation, but, he declared, "we do insist that we shall not join Tammany in making the nomination!" [67] Oklahoma stood firm and the Wilson men began a wild counterdemonstration that lasted fully fifty-five minutes.

The tenth ballot continued without any further material change in the voting. When, on the eleventh ballot, the Underwood delegations stood firm, it became suddenly apparent that Clark's expected landslide had signally failed to materialize. Manifestly, the Underwood delegates, by standing firm against the Clark onslaught, prevented the nomination of the Missourian. It was true that the one hundred-odd votes Manager John H. Bankhead might have added to Clark's majority would not have given the Speaker the requisite two thirds. But it would have made his nomination inevitable. Why, then, if the Underwood men had the power to decide the contest, did they not effect Clark's nomination? Why did they not accept the vice-presidential nomination for Underwood that the Clark managers probably offered them? In the first place, Wilson, not Clark, was the second choice of a good majority of the Underwood delegates; and in the second place, Underwood and his managers were after nothing less than the presidential nomination. Under no circumstances would Underwood have accepted the vice-presidential nomination.[68] The Underwood delegates still expected that both Clark and Wilson

67. *Ibid.*, p. 220.
68. This fact is attested to by Underwood's absolute refusal to accept the vice-presidential nomination when Wilson later offered it to him.

would fail to win the nomination and that it would eventually fall to the Alabamian.

The skillful bargaining of Wilson's managers, moreover, was probably the decisive factor in deciding Clark's defeat. They decided early in the balloting that since the Underwood delegations constituted the balance of power in the convention, it was "absolutely essential that some arrangement should be made with his forces by which we could supplement the Wilson forces with enough votes to block the convention." [69] Gregory, McCombs, and other Wilson managers had long conferences with leaders in the Underwood delegations and promised that if "Wilson should be put out of the race at any stage of the game" they would use their influence to throw the weight of the Wilson forces to the Alabamian. In return, the Underwood men agreed to remain loyal to their candidate.[70] Thus, a vote for Underwood was as good as a vote for Wilson and his managers were able to prevent the nomination of Champ Clark.

There yet remained the danger that McCombs, oftentimes nervous and panic-stricken, might take a fatal step that would ruin Wilson's chances for the nomination. Sen. William J. Stone, Clark's manager, had sent a telegram to Wilson, urging him to withdraw and insisting that party tradition demanded that Clark be nominated. Wilson had previously declared his opposition to the two-thirds rule on the ground that it was undemocratic,[71] but that was at a time when it appeared that it would militate against his chances for the nomination. Early Saturday morning, June 29, McCombs called Wilson on the telephone. He was very discouraged and suggested that Wilson give him an authorization to withdraw his name from the balloting. Wilson accordingly sent a telegram to that effect and even considered sending Clark a message of congratulations.[72] Later in the morning, when McAdoo discovered what McCombs had done, he immediately telephoned Wilson and urged him by no means to consider withdrawing from the contest because he was steadily gaining in strength and would

69. Gregory to House, *American Historical Review,* L (July 1945), 768–775.
70. *Ibid.;* Thomas P. Gore to the author, August 15, 1942.
71. Wilson to E. M. House, October 24, 1911, House Papers.
72. Joseph P. Tumulty, *Woodrow Wilson As I Know Him* (Garden City, N.Y.: Doubleday, Page & Co., 1921), p. 121.

eventually be nominated. Wilson authorized McAdoo to counter-
mand the withdrawal authorization he had given McCombs and
the danger was averted.[73]

The convention assembled on Saturday—the fifth day—to take
up again the laborious and monotonous task of balloting for the
nomination. The air was even yet charged with the excitement
of the preceding day. Had Clark's managers secured the two
hundred votes the Missourian needed for the nomination? The
succeeding ballots revealed that they had not. On the twelfth
ballot, Clark lost seven votes; Wilson lost half a vote. On the
thirteenth, the Missourian gained seven and a half; Wilson gained
two.[74]

Bryan had been profoundly disturbed when Murphy threw
New York's strength to Clark on the tenth ballot. Did not this
confirm the charge made by his brother that there had been a
bargain between Clark's managers and Tammany?[75] A number
of the Nebraska delegates demanded that their delegation cease
supporting Clark and go to Wilson's aid. Bryan, spokesman of
the Nebraskans, hesitated; he thought New York would go to
Underwood and Clark would then be nominated by the progressives. But he had promised the Nebraskans that he would not
support a Tammany candidate. Consequently he prepared a written statement explaining his change from Clark to Wilson which
he planned to use when it became necessary for him to desert
the Speaker.[76]

On the fourteenth ballot, Sen. Gilbert M. Hitchcock went
to the speaker's platform and demanded that Chairman James
take an official poll of the Nebraska delegation. When Bryan's
name was called, he rose and asked the convention's permission
to explain his reason for casting his vote as he was about to cast
it. Bryan declared that Nebraska was a progressive state and would
not participate in the nomination "of any man whose nomination

73. *Ibid.,* pp. 121–122; McAdoo, pp. 153–154; Josephus Daniels to the author, January
24, 1942; Robert S. Hudspeth to R. S. Baker, November 11, 1927, Baker Papers. The evidence
to support this position is simply overwhelming. McCombs in his completely unveracious
memoir, *Making Woodrow Wilson President* (New York: Fairview Publishing Co., 1921),
pp. 143–144, relates that he prevented Wilson from withdrawing.

74. *Proceedings of the Convention,* pp. 226–227, 230–231.

75. Bryan states that he "never heard anything other than circumstantial evidence
to support this charge," and, he says, he never made it himself. (Mary B. Bryan, p. 179.)

76. *Ibid.,* p. 182.

depends upon the vote of the New York delegation." He declared that he would withhold his vote from Clark so long as New York's vote was recorded for him. Although he cast his vote for Wilson, Bryan declared that he stood ready to withdraw his support from him should New York give him its support.[77]

Bryan's desertion of Clark infuriated the Speaker's supporters. They joined in a terrific onslaught of boos, hisses, and jeers against the Commoner. John B. Stanchfield of New York severely arraigned Bryan and said what many delegates were thinking but not publicly declaring. He shouted that "no man can go forth from this Convention stigmatized and branded with Bryanism, and come within half a million votes of carrying the state of New York."[78] In Washington, Champ Clark was furious. After a conference with his managers and William R. Hearst, he gave out a statement declaring that Bryan's charge was "an outrageous aspersion" and demanded immediate "proof or retraction" of Bryan's charges.[79] Clark went in haste to Baltimore to meet Bryan's challenge. Perhaps he might have started a stampede in his favor had he reached the convention in time. But he never got the chance, for the convention adjourned just as he was arriving.[80]

The balloting continued throughout Saturday, June 29. Bryan's conversion to Wilson on the fourteenth ballot did the New Jersey governor slight immediate good. Although he gained twelve votes from Nebraska, he lost several votes from various delegations. Clark's lines held firmly; he lost only one and a half votes. On the twentieth ballot, Kansas cast its twenty votes, which had hitherto been given to Clark, to Wilson.[81] The balloting was tedious and monotonous, but slowly Wilson gained new strength. His gains were so slight as to appear imperceptible; but when the convention adjourned on Saturday at the end of a hectic and

77. *Proceedings of the Convention,* pp. 233–237.
78. *Ibid.,* pp. 282–283
79. Baltimore *Sun,* June 30, 1912.
80. Clark never forgave Bryan for his action on the fourteenth ballot. Years later, he wrote that the Nebraskan, dishonestly and hypocritically, had endeavored to cause a deadlock "and grab off the nomination for himself." *My Quarter Century of American Politics,* 2 vols. (New York and London: Harper & Brothers, 1920), II, 424.
81. The change in the Kansas vote can hardly be ascribed to Bryan's influence. Wilson was the definite second choice of the Kansas delegation, which had instructions to vote for him when Clark's nomination appeared impossible.

exhausting week, Wilson had gained some sixty votes and Clark had lost Massachusetts to Governor Foss and Kansas to Wilson.[82]

June 30 was Sunday and, although the rank and file of the delegates enjoyed a much-needed rest, the political managers redoubled their efforts at the manipulation of bargains and trades. Wilson's opponents charged that his managers were making promises of patronage in order to secure blocs of delegates. Only once during the convention, according to Tumulty, did Wilson betray feelings of irritation. It was when he read these charges in the press.[83] Wilson wanted it understood that he would not be bound by any agreements. "There cannot by any possibility be any trading done in my name; not a single vote can or will be obtained by means of any promise," he declared.[84] His protests were undoubtedly well-meant, but McCombs, Burleson, and the other Wilson managers were on the ground at Baltimore and knew a great deal more about the necessities of the situation than he did. Already they had concluded very important agreements with Roger Sullivan and the Underwood delegations, and other important bargains and "promises" would follow.

Several of Wilson's managers dreaded lest Bryan might, at some dramatic moment, rally the progressives and capture the nomination for himself. His very actions throughout the length of the prenomination campaign led to such suspicions. Many observers thought that his policy of neutrality as between Clark and Wilson was an ill-disguised attempt to prevent either from securing a decisive majority of the convention vote.[85] On June 30, at a time when Wilson was gaining steadily in strength, the Commoner angered Wilson's managers by declaring that there was no reason why the delegates should not conclude their work the following day by nominating a President and vice-president.

82. The vote at the end of the twenty-fifth ballot stood: Clark, 469; Wilson, 405; Underwood, 108; Harmon, 29; Marshall, 30. *Proceedings of the Convention,* p. 272.

83. Tumulty, p. 117.

84. New York *World,* July 1, 1912.

85. Carter Glass later wrote that, several weeks before the convention, Bryan endeavored to persuade him that Wilson's nomination would mean suicide for the Democratic party. By the facility with which the Nebraskan eliminated all other Democratic candidates but himself, Glass concluded that he wanted the nomination for himself. (Carter Glass to Maurice F. Lyons, October 27, 1925, copy in Baker Papers.) Col. George Harvey was at the convention and wrote a friend that Bryan was greatly disappointed because he did not think he could be nominated. (E. S. Martin to E. M. House, July 24, 1912, House Papers.)

"There is every reason why the progressives should get together and select a ticket," he declared, adding that either Senator Kern, Ollie James, Senator O'Gorman, Senator Culberson, or Sen. Isidor Rayner of Maryland would be an acceptable candidate.[86] Bryan's selection of such political "light-weights" infuriated the Wilson men who were sure that the Commoner meant, by implication, to put his name at the head of the list. The Wilson leaders, furthermore, resented the fact that not once during the convention did Bryan publicly or privately advocate Wilson's nomination. They remembered that Bryan had voted for Wilson, not because he thought him the best candidate, but simply because New York had voted for Clark. And it is still a moot question whether Bryan had his eye on the nomination.[87]

In the meantime, the Tammany bosses and other conservative leaders, seeing that they could not defeat Wilson by direct assault, endeavored to undermine his strength by drawing away from him his supporters. John J. Fitzgerald and Murphy of Tammany, Roger Sullivan of Illinois, and Thomas Taggart of Indiana attempted to persuade Burleson and Palmer to withdraw Wilson's name from the contest. If they could persuade Wilson to withdraw, Murphy promised, "we will nominate [A. Mitchell] Palmer for President."[88] When this suggestion was instantly rejected by Palmer himself, the Tammany group turned next to the Texas delegation. They thought that if they could draw the Texans from the Wilson ranks, Wilson's candidacy would collapse. The Tammany men promised to support Culberson for president if the Texas delegation would lead the way by voting for him; but the entire delegation, including Culberson himself, indignantly rejected the suggestion.[89]

On Monday, July 1, the balloting for the presidential nomination was resumed. On the second ballot of the day, Taggart startled the convention by casting Indiana's twenty-nine votes, hitherto given to Marshall, to Wilson. When Iowa took fourteen votes from Clark and cast them for Wilson, he for the first time had

86. New York *Times*, July 1, 1912.

87. On the other hand, we have Mary B. Bryan's word that, although she tried to persuade her husband to endeavor to secure the nomination, he refused. (M. B. Bryan, pp. 334–335.)

88. R. S. Baker, "Memorandum of a Conversation with A. S. Burleson, March 17–19, 1927," Baker Papers.

89. *Ibid.*; San Antonio *Express*, July 1, 1912.

a greater vote than Clark.[90] In quick succession, the delegations from Vermont, Wyoming, and Michigan left the Clark ranks and joined the growing Wilson forces. Despite the gains made during the day, the Wilson leaders were still uncertain of success. True it was that Wilson had almost five hundred votes and was definitely in the lead. But his managers knew perfectly well that they had come to the end of their rope, that they had corralled practically every vote they could possibly hope to secure, and that unless either Roger Sullivan of Illinois or John H. Bankhead of Alabama committed their delegations to him, the Wilson movement would collapse as surely as had Clark's.

Sullivan had probably looked with favor upon the prospect of Wilson's nomination from the beginning. His son, a Princeton alumnus and an ardent Wilson supporter, had argued Wilson's cause consistently with his father.[91] The Illinois boss promised McCombs that when the Wilson men had secured sufficient strength to make Wilson's nomination appear probable he would come to their aid.[92] Something more than simple altruism motivated this veteran politician. In the first place, the Hearst-Harrison faction of the Illinois Democracy, Sullivan's archenemies, had first claims on Champ Clark, and Sullivan knew that if the Speaker were elected President he would receive few favors from the White House. It was better to support Wilson, who was not particularly his friend, Sullivan may have reasoned, than to give aid and comfort to his enemies. Moreover, the Illinois boss had not forgotten that the aid he received from the Wilson men in the contest over the Chicago delegation had enabled him to secure complete control of that delegation. And Roger Sullivan was not a man who forgot his "friends." On the first ballot taken in the convention on Tuesday, July 2, Sullivan accordingly fulfilled the promise he had made to the Wilson men on the preceding day and cast Illinois's fifty-eight votes for Wilson and gave the governor a majority of the convention vote.[93]

90. The vote on this, the thirtieth ballot, was: Wilson, 460; Clark, 455; Underwood, 121½; Harmon, 19. *Proceedings of the Convention*, p. 302.

91. The Trenton *True American*, July 6, 1912, has an interesting discussion of this point.

92. Thomas P. Gore to the author, August 15, 1942.

93. *Proceedings of the Convention*, p. 337.

In the meantime, Willard Saulsbury of Delaware had been assiduously pleading with the Democratic leaders from Kentucky, West Virginia, Maryland, and Virginia to cast in their lot with Wilson. McCombs, Saulsbury, and Sen. John W. Smith of Maryland met on the evening of June 30 with representatives from these states who agreed that, when the most favorable opportunity to nominate Wilson arose, they would transfer their delegations to him.[94] Sen. Clarence E. Watson of West Virginia decided to deliver his state's votes to Wilson,[95] while Sen. Thomas S. Martin startled the Virginia delegation by suggesting that they vote as a unit for Wilson. The Virginia Wilson men, who had consistently fought the application of the unit rule when it would have been a disadvantage to them, objected, but Martin was adamant and insisted that the state give its unanimous support to its native son.[96]

The dramatic swing-over of Illinois to Wilson on the forty-third ballot was the signal for Watson and Martin to act. When Virginia was called, Martin arose and delivered Virginia's twenty-four votes to Wilson. Immediately afterward, Watson, one of the original anti-Wilson men, made his peace with the progressives and cast West Virginia's sixteen votes for the New Jersey governor. Although Wilson now had over six hundred votes, his chances of securing the nomination were not entirely certain. The loyal Clark and Underwood delegates, together with New York's ninety votes, proscribed by Bryan, could easily maintain a deadlock and block forever Wilson's nomination.

The Underwood leaders were even yet hopeful that the Alabamian would be nominated. Sullivan, according to several accounts, promised Bankhead that he would deliver the Illinois delegation to Underwood sometime during July 2. But when the forty-fifth ballot passed and Sullivan did not fulfill his promise, Bankhead, J. Thomas Heflin, and Henry D. Clayton decided that it was time to call his hand. When they asked Sullivan what he

94. Lyons, pp. 98–100.

95. Memorandum of Charles H. Grasty in Baker Papers. Watson agreed to support Wilson if Grasty would give him full credit in the Baltimore *Sun* for his action. Grasty was happy to publicize Watson's swing-over to Wilson.

96. Richmond *Times-Dispatch*, July 3, 1912.

intended to do, the old veteran replied that he was going to swing Illinois back to Clark on the forty-sixth ballot.[97]

The forty-fifth ballot marked the major crisis for Wilson at Baltimore. Burleson and McCombs were convinced that if he could not gain the support of the Underwood delegations, Wilson would surely be defeated. Burleson was greatly excited and pleaded with Bankhead to release the Underwood delegates.[98] Bankhead, Heflin, and Clayton immediately decided to withdraw Underwood's name. This, they believed, would break the deadlock and result in Wilson's nomination.[99] When Alabama was called on the forty-sixth ballot, Senator Bankhead went quickly to the platform and withdrew Underwood's name. The convention was by this time in wild confusion. Senator Stone released the Clark delegates but announced that Missouri would cast her last vote for "old Champ Clark." John J. Fitzgerald of New York moved that Wilson be nominated by acclamation. Senator Reed objected; Missouri had no resentment toward Governor Wilson, but she must insist on casting her last ballot for Clark. The Harmon delegates were released and Wilson received 990 votes on the forty-sixth ballot. Amid the wildest confusion and tumult, the governor of New Jersey, at 3:30 in the afternoon of July 2, was made the Democratic nominee for President of the United States.[100]

The delegates were completely exhausted and wanted to go home as quickly as possible. The Wilson managers were almost physical wrecks; McCombs had had hardly an hour's sound sleep for more than a week.[101] But two important tasks had yet to be completed; the nomination of a vice-president and the adoption of a platform. Wilson did not know that McCombs had traded the vice-presidential nomination to Indiana in return for her votes and insisted that Burleson go to Washington and sound out Un-

---

97. Birmingham *Age-Herald*, July 4, 5, 7, 1912. Clark, who was following the events of the convention in Washington, made a hurried visit to Baltimore when he learned that Sullivan had deserted him. Seated in a cab outside the convention hall, Clark pleaded with Sullivan to return to his standard. Sullivan declared that he had promised the Wilson leaders to vote for Wilson, but that he would bring Illinois back to the Clark fold on the forty-sixth ballot. (T. P. Gore to the author, August 15, 1942.) Clark had probably agreed to recognize Sullivan as leader of the Illinois Democracy in the distribution of the patronage.

98. New Orleans *Times-Democrat*, July 3, 1912.

99. C. E. Stewart in Birmingham *Age-Herald*, July 4, 1912.

100. *Proceedings of the Convention*, pp. 345-353.

101. Gregory to House, *American Historical Review*, L (July 1945), 768-775.

derwood whom he desired as a running mate.[102] Fortunately for McCombs, Underwood refused to accept the nomination and it was consequently given to Gov. Thomas R. Marshall.[103] After adopting a progressive platform,[104] the convention adjourned.

Historians have for some reason or another written that Bryan's decision to vote for Wilson caused the latter's nomination,[105] and now a motion picture has given popularity to this interpretation. Certainly no person acquainted with the history of the Baltimore convention would underestimate the important work done by Bryan during the first struggles in the convention, during which time he became the acknowledged leader of the progressives. Hig fight against Parker undoubtedly forced a more or less clear-cut alignment between conservatives and progressives before the balloting had begun. It is not the present writer's intention or purpose to imply that Bryan did not have a considerable share in achieving Wilson's nomination; he desires, however, to emphasize the fact that there were other influences and persons at work which were perhaps just as important. It should be remembered, for example, that by voting for Wilson, Bryan did not deal the deathblow to the Clark candidacy, for by the

102. R. S. Baker, "Memorandum of Conversation with A. S. Burleson, March 17–19 1927," Baker Papers.

103. *Proceedings of the Convention,* p. 388.

104. The platform attacked the Republican protective tariff policy and promised that the Democrats would enact laws to destroy the trusts and regulate business; commended the proposed amendments for the adoption of the income tax and direct election of senators; pledged the Democratic candidate to the principle of a single term; and voiced Democratic opposition to the Aldrich plan or the establishment of a central banking system. With the blessing of Samuel Gompers, the Democrats adopted a plank which demanded jury trial in cases of criminal contempt of court and declared that labor organizations should be exempted from the provisions of the Sherman Antitrust Act. The platform further declared that it was Democratic policy to recognize the independence of the Philippine Islands as soon as a stable government might be established, and commended to the nation numerous other reforms. (*Proceedings of the Convention,* pp. 365–376.)

105. See, for example, Charles Seymour, *The Intimate Papers of Colonel House,* 4 vols. (Boston and New York· Houghton, Mifflin Co., 1926–1928), I, 66–67; Arthur D. Howden Smith, *Mr. House of Texas* (New York and London; Funk & Wagnalls Co., 1940), pp. 52–53; Samuel E. Morison and Henry S. Commager, *The Growth of the American Republic,* 2 vols. (New York: Oxford University Press, 1937), II, 422–423; Matthew Josephson, *The President Makers* (New York· Harcourt, Brace and Co., 1940), pp. 445–446; Gerald Johnson, *Woodrow Wilson* (New York and London: Harper & Brothers, 1944) p. 66; Dwight L. Dumond, *Roosevelt to Roosevelt* (New York: H. Holt and Co., 1937), p. 100; Louis M. Hacker and Benjamin B. Kendrick, *The United States since 1865* (New York: F. S. Crofts & Co., 1935), p. 452; Jeanette P. Nichols, *Twentieth-Century United States* (New York and London: D. Appleton-Century Co., 1943), pp. 161–162.

fourteenth ballot Clark's candidacy was a great deal less menacing than it had been on the tenth. He had already shown that he could not, under the best possible circumstances, win two thirds of the convention. Clark's boom was headed off, then, not by Bryan's belated action, but by virtue of the fact that the Wilson and Underwood delegates co-operated and held their ground. Consequently, the threat of Clark's nomination had passed when Bryan announced his vote for Wilson. If Bryan had been intent upon destroying Clark's chances for the nomination, it does appear logical that he would have come out against him on the eleventh, not the fourteenth ballot. In the second place, the balloting which followed Bryan's shift to Wilson further revealed that the Commoner's action had only an inconsequential effect on the voting. The reason for this is quite clear: Bryan's influence among the various delegations from the Underwood states and from the Northeast was practically nonexistent; his influence was strongest among the Clark delegations of the West, whom he alienated by his desertion of the Speaker. As a result of Bryan's voting for Wilson, the New Jersey governor eventually gained—by a liberal estimate—thirteen from Nebraska, fourteen from Iowa, and six from Wyoming—in all, only thirty-three votes and certainly not of sufficient importance to warrant the statement of a distinguished historian that "Bryan gave the word at last and Wilson was nominated." [106] As a matter of fact, Bryan was really on the periphery during the convention, as far as the Wilson managers were concerned. He never once identified himself with the Wilson leaders and never participated in their deliberations. The truth of the matter was that, after his action on the fourteenth ballot, Bryan played a role of inconsequential importance in the convention.

It is a part of the general irony of history that the nomination of Woodrow Wilson was made possible by the very men who had been his bitterest antagonists and who represented the forces against which he was struggling. Assuredly, it must be indelibly clear that without the support of the master politicians and political bosses—Roger Sullivan, Tom Taggart, Clarence E. Watson, Thomas S. Martin, and John H. Bankhead—Woodrow Wilson would not have received the Democratic nomination in 1912. It

106. William E. Dodd, "The Social and Economic Background of Wilson," *Journal of Political Economy;* XXV (March 1917), 279.

can be said with certainty that Wilson's nomination was not due to the work or influence of any single man or group of men. It is a long story from George Harvey's Lotos Club speech in 1906, suggesting Wilson for the presidency, to the Baltimore convention. Wilson's own political activities brought him first into the public consciousness; the labors of the little group of men in the national organization at 42 Broadway in New York City furthered his presidential movement; the important work of state politicians and editors won him support among the people; Bryan's fight at Baltimore emphasized the progressive character of Wilson's leadership and generated a widespread popular agitation for his nomination; the Underwood delegates helped prevent Clark's nomination at a critical time and, later during the balloting, definitely turned the tide in Wilson's favor; and, finally, the support of machine politicians brought over the votes without which Wilson could never have been nominated.

16

Theodore Roosevelt and the South in 1912

THE momentous schism in the Republican party which occurred at Chicago in June 1912 probably decided the outcome of the presidential campaign.[1] When Theodore Roosevelt, defeated by William Howard Taft for the Republican presidential nomination, led his angry followers out of the convention hall, he made it clear that he would accept the presidential nomination on the condition that a new party be organized. Accordingly, a call was issued for a convention of Roosevelt's supporters to meet in early August to organize the Progressive party.[2]

The Progressive convention which assembled in Chicago in August 1912 was one of the most remarkable political gatherings the country had witnessed. Social and economic reformers, disgruntled politicians, representatives of big business, idealists, and

Reprinted from the *North Carolina Historical Review,* XXIII (July 1946), 313–324, by permission of the Editor.

1. Research on this article was made possible by a grant from the Julius Rosenwald Fund.

2. The literature on the Progressive party is voluminous. Henry F. Pringle's *Theodore Roosevelt* (New York: Harcourt, 1931) and *Life and Times of William Howard Taft,* 2 vols. (New York: Farrar, 1939), are particularly good. The most recent and exhaustive work on the subject is George E. Mowry, *Theodore Roosevelt and the Progressive Movement* (Madison: University of Wisconsin Press, 1946). There is abundant material on the presidential campaign of 1912 in the Theodore Roosevelt Papers, Library of Congress, Washington, D.C.; hereinafter cited as Roosevelt Papers.

sundry others made up the motley crowd. Roosevelt was also there, feeling like a "Bull Moose."

In his "Confession of Faith," his keynote address to the Progressive convention, Roosevelt came out squarely in favor of a positive social democracy and championed practically every social and economic reform that had been proposed and had failed of accomplishment in the country. He emphasized the necessity for a central government powerful enough to regulate effectively the trusts and interstate corporations, determine fair minimum wages and hours for industrial laborers, and in every way possible exert its influences to safeguard the welfare of the people. Social justice, political reform, a sort of state socialism, and moral regeneration were the Bull Moose candidate's chief themes. "We stand at Armageddon, and we battle for the Lord," shouted Roosevelt as he concluded his keynote to a convention that resembled an old-fashioned religious revival more than a political convention.[3]

Southern editors, like their colleagues throughout the country, had always given Roosevelt priority on the front pages of their newspapers. And now this new third party constituted a threat to southern Democratic solidarity, for from the very start Roosevelt and the Progressives emphasized the national character of their organization and extended a hearty welcome to southerners to join with them in their fight for social justice. Roosevelt began the campaign by specifically declaring that the Progressive appeal was made "equally to the sons of the men who fought under Grant and to the sons of the men who fought under Lee, for the cause we champion is as emphatically the cause of the South as it is the cause of the North."[4] The colonel was almost pathetically anxious to break the solid South. "Really, if I could carry one of the eleven ex-Confederate States," he wrote, "I should feel as though I could die happy."[5] And he expected in 1912 to capitalize upon the discontent of southern businessmen and manufacturers with the new progressive leadership within the Democratic party. All that was necessary, he thought, was that

3. New York *Times* August 7, 1912.
4. Charleston *News and Courier*, June 24, 1912.
5. Roosevelt to John M. Parker, July 15, 1912, Roosevelt Papers.

the Progressive party should be completely disassociated from Republican traditions.[6]

After Roosevelt set forth his political and economic program in his "Confession of Faith," some liberal southern editors observed that many of his proposals were eminently desirable and that he was undoubtedly sincerely interested in the welfare of the people. His proposals to establish minimum wages and hours, for example, evoked warm praise from at least two progressive newspapers.[7] But liberal southern editors in general declared that, although Roosevelt's suggestions were commendable, they were either impossible of solution or impracticable in theory. Sincere progressives, these editors declared, should rally behind Woodrow Wilson, the only progressive candidate who could bring about the reforms the nation urgently needed.[8]

Most southern editors, however, had few kind words to say for the third party and its candidate. Perhaps they were determined to assail the prophet of the New Nationalism on any pretext. Several editors objected to him personally: they resented his obvious egotism and political methods. For example, Roosevelt's utterances sounded to one editor like the "caterwauling of monster alley cats,"[9] while other editors feared that the Progressive candidate was endeavoring to "carry out his treacherous ambition to destroy the government created by the founders,"[10] or to force a wild brand of resurrected populism or unmitigated socialism upon the country.[11]

Henry Watterson was guilty of the severest diatribes against the Progressive candidate. Old "Marse Henry" had quarreled with Wilson during the preconvention Democratic campaign and had become one of his bitterest critics prior to the New Jersey governor's nomination. But since it was not exactly politic for him to

6. Roosevelt to the members of the Progressive National Committee, undated letter in Roosevelt Papers.

7. Richmond *Times-Dispatch*, August 7, 1912; Mobile *Register*, August 7, 1912.

8. Dallas *Morning News*, August 8, 1912; Oklahoma City *Daily Oklahoman*, September 26, 1912; Nashville *Tennessean and American*, August 10, 1912; Richmond *Times-Dispatch*, August 7, 1912; Mobile *Register*, August 7, 1912.

9. Wilmington (N.C.) *Morning Star*, September 10, 1912.

10. Chattanooga *Daily Times*, August 7, 1912.

11. Montgomery *Advertiser*, August 8, 1912; Louisville *Times*, August 7, 1912; Charlotte *Daily Observer*, August 7, 1912.

continue his attacks against the Democratic presidential nominee, the old Kentuckian turned the full fury of his seething wrath against the colonel. Even before the Baltimore convention, "Marse Henry" had devoted one full editorial page of the *Courier-Journal* to a detailed and serious argument attempting to prove that Roosevelt was insane. How else, he asked, could one explain "The devilish streak of viciousness, the ignoble malignancy, the illogical intensity and inaccuracy of the lunatic?" [12] Roosevelt presented, Watterson later wrote, "the hideous spectacle of an ex-President, bawling like a drunken harlot from one end of the land to the other."[13] The old editor was in his happiest role as a maligner and carper and spent the summer lambasting the Progressive candidate.[14]

Like Watterson, other southerners utterly threw to the winds all discretion and temperance of judgment and completely went off balance in their denunciation of Roosevelt. Sen. Ben Tillman of South Carolina expressed the sentiment of many southern Democrats when he wrote, "It seems to me that the Devil has more to do with the world now-a-days than God Almighty." Otherwise he could not understand how "a crazy liar and all-round scoundrel like Roosevelt" could deceive so many people.[15] Even the responsible Nashville *Banner* charged that Roosevelt was without moral scruples and that he would "violate any law, overthrow any established usage, disregard his own plighted faith, or stab his nearest friend." [16] Another usually sane editor likewise wrote that the colonel was a "big, burly fellow, with the muscles of a thug, the voice of a bull of Bashan, and the assurance of a brass monkey." [17]

12. Louisville *Courier-Journal*, May 7, 1912.

13. Louisville *Courier-Journal*, May 23, 1912.

14. One of the best of these editorials is in the Louisville *Courier-Journal*, August 24, 1912.

15. B. R. Tillman to F. E. Barber, August 5, 1912, B. R. Tillman Papers, University of South Carolina, Columbia, S.C.

16. Nashville *Banner*, April 29, 1912.

17. "He is a great exaggerator," the editor added, "a great prevaricator; a great pilferer of other men's ideas; a great braggart; a great dodger; a great kicker when things don't go his way; a great baby when some bauble is given him; a great spender of other people's money; a great hand at being on both sides of every issue; a great hand at inventing facts to suit the occasion; he has a great lust for power." (Norfolk *Virginian-Pilot*, April 25, 1912.)

But illogical personal prejudice was not the only reason southerners objected to the Progressive movement and its leaders. The lily-white movement within the new party and its relation to the South alternately frightened and amused southern Democrats. Theodore Roosevelt meant to make a direct personal appeal to the southern people to break away from Democratic traditions and to join with him in what he thought was his movement for social and political regeneration. Many Negroes both in the North and in the South looked to him as their deliverer and hastened to join the Progressive ranks. But, manifestly, if the Progressive party was to gain a considerable number of adherents in the South, it had first of all to divorce itself from the Negro voters who, in the deep South at least, constituted the backbone of the old Republican party. This much was clear to John M. Parker of New Orleans, Roosevelt's chief southern political adviser, who warned the colonel that "this should be a white men's party, recognizing the superior ability of the white man and his superior civilization." The South, Parker added, "cannot and will not under any circumstances tolerate the Negro, and my firm belief is that a plank on these lines, diplomatically arranged would be productive of immense good." [18] In other words, the Progressive party had to be "lily-white" or a "white man's party" if it was to make any progress in the South.[19]

Roosevelt, however, was at first loath to make any conspicuous stand on the issue for fear of alienating many Negro voters in the North. In the latter part of July, he announced that the problem of the composition of the several state delegations to the national convention would have to be settled by the various state organizations.[20] This effort to sidestep the issue was entirely unsuccessful because in Georgia, Florida, Alabama, and Mississippi, rival white and Negro Progressive parties were organized and each sent a delegation to the national convention claiming to be the legitimate representatives of the party. And when these Negro delegates actually appeared in Chicago to contest the seating

18. J. M. Parker to Roosevelt, July 24, 1912, Roosevelt Papers; published in Arthur S. Link, editor, "Correspondence Relating to the Progressive Party's 'Lily-White' Policy in 1912," *Journal of Southern History*, X (November 1944), 481.

19. See also Julian Harris to Roosevelt, August 3, 1912, Roosevelt Papers; published in *Journal of Southern History*, X (November 1944), 488–490.

20. Charlotte *Daily Observer*, July 28, 1912.

of the white delegations, there was nothing left for Roosevelt to do except take a definite stand on the question.[21]

As a consequence, before the assembling of the Progressive national convention, Roosevelt, in a letter to Julian Harris,[22] set forth his position with regard to the Negro and his relation to the Progressive party. The traditional Democratic policy of setting whites against Negroes, and the Republican practice of setting Negroes against whites, had led to an almost ruinous situation, Roosevelt asserted. Since the Civil War, Republican delegates from the South had been largely Negroes who were easily bought and more easily controlled; the Progressive party could not deal with these black politicians from Dixie. The colonel made it plain to the country that the Progressives would appeal "to the best white men in the South, the men of justice and vision." By placing the Progressive movement in their hands from the outset, "we shall create a situation by which the colored men of the South will get justice as it is not possible for them to get justice if we are to continue and perpetuate the present conditions."[23]

In the meantime the Progressive provisional national committee was endeavoring to decide the question as to whether the white or Negro delegations from the South should be seated. The contest between the rival Florida delegations was so bitter that the state was allowed to go unrepresented. The white delegations from the other deep southern states were seated. And when the Progressive convention assembled at Chicago a few days later, Roosevelt revealed to an astonished South that his dictum against the Negro in politics pertained only to the would-be black Bull Moosers from below the Potomac. The convention on August 6, 1912, adopted the report of the credentials committee which excluded every Negro delegate from the South; but Negro delegates from the North were cordially welcomed by the Bull Moose leader who declared in a fulsome tribute to northern Negroes that since they "had won the respect of their communities" and were "the

21. George E. Mowry, "The South and the Progressive Lily-White Party of 1912," *Journal of Southern History*, VI (May 1940), 240.
22. Editor of *Uncle Remus's Home Magazine* (Atlanta) and one of the few prominent southern Roosevelt men.
23. Roosevelt to Julian Harris, August 1, 1912, Roosevelt Papers; published in Arthur S. Link, editor, "Correspondence Relating to the Progressive Party's 'Lily-White' Policy in 1912," *Journal of Southern History*, X (November 1944), 481–488.

peers of the white men," the Progressives by admitting them were setting a high standard for the southern states "to which we hope that our colored brethren [from the South] will come up." [24]

Few southerners believed that Roosevelt was sincere in his policy of North-South racial discrimination. They believed that it was simply a bid for southern Democratic support on the one hand and northern Negro votes on the other. "The great Bull Moose leader has summarily ejected the black mooses that hail from the sunny land of Dixie from his herd," one editor humorously commented.[25] Southern Democrats did not let Roosevelt forget, furthermore, that his convictions regarding the place of the Negro in southern politics were of too recent an origin not to warrant suspicion. They recalled the Crum incident, the suspension of the Indianola, Mississippi, post office, and the Booker T. Washington dinner at the White House. The colonel never once intimated that he had changed his democratic views concerning Negro-white relations in general, but southern newspapers implied that he had and when he dined with two Negro Progressives in Providence, Rhode Island, southerners were assured that Roosevelt still endorsed "social equality" for the races.[26]

The lily-white policy of the Progressive party was not the only basis for southern criticism of Theodore Roosevelt. His southern critics charged that he was a pawn in the hands of the trusts. That George W. Perkins of the harvester and steel trusts

24. "Extract from Mr. Roosevelt's Speech at the Coliseum, August 6, 1912. On the Negro Question." Manuscript in Roosevelt Papers.

25. Nashville *Banner,* August 6, 1912.

26. Providence *Bulletin,* August 17, 1912; Montgomery *Advertiser,* November 2, 1912. On the other hand, the Charleston *News and Courier,* August 12, 1912, and Columbia (S.C.) *State,* August 10, 1912, commended Roosevelt's seeming conversion to the southern viewpoint on the Negro's place in southern politics.

Josephus Daniels's pronouncement on the issue was a plain statement of the prevailing southern conviction regarding the Negro in politics. Out of her bitter experience, Daniels wrote, the South had evolved certain paramount convictions. The region was seeking not merely a sectional policy, but a national policy on the subject of the race question. The South would attain security, Daniels added, only by the general acceptance of a national policy embodying southern racial ideas and practices. If Roosevelt would emancipate the South, the Tar Heel editor insisted, he should recognize the justice of the southern claim "that the subjugation of the Negro, politically, and the separation of the Negro, socially, are paramount to all other considerations in the South, short of the preservation of the Republic itself." This, he asserted, was the *"Anglo-Saxon instinct of self-preservation,"* more profound than reason and deeper than experience. (Raleigh *News and Observer,* October 1, 1912.)

was Roosevelt's chief financial supporter was bad enough, southerners declared. But when Sen. Robert M. La Follette made known the fact of the rapid growth of trusts during the years of the Roosevelt presidency, Democratic critics could with some reason declare that the Bull Moose had been no consistent enemy of the trusts.[27] They insisted, moreover, that Roosevelt as President had proved unfaithful to his promise to support the Constitution when he allowed Morgan and Gary to incorporate the Tennessee Iron and Coal Company into the United States Steel Corporation. Josephus Daniels extravagantly labeled this act "The greatest crime that has ever been committed by any president of any Republic."[28] Southern editors generally ridiculed the Progressive candidate's promises that he would effectively regulate the trusts if he were elected President. They thought that, instead, the trusts would control Roosevelt.[29]

The disclosures of a Senate investigating committee in the fall of 1912 furnished southern critics with new ammunition to fire at Roosevelt. It was revealed authoritatively for the first time that the railroad magnate, Edward H. Harriman, had contributed personally $50,000 and had collected $200,000 for the Roosevelt campaign fund in 1904.[30] To make a bad situation worse for Roosevelt, it was further revealed that John D. Archbold gave $100,000 for Standard Oil and that George W. Perkins gave $50,000 for the New York Life Insurance Company. Roosevelt branded as false Harriman's statement that it was at the colonel's request that the railroad executive collected a quarter of a million dollars from Wall Street; and he declared that he knew nothing whatever about the Standard Oil contribution, but vigorous rebuttals from the men involved placed Roosevelt in a suspicious light. Southern editors, in "righteous anger," endeavored to paint his past record in the darkest colors and most sinister light. One critic was particularly harsh. Roosevelt was, he declared, a "wolf in sheep's clothing,—a decoy duck, an emissary of legalized piracy masquerading as a reformer."[31] An Arkansas editor thought Roosevelt was "not

27. Raleigh *News and Observer*, September 7, 1912.
28. Raleigh *News and Observer*, October, 6, 1912.
29. See also the Chattanooga *Daily Times*, September 10, 1912; Raleigh *News and Observer*, July 20, 1912; Houston *Post*, August 18, 1912; Little Rock *Arkansas Democrat*, August 17, 1912.
30. Louisville *Times*, October 3, 1912.
31. Norfolk *Virginian-Pilot*, July 7, 1912.

only the biggest hypocrite alive, but is entitled to all the other epithets that may be applied to an ungrateful master and subservient public servant."[32]

The Progressive candidate's allegations that the Democratic and Republican parties were boss-ridden and boss-controlled puzzled southern editors,[33] many of whom thought that Roosevelt himself was the most arrogant political boss in the country. They pointed, furthermore, to the obvious fact that William Flinn of Pennsylvania, a ringleader in Bull Moose councils, had the reputation of a corrupt and unscrupulous politician. Southern Democrats also objected to the high degree of governmental centralization envisaged in the New Nationalism. One editor saw the struggle between the New Freedom and the New Nationalism as *"a conflict between a government of delegated powers and a government of absolute powers, between Anglo-Saxon law and Roman law, between Democracy and Socialism."*[34] Southern progressives and conservatives alike voiced their opposition to Roosevelt's proposals for a protective tariff, the benefits of which were to be distributed to all the people. They feared that with his proposed Tariff Commission, his Trust Commission, and his numerous other suggested commissions, Roosevelt would inaugurate a regime of government by commission for the nation.[35]

Despite the impression of an apparent unanimity of feeling against Theodore Roosevelt and his Progressive program that one gets from the southern newspapers, there was considerable difference of opinion at the time as to the actual strength of the new party in the South. The New York *Times* attempted to probe southern political inclinations by gathering from leading Democrats in the region their opinions as to whether Roosevelt would carry any of the states below the Potomac. The southerners replied almost unanimously that they had no fear that the Progressives would make serious inroads in their respective states.[36]

32. Little Rock *Arkansas Democrat*, August 22, 1912.

33. Roosevelt to Eugene Thwing, July 16, 1912, Roosevelt Papers; see also T. Roosevelt, "Platform Insincerity," *Outlook*, CI (July 27, 1912), 660–662.

34. Atlanta *Journal*, September 1, 1912.

35. Atlanta *Journal*, September 29, 1912; Birmingham *Age-Herald*, July 12, 1912; Raleigh *News and Observer*, August 7, 1912; Dallas *Morning News*, August 8, 1912; Richmond *Times-Dispatch*, August 7, 1912; Norfolk *Virginian-Pilot*, July 29, 1912; Oklahoma City *Daily Oklahoman*, September 26, 1912.

36. New York *Times*, August 19, 1912.

But in every southern state except Oklahoma a lily-white Progressive party was organized. In Tennessee, Kentucky, North Carolina, and Virginia—states in which the Republicans were normally respectable minorities—the rise of the new party only caused a division within the Republican ranks; but in Georgia, Arkansas, and Alabama, thousands of enthusiastic Bull Moose supporters worked for Roosevelt's election.[37] In the remainder of the Deep South, the third party made little progress. It was in that section, according to one Mississippi editor, like the proverbial Panamanian army, a force with several hundred generals and but two privates.[38] At least two southern newspapers, the Memphis *News-Scimitar* and the Burlington (N. C.) *State-Dispatch,* espoused the Progressive cause, but only two men prominent in southern life—John M. Parker of New Orleans and Julian Harris of Atlanta—advocated Roosevelt's election.

Roosevelt himself felt that he had a great personal following in the South who would rally to his support if he could only deliver his appeal to them.[39] He determined, accordingly, to carry the fight to the heart of the enemy, to make a campaign tour in the South. Roosevelt opened his southern campaign "swing around the circle" at Little Rock, where he addressed a session of the Lakes-to-the-Gulf Deep Waterway Association on September 24, 1912. He confined himself largely to a discussion of flood control on the Mississippi River and offered the startling suggestion that the equipment used to build the Panama Canal be transported to the Mississippi Valley, once the Canal was completed, and "then we will have flood prevention, water conservation and river traffic."[40]

37. In Georgia, Roosevelt polled 22,010 (16.14% of the total vote), and Taft polled 5,190 votes (4.27% of the total vote). Arkansas gave 21,673 (17.66% of the total vote) to Roosevelt, and 24,297 votes (19.62% of the total vote) to Taft. Roosevelt polled 22,689 (19.26% of the total vote) and Taft 9,731 votes (8.26% of the total vote) in Alabama. *World Almanac, 1916, passim.*

38. New Orleans *Times-Democrat,* September 24, 1912, quoting Jones County (Miss.) *News.*

39. There can be no doubt that Roosevelt was something of a popular idol with many southerners. The numerous letters written by Progressives in the South to their leader testify to this fact. See, for example, James M. Williamson, Jr., to Roosevelt, June 7, 1912, and M. F. Anderson to Roosevelt, May 7, 1912, both in Roosevelt Papers.

40. Little Rock *Arkansas Democrat,* September 25, 1912.

At Memphis, on September 26, the colonel addressed a crowd of almost 5,000 persons at a meeting of the Interstate Levee Association and advocated a broad policy of flood control which would include every phase of soil reclamation, the building of reservoirs for the storage of flood waters, reforestation, the generation of electrical power from the water power accumulated, and the completion and strengthening of the levee system. At the state fairgrounds, he braved a pouring rain to shake hands with a crowd estimated by the local newspaper at 17,000.[41]

In his two addresses at Little Rock and Memphis, Roosevelt had carefully avoided a discussion of politics, but at New Orleans, on September 27, he set forth plainly his political appeal to the South. There was popular enthusiasm aplenty and the crowd gave the colonel a welcome that must have gladdened his heart. His southern manager, John M. Parker, introduced Roosevelt with an impassioned plea to the southern people to cast aside the fetters of political tradition and to join in the movement for economic and political regeneration. The colonel emphasized the necessity for federal control of the Mississippi and its levees, advocated protection for the cane and beet sugar industries, and pleaded for the abolition of what he called "artificial political lines" in the South. "I come here not to ask you to follow me," he declared, "but to ask you to join me." [42] It was in the interest of the South, he said, that he had come into the region to make his appeal in behalf of the Progressive party. "I want you to feel free to vote as your conscience inclines you to. If we win I want you to take your share in steering the wheels of the nation. I am less engaged in pleading my cause than in pleading yours." He ended his address by appealing to southerners who believed as he did to disregard tradition and join in the new political crusade.[43]

Roosevelt made a similar appeal in Montgomery on the morning of September 28,[44] but in Atlanta, during the evening of the same day, he launched an attack upon Woodrow Wilson before an audience numbering more than 10,000. He charged that Wilson had grossly and deliberately misrepresented his views in

41. Memphis *Commercial Appeal,* September 27, 1912.
42. New Orleans *Times-Democrat,* September 28, 1912.
43. Louisville *Courier-Journal,* September 28, 1912.
44. Montgomery *Advertiser,* September 29, 1912.

his campaign speeches and that the New Jersey governor was totally ignorant of present-day thought on political and economic questions.[45]

The Progressive candidate continued his "swing around the circle" in the South by going to Chattanooga for an address on the evening of September 30,[46] and concluded his southern tour with an address in Raleigh on October 1. At Raleigh, he recalled North Carolina's history and declared, "with such a history behind you, I think I have the right to come here and appeal to you to join us in the greatest movement for regeneration that you have seen or will see, as I believe." He further declared that the South, with "its old and native goodness," had the opportunity to aid in political regeneration. "I wish to see the South," he concluded, "come back into its position of national importance which it formerly had, and which by right it should have." [47]

The tumultuous reception Roosevelt received in every southern city in which he spoke could not have failed to increase his hopes of capturing at least one southern state, for his campaign proved one very definite thing: that, despite the onslaught of press and politicians, Roosevelt was popular with the southern people. Woodrow Wilson himself could have received no warmer welcome.

Roosevelt found, however, that it was his misfortune that people often shout one way and vote another, and he got only a small minority of the votes in the South. Why did the Progressives fail in their effort to win the support of southern progressives and liberals? Roosevelt received little support from southern liberals mainly because their own leader, for whom they had long been struggling, was now the Democratic presidential nominee. Southern progressives were generally convinced, furthermore, that Wilson was a true progressive leader, whereas many of them thought that Roosevelt was an opportunist and a demagogue. These liberals stood to gain everything politically should the Democratic candidate become President of the United States, and they were naturally unwilling to desert the candidate for whom they had been fighting, to become the advocates of an obviously lost cause. Southern conservatives, on the other hand, opposed

45. Atlanta *Constitution,* September 29, 1912.
46. Chattanooga *Daily Times,* October 1, 1912.
47. Raleigh *News and Observer,* October 2, 1912.

Roosevelt for different reasons. Although some of them might look with favor upon his protective tariff policy, they viewed with suspicion and distrust his program of social, political, and economic reform. Wilson was too "radical" to suit their tastes, but even he was not as "radical" in their eyes as was Roosevelt.

After the furor and name-calling of the campaign had given way to a serious consideration of Roosevelt's mission, however, progressive southerners must have agreed with the editor of the Richmond *Times-Dispatch* who wrote that the Progressive candidate was not a "vulgar charlatan, or a cheap demagogue," but that he was a spokesman for the discontent of the American people. The idealism of the Progressive movement, the editor concluded, still lived and reigned. There was no defeat at Armageddon, for Woodrow Wilson's dream of the ideal republic might yet be realized if all good men set their hearts and their hands to the great work of reconstructing the American commonwealth.[48]

48. Richmond *Times-Dispatch,* November 6, 1912.

17

The Negro as a Factor in the Campaign of 1912

NOTWITHSTANDING the divergent interpretations of southern political history from the Populist movement to the present, all historians of the South agree substantially that the Negro was effectively and almost completely disfranchised by the southern states after 1890.[1] The Populist movement split the Democratic party in several southern states, brought again to the front the question of the Negro's participation in politics, and ended with a general agreement between the agrarian and Bourbon leaders that the Negro should be removed, once and for all, from the southern political scene. From 1890 to 1910, eight states adopted amendments to their constitutions that had the effect of denying the ballot to the Negro,[2] while the remaining southern states engineered, by statutory restriction, a disfranchisement that was just as effective.[3]

Reprinted from *The Journal of Negro History*, XXXII (January 1947), 81–99, by permission of the Editor.

1. This paper was read at the thirty-first annual meeting of the Association for the Study of Negro Life and History in Philadelphia on October 26, 1946. The author wishes to acknowledge his indebtedness to the Julius Rosenwald Fund, whose grants financed research on this article.

2. Mississippi in 1890, South Carolina and Louisiana in 1895, North Carolina in 1900 and 1905, Alabama and Virginia in 1901, Georgia in 1908, and Oklahoma in 1910.

3. The most convenient summary of the disfranchisement movement is Paul Lewinson, *Race, Class, and Party* (London and New York: Oxford University Press, 1932), pp. 79–97.

The explanation most freely given by southern Democratic leaders for this assault upon the political rights of Negro citizens was that the Negro constituted a debauching influence in the region's political life and that the whites could never divide on political and economic issues until their fears of "Negro domination" had been laid permanently to rest. Although we are concerned here with neither the sincerity nor the truth of these asseverations, it might not be amiss to point out that the southern leaders succeeded in disfranchising a considerable number of lower class whites along with the Negroes. At any rate, the presumption would seem to be that the Negro, as an issue in political controversies, would cease to play a significant role in southern life. Such, of course, was not to be the case. From 1890 until the recent enfranchisement movement of the 1940s, the Negro has played a role of major importance in southern politics. But it has been a negative role that he has played, negative in providing an eternal whipping boy for southern demagogues; in furnishing for politicians with their backs to the wall a bogus issue with which to becloud the real issues at stake; in offering an ever-present scapegoat upon which the southern white masses might vent their frustrated emotions.

One case in point is the Democratic preconvention campaign of 1911–1912, which constitutes a springboard for our discussion of the Negro in the campaign of 1912. The rise of Woodrow Wilson to political leadership from 1910 to 1912 is one of the most amazing success stories in American history. Beginning his public career as a progressive reform governor of New Jersey, Wilson succeeded in making a strong bid for the Democratic presidential nomination in 1912 and for national party leadership. Campaigning throughout the nation in his fight for the nomination, he appealed especially to the progressive Democrats in the South for support. Such support was indeed forthcoming, but the rising tide of Wilson-progressive sentiment in the South engendered also a political reaction in the form of the candidacies of Oscar W. Underwood of Alabama and Champ Clark of Missouri. The result was a bitter preconvention struggle in the South.

Even in a campaign such as this, in which the Negro, by no conceivable stretch of imagination, was an issue, the South could not escape the disgrace of witnessing the injection of the race question by unscrupulous politicians. By far the worst offender was Tom Watson, erstwhile Populist congressman from Georgia and once a leader in the reform movement in that state. By 1912, Watson had long since abandoned his progressive economic and racial ideas and was now one of the chief pillars of support of the reactionary Joseph M. Brown Democratic faction in Georgia. Undertaking personally to defeat the Wilson movement in the state in 1912, Watson published, through the medium of his weekly newspaper, *The Jeffersonian,* as scurrilous and abusive a series of attacks on Wilson as were to be found in the country.

Watson attacked Wilson on all sides—as a Tory, an enemy of the workingman and farmer, a slave of the Pope, ally of Hoke Smith, and, above all, as a friend of the Negro. Wilson, Watson asserted, was "ravenously fond of the Negro," because he had sent to Booker T. Washington a message of condolence and confidence, "when that coon was caught at a white woman's bed-room door, and was deservedly beaten for it." [4] Watson objected, besides, because Wilson had allegedly been president of "a social equality college, where negro youth were admitted on the same terms as the white boys," and because in his letters to eminent Negroes, Wilson addressed them "in the same way he would address . . . any other distinguished white man." [5] Watson's influence among the farmers of Georgia, unfortunately for the state, was immense, and certainly his abusive attacks on Wilson were in large measure responsible for Wilson's defeat in the Georgia presidential primary.[6] It should be noted that although the Underwood newspapers in the South refused to echo Watson's charges, the conservative politicians in Georgia welcomed his support, and Underwood personally acknowledged his indebtedness to the Georgia demagogue.[7]

On the other hand, Watson's allegations that Wilson treated Negroes like human beings were taken up by a Clark manager in Fort Worth, Texas, who published and circulated some 15,000 copies of a malicious pamphlet entitled, "The Nigger and the

4. *The Jeffersonian* (Thomson, Ga.), April 11, 1912.
5. T. E. Watson to W. J. Jelks, December 21, 1912, Thomas E. Watson Papers, University of North Carolina, Chapel Hill, N.C.
6. See Arthur S. Link, "The Democratic Preconvention Campaign of 1912 in Georgia," *Georgia Historical Quarterly,* XXIX (September 1945), 143-158.
7. O. W. Underwood to T. E. Watson, published in *The Jeffersonian,* May 9, 1912.

Governor of New Jersey."[8] This maneuver so alarmed Wilson's managers in Texas that they obtained from Wilson personally a specific denial that he had ever sent the alleged message of condolence to Booker T. Washington.[9]

After a protracted struggle in the national convention at Baltimore, Wilson was nominated for the presidency on July 2, 1912. From that day forward, he of course became the acknowledged leader and spokesman of the national Democracy, and consequently charges accusing him of friendship toward the Negro ceased in the South. Strictly speaking, there was no race issue in the presidential campaign that followed in the North and East in 1912. On the contrary, the apparent closeness of the three-cornered campaign among Wilson, Taft, and Roosevelt even drove the Democratic managers to the unprecedented step of seeking the Negro vote in the North. In the South, on the other hand, the attempt by Theodore Roosevelt to organize a lily-white Progressive party stirred up the Negro issue anew and afforded southern Democratic spokesmen an opportunity to dilate at length on the subject.

Let us consider first the Democratic campaign in the North as it affected the Negro voter. The day had not yet arrived when the Democratic party assiduously courted the Negro vote, or when the Negroes held a delicate balance of power in the large northern states. Yet the Wilson managers in 1912 did make an open bid for Negro support that has hitherto gone unnoticed by historians.

Democratic approval was given, for example, to the organization in September of a National Negro Wilson League in Richmond, Virginia, for the purpose of providing Negro orators for the Democratic national committee in the North. The League issued an address to the Negro voters of the United States, calling on the Negroes of the South to cooperate with their southern white neighbors and appealing to the Negro voters of the North to break their traditional allegiance to the Republican party. One wonders, however, whether this organization's activities among northern Negro groups did not do more harm than good to the Wilson cause, in light of the fact that its announced purpose was

8. T. B. Love to E. M. House, May 5, 1912, Edward M. House Papers, Library of Yale University, New Haven, Conn.
9. Dallas *Morning News*, May 2, 1912.

the promotion of sympathy for the southern white point of view on the race question.[10]

Wilson, moreover, personally recognized the National Independent Political League of Washington, a Negro Democratic organization, as one of his representatives, and the publications of the League had the approval of the national committee.[11] In addition, a total of $52,255.95 was expended by the New York office of the Democratic campaign headquarters for the purpose of obtaining Negro votes.[12]

Unfortunately, there are no pamphlets in the Wilson Papers or other depositories issued by the Democratic campaign committee to the Negro voters. There exists, however, one recorded Democratic appeal that indicates the extent to which the Democratic politicians were willing to go. Entitled "Quo Vadis?" and published in the November issue of the *Crisis,* the appeal asserted that the Negro had suffered politically because of his unfaltering loyalty to the Republican party, that the party of Lincoln had failed to protect his civil and political rights. Negro delegates had nominated Taft at Chicago, yet the Taft supporters had refused to insert a radical plank on the race question in the Republican platform. Theodore Roosevelt had deserted the Negroes in the South. Where could the Negro go for justice? He must find protection in the Democratic party, which believed in equal rights to all.[13] Actually, this appeal was a masterpiece of evasion, for nowhere did it specifically promise that the Democratic party would henceforth defend the political rights of the Negro, or cease to be dominated ideologically by the southern wing. Yet it is significant at least for what it represents—an open appeal by Democrats for Negro support.

It required more than propaganda and the expenditure of thousands of dollars to convince the Negroes that the Democratic party had become, overnight, the friend and protector of their race. With good cause, the intellectual Negro leaders feared that a Democratic Congress and administration controlled by southern

10. Richmond *Times-Dispatch,* September 5, 1912.
11. See J. M. Waldron and J. D. Harkless, *The Political Situation in a Nut-Shell. Some Un-Colored Truths for Colored Voters* (Washington: Trades Allied Printing Council, 1912), for an example of this organization's appeal for Negro support for Wilson.
12. Rolla Wells, *Report of the Treasurer, Democratic National Committee. Presidential Campaign of 1912* (St. Louis: Allied Printing, 1913), p. 172.
13. "Quo Vadis?" *The Crisis,* V (November 1912), 44–45.

white men might enact legislation hostile to their interests. They knew, for example, that James K. Vardaman of Mississippi had been elected to the United States Senate in 1911 on a platform demanding the modification of the Fourteenth and the repeal of the Fifteenth Amendments. What, except hostility and an attitude of scorn and contempt, could the Negroes expect from the Democratic party when a responsible Democratic spokesman and Wilson manager, Josephus Daniels, published an editorial in the fall of 1912 in which he announced that the South would never feel secure until the whole southern program of political oppression and social segregation had been adopted by the northern and western states! [14]

Negroes feared, moreover, that Wilson was a southerner who had inherited all the usual baggage of southern racial prejudices. As one Negro editor put it: "The New York *Age* does not see how it will be possible for a single self-respecting Negro in the United States to vote for Woodrow Wilson. . . . Both by inheritance and absorption he has most of the prejudices of the narrowest type of southern white people against the Negro." [15] W. E. Burghardt Du Bois, certainly the most responsible spokesman of militant Negro opinion, expressed the same foreboding more temperately when he wrote, "On the whole, we do not believe that Woodrow Wilson admires Negroes." [16]

The truth is that, although he never shared the extreme anti-Negro sentiments of many of his contemporaries, Wilson remained throughout his life largely a southerner on the race question. He had an extravagant and romantic love for the South, which increased in direct ratio to his absence from the region. Not once in his entire career before 1912 had he lifted his voice in defense of the minority race. As president of Princeton University he had, by evasion, prevented Negroes from enrolling. [17] As a matter of fact, Mrs. Wilson felt much more strongly about drawing the color line than did her husband, but both were opposed to social relations between the races. [18]

14. Raleigh *News and Observer,* October 1, 1912.
15. New York *Age,* July 11, 1912.
16. *The Crisis,* IV (August 1912), 181.
17. See Stockton Axson to R. S. Baker, October 31, 1928, Ray Stannard Baker Papers, Library of Congress, Washington, D.C., for a discussion of this point.
18. R. S. Baker, "Memorandum of an interview with Jessie W. Sayre, December 1, 1925," manuscript in Baker Papers.

262 The Higher Realism of Woodrow Wilson

The Negro question was one of those ticklish problems, like the liquor question and woman suffrage, that Wilson would have preferred to ignore. He was badgered so constantly by his reformer friends and by the Negroes themselves, however, that soon after the Baltimore convention he was forced to deal with the spokesmen of the race. On July 16, he conferred with the Reverend J. Milton Waldron and William Monroe Trotter, representatives of the National Independent Political League of Washington; two weeks later, he spoke to a delegation from the United Negro Democracy of New Jersey, who called at Sea Girt. "I was born and raised in the South," he declared:

There is no place where it is easier to cement friendship between the two races than there. They understand each other better there than elsewhere. You may feel assured of my entire comprehension of the ambitions of the negro race and my willingness and desire to deal with that race fairly and justly.[19]

This, of course, sounded like the apologies for racial discrimination that any southern Bourbon might make; something more definite and assuring was necessary before Negro leaders would give Wilson their approval. Oswald Garrison Villard, grandson of William Lloyd Garrison, crusading editor of the New York *Evening Post*, and one of the founders of the National Association for the Advancement of Colored People, was in 1912 unquestionably the leading white champion of Negro rights in the United States. He was, moreover, on fairly intimate terms with Wilson, because he had given Wilson his own and his newspaper's enthusiastic support in the gubernatorial contest in 1910 and in the hotly disputed battle for the Democratic nomination. It was natural, therefore, that he should become Wilson's chief adviser on the race question, and that Wilson should turn time and again to him for advice.

On August 13, a month after the Baltimore convention, Villard went to Trenton for a three hours' conference with the Democratic nominee. Their conversation centered about four subjects in which Villard was particularly interested: woman suffrage, the navy question, the New York political situation, and the general question of the Negro. Villard was not entirely satisfied with Wilson's

19. Trenton *Evening Times*, July 31, 1912.

attitude on the first three issues, but he was delighted by Wilson's pronouncements on the race question. Among other things, Wilson told him that of course he would attempt to be President of all the people and that, in the matter of appointments, merit, and not race or creed, would be the deciding factor.[20] He said, furthermore, that he would gladly speak out in denunciation of lynching—"every honest man must do so"—but he did not want the Negro people to form the impression that he, as President, could help them in this matter. Finally, Wilson promised to send to Villard a statement of his attitude toward the problem for publication in the *Crisis* and the New York *Evening Post*.[21] The day following the Trenton meeting, Villard wrote to Wilson, strongly urging him to go as far as he consistently could in assuring the Negroes that they would have equal treatment before the law and that he also would not discriminate against them, either in the matter of appointments, or in other ways.[22]

Meanwhile, as has been briefly noted above, Wilson conferred at Trenton on July 16 with the Reverend J. Milton Waldron and William Monroe Trotter. After the meeting was over, Waldron apparently attempted to set down from memory the details of Wilson's conversation. The result was an unauthorized statement that was printed in the September issue of the *Crisis*, in which Wilson was quoted as having said that he needed and sought Negro support in the campaign and pledged himself to deal with Negroes, if he were elected President, as he would deal with other citizens, both in executing the laws and in making appointments. Wilson, moreover, allegedly assured Waldron and Trotter that Negroes had nothing to fear from a Democratic Congress and that if, by some accident, Congress should enact legislation inimical to the Negro's interest, he would veto such laws.[23]

The publication of the Waldron statement caught Wilson off balance; he apparently had not seen a copy of what Waldron

20. "The only place," Wilson said, "where you and I will differ is as to where the entering wedge should be driven." Wilson stated that he would not make an appointment like that of Crum at Charleston, because he felt such appointments resulted in very great injury to the Negro people and increased racial antipathies.

21. Oswald Garrison Villard, memorandum, dated August 14, 1912, of an interview with Wilson on August 13, 1912. Manuscript in the private papers of O. G. Villard, New York City. All materials from these papers are used by permission of Mr. Villard.

22. O. G. Villard to Wilson, August 14, 1912, Villard Papers.

23. For which, see *The Crisis*, IV (September 1912), 216–217.

published until Villard sent him one on August 14, and he was irritated and alarmed beyond measure. In great haste, Wilson wrote to Villard on August 23 that he had just read with amazement the Waldron statement. He of course had said that he would seek to be President of the whole country, and he had declared that the Negroes had nothing to fear from a Democratic Congress. On the other hand, he had not promised to veto legislation inimical to the Negro's interest, for he would make no such promise to any man; he had not said that he felt himself in need of Negro votes; and he had not given his listeners any assurances about appointments, "except that they need not fear unfair discrimination." Wilson concluded with an urgent plea that Villard prepare a general statement along the lines of what he, Wilson, had just written, which might be issued as Wilson's own statement.[24]

A few days later, Villard replied to this appeal by sending to Wilson a statement that W. E. B. Du Bois had drawn up. Villard was obviously disturbed by Wilson's refusal to commit himself to the Waldron statement. Thus he wrote:

So far as your proposed statement is concerned, I feel very strongly that nothing important can be accomplished among the colored people until we have an utterance from you which we can quote. They not unnaturally mistrust you because they have been told that Princeton University closed its doors to the colored man (and was about the only Northern institution to do so) during your presidency. They know that besides yourself, both Mr. McAdoo and Mr. McCombs [25] are of Southern birth, and they fear that the policy of injustice and disfranchisement which prevails not only in the Southern states, but in many of the Northern as well, will receive a great impetus by your presence in the White House. Again, as I explained to you, they want some assurance that they will not wholly be excluded from office, office meaning so much to them because the bulk of their race are absolutely deprived of any self-government, even in the smallest matters such as schools and the making of the town ordinances in which they live.[26]

23. For which, see *The Crisis*, IV (September 1912), 216–217.

24. Wilson to Villard, August 23, 1912, Villard Papers.

25. William G. McAdoo and William F. McCombs, vice-chairman and chairman, respectively, of the Democratic national committee in 1912.

26. Villard to Wilson, August 28, 1912, Villard Papers.

The conclusion is inevitable that the Du Bois statement, although it was exceedingly moderate in tone, went entirely farther than Wilson was willing to go. Obviously, he was not willing to assure the Negroes, as Du Bois had suggested, that the Democratic party sought and would welcome their support as American citizens, and that the Democrats were opposed to disfranchisement on account of race.[27]

The limit to which Wilson was willing to go was made evident in October. Bishop Alexander Walters of the African Zion church, who had joined the Democratic party in 1909 and who was in 1912 president of the National Colored Democratic League, invited Wilson to speak before a mass meeting of the League in New York City. Wilson replied that he could not attend the meeting because he had cancelled his speaking engagements until Roosevelt, who had recently been shot by an anti-third term fanatic, was again on the stump. On the other hand, there were certain things that he did want to say to the colored people: that he earnestly desired to see justice done them in every matter, "justice executed with liberality and cordial good feeling," and that his sympathy with the Negroes in their struggle for advancement was

27. The statement is of such great importance that it is here given in full:
   The time has come when the attitude of the Democratic Party toward Americans of Negro descent may be easily and clearly defined. The Democratic Party as a political organization working for the best governing of men recognizes no distinctions of race or caste among citizens. It asks the votes of citizens not because they are Italian, German or Negro, but because they are Americans. It offers no bribe of office or special class legislation but only the legitimate bribe of good government. If American Negroes desire more equitable tariff taxes, a wider participation of the people in government, a curbing of the sinister political power of accumulated wealth, then they should vote for the Democratic Party and the Party will welcome their support. On the other hand, no class of rich or poor, black or white, has anything to fear from the triumph of this party. We are not in favor of unfair discriminating laws against any class or race, and we believe that the qualifications for voting should be the same for all men. If ignorance and crime be a bar to the suffrage, it should be just as much a bar to white men as to black.
   On this broad platform, without special promises or discrimination of any kind, the Democracy appeals to the Voters of all races represented in our cosmopolitan citizenship. I shall be, if elected, President of the whole nation and treat every citizen according to the spirit of our institutions. I am glad of this opportunity to deny the published reports of many negro newspapers that I am hostile to the colored people, and that if I am elected no colored man will be appointed to office. It would seem as if my record as Governor of New Jersey would forbid anyone misrepresenting me by saying that I will connive at any form of civic wrong or injustice. (Manuscript in the Villard Papers.)

of long standing. "I want to assure them through you that should I become President of the United States," Wilson concluded, "they may count upon me for absolute fair dealing and for everything by which I could assist in advancing the interests of their race in the United States." [28]

Apparently, this unequivocal promise of fair dealing, although stated in vague and general terms, had the effect of swinging Du Bois and many other leaders of militant Negro opinion in the North to the Wilson ranks.[29] Although Du Bois had profound misgivings about supporting Wilson, he distrusted Taft and Roosevelt even more, and resigned his membership in the Socialist party in order to support the Wilson cause. It was better, he concluded, "to elect Woodrow Wilson President . . . and prove once for all if the Democratic party dares to be Democratic when it comes to the black man." The party had proved that it could be democratic in many northern cities and states. "Can it in the nation?" Du Bois asked. "We hope so and we are willing to risk a trial." [30]

During the fall and summer of 1912, be it noted, not one word was said by southern Democratic newspapers or spokesmen of Wilson's overtures to the Negroes. Such maneuvers were, it would seem, an apt example of not letting one's right hand know what his left hand doeth! In the southern states, however, Democratic leaders were more concerned about the lily-white movement in the newly-organized Progressive party.

Theodore Roosevelt meant to make a direct personal appeal to the southern people to break away from Democratic traditions and to join with him in what he asserted was his movement for social and political regeneration. Many Negroes, both in the North and in the South, looked to him as their deliverer and hastened to join the Progressive ranks. Yet the Roosevelt leaders in the South believed that if the Progressive party was to win a large following in the region, it had first of all to divorce itself from the few Negro voters who, in the deep South at least, constituted

28. Letter published in Alexander Walters, *My Life and Work* (New York: Fleming H. Revell Co., 1917), pp. 194–195.

29. W. E. B. Du Bois, *Dusk of Dawn; an Essay toward an Autobiography of a Race Concept* (New York: Harcourt, Brace and Co., 1940), p. 234.

30. *The Crisis*, V (November 1912), 29.

the backbone of the old Republican party. So thought John M. Parker of New Orleans, Roosevelt's chief southern adviser, who warned the colonel, "this should be a white men's party, recognizing the superior ability of the white man and his superior civilization." The South, Parker added, "cannot and will not under any circumstances tolerate the Negro, and my firm belief is that a plank on these lines, diplomatically arranged, would be productive of immense good." [31] In other words, the Progressive party had to be lily-white if it was to make any progress in the South.[32]

Roosevelt was at first loath to take any conspicuous stand on the issue for fear of alienating many Negro voters in the North. In the latter part of July, for example, he announced that the problem of the composition of the several state delegations to the national convention would have to be settled by the various state organizations.[33] This effort to sidestep the issue was unsuccessful because, in Georgia, Florida, Alabama, and Mississippi, rival white and Negro progressive parties were organized, and each sent a delegation to the national convention claiming to be the legitimate representatives of the party. And when these Negro delegates actually appeared in Chicago to contest the seating of the white delegations, there was nothing left for Roosevelt to do except take a definite stand on the question.[34]

In a letter to Julian Harris of Atlanta, Roosevelt on August 1 set forth his new position with regard to the Negro in southern politics. There is no doubt that he felt considerable resentment against the action of the southern Negro delegates at the Republican national convention in supporting Taft for renomination; in his letter to Harris, he asserted that the practice of sending Negro delegates from the South to Republican national conventions had finally been responsible for "the disruption and destruction" of the Republican party. Perhaps this in large measure accounts for

31. J. M. Parker to Roosevelt, July 24, 1912. Theodore Roosevelt Papers, Library of Congress, Washington, D.C.; also published in Arthur S. Link, editor, "Correspondence Relating to the Progressive Party's 'Lily-White' Policy in 1912," *Journal of Southern History,* X (November 1944), 481.

32. For an expression of the same point of view, see Julian Harris to Roosevelt, August 3, 1912, Roosevelt Papers; published in *Journal of Southern History,* X (November 1944), 488–490.

33. Charlotte (N.C.) *Daily Observer,* July 28, 1912.

34. George E. Mowry, "The South and the Progressive Lily-White Party of 1912," *Journal of Southern History,* VI (May 1940), 240.

his determination to build his party in the South on an exclusive white basis.

Roosevelt's letter to Harris was long and involved; it covers almost seven closely printed pages. It abounds with expressions of a friendly feeling and concern for the welfare of the southern Negroes. The result, nonetheless, was the same: Roosevelt unreservedly capitulated to the southern white argument against the Negro's participation in the political life of the South. The traditional Democratic policy of setting whites against Negroes, and the Republican practice of setting Negroes against whites had led to an almost ruinous situation, he asserted. Since the Civil War, Republican delegates from the South had been largely Negroes who were easily bought and more easily controlled; the Progressive party could not deal with these Negro politicians. On the contrary, Roosevelt made it plain that the Progressives would appeal "to the best white men in the South, the men of justice and vision." By placing the Progressive movement in their hands from the outset, he added, "we shall create a situation by which the colored men of the South will get justice as it is not possible for them to get justice if we are to continue and perpetuate the present conditions." On the other hand, the Progressive party was appealing for the support of the better class of Negro voters in the northern states, and there would be many Negro delegates from these states in the Progressive convention. "Our only wise course from the standpoint of the colored man himself," he concluded, "is to follow the course that we are following toward him in the North and to follow the course we are following toward him in the South." [35]

Meanwhile, the Progressive provisional national committee was endeavoring to decide the question whether the white or Negro delegations from the South should be seated. The contest between the rival Florida delegations was so bitter that the state was allowed to go unrepresented. On August 3, the committee refused to seat twelve Negroes and seated as many white delegates from Alabama.[36] The fight over the Mississippi delegation was particularly bitter. The Negro delegates who were unseated by

35. The original letter is in the Roosevelt Papers; it is published in the *Journal of Southern History*, X (November 1944), 481–488.
36. Birmingham *Age-Herald,* August 4, 1912.

the provisional national committee appealed on August 6 to the credentials committee of the convention; after a heated controversy in that committee, they were refused their seats by a vote of 17 to 16.[37] On the same day, the convention adopted the report of the credentials committee that excluded every Negro delegate from the South. On the other hand, Roosevelt, in his speech accepting the presidential nomination, cordially welcomed Negro delegates from the North. They were, he declared, the peers of white men; by admitting them, the Progressive convention had set high standards for the southern states, "to which we hope that our colored brethren [from the South] will come up." [38]

Clearly, however, Roosevelt was not about to embark upon any crusade for the Negro, and this fact was made certain when he refused to allow the adoption of a Negro rights plank in the Progressive platform. Du Bois, who had at first greeted Roosevelt's movement with great enthusiasm, had written a proposed plank for the platform, demanding the repeal of discriminatory laws and a guarantee for the Negro's right to vote. The resolution was taken to Chicago by Joel Spingarn, an official of the NAACP; at the convention, Spingarn, Henry Moskowitz, and Jane Addams labored in vain for its adoption.[39]

In the South, Democratic spokesmen refused to believe that Roosevelt was sincere in his policy of North-South racial discrimination, or that his appeal to the white men of the region was anything more than a bid for southern Democratic support. Democratic editors in the South did not allow their readers to forget that Roosevelt had appealed for the support of northern Negroes, and that, of course, was in their eyes almost a capital crime. As one editor put it, "Mr. Roosevelt, instead of making himself strong with the Democrats in the South, as he is studiously attempting to do, will succeed in disgusting the Southern Democrats. They will think none the more of him as a political leader so long as he advocates the recognition of the negro as a real factor, North or South." [40] Southern editors, moreover, rang the changes on

37. Atlanta *Journal,* August 6, 1912.

38. "Extract from Mr. Roosevelt's Speech at the Coliseum, August 6, 1912. On the Negro Question." Manuscript in the Roosevelt Papers.

39. W. E. B. Du Bois, *Dusk of Dawn,* pp. 233–234.

40. Little Rock *Arkansas Democrat,* August 6, 1912.

Roosevelt's open friendship for the black race during his presidency; they recalled the Crum incident in Charleston, South Carolina, the suspension of the Indianola, Mississippi, post office for refusing to accept a Negro postmaster, and the famous dinner at the White House in honor of Booker T. Washington.[41] And when the story that Roosevelt had eaten with two Negro Progressives in Providence, Rhode Island, was published in the South, southern editors could proclaim with an air of obvious delight that he sti'' believed in social equality for the Negro and for that reason was unacceptable to the southern people.[42]

The story of the Providence dinner was published in many of the southern newspapers on the eve of the election. Few newspapers, however, went as far as the Montgomery *Advertiser*, which warned the Democrats of Alabama on November 2 that white supremacy was at stake in the campaign. Actually, there was no necessity for injecting the race question, even as a smoke screen, because by early fall it was obvious that Wilson would carry the election by an overwhelming majority in the electoral college. A strong and vociferous Progressive party was organized in many of the southern states, but the Progressive campaigners made no appeals whatsoever for Negro support.[43]

In conclusion, it is impossible for various reasons to estimate the effect on the Negro voters of Wilson's carefully calculated appeal for their support and of Roosevelt's erratic policies. We may be confident that Wilson did receive many Negro votes, more, probably, than any other Democratic presidential candidate had ever received. The Negro leaders who were supporting Wilson estimated that, in the North, 100,000 Negroes had voted the Democratic ticket, and these leaders regarded as successful their efforts to divide the Negro vote.[44] In view of the fact that the Republicans were split, however, Wilson's pluralities were large in all the great

41. Atlanta *Journal,* September 15, 1912; Raleigh *News and Observer,* October 1, 1912; Wilmington (N.C.) *Morning Star,* August 8, 1912; Charleston *News and Courier,* August 12, 1912; Jacksonville *Florida Times-Union,* August 7, 1912.

42. Atlanta *Journal,* November 1, 1912; Charleston *News and Courier,* August 20, 1912; Montgomery *Advertiser,* November 2, 1912.

43. For a general discussion of the Progressive campaign in the South, see "Theodore Roosevelt and the South in 1912," pp. 252–255, this volume.

44. Du Bois, *Dusk of Dawn,* p. 235.

northern states, and it is questionable whether the Negro vote made much difference one way or another.

We may be sure, on the other hand, that Roosevelt's proscription of Negro support in the South for the Progressive ticket turned away from his ranks most of the militant Negroes in the North. It caused, also, some idealistic northern white men to abandon his movement. As one outraged former Progressive wrote in August, "The action of Colonel Roosevelt and the party on the Negro question is amazing and intolerable. For a large section of the country it has done what no party has done before, drawn a race deadline." [45] Finally, it is probably safe to assume that the majority of northern Negroes remained loyal to the Republican party and voted for Taft.

45. Edwin C. Walker to Edward H. Hill, Jr., August 8, 1912, Jane Addams Papers, Library of Congress, Washington, D.C.

18

The Progressive Movement
in the South, 1870–1914

BEFORE assessing the nature and extent of progressive democracy
in the South, a definition of terms, as they are meant to be understood in this discussion, is necessary.[1] Conservatism, as it is generally understood, connotes a tendency to maintain the status quo
and a disposition of hostility to innovations in the political, social,
and economic order. Oftentimes the classes that possess a conservative point of view are the wealthy classes, but, of course, this
is not always the case. In short, conservatism is usually a reasoned
or unreasoned resistance to change.[2] Progressivism, on the other
hand, implies a philosophy that welcomes innovations and reforms
in the political, economic, and social order. Progressives are
usually persons who strive for reforms that alleviate the ills of
society, that assure to the people a broader control of their governments, and that look toward affording greater economic, political,
and social justice to the people. These progressives are the so-
called "liberals," not "radicals"; they have been, as a general rule,

Reprinted from *The North Carolina Historical Review*, XXIII (April 1946), 1–24, by
permission of the Editor.
    1. Research on this article was made possible by a grant from the Julius Rosenwald
Fund.
    2. See Edwin R. A. Seligman, editor, *Encyclopaedia of the Social Sciences*, 15 vols. (New
York: Macmillan, 1930–1935), IV, 230–232, for a discussion of conservatism.

essentially conservative insofar as basic property rights and the fundamental capitalistic structure are concerned.[3]

The popular notion that such a thing as progressive democracy in the South was non-existent during the period 1870-1914, or practically so, that the southern states were ruled by tyrannical political machines, that they were almost unbelievably backward, economically, politically, and socially, has become so persistent that it is hard to down. Most writers ignore the progressive movement in the South altogether; those that do recognize its existence characterize it as a result of Western progressivism. The extremists's view that there was no progressive democracy in the South was expressed by the late Sen. Robert M. La Follette, himself a foremost progressive, in a speech at Saginaw, Michigan, on New Year's day, 1912. He said:

I don't know of any progressive sentiment or any progressive legislation in the South. . . . A true American believes in democracy. He believes men and women are equal and entitled to an equal chance. But the Democratic party of the South is not by inheritance that sort of organization. All the strength of the party is the aristocracy. The Southern Democrat despises alike the poor white and the negro and that is not the sentiment that makes for popular government.[4]

Despite Senator La Follette's blanket indictment, only his ignorance prevented him from knowing that there was in 1912, and had been for some decades, a far-reaching progressive movement in the South. Basically and primarily it was, before 1900, agrarian in composition and principle, generated by agricultural unrest that came as a result of social, political, and economic causes. Farmers throughout the nation saw control of the national government pass from their hands into the hands of the industrial class after the Civil War. They saw the formation of large combinations in industry, which enabled the industralists to eliminate competitors and to maintain a monopolistic price level. They saw themselves economically oppressed by the railroads by means

3. For a discussion of the idea, see David J. Saposs's provocative article, "The Role of the Middle Class in Social Development, Fascism, Populism, Communism, Socialism," in *Economic Essays in Honor of Wesley Clair Mitchell* (New York: Columbia University Press, 1935), pp. 395-424, especially p. 399.
4. San Antonio *Express*, January 2, 1912.

of discriminations between persons and places, unjustly high freight rates, pools, and the granting of rebates. They felt themselves economically injured by the national bank system that furthered the interests of the business groups and prevented a free flow of credit to agricultural communities.

The Granger movement was the first attempt by the farmers to strike back at the industrial and railroad giants oppressing them. The economic platform of the Grange is illustrative of this point. It advised farmers to dispense with middlemen and commission agents, expressed violent opposition to monopolies and trusts, demanded regulation of the railroads by the state and national governments in the interests of the producers, and advocated agricultural and industrial education.[5] The year 1871 saw the introduction of the Grange into South Carolina, Mississippi, and Kentucky; and by the end of 1872, the movement had spread widely throughout the South. By the end of that year, for example, South Carolina ranked next to Iowa in the number of granges.[6] The influence of the movement is clearly discernible in the demand for railroad regulation that made headway in the southern states in the 1870s. There are numerous instances of Granger agitation for railroad regulation in the South. The state grange of Arkansas petitioned the legislature in 1877 for a law establishing maximum rates. In Virginia and Tennessee, the state granges were interested in efforts to secure reduced rates by negotiation with the railroad companies. The state grange of South Carolina appealed to the legislature in 1877 and again in 1878 for laws to prevent unjust rates, discrimination, and other railroad malpractices.[7] Obviously, the movement for railroad regulation was an early manifestation of the southern progressive movement. Numerous co-operative stores, banks, manufactories, and insurance companies were also begun by the Grange leaders in the South.[8]

Many causes were responsible for the decline and failure

5. Solon J. Buck, *The Granger Movement* (Cambridge: Harvard University Press, 1913), p. 64.

6. Buck, *Granger Movement*, pp. 52–55.

7. Buck, *Granger Movement*, pp. 252–273. See also Francis B. Simkins, *The Tillman Movement in South Carolina* (Durham, N.C.: Duke University Press, 1926), p. 17.

8. For Texas, see Ralph A. Smith, "The Grange in Texas, 1873–1900," *Southwestern Historical Quarterly*, XLII (April 1939), 297–315.

of the Granger movement in the South and in the nation.[9] Even after the passing of the organization as a powerful body, its influence lived on and subsequent agrarian movements became its heirs. The Grangers organized to do battle with the new capitalism—the railroads, the middlemen, the trusts, and the bankers—and, having failed to gain all their objectives, retired from the field.

The Greenback-Labor movement was the successor to the Granger movement; but primarily because it was a third party organization, it made little headway in the South. In 1880, a state convention of the Alabama Greenback-Labor party adopted a platform which demanded adequate educational facilities, denounced the convict-lease system, and demanded an equalization of the tax burden.[10] Alabama was the only state in which the party made any headway at all, but in that state "Greenbackism . . . was a significant experiment in political discontent, and gave impetus to Populism as its successor in the state."[11]

The most significant and the largest farmers' organization in the nineteenth-century South was the Farmers' Alliance. The Southern Farmers' Alliance had its origin in a cattlemen's association in Lampasas County, Texas, in the middle 1870s. Within a decade, the Texas Alliance had spread throughout the state, and under the guidance of its leader, C. W. Macune, began in the late 1880s to absorb similar farmers' organizations in other southern states. By 1890, the Southern Alliance boasted a membership of over a million and was the most powerful farmers' organization in the country. It was the spearhead of the last great concerted agrarian effort in this country. It and its political successor, the People's party, marked the culmination of the agrarian progressive movement in the South.

9. Among the causes for the decline of the Granger movement may be listed (1) the laxness of organization permitted many persons who were not interested in the farmer and his problems to join—for example, it was not uncommon for politicians to use the Grange for their own political advancement; (2) the huge, unwieldy mass within the organization, which led to dissension within the ranks; (3) the connection of the Grange with a number of political movements, which led to its decline; (4) failure of the Grange to secure permanent and effective railroad regulation; (5) the main cause, which was the failure of the Granger co-operative endeavors, which went to pieces and left a burden of discredit and indebtedness. (Buck, *Granger Movement*, pp. 70–74.)

10. John B. Clark, *Populism in Alabama* (Auburn, Ala.: Auburn Printing Co., 1927), p. 25.

11. Clark, *Populism in Alabama*, p. 28.

When agrarian efforts to liberalize the Democratic party failed, southern farmers joined their comrades in the West and launched, in 1892, the People's party. The platform of the agrarian Democrats and the Populists, as members of the People's party were called, comprehended a broad program of economic and political reforms in the interest of the agrarian and debtor classes. Since the third party was organized in every southern state, it is possible to see the objectives for which these progressives were fighting. The populistic group in Alabama adopted a platform in 1892 that included the progressive demands of the Democrats and also called for fair elections and a national graduated income tax, and denounced national banks and trusts. A platform of 1894 demanded that the use of convicts as mine-workers be stopped and that child labor be prohibited in the mines.[12] The Alliance-controlled Democratic party in Tennessee in 1890 demanded free coinage of silver, extension of the public school system, lien laws to protect laborers and mechanics, good roads, and abolition of the convict-lease system.[13] The Democracy in Georgia in 1890, in the control of the Alliance, came out in favor of an enlargement of the powers of the state railroad commission, abolition of the convict-lease system and other prison reforms, revision of the tax system, extension of the public school system, and laws to ensure fair primaries and elections.[14] The 1892 North Carolina Populist platform called for economy in state government, adequate aid to the state educational institutions, reduction of the legal rate of interest to six percent, adequate taxation of the railroads, and a ten-hour day for laborers in mines, factories, and public works.[15]

All of the southern state parties endorsed the national Populist platform, but none had so complete a program as did Texas Populism. The 1892 Texas platform reaffirmed the traditional American doctrine of the equality of man and demanded the

---

12. Clark, *Populism in Alabama*, pp. 133, 152.

13. Daniel M. Robison, *Bob Taylor and the Agrarian Revolt in Tennessee* (Chapel Hill, N.C.: University of North Carolina Press, 1935), pp. 144–145.

14. Alex M. Arnett, *The Populist Movement in Georgia* (New York: Columbia University, 1922), pp. 105–106. See also James C. Bonner, "The Alliance Legislature of 1890," in J. C. Bonner and Lucien E. Roberts, editors, *Studies in Georgia History and Government* (Athens: University of Georgia Press, 1940), pp. 155–171.

15. Simeon A. Delap, "The Populist Party in North Carolina," *Historical Papers of the Trinity College Historical Society*, XIV (1922), 52.

elimination of certain economic inequalities that weighed heavily upon the farmers. It demanded the recovery of Texas land from railroads and corporations and the prohibition of alien ownership. The Texas Populists advocated, moreover, government construction of railroads, abolition of national banks, free silver, and the issuance by the federal government of legal tender notes to the amount of fifty dollars per capita, while the subtreasury plan was the means by which the money would be put into circulation. The taxation system and Democratic extravagances in government were criticized. An antitrust program was endorsed; and a labor program which included an eight-hour day, mechanics' lien laws, the establishment of a state board of labor and arbitration, and the abolition of the convict-lease system was adopted. Such political reforms as the direct election of senators, the President, and the vice-president, proportional representation, and the initiative, referendum, and recall were also endorsed.[16]

The influence of the Alliance and Populist movements in the South was so profound and of such portent to southern political life that its significance can be understood only when it is realized that it shook the very foundations of Democratic supremacy in the region. Although, with the single exception of North Carolina, the Populists failed to gain control in any southern state, the agrarians in the Farmers' Alliance seized control of the Democratic party machinery and elected governors and Congressmen in several southern states. And Populism itself, despite the paucity of its actual gains, had a significant influence on the political life of the South. The movement effected, for the first time since the Civil War, a real cleavage within the Democratic ranks and forced the retirement of many of the old conservative leaders. What is more important, it forced the southern Democratic party, at least for a time, to become almost as progressive as the Populist party.

An examination of the history of the several southern states during the 1890s will illustrate this point. In Texas, in 1894, the

---

16. Roscoe C. Martin, *The People's Party in Texas* (Austin: The University, 1933), pp. 46–54. This is the best of the state studies on southern Populism. Again, it should be emphasized that the national Populist platform concerning land, money, and railroad regulation was heartily approved by southern Populists. It will be remembered, also, that the "sub-treasury" plan was a southern invention and was one of the chief planks of southern Populism.

Democrats adopted the Populist program with regard to convict labor. In 1896, they approved the national Populist planks calling for free silver, the issuance of legal tender notes by the federal government, the abolition of national banks as banks of currency issue, the election of United States senators by the people, and the institution of the income tax. A railroad commission had been established and an alien land law had been passed early in the 1890s by the legislature.[17] The Democrats of Alabama in 1892 adopted a platform demanding free silver, the abolition of the convict-lease system, adequate support for the public school system, primary election laws, and the secret ballot.[18] A farmer-controlled legislature in Tennessee in 1890 and 1891 passed a stringent antitrust law, drastically raised taxes on corporations, and passed a resolution calling on Tennessee's congressmen and senators to support a constitutional amendment for the direct election of United States senators.[19] By 1896, the Democratic party in that state had become almost completely converted to Populism. Its platform demanded free silver, the abolition of national banks, the repeal of the tax on state bank notes, and a national income tax.[20] In South Carolina, Benjamin R. Tillman led the white small farmers to victory in 1890 and subsequently inaugurated a number of reforms, many of which were in the interests of the farmers.[21] In Virginia, the conservative Thomas S. Martin organization was forced to take a stand in favor of free silver, and the Democratic convention of 1896 was a free-silver carnival.[22]

An Alliance legislature in Georgia, 1890–1891, led by Alliance Governor W. J. Northen, extended the jurisdiction of the state railroad commission, instituted certain reforms in the banking laws of the state, extended the system of state inspection of fertilizers,

---

17. Martin, *People's Party in Texas*, pp. 266–267.
18. Clark, *Populism in Alabama*, p. 132.
19. Robison, *Bob Taylor*, pp. 152–153.
20. Robison, *Bob Taylor*, p. 197.
21. Simkins, *Tillman Movement*, chapters VI, VII, and VIII. Some of the reforms of the Tillman regime were increased aid to the agricultural college, establishment of a woman's college, reorganization of the insane asylum, raising the valuation of corporation property for taxation purposes, the establishment of a more powerful railroad commission in 1892, a bill limiting the hours of labor in industry, and the famous dispensary system.
22. William DuBose Sheldon, *Populism in the Old Dominion* (Princeton, N.J.: Princeton University Press, 1935), chapter V.

and established a Negro agricultural and mechanical college.[23] By 1896, the Georgia Democratic convention was demanding free silver, the repeal of the Resumption Act that gave President Cleveland authority to issue United States bonds in order to maintain the gold reserve in the Treasury, the repeal of the federal tax on state bank notes, an income tax amendment, and a revenue tariff.[24] In North Carolina, the Farmers' Alliance had captured the legislature by 1890, and in 1891 a state railroad commission was established and endowed with complete rate-making authority.[25] In 1895, a fusion Populist-Republican legislature passed an election law aimed at wiping out entirely corruption at the ballot boxes. The election machinery was made completely bipartisan. The people were given the right to elect county commissioners; the legal rate of interest was set at six percent; increased appropriations for public institutions were made, while all corporations which had been exempted from taxation were hereafter to be subject to taxation.[26]

Such were the objectives and achievements of southern agrarianism and Populism. Of course, the fact that the Populist revolt had forced out the conservative Bourbon leadership within the Democratic party and had necessitated a reorganization and reorientation within the party is not particularly surprising. The movement was nationwide. It resulted in the expulsion of the Cleveland Democrats of the conservative East from power in party circles in 1896 and the inauguration of the progressive, Bryan-dominated era. Moreover, the return of large numbers of former Populists to the Democratic party upon the fusion of the Populists with the Democrats in 1896 further stimulated the progressive leaven within the Democratic party. The result of a decade of agitation was a much greater emphasis in the South on popular education and social and economic reform. Populistic and agrarian agitation against the railroads and banks resulted in increased regulation of these institutions by the state governments. The activities of state departments of agriculture were expanded and

23. Bonner, "The Alliance Legislature of 1890," pp. 155–171. See also Arnett, *Populist Movement in Georgia*, p. 121.

24. Arnett, *Populist Movement in Georgia*, pp. 194–195.

25. John D. Hicks, "The Farmers' Alliance in North Carolina," *North Carolina Historical Review*, II (1925), 174–175.

26. Delap, "Populist Party in North Carolina," pp. 57–59.

greater emphasis was given to agricultural and vocational education. Significant reforms in the political machinery of the states were effected by the utilization of the party primary instead of the state convention as the method of nominating party candidates, the replacement of the old party ballot with the secret ballot, and the adoption by many southern cities of the commission form of city government.

Although the Populist revolt caused the downfall of the Bourbon domination, it brought to the fore in southern political life a new type of leadership, the leadership of the demagogues. Men like Cole L. Blease of South Carolina, Jeff Davis of Arkansas, and Theodore G. Bilbo of Mississippi were typical demagogues who stirred the people to democratic revolt and who rose to power by class agitation and race hatred, but who offered their constituents few measures of progressive legislation.

Throughout the decades of agrarian revolt, class agitation, and conflict, there remained a great number of Democrats who were neither Bourbons nor Populists, but middle-of-the-road progressives. As a general rule, this group found its recruits in the middle classes of the South among the more prosperous farmers, small businessmen, schoolteachers, editors, and other professional groups. They looked askance alike at the defection of the Populists and the conservatism of the Bourbons. But to a great degree, the aims of the southern progressives—popular education, reforms looking toward greater popular control of the state governments, and the abandonment by the state governments of laissez-faire as a guide for economic and social action—were much the same as those of the Populists. In Virginia, the progressives were led by Carter Glass, Andrew J. Montague, and William A. Jones; in North Carolina, by Charles B. Aycock, Josephus Daniels, Claude and William Kitchin, and Walter Clark. In Georgia, Hoke Smith and Thomas W. Hardwick; in Florida, Frank L. Mayes; in Alabama, Benjamin B. Comer; in Louisiana, John M. Parker; in Kentucky, Ollie M. James and John C. W. Beckham; in Oklahoma, Robert L. Owen and Thomas P. Gore; and in Texas, James Stephen Hogg, Charles A. Culberson, and Robert L. Henry were representatives of this middle-class progressivism. Indeed, the statement might perhaps be made that no region of the country, in proportion to its population, could boast a greater galaxy of progressive leaders.

After 1900, the southern progressive movement reveals itself in a somewhat different light from the nineteenth-century agrarian radicalism. In the first place, the farmers of the South and of the nation as well entered upon a period of relative prosperity around 1897 which continued with few interruptions until 1920. As money became more plentiful, farm prices rose and consequently agrarian demands for extreme financial reforms diminished. In the second place, what was perhaps the farmers' paramount problem—adequate regulation of railroad rates and services—was gradually being taken care of by federal and state action. As a consequence, there was a gradual shift in emphasis in the southern progressive platform. It ceased to be almost entirely agrarian in outlook, while the leadership of the movement passed from the hands of the farmers to progressive editors, politicians, and other urban groups. The chief issues of the progressive movement in the early part of the twentieth century, from 1900 to 1914, were primarily political. Once again, it should be pointed out that this development within progressive ranks was nationwide.

The culmination of the southern progressive movement came as a result of a national development—the Woodrow Wilson presidential campaign both before and after the Baltimore convention of 1912. Even by 1911, Wilson was displacing Bryan as leader of the progressive Democrats, and liberal southerners hastened to join the New Jersey governor's ranks. Wilson's New Freedom philosophy and program had a powerful appeal to certain groups in southern society. The fact that he had taken the lead in smashing a reactionary political machine in New Jersey won him the support of liberals in every southern state who were fighting to overthrow conservative political organizations. The most significant fact about the Wilson movement in the South was that these southern progressives seized upon it as a weapon to use against the conservatives in order to gain control of their own state governments. Wilson's economic philosophy was very much like Bryan's and the New Jersey governor's campaign against the "money trust," big business, and in favor of a revenue tariff naturally won him the support of the old Bryan men. The educational leaders in the South—from the universities and colleges to the country schools—played an important role in the movement. Southern teachers were naturally gratified to see one of their fellows step from college halls to the national political stage and the remarks of anti-Wilson editors which reflected on the candidate because he had been a professor drove thousands of teachers into the Wilson ranks. Wilson was popular, not only with the educators in the South, but also with the college students and the enthusiasm for him which swept through college campuses was phenomenal. As Wilson was supported by southern educators, so was he likewise supported by many southern clergymen. Wilson's adherence to and profession of the Christian faith, and his Christian life were reasons enough for thousands of ministers and members of the church to enlist in his cause. The religious press, abandoning its usual hands-off policy in political campaigns, generously supported Wilson in the pre-nomination campaign of 1912.[27]

If the writer had to single out the group of men that made the greatest contribution to the Wilson movement in the South, he would almost inevitably name the southern editors who heralded the coming of the New Freedom. Their work in presenting the man to the people and in engendering enthusiasm and support for his cause was the foundation stone of Wilson's campaign in the South. It is not strange that many of the strongest Wilson editors—Josephus Daniels, William E. Gonzales, Frank L. Mayes, and Luke Lea—were also devoted followers of William Jennings Bryan. Nor is it strange that most of the anti-Bryan editors were also antagonistic to the New Jersey governor. The powerful leavens of progressivism and conservatism necessitated such an alignment. Many of the southern editors were also politicians of influence.[28]

The Wilson movement in the South became in effect a struggle for progressive Democracy, and progressive southern politicians were in the vanguard of the movement. Men who had been

27. See, for example, *Christian Advocate* (Nashville), March 8, 1912; Birmingham *Age-Herald*, August 20, 1912; Raleigh *News and Observer*, April 2, 1912; Atlanta *Constitution*, February 5, 1912; Atlanta *Journal*, April 16 and 26, 1912; *Presbyterian Standard* (Charlotte), March 24, 1911, April 24, and July 17, 1912; *Presbyterian of the South* (Richmond), February 8, 1911.

28. Daniels and Robert Ewing were national committeemen, respectively, from North Carolina and Louisiana. Gonzales dominated the progressive faction of the party in South Carolina. Lea and E. B. Stahlman were spokesmen for the progressive Democrats in Tennessee. James R. Gray of the Atlanta *Journal* was allied with the political fortunes of Hoke Smith and the progressive faction of the Georgia Democracy.

Bryan's spokesmen for nearly sixteen years—Daniels, Tillman, Gonzales, Hoke Smith, Frank L. Mayes, Nathan P. Bryan, Braxton B. Comer, Luke Lea, Charles A. Culberson, Robert L. Henry, William H. Murray, and Thomas P. Gore—perhaps realized that the Commoner's day as a presidential candidate had passed, and they found a new leader in Woodrow Wilson. There were, of course, Bryan men in the South who supported Champ Clark, who was running as a progressive. On the other hand, the consistent opposition of the conservative southern state organizations came as a result of the liberalism of the Wilson movement.

The Wilson movement was moderately successful in achieving its immediate goal, the winning of the southern delegations. Wilson won proportionately as much support in the South as in any other section of the country. From the long-range point of view, the movement was significant in that it became the spearhead of a great progressive revolt. It brought to the fore important issues which demanded solution; it engendered a tremendous amount of discussion concerning popular government and progressive reform.[29]

So much for the general development of the progressive movement in the South from the Granger movement to the Wilson era. An interrogator might reasonably ask: if the South had such a considerable body of progressives and was so visibly affected by the progressive movement, why did not the region show results by way of progressive reforms? Such a question creates a perplexing problem in the establishment of a yardstick of progressivism. It might be helpful to consider the reform measures that were outstanding during this period and to analyze the accomplishments of the southern states.

One example of progressive reform in which southern states were virtual pioneers was the difficult problem of railroad regulation. In the rebuilding of the railroads in the South after the destruction that occurred during the Civil War, northern capitalists

---

29. Spatial limitations have required that the writer merely summarize the general characteristics of the Wilson movement in the South. For a fuller discussion, however, see Arthur S. Link, "The South and the Democratic Campaign of 1910–1912" (Ph.D dissertation, University of North Carolina, 1945); "The Wilson Movement in Texas, 1910–1912," pp. 155–171, this volume; and Arthur S. Link, "The Democratic Pre-Convention Campaign of 1912 in Georgia," *Georgia Historical Quarterly*, XXIX (September 1945), 143–158.

played an influential part. And with the subsequent consolidation of southern railroads into large systems also came the attendant evils of monopolistic control. The railroads levied fares and freight rates at their pleasure and often to the oppression of the people, while stock watering, discrimination in rates, the free-pass evil, and under-assessment for taxes were frequently practiced. The political corruption attendant upon the railroads' suspicious and frequent sorties into politics, as well as the malpractices mentioned above, led soon after the restoration of home rule to a popular demand that the railroads be subjected to public control.

Virginia took the first step, and in 1877, the legislature of that state established a state advisory railroad commission on the order of the Massachusetts type.[30] The powers of the Virginia commission were purely supervisory and recommendatory, and it was not until 1901 that popular agitation for a commission with power to set rates finally culminated in the establishment of a powerful Corporation Commission with complete administrative, legislative, and judicial powers over railroads and other corporations.[31] A year after the establishment of the first Virginia commission, South Carolina set up an advisory railroad commission modeled after it.[32] Four years later, however, the legislature amended the law so as to endow the commission with full power to set freight and passenger rates.[33]

Georgia was the first southern state and, along with California, the first state in the country effectively to regulate railroad rates and operations.[34] The Georgia constitution of 1877 made the establishment of a railroad commission by the legislature mandatory and, in compliance with this emphatic directive, the legislature in 1879 established the state commission. The Georgia commission had extraordinary powers to fix and compel fair and uniform rates, to forbid discrimination among persons and places, and to abolish

30. *Acts of the General Assembly of the State of Virginia,* 1876–1877, chapter 254, pp. 254–257.
31. See the *Virginia Constitution of 1902,* article XII, sections 155–156, in *Acts of the General Assembly of the State of Virginia,* 1902–1903–1904, pp. 31–37.
32. *Acts and Joint Resolutions of the General Assembly of the State of South Carolina,* 1878, chapter 662, pp. 789–792.
33. South Carolina, *Acts,* 1881–1882, chapter 595, pp. 791–841.
34. The earlier legislative efforts of the midwestern states of Illinois, Minnesota, Wisconsin, and Iowa during the heyday of the Granger movement were ineffective and short-lived.

the discrimination inherent in the long-and-short-haul practice. Schedules of rates established by the commission were to be accepted as just and fair by the state courts, while railroad companies were compelled to submit to the commission their records and business files.[35] The Georgia commission was exceedingly effective in bringing the railroads of the state under its control, and it secured reductions in passenger and freight rates of between fifty and sixty percent.[36] In addition to the fact of its successful career, the Georgia commission is significant in that practically all other southern states subsequently established commissions modeled after it. In 1907, largely due to the persistent efforts of Hoke Smith, leader of the progressive wing of the Democratic party in Georgia and governor of the state in 1907, the legislature reorganized the railroad commission and greatly extended its jurisdiction. It was in reality transformed into a corporation or public utilities commission. The most interesting feature of the new law was a provision which made it the commission's duty to promulgate such rules regarding the issuance of stocks and bonds as would put an end to over-capitalization and guarantee honest values to purchasers of securities.[37]

Kentucky, in 1879, established an advisory railroad commission.[38] The commission was, however, deprived of all authority to supervise railroad rates by a decision of the Kentucky Court of Appeals in 1896, but an act of the legislature in 1900 conferred the authority upon the commission to prescribe "reasonable and just" freight and passenger rates.[39] After a prolonged battle with the Louisville and Nashville Railroad, the commission's right to prescribe reasonable maximum intrastate rates was confirmed by the Supreme Court of the United States.[4]

The Alabama legislature, in 1881, established a railroad commission, but withheld from it the authority to fix rates and fares.

35. *Acts and Resolutions of the General Assembly of the State of Georgia*, 1878–1879, chapter 269, pp. 125–131.

36. Jim David Cherry, "The Georgia Railroad Commission, 1879–1888" (M.A. thesis, University of North Carolina, 1940).

37. Georgia, *Acts*, 1907, chapter 223, pp. 72–81.

38. *Acts of the General Assembly of the Commonwealth of Kentucky*, 1879, chapter 1019, pp. 92–95.

39. Kentucky, *Acts*, 1900, chapter 2, pp. 5–7.

40. Maxwell Ferguson, *State Regulation of Railroads in the South* (New York: Columbia University, 1916), pp. 123–124. This is the only general work on the subject.

The carriers were required to submit to the commission their tariffs of freight and passenger charges for examination and if the commission should find any charge which it deemed unreasonable, it was directed to notify the railroad in question.[41] The provisions of the Alabama law were a decided improvement upon the law establishing the Virginia commission but were obviously inadequate effectively to deal with the problem of railroad regulation. Consequently, in 1883, the legislature gave the commission authority to determine reasonable rates.[42] The Alabama commission was successful in decreasing tariff charges, but there was considerable popular agitation for an act to increase the commission's powers. The leader of the movement for more effective regulation after 1900 was Braxton Bragg Comer, who was elected president of the commission in 1904. In 1906, Comer was elected governor on a railroad-regulation platform; and in 1907, he called upon the legislature to abolish the "debauching lobby" maintained by the railroads at Montgomery and to pass laws providing for thorough railroad regulation.[43] In compliance, the legislature passed a series of acts which extended the jurisdiction of the commission to include most of the public utility companies of the state, reduced the freight rates on one hundred and ten articles of common production, and reduced passenger rates to two and one-half cents a mile.[44] A bitter fight between Governor Comer and the Louisville and Nashville Railroad resulted. In 1913, however, this railroad gave up its fight against the Alabama commission and accepted its schedules.[45]

Tennessee, in 1883, established a railroad commission and authorized it to set just and reasonable rates,[46] but the railroads of the state were able to halt the work of the commission by use of judicial injunctions. As a consequence, the commission

41. *Acts of the General Assembly of Alabama,* 1880-1881, chapter 91, pp. 84-95.

42. Alabama, *Acts,* 1882-1883, chapters 103 and 104, pp. 177-178.

43. Albert B. Moore, "Braxton Bragg Comer," *Dictionary of American Biography,* 21 vols. (New York: Scribner, 1928-1944), IV, 329-330.

44. General Laws of the Legislature of Alabama, 1907, chapter 17, p. 80; chapter 30, p. 104; chapter 31, pp. 105-107; chapter 69, pp. 135-166; chapter 329, pp. 404-405.

45. Ferguson, *State Regulation,* p. 138. For a discussion of Comer's battle with the Louisville and Nashville Railroad, see Rupert B. Vance, "Spell-Binders of the New South," unpublished manuscript in possession of Professor Vance.

46. *Acts of the State of Tennessee,* 1883, chapter 199, pp. 271-279.

law of 1883 was repealed in 1885. However, in 1897, a new commission was established and endowed with full authority to regulate rates and tariffs.[47] It was successful in effecting a drastic reduction in transportation charges.[48] The Mississippi legislature in 1884 established a commission[49] which effectively reduced freight rates during 1886 and 1887. Passenger rates, because of the competitive practices of the Mississippi railroads, were already exceedingly low.[50] Florida, in 1887, established a commission modeled almost exactly after the Georgia commission of 1879.[51] The Florida legislature, however, abolished the commission in 1891 because it did not approve of the new chairman appointed by the governor, and it was not until 1897 that the commission was reestablished.[52] In 1899, the legislature considerably strengthened the commission's authority by more clearly defining its powers and giving it judicial authority,[53] and in 1901 it promulgated a comprehensive freight rate schedule.[54]

After many years of agitation, the legislature of North Carolina, in 1891, dominated by members of the Farmers' Alliance, established a railroad commission based on the Georgia model.[55] Within less than a year's time, freight and passenger schedules were promulgated that brought about numerous reductions.[56] In 1899, the railroad commission was transformed into a corporation commission, one of the first of its kind in the United States. The powers and duties of the old railroad commission were transferred to it, but its jurisdiction was extended to cover all carriers, as well as telephone companies, public and private banks, loan and trust companies, and building and loan associations.[57] The North Carolina commission attempted to bring to an end the discriminatory rates levied by the Virginia railroads to favor Virginia

47. Tennessee, *Acts,* 1897, chapter 10, pp. 113–126.
48. Ferguson, *State Regulation,* pp. 140–146.
49. *Laws of the State of Mississippi,* 1884, chapter 23, pp. 31–41.
50. Ferguson, *State Regulation,* pp. 148–151.
51. *Acts and Resolutions Adopted by the Legislature of Florida,* 1887, chapter 3746, pp. 118–126.
52. Florida, *Acts,* 1897, chapter 4549, pp. 82–94.
53. Florida *Acts,* 1899, chapter 4700, pp. 76–93.
54. Ferguson, *State Regulation,* pp. 154–161.
55. *Laws and Resolutions of the State of North Carolina,* 1891, chapter 320, pp. 275–288.
56. Martha F. Bowditch, "The North Carolina Railroad Commission, 1891–1899" (M.A. thesis, University of North Carolina, 1943).
57. North Carolina, *Laws,* 1899, chapter 164, pp. 291–307.

cities and to eliminate the discrimination practiced by the north-south lines running through the state.[58]

The trans-Mississippi southern states kept well abreast of the southeastern states in the perplexing and difficult business of railroad regulation. Texas, in 1891, under the progressive leadership of Gov. James Stephen Hogg, established a railroad commission to set reasonable rates,[59] and in 1893 the legislature enacted a stock-and-bond law designed to prevent the railroads from increasing and collecting fictitious debts by means of increasing the rates.[60] In Arkansas, a railroad regulation amendment to the state constitution was adopted in 1897; and in 1899, the legislature established a commission. The railroads were required to furnish rate schedules to the commission, to keep rate schedules posted, and to furnish facilities for the care of persons and property transported. Discriminations of any sort, rebates, pooling, and the long-and-short-haul practice were prohibited. The commission was empowered to determine the valuation of the railroads, to conduct hearings, and to regulate freight, express, and passenger rates.[61] In 1907, the commission's jurisdiction was extended to sleeping car companies.[62] A railroad commission was established in Louisiana by a provision of the constitution of 1898. The commission was directed to set reasonable rates and was given authority over sleeping-car, express, telephone, and telegraph companies, and steamboats and other watercraft, as well as the railroads.[63] The first endeavor of the commission was to put an end to the disastrous competition between the railroads and steamboats, while numerous reductions in freight rates were effected.[64] Oklahoma's progressive constitution of 1907 restricted railroad and corporate activities in many ways. Considerable space was given to expressing the limitations and regulations of railroads and other

58. Ferguson, *State Regulation,* pp. 174–177.

59. *Revised Civil Statutes of the State of Texas,* 1895, chapter 13, pp. 909–920.

60. Texas, *Statutes,* 1895, chapter 14, pp. 920–928.

61. William F. Kirby, editor, *A Digest of the Statutes of Arkansas,* sections 6788–6826, pp. 1407–1415.

62. Charles W. Fornoff, "The Regulation of Public Service Corporations," in David Y. Thomas, *Arkansas and Its People, a History, 1541–1930,* 4 vols. (New York: American Historical Society, 1930), I, 338–341.

63. *Constitution of the State of Louisiana,* 1898, articles 283–289.

64. Ferguson, *State Regulation,* pp. 180–184.

public corporations which were regulated by a corporation commission of three members.[65]

In concluding this discussion of state railroad regulation in the South, it may reasonably be said that commissions in every southern state regulated the transportation companies, for the most part, in the public interest and that the movement was successful in bringing benefits to the people in the form of reductions in rates, uniformity of schedules, and increased taxation of the railroads. It is the conclusion of the only authority in the general field that state regulation in the South effectively ended discrimination and reduced freight and passenger rates to an unjustly low level.[66]

The southern movement for railroad regulation was manifestly a part of the nationwide movement, and it is interesting to note that southerners exercised considerable influence in the national movement for railroad reform. It is a well-known fact that John H. Reagan of Texas was regarded as the father of the Interstate Commerce Act of 1887. Robert M. La Follette, writing years later, declared that "To Reagan of Texas, more than any other man in the House, belongs the credit for the passage of the act." [67] La Follette also wrote that he and his progressive lieutenants in Wisconsin had profited greatly from Reagan's wise advice when they drew up Wisconsin's railroad regulation law.[68] The advocates of national railroad legislation always had the overwhelming support of southern representatives and senators, and Sen. Ben Tillman of South Carolina gave conspicuous service to the Roosevelt administration when he piloted the Hepburn rate bill through the Senate in 1906.[69]

In any discussion of the program of the progressive movement, the measures advocated by progressives directed toward the reform of the party machinery loom large. One of the most

65. *Constitution of the State of Oklahoma,* 1907, article X, sections 2-35.
66. Ferguson, *State Regulation,* pp. 207-212.
67. R. M. La Follette, *La Follette's Autobiography* (Madison, Wisconsin: Robert M. La Follette Co., 1913), p. 119.
68. La Follette, *Autobiography,* pp. 119-120.
69. Henry F. Pringle, *Theodore Roosevelt* (New York: Harcourt, Brace & Co., 1931), pp. 420-425; Claude G. Bowers, *Beveridge and the Progressive Era* (Boston: Houghton Mifflin Co., 1932), pp. 225-226. Tillman received considerable support from Sen. Joseph Weldon Bailey of Texas in the fight for the Hepburn bill.

important of these measures was the direct primary, by means of which reformers hoped to wrest control over the nominating process from the political bosses and to restore it to the people. Under La Follette's leadership, Wisconsin in 1903 adopted the mandatory statewide direct party primary. Before 1890, however, every county in South Carolina used the primary system for the nomination of local officers and legislators, and in 1896 the statewide Democratic party primary was inaugurated.[70] As early as 1897, the legislature of Arkansas had legalized primary elections.[71] The Mississippi legislature in 1902 enacted a law requiring that all nominations for state, district, county, and county district officials be made by primary elections.[72] The primary system was in use in Virginia at least by 1905, and in that year the United States senatorial primary was adopted by the Democratic party.[73] The first statewide primary in Georgia was held on June 7, 1898, and the primary system was used regularly by the Democrats thereafter.[74] In 1902, Alabama Democrats adopted the primary system for nominating their candidates. Following the primary for state officers in 1902, the friends of the primary system began to agitate for a senatorial primary by means of which the voters could instruct the members of the state legislature upon their preference for United States senator. The system was adopted

70. David D. Wallace, *History of South Carolina,* 4 vols. (New York· American Historical Society, 1934), III, 336, 356. The South Carolina legislature in 1896 enacted a statute to prevent frauds at the primary elections, but the party primary was not made legally mandatory nor brought within the protection of the general election laws. (South Carolina, *Acts and Joint Resolutions,* 1896, chapter 25, p. 56.)

71. Kirby, editor, *Statutes of Arkansas,* 1904, chapter 57, sects. 2892-2897, pp. 705-706. In 1917, an act adopted by the initiative required primary elections of the major parties. (T. D. Crawford and Hamilton Moses, editors, *Digest of the Statutes of Arkansas,* 1919, chapter 54, sects. 3757-3872, pp. 1075-1083.)

72. Mississippi, *Laws,* 1902, chapter 66, pp. 105-112. Section 18 of this law also provided for the nomination of United States senators by the senatorial primary.

73. Robert C. Glass and Carter Glass, Jr., *Virginia Democracy,* 3 vols. (Springfield, Ill.: Democratic Historical Association, 1937), I, 292. In 1912, the Virginia legislature passed an act "to establish and regulate the holding of primary elections." (Virginia *Acts,* 1912, chapter 307, pp. 611-619.)

74. Walter G. Cooper, *The Story of Georgia,* 4 vols. (New York: American Historical Society, 1938), III, 370. A Georgia law of 1900 provided that primary elections should be held under the regulations prescribed by the party, but also provided that clerks of the superior courts should receive and count the election returns. (Georgia, *Acts,* 1900, chapter 117, pp. 40-41.)

in 1906.[75] Gov. William S. Jennings, elected in 1900, was the last governor of Florida nominated by a political convention. The legislature, early in his administration, enacted the primary system into the body of Florida laws.[76] By 1908, at least, Florida had instituted the senatorial primary.[77] The primary system had been in operation in Tennessee for some time before 1901, for in that year the state legislature enacted a law to legalize and regulate party primaries. All primary elections in the state were to be conducted under the provisions of the general election laws.[78] During the administration of Gov. John C. W. Beckham, around 1905, the Kentucky Democratic party adopted the primary system,[79] while Texas [80] and Oklahoma [81] adopted the system in the early years of the twentieth century. Although the primary system had been in use since 1900 in the counties of North Carolina, it was not until 1915 that the legislature made its use mandatory on a statewide basis.[82] Thus it would appear that the primary election idea was almost indigenous to the South, as far as its

75. Albert B. Moore, History of Alabama, 3 vols. (New York: American Historical Society, 1927), I, 909–910. In 1903, the Alabama legislature enacted a law which gave legal sanction and protection to all party primaries that might be held in the state. (Alabama, General Laws, 1903, chapter 417, pp. 356–365.)

In 1911, the legislature made a sweeping revision of the primary act and exempted from its application parties that polled less than 25 percent of the votes at the general election. (Alabama, General Laws, 1911, chapter 479, pp. 421–449.)

76. The Florida law was passed in 1901. It provided for complete state regulation of party primaries. (Florida, Acts, 1901, chapter 5014, pp. 160–165.)

77. Harry Gardner Cutler, History of Florida, 3 vols. (Chicago and New York: Lewis Publishing Co., 1923), I, 179.

78. Tennessee, Acts, 1901, chapter 39, pp. 54–59. The poll tax requirement for voting did not apply in the primary election.

79. George Lee Willis, Kentucky Democracy, 3 vols. (Louisville: Democratic Historical Society, 1935), I, 391–392. In 1912, the Kentucky legislature instituted the mandatory primary system which included the United States senatorial primary. (Kentucky, Acts, 1912, chapter 7, pp. 47–77.)

80. A Texas law of 1905 made primary nominations mandatory for all candidates for state, district, and county offices. The law affected at the time, however, only the Democratic party, since it applied only to parties polling more than 100,000 votes. (Texas, General Laws, 1905, chapter 11, pp. 543–565.) See also O. Douglas Weeks, "The Texas Primary System," in Frank Carter Adams, editor, Texas Democracy, 4 vols. (Austin: Democratic Historical Association, 1937), I, 531–554, especially p. 531.

81. Oklahoma in 1909 adopted the mandatory primary as the method by which all political parties were to nominate candidates for all state offices. (Oklahoma, Session Laws, 1909, Senate Bill No. 5, pp. 270–274.)

82. North Carolina, Public Laws, 1915, chapter 101, pp. 154–168. See also Robert D. W. Connor, North Carolina, Rebuilding an Ancient Commonwealth, 4 vols. (Chicago and New York: American Historical Society, 1929), II, 481–482.

use in this country is concerned. It is clearly evident that a good majority of the southern states were using the system by the time Wisconsin adopted it.

Another measure of reform advocated by progressives in the early part of the twentieth century was corrupt practices legislation, designed to purify the election process. By the end of the Wilson period, every southern state had enacted legislation making it a criminal offense to give bribes to influence a voter, and every southern state except Florida had enacted severe legislation against the receiving of such bribes. Arkansas, Louisiana, Mississippi, North Carolina, Oklahoma, Tennessee, and Texas prohibited candidates from promising appointments before elections, while Arkansas and Texas had declared it unlawful for candidates to pay for the conveyance of voters to the polls. Alabama, Arkansas, Louisiana, and Mississippi denied party leaders the right to solicit campaign funds from candidates. By 1919, every southern state had enacted laws of varying effectiveness and severity prohibiting the intimidation of voters, while Alabama, Texas, Mississippi, Tennessee, Florida, and Kentucky had made it unlawful for employers to intimidate or attempt to influence the voting of their employees. Arkansas, Florida, Kentucky, Oklahoma, Tennessee, and Texas also required employers to give their employees ample time to vote on election day. Tennessee, South Carolina, Oklahoma, Alabama, Georgia, Kentucky, Louisiana, Mississippi, and North Carolina passed legislation prohibiting illegal and unqualified registration, while all of the southern states endeavored to prevent illegal and fraudulent voting. Kentucky, Louisiana, Mississippi, and Tennessee prohibited distinguishing marks or signs on election ballots, and Louisiana, Tennessee, and Virginia made it unlawful for a person to participate in a primary or convention of a party other than his own. Alabama, Arkansas, Florida, Texas, and Virginia required that political advertisements in newspapers be clearly denoted as such, while North Carolina, Louisiana, Mississippi, Florida, Arkansas, and Alabama required that political posters and advertisements bear the names and addresses of the persons responsible for issuing them. Florida and Virginia made it unlawful for a candidate to purchase editorial support in a political campaign. In the matter of campaign expenditures, Alabama, Arkansas, Florida, Kentucky, Louisiana, North Carolina, Oklahoma, South Carolina, and Virginia limited the amounts a candidate for governor might expend in his campaign for nomination and election. The sums varied from $3,000 in Oklahoma to $10,000 in Alabama. Virginia allowed an expenditure of fifteen cents for every voter who cast his vote for the highest party candidate at the last election. All of the states except Mississippi and Tennessee required candidates to file statements of their campaign expenditures either before or after the primary and election, or both. Alabama, Florida, Georgia, Kentucky, Louisiana, Mississippi, North Carolina, Oklahoma, Tennessee, and Texas attempted either to prohibit or to regulate the contributing by corporations to campaign funds.[83]

Four other political reforms were prominently in vogue in 1912: the presidential preferential primary, the commission form of city government, the direct election of senators, and the initiative, referendum, and recall. During the presidential prenomination campaign of 1912, the issue of the presidential primary, in which the voters instructed delegates to the national convention to vote for their specified candidate, arose. The system, which supposedly deprived the political bosses of the power to select presidential candidates, was adopted in the South in 1912 by Florida, Georgia, and Mississippi. In 1913, a preferential primary law was enacted by the Texas legislature.[84]

The commission form of city government originated in Galveston, Texas, in 1900, under extraordinary circumstances.[85] What was begun as an emergency administrative measure proved so effective a method of city government that it was not only retained in Galveston, but spread throughout the country. By 1914, commission government was operative in most of the larger southern cities—in Galveston, Birmingham, Mobile, Montgomery, Shreveport, New Orleans, Wilmington, Oklahoma City, El Paso, Columbia, Chattanooga, Knoxville, Memphis, Dallas, San Antonio, Fort Worth, Houston, and Austin—and in many of the smaller cities,

---

83. This discussion of corrupt-practices legislation in the southern states is based upon Earl R. Sikes, *State and Federal Corrupt-Practices Legislation* (Durham, N.C.: Duke University Press, 1928), and is taken directly from the tables in pp. 258–291. It is difficult to determine the effectiveness of the laws. Sikes deals only with the legislation and not with the application of the laws.

84. Weeks, "The Texas Primary System," p. 532.

85. In 1900, a great hurricane and flood swept over the city and, in order to facilitate the progress of reconstruction, the citizens of Galveston placed the government and job of rebuilding in the hands of a business commission.

as well.[86] It is interesting to note in this connection that Staunton, Virginia, was the first city in the country to adopt the city manager form of government.[87]

There was, and had been since the days of the agrarian revolt, a widespread demand in the South for the adoption of a constitutional amendment providing for the popular election of United States senators.[88] As a matter of fact, by the time the amendment went into effect senatorial candidates in every southern state were first nominated by the people in a party primary. The principles of the initiative, referendum, and recall never found widespread acceptance in the South, although Oklahoma in 1907 and Arkansas in 1909 wrote the reforms into their bodies of law.[89]

Although southern progressives gave emphasis to the struggle for political reform, they by no means were oblivious of the necessity of reform in the economic and social fields. As early as 1889, the Georgia legislature passed a law limiting work in the textile mills to sixty-six hours a week,[90] and, in 1882, South Carolina enacted a similar law.[91] In 1911, both Georgia and North Carolina set the maximum number of hours per week operatives

86. Aside from the cities named above, the following places had the commission form of government by 1914: Anthony, Beaumont, Corpus Christi, Denison, Kennedy, Lyford, Marshall, Marble Falls, Palestine, Port Lavaca, Sherman, Waco, and Greenville, Texas; Ardmore, Bartlesville, Duncan, Enid, Miami, McAlester, Muskogee, Sapulpa, Tulsa, and Wagner, Oklahoma; Bristol, Clarksville, Etowah, and Richmond City, Tennessee.

Commission city government was almost unanimously favored by the press of the South. See, for example, editorials in Raleigh *News and Observer,* March 15, 16, 17, 1911; Wilmington *Morning Star,* December 20, 1910, March 14, 15, 1911; Charlotte *Daily Observer,* November 16, 1911; Pensacola *Evening News,* January 13, 1912; Columbia *State,* April 13, 1911; San Antonio *Express,* January 9, 1911; Mobile *Register,* December 24, 1910; Petersburg (Va.) *Daily Index-Appeal,* February 19, 20, 21, 22, 23, 1911; Oklahoma City *Daily Oklahoman,* March 11, 1911; Birmingham *Age-Herald,* May 2, 1911.

87. Benjamin P. De Witt, *The Progressive Movement* (New York: Macmillan, 1915), pp. 309–310.

88. See, for example, editorials in Tulsa *World,* February 25, 1911; New Orleans *Times-Democrat,* December 19, 1910; Nashville *Tennessean and American,* December 20, 1910.

89. Arkansas adopted only the initiative and referendum. (Thomas, *Arkansas and Its People,* I, 320.) For Oklahoma, see Grant Foreman, *History of Oklahoma* (Norman: University of Oklahoma Press, 1942), p. 314. For editorials favorable to the initiative, referendum, and recall, see New Orleans *Times-Democrat,* December 15, 1910; Nashville *Tennessean and American,* December 21, 1910; Oklahoma City *Daily Oklahoman,* February 17, 1911; Mobile *Register,* December 30, 1910; Columbia *State,* May 24, 1911; Little Rock *Arkansas Democrat,* December 2, 1910.

90. Elizabeth H. Davidson, *Child Labor Legislation in Southern Textile States* (Chapel Hill, N.C.: University of North Carolina Press, 1939), pp. 69–70.

91. Davidson, *Child Labor Legislation,* p. 90.

could work in textile factories at sixty.[92] In the matter of child-labor legislation, southern progressives were likewise active. "There are only a few characteristics of the child labor struggle in the South which differentiate it from the movement in the nation at large, and even in them the difference is largely one of degree rather than of kind," writes the authority on this movement.[93] The leader in the struggle for child labor legislation in the South was Edgar Gardner Murphy of Alabama, who was chiefly instrumental in the organization of the National Child Labor Committee.[94] Alexander J. McKelway, a Presbyterian minister of Charlotte, was the executive secretary in the South for the committee and for years carried on a struggle for child labor reform. The advocates of child labor legislation were not successful in accomplishing all of the objectives for which they were striving, but they did secure a number of reform laws in the textile states and presented vividly the child labor problem to the southern people.[95]

It is undoubtedly true that southern editors led the fight for progressive reforms in the South.[96] Especially was this true in the fight against the notorious convict-lease system and the iniquitous fee system that make crime profitable to sheriffs and constables. The editor of the Mobile *Register,* editors Frank L. Mayes of the Pensacola *Journal,* Fred Seeley of the Atlanta *Georgian,* and Edward W. Barrett of the Birmingham *Age-Herald* led in the fight against these twin evils.[97] Progressive editors and leaders were also active

92. Davidson, *Child Labor Legislation,* pp. 163, 206.
93. Davidson, *Child Labor Legislation,* p. 2.
94. Davidson, *Child Labor Legislation,* p. 125.
95. Miss Davidson (*Child Labor Legislation,* pp. 275–278) lists in a table the laws controlling child labor passed by the southern states.
96. Among the progressive newspapers in the South during the period after 1900, the following were outstanding: Mobile *Register,* Raleigh *News and Observer,* Petersburg *Daily Index-Appeal,* Columbia *State,* Atlanta *Georgian,* Atlanta *Journal,* Pensacola *Journal,* Birmingham *Age-Herald,* Birmingham *News,* Nashville *Tennessean and American,* New Orleans *Times-Democrat,* Little Rock *Arkansas Democrat,* Galveston *Daily News,* Dallas *Morning News,* Houston *Chronicle,* Louisville *Post,* Oklahoma City *Daily Oklahoman,* and Richmond *Times-Dispatch.*
97. The following editorial comment from the Mobile *Register,* October 10, 1911, is characteristic of the anticonvict-lease editorials:
"The Register has constantly fought this leasing system and has shown up its abuses and inhumanity. It is a relic of barbarism which is a stain on Alabama. . . . The leasing system is wrong in principle, unsafe in operation and cruel in effect."

during this period in an effort to secure adequate public health programs and insurance laws.[98]

Insofar as the foregoing movements for reform were progressive, it can be stated that there was a well-organized progressive movement in the South aimed at remedying the ills of the region's social and economic and political order. It, of course, had serious deficiencies. None of the southern editors, as far as this writer knows, who were agitating for political reforms gave any consideration to the ominously steady increase in farm tenancy. The perplexing problems of the economic, social, and political development of the Negro likewise escaped serious attention from southern editors. Although practically all the southern editors severely condemned lynching, none dared to advocate political rights for the black man. As far as progressive democracy went in the South, it was progressive democracy for the white man.

It is only too apparent to the student of recent southern history that many southern institutions and practices were, during this period, antiquated and backward. Bearing this fact in mind, it may none the less be stated with emphasis that there were few sections of the country in which the masses of the people were more powerful than in the South. Certainly many of the dominant southern political leaders during this period were not representative of the conservative classes. Demagogues like James K. Vardaman of Mississippi, Jeff Davis of Arkansas, or Cole Blease of South Carolina ostensibly represented the lower classes in a very definite class movement against the Bourbon conservatives. Progressives like Hoke Smith of Georgia; Robert L. Owen of Oklahoma; Charles A. Culberson, James S. Hogg, Thomas W. Gregory, and Robert L. Henry of Texas; Andrew J. Montague, William A. Jones, and Carter Glass of Virginia; Ollie M. James and J. C. W. Beckham of Kentucky; Luke Lea of Tennessee; Josephus Daniels, Claude and William W. Kitchin, and Walter Clark of North Carolina; Frank P. Glass and B. B. Comer of Alabama; William E. Gonzales, Ira B. Jones, and Ben R. Tillman of South Carolina; John M. Parker, Arsène Pujo, and Newton Blanchard of Louisiana; or Nathan P. Bryan and Frank L. Mayes

98. For the early years of the North Carolina public health board, see Hilda Jane Zimmerman, "The Formative Years of the North Carolina Board of Health, 1877-1893," *North Carolina Historical Review*, XXI (1944), 1-34.

of Florida continually fought the reactionaries and conservatives and were in the vanguard of the progressive movement, not only in the South, but in the nation as well.

19

The South and the "New Freedom":
An Interpretation

THE election of Woodrow Wilson and Democratic majorities in the House and Senate in 1912 confronted the Democrats of the South with their most serious challenge since before the Civil War. They had come to power more because of the disruption of the Republican party than because their party now represented the majority opinion of the country, and the future of the Democratic party for many years to come would depend upon their performance during the next two years. But the question whether they were not too much rent by personal factionalism and too sectionally conscious to govern in the national interest remained yet to be answered.

Southern Democrats in 1913 controlled practically all important congressional committees; they had a large majority in the Democratic caucuses in both houses; they had a President apparently responsive to their wishes, and they had a goodly representation in the Cabinet. Judged by all superficial appearances, at least, the South was "in the saddle." These, however, were only the outward signs of control. The fact that southerners happened to be chairmen of certain committees may or may not be important. The important question is whether they used the power

Reprinted from *The American Scholar*, XX (Summer 1951), 314–324; copyright 1970, Arthur S. Link.

they possessed to achieve political and economic objectives that the South especially desired, and whether they helped to shape the character of Wilsonian reform.

Wilson came to the presidency in 1913 with a clear conception of what the Democratic party should do to right the wrongs that special privilege had allegedly perpetrated through the Republican party. He would have the Democrats revise the tariff to eliminate all features of special privilege to domestic industries, bring the national banks into effective co-operation and control, and work out a new code for business in order to restore competition and make impossible the misuse of power by the giant corporations. This was the sum and substance of the "New Freedom." The political and economic millennium was to be achieved by these simple expedients, all of which were based upon the assumption implicit in Wilson's campaign addresses of 1912, namely, that the limits of federal authority under the Constitution would not permit, and wise statesmanship would not desire, the extension of federal authority directly into business operations or the use of that authority to change the social and economic relationships then existing among the various interest groups.

Wilson originally conceived of the New Freedom as the political means of implementing the doctrines of laissez-faire, by removing all kinds of special class legislation. It was, therefore, a program intended to meet the needs primarily of the business community. There was nothing in it for the farmers or laborers directly, although these groups presumably would benefit from lower tariff rates and the restoration of competition in business. But Wilson had no more idea of legislating to advance the interests of these particular groups than he did of granting subsidies to American manufacturers. It can be said, in brief, that the Wilsonian program had the one supreme objective of taking the government out of the business of subsidizing and directly regulating economic activity and of taking the country back to some mythical age when there was a perfect natural identification of economic interests.

The most significant fact about the first Wilson administration is that the New Freedom, as it was originally conceived by its author, survived for only a few months. It required only short contact with reality to convince Wilson that his elaborate doctrines of 1912 were inadequate to deal with such great concentrations of economic power as existed at the time. More important as a factor in moving him away from his laissez-faire position, however, were certain powerful political forces over which Wilson and his administration had no control and which, as it were, seized control of administration policy and pushed it far beyond the bounds that Wilson and his advisers had originally thought desirable. In effect, what occurred from 1913 to 1917 was that Wilson adopted many of the assumptions and almost the whole platform of Theodore Roosevelt's New Nationalism.

This metamorphosis in the Wilsonian program is the key to understanding the first Wilson administration. The southern contribution toward bringing the administration to an advanced position with regard to the exercise of federal authority was considerable, but the character of this contribution was different from what has been generally assumed. Southern Democrats in Congress were divided roughly into two factions. First, there was what might be called the administration faction, consisting mainly of committee chairmen like Oscar W. Underwood and Carter Glass, who, by and large, represented a political tradition and constituencies whose interests were more or less divergent from those of the more numerous southern group. Members of the administration faction were for the most part conservatives, although most of them had no fundamental political principles, were loyal party men, and would follow Wilson's lead. Second, there was a larger faction that represented more accurately the political traditions and economic interests of the South—the spokesmen for the agrarian interests of the South, men like Claude Kitchin, Otis Wingo, James K. Vardaman, and Robert L. Henry.

The southern agrarians of the Wilson period were the direct inheritors and now the prime articulators in the Democratic party of the philosophy underlying the agrarian crusade—namely, that it was government's duty to intervene directly in economic affairs in order to benefit submerged or politically impotent economic interests. As it turned out, the existence and power of the southern agrarian group had important consequences for the Democratic party, the Wilson administration, and the nation. Whereas the administration faction usually followed the regular party line, the southern agrarians were often far to the left of it; and in the end they helped to make Wilson an advanced progressive and helped

to commit his administration to a broad program of welfare legislation.

The program of the southern agrarians was aimed at benefit-
ing the farmers almost exclusively. Although this had been true
also of the Democratic program in 1896, Bryan and progressive
Democrats in the North and West had moved beyond the almost
pure agrarianism of 1896. There was a growing concern for the
plight of submerged groups from about 1890 to 1913 and a consequent rise of a great movement for social justice. This phase
of progressivism had not been totally absent in the South, but
the southern states were still overwhelmingly rural, and most
southerners had no conception of the grave social and economic
problems raised by industrialization and urbanization.

Hence southern progressives were more concerned with
strengthening the political and economic position of the farmers,
through regulation of railroads and corporations, a low tariff, the
direct primary, and the like, than with tenement reforms, minimum wage legislation, or workmen's compensation legislation.
But the important point about the southern agrarian program is
not that it was limited in scope, but that its advocates were an
important element in the Democratic party and that they were
now in a position to give voice to their own demands.

The brief period when the philosophy of the New Freedom
had any real authority was the few months in 1913 when the
Underwood tariff bill was under discussion in Congress. There
was little disagreement among Democratic congressmen, progressive or conservative, over the provisions of the bill, except for
minor differences on the wool and sugar schedules. There was
a much greater difference of opinion between the conservatives
and the agrarian radicals, however, on the question of the reorganization of the banking system and the control of the money
supply. It was here that the southern agrarians, acting with their
colleagues from the West, first helped to move their party away
from laissez-faire tpward a dynamic concept of government.

In line with his New Freedom principles, Wilson was inclined
to favor the banking and monetary system proposed by the National Monetary Commission, one providing for a reserve association or associations owned and controlled by the bankers
themselves. The original Glass bill, which had the tentative endorsement of the administration, provided for such an arrangement.

But even before the Federal Reserve bill emerged from the House Banking Committee, there occurred a momentous struggle within the party councils that was not ended until the agrarian leaders had won all their important demands. Secretary of State Bryan and Louis D. Brandeis persuaded the President that a banking bill which did not provide for exclusive governmental control, on the top level, was not only unwise but also would never be approved by the House caucus. This was true, incidentally, regardless of the position Bryan might have taken in the controversy.

Wilson was won over by the persuasive arguments of Bryan and Brandeis and the threats of the radicals. Thus the Glass bill, as it finally emerged from the House committee, provided for a decentralized reserve system, for government issue of federal reserve currency, and for an over-all supervision and limited control of the new system by a central reserve board composed exclusively of presidential appointees. It marked, to all practical purposes, the demise of the New Freedom and the beginning of the rise to dominance of the progressives in the Wilson administration.

Bryan and the western Democrats were now satisfied, but not the southern agrarian leaders. In spite of the radical changes that had been effected, the new banking system still would operate exclusively for the benefit of the business community. Here was the rub, as far as the southern radicals were concerned. After tariff reform had been accomplished, their main objective was the establishment of a system by which farmers could obtain easier and cheaper credit. When the Glass bill was published, and the southern agrarians discovered that it included no provision for agricultural credit, they rose in rebellion and declared that they would help the Republicans defeat the measure if the administration did not concede their demands. The fight between the administration forces and the southern agrarians was bitter, and for a time threatened to defeat banking reform altogether. Suffice it to say that, in spite of the ridicule of the eastern press and in spite of the opposition of the administration and of Wilson's spokesmen in the House, the Federal Reserve bill as finally passed by Congress contained ample provisions for short-term agricultural credit. And this was true because Wilson realized that he must give in to the demands of the southerners.

The philosophic foundations of the New Freedom were dealt

another heavy blow during the formulation of an antitrust policy by administration leaders. It was Wilson's original idea that all that was required was to define precisely what constituted an unfair trade practice or illegal restraint of trade, so as to remove all element of doubt from the laws. The enforcement of the anti-trust laws would be delegated, as before, to the Justice Department and the courts. Some of the southern radicals proposed more drastic remedies, such as prescribing by law the percentage of the total production of a field of industry which one corporation would be allowed to control, or a high excess profits tax which would increase in direct proportion to the size of the industry; but they made no determined fight for these proposals. Wilson, therefore, gave the job of drawing up the measure to Representative Clayton of Alabama, chairman of the Judiciary Committee, and the bill that came out of his committee was simply a synthesis of current ideas, most of which were already embodied in the laws of many states. In addition, Representative Covington of Maryland drew up at Wilson's request a bill providing for an interstate trade commission, which was to be an enlarged Bureau of Corporations and without any real authority over business practices.

Thus far, Wilson had proceeded in line with his New Freedom concepts. At this point, however, an important turn in administration policy occurred. Brandeis, George L. Rublee, and Representative Stevens of New Hampshire visited the President and persuaded him to change the character of his antitrust program entirely. Under their direction, the Clayton bill was rewritten so as to provide for greater flexibility in defining an unfair trade practice and, more important, the interstate trade commission was reconstituted as the Federal Trade Commission and given apparently vast authority over the day-to-day operations of the business world. The Covington bill had provided for nothing more than an investigatory body to serve as an adjunct of the Justice Department. In the revised bill, the Commission was established as an independent regulatory agency, empowered to supervise business practices and to issue cease and desist orders when it found that corporations were engaging in unfair practices. This last change marked the complete adoption by the Wilson administration of Roosevelt's program for the regulation of business.

The southern leaders in Congress had nothing to do with bringing about this profound change in Wilson's antitrust policy. The southern and western agrarian radicals, acting with a small labor bloc in the House, worked hard, however, to have a provision inserted in the Clayton bill exempting farm and labor unions from the operation and application of the antitrust laws. This had been one of the major objectives of the American Federation of Labor since 1906 and had been given Democratic approval in the platforms of 1908 and 1912. Although Wilson was rapidly abandoning his New Freedom assumptions, he was not yet ready to go so far as to approve what was obviously legislation in the interest of particular classes. Since the first days of his administration, he had resisted bitterly this move, and a bill specifically exempting farm and labor unions from antitrust prosecutions, which had been passed by the House in the previous session, was blocked by administration pressure. When the Clayton bill was under discussion in the House committee, however, the agrarian and labor bloc declared that they would guarantee its defeat unless Wilson gave in to their demands.

Thus faced with another major revolt within his party, Wilson resolved his dilemma by resorting, it must be admitted, to one of the most artful dodges in the history of American politics. The famous labor provisions of the Clayton bill were drawn by Rep. E. Y. Webb of North Carolina, who had succeeded Clayton as chairman of the Judiciary Committee, and represented Wilson's attitude perfectly. On the face of it, the new provision did indeed seem to give the exemption and immunity from antitrust prosecutions that the farm and labor spokesmen were demanding. Actually, this was not the case at all. Farm and labor organizations were not to be construed by the courts as being, per se, combinations in restraint of trade, but they were in no way freed from the threat of prosecution if they violated the antitrust laws.

Wilson had completed his program of domestic reform by the fall of 1914. In his letters and public statements at the time, he made it clear that he thought everything had been done that was necessary to clear away special privilege and put all classes on an equal footing. Under the operation of the beneficent new laws, Wilson was sure that the nation would enjoy a long period of prosperity and economic freedom. As we have seen, he had been forced partially to abandon his earlier position and to make important concessions in order to get his program across. He was reconciled to the concessions he had been compelled to make, but he was absolutely determined to draw the line at the point it had reached by the fall of 1914.

In fact, a pronounced reaction against progressive policies had set in among Wilson and his advisers during the spring of 1914, and relations between the President and progressive leaders became exceedingly strained at this time. The following year, 1915, was practically barren of progressive accomplishments, except for the La Follette Seamen's Act, which the administration had opposed and which Wilson almost vetoed. There were, however, several great political forces at work which were so strong that Wilson would be compelled to accommodate his program to satisfy their demands. One was the well-organized agrarian movement for the establishment of a federal system of long-term rural credits. Another was the movement in behalf of federal social legislation, which was rapidly gaining momentum during this period. Another was the movement for woman suffrage, which was becoming so powerful that it would soon be dangerous for any politician to oppose it. Finally, there was the fact that the Progressive party was obviously disintegrating after 1914 and that the only hope the Democrats had of obtaining a national majority in 1916 was in winning a large minority of the former Bull Moosers to the Democratic side.

Wilson resisted this movement to extend the intervention of the federal government into the fields mentioned here as long as he could do so safely. Then, when it became evident that the Democrats could win the election of 1916 only by adopting the New Nationalism, lock, stock, and barrel, Wilson capitulated and supported the very demands he had so long opposed, as strongly as if he had been their originator. We do not have the space to discuss this last and most important phase of Wilsonian reform in any detail, except to consider the extent to which the southern leaders contributed to the administration's final, complete surrender to the New Nationalism.

The main objective of the southern agrarian progressives after 1914 was the adoption of a federal rural credits bill. The first nationwide movement for long-term federal rural credit facilities had been inaugurated by the Southern Commercial Congress in 1913, and during the next year or two, there was widespread discussion of the subject all over the country. In the spring of 1914, a joint subcommittee drew up the bill which was finally passed in 1916 and which would have passed in 1914 had not Wilson let it be known that he would veto the bill if Congress enacted it. Both Wilson and the agrarian leaders proclaimed themselves advocates of a rural credits measure. What, therefore, was the root of the difference between them? Wilson would not agree to the establishment of a system involving direct subsidies or financial support by the government, and Wilson, Secretary of Agriculture Houston, and Carter Glass were insistent that the government should do no more than provide for the structure of a rural credits system, with capital and management to be provided by private sources. The agrarian spokesmen, on the other hand, contended that any system which was not operated and financed by the government was bound to fail. But as this involved the direct intervention by the government in behalf of a special class, Wilson was absolutely adamant against it. The result was an impasse, with both sides holding out stubbornly for their own proposals until 1916, when Wilson accepted the agrarian proposal for reasons of political expediency.

It was, in fact, in agricultural legislation that the southern agrarians had the greatest influence in the shaping of the later Wilsonian program. Their greatest contribution was undoubtedly the forcing of the Rural Credits Act of 1916, but they were also able to obtain the adoption of the Lever Warehouse Act in 1914, the Smith-Lever Act for rural extension work of the same year, the Smith-Hughes Act for vocational education, and the program of federal subsidies for highway improvement in 1916.

Southern influence was practically negligible, however, in the formulation of the remaining great social and economic legislation of 1916—the federal Workmen's Compensation Act, the Child Labor Law, the Adamson Act, and the act establishing the Federal Tariff Commission. But there still remain three other areas of legislation in which the influence of the southern agrarians was decisive and which merit notice here.

The first involved the question of what sort of military and naval bills Congress should enact in 1916. On this controversial subject, the southern progressives joined with radicals throughout the country in resisting the administration's designs greatly to increase the navy and to establish a large volunteer army. They were not successful in blocking the movement for a large navy, because the pressure here was too great. But they were signally successful in blocking Wilson's plans for military preparedness, indeed, in emasculating them.

The second field of legislation in which southern progressive influence was decisive was the area of federal fiscal policy. Before the outbreak of World War I, Wilson and McAdoo were able to keep a firm grip on the formulation of tax policies, and their influence was conservative indeed. The tax structure that the Republicans had erected and which was weighted so heavily in favor of the upper classes was left practically undisturbed by the Wilson administration. An income tax provision was included in the Underwood Tariff Law, to make up the anticipated deficit resulting from the lower duties, but the rates were very low and the administration was quick to make it clear that it had no intention of using the income tax to effect a redistribution of wealth.

The outbreak of the war in Europe in the summer of 1914 caused a temporary disarrangement of the finances of the United States and resulted in a sharp decline in imports, which meant that the administration was faced with an alarming decline in revenues. To meet this emergency, McAdoo proposed a series of new excise taxes and a tax on freight shipments, such as had been applied during the Spanish-American War. The southern and western agrarians rebelled at the administration's emergency tax program, claiming that it would throw the whole burden of carrying the country through the crisis on the masses and demanding instead an increase in the income tax. They were successful in eliminating the tax on freight shipments and in getting most of the new taxes put on alcoholic beverages and other luxuries. Even so, they did not like the emergency tax law and vowed that they would continue to fight all such consumption taxes.

With the opening of Congress in December 1915, the southern progressives found themselves virtually in control of the House Ways and Means Committee. Long before the new session convened, a majority of the committee declared in writing to the new chairman, Claude Kitchin of North Carolina, their determination to overhaul the tax structure and make it more democratic. The result was that, during the winter and spring of 1916, the control of federal tax policy was literally taken out of the hands of the administration leaders and assumed by these southern agrarians and their western allies. It was obvious by this time that some kind of preparedness measures would be adopted, and that either the government would have to find new sources of revenue or else resort to borrowing. The Republicans proposed a bond issue; the administration proposed new consumption and excise and increased income taxes. The Ways and Means Committee, however, replied with one of the most startling and significant tax bills in the history of the country. The southern agrarians, who had bitterly resisted the preparedness movement, saw now that new defense measures were inevitable; but they were determined that the people of the East, who had been most vociferous in support of preparedness, should pay for it. Kitchin said as much, in fact, before the House caucus when he explained the new tax bill, which greatly increased the income tax, levied the first federal inheritance tax in our history, and placed an excess profits tax on munitions manufacturers.

The last area in which southern influence was decisive in determining the policies of the Wilson administration was the federal government's policy toward Negroes. Here the southern contribution was definitely retrogressive and proved that it was impossible for white southerners of all shades of opinion to get much beyond the rationale of slavery. Suffice it to say that Wilson practically sacrificed the Negroes on the altar of political expediency, by allowing segregation in the government departments, dismissal and downgrading of Negro civil servants in the South, and the like, in order to win southern support for his program.

Yet in spite of this and other blind spots in the southern progressive program, it must be concluded that the contributions of the southern agrarians were undoubtedly in many ways decisive in moving the Wilson administration away from a static laissez-faire program, to which it was originally dedicated, toward a dynamic, positive program of federal action. Although their program was limited in scope and motivated largely by class interests, the southern progressives could claim as much credit as could several other major groups for the amazing metamorphosis in Democratic policy that occurred from 1913 to 1916. That is the real significance of their contribution.

20

The Cotton Crisis, the South, and Anglo-American Diplomacy, 1914–1915

THE outbreak of the First World War in early August 1914 disorganized international trade and commodity markets, provoked a near panic on Wall Street, and deepened a business depression that had begun during the last months of 1913. But nowhere in the United States was the impact of the war more disastrous than in the South. Since 1897, southerners had ridden the crest of the wave of inflation in commodity prices that had brought almost unparalleled prosperity to the rural areas. Between 1897 and 1913, the production of cotton had increased from roughly 10,900,000 to 14,000,000 bales, yet prices had also steadily risen under the pressure of a seemingly insatiable world demand. We do not need to belabor the obvious consequences of this phenomenon, for cotton was still the king of the southern economy.

The happy economic world of the South fell with a crash in the late summer and autumn of 1914, as the foundations of the cotton market sagged and then collapsed altogether. The prime cause of the cotton panic was the fear of an enormous domestic oversupply, stimulated by reports of the largest cotton crop in

Reprinted from J. Carlyle Sitterson, editor, *Studies in Southern History in Memory of Albert Ray Newsome, 1894–1951* (Chapel Hill, N.C.: University of North Carolina Press, 1957), pp. 122–138, by permission of the Director of the University of North Carolina Press.

American history, by the anticipation of a decrease in normal British purchases, and above all by the fear that the large central European market, which absorbed more than one fourth of the American cotton exported in 1913, or about 2,500,000 bales, would be closed because of the lack of neutral shipping and perhaps because of British restrictions on seaborne commerce to the Central Powers.

Whatever the causes, the consequences of the cotton panic were dire indeed. In order to protect the brokers, the New York, Liverpool, New Orleans, and other important cotton exchanges closed within a week after the outbreak of hostilities in Europe. Thus almost overnight the normal market ceased to exist, and prices fell, when buyers could be found at all, from about twelve and one half cents a pound in July to between six and seven cents a pound by mid-October 1914. For the South as a whole, this meant a potential loss of half the value of the cotton crop, or some $500,000,000, with catastrophic consequences for the merchants, factors, and bankers who financed the crop and served the rural areas and above all for the thousands of cotton growers, large and small, who were most immediately affected.

The response of the southern leaders to this, the most portentous threat to southern prosperity since the depression of the 1890s, came almost simultaneously with the outbreak of the panic. On August 3, 1914, while the European nations were still busy declaring war on one another, E. J. Watson of Columbia, Commissioner of Agriculture of South Carolina and president of the Southern Cotton Congress,[1] summoned southern governors, commissioners of agriculture, bankers, merchants, and farm leaders to meet in Washington on August 13 and 14 with members of the Wilson administration and southerners in Congress to discuss ways and means of averting wholesale panic. "In two days the price of cotton has begun to fall startlingly," Watson warned. "Cotton is about to move to the markets; the markets are about to be curtailed by millions of bales and closed. . . . It is clear that great damage has already been done."[2] On August 4, the day following Watson's call, moreover, representatives and senators from the cotton states,

1. Formed in Montgomery, Alabama, in 1911 by representatives of the National Farmers' Union, cotton growers, and southern businessmen and bankers.
2. E. J. Watson to "the People of the Cotton Belt," August 3, 1914, copy in the Papers of Daniel A. Tompkins, University of North Carolina, Chapel Hill, N.C.

led by Rep. A. F. Lever of South Carolina and Sen. Hoke Smith of Georgia, met on Capitol Hill to make plans for the coming meeting and to draw administration leaders into discussions.[3]

The so-called cotton conference met in the Pan-American Building in Washington on August 24 and 25, 1914, with some two hundred southern farm and business leaders in attendance. One speaker from Louisiana demanded that the federal government offer to buy cotton at forty dollars a bale, while a Mississippi congressman proposed that Congress permit state banks to issue currency on a basis of warehouse receipts for cotton. But on the whole it was a tame affair, and the delegates listened patiently while Secretary of the Treasury William G. McAdoo condemned such "perfectly wild and ridiculous" schemes and explained the administration's plans to meet the cotton crisis. There could be no thought, he insisted, of projecting the federal government into direct support of the market; the only feasible solution was the extension of short-term credit to enable the southern farmers to hold their surplus cotton.[4]

There was a momentary return of confidence during early September, encouraged by the "buy a bale of cotton" movement, which began in the South around September 1, 1914, and spread to the North three weeks later. "There is no reason, in my opinion, for pessimism in the South about cotton," McAdoo declared reassuringly on September 21.

The assistance which the Federal Government is extending to the banks, through the issuance of national bank currency notes secured by cotton warehouse receipts, has already greatly improved the situation, and if the banks, the merchants, and the manufacturers throughout the South

3. New York *World*, August 5 and 19, 1914.

4. New York *Journal of Commerce*, August 25 and 26, 1914; New York *Times*, August 25 and 26, 1914.

McAdoo explained his relief plan in explicit detail in a public statement issued two days after the end of the cotton conference. He would, the Secretary promised, issue emergency currency authorized by the Aldrich-Vreeland Act of 1908 to groups of national banks on a basis of short-term notes secured by warehouse receipts for cotton or tobacco, at 75 percent of the face value of the notes. In this manner, he continued, southern merchants and bankers could obtain ample credit to carry the farmers through the next critical four months. (New York *Times*, August 28, 1914.)

Studying McAddo's plan, a committee appointed by the Secretary at the cotton conference approved and suggested that southern banks lend to the farmers on a basis of eight cents a pound for cotton. (*Financial Age*, XXX [September 5, 1914], 418.)

will quit taking counsel of fear and will go forward with confidence, the situation will, I believe, improve still further.[5]

Yet developments in the South were generating a new and more critical phase of the cotton crisis even as McAdoo spoke. Experience soon proved that the currency machinery authorized by the Aldrich-Vreeland Act was too cumbersome and inadequate to provide any substantial credit relief. For one thing, the emergency currency authorized by this measure had to be redeemed within four months, and it was obviously impossible to move the cotton crop of 1914 within so short a time.[6] For another, the great mass of banks that served the southern farmers and merchants, the country banks, were not members of the national banking system and could not participate in the so-called national currency associations formed under the Aldrich-Vreeland Act for the purpose of issuing emergency currency. In many cases, moreover, the state banks found it simply impossible to borrow the emergency currency from the larger commercial banks. Clarence Poe of Raleigh, North Carolina, editor of the *Progressive Farmer* and one of the leading southern agrarian spokesmen, contrasted McAdoo's optimistic forecasts with reality in early October 1914:

The facts are that we have not been able to get from the banks the help indicated by the foregoing utterances [by the Secretary of the Treasury]. . . . The State banks . . . report that they can't get additional currency from their National banking correspondents. Even the offer to issue emergency currency to 75 per cent of the value of warehouse receipts was illusive. . . . In a word, the banks have fallen down on their job—not voluntarily perhaps, but involuntarily. They have been framed for serving commercial interests, and they are afraid to risk making heavy loans to agricultural interests.[7]

As the bottom dropped out of the market when cotton began to move in large quantities during early October, a gripping fear and a demand for speedy federal action spread through the South. "It seems to me that unless we are given relief and that in short order," one South Carolina country banker wrote, "the whole south will be put into bankruptcy and ruin."[8] "Ruin [is] now

5. New York *Times*, September 22, 1914.

6. As Gov. Oliver B. Colquitt of Texas pointed out. See Colquitt and C. H. Terrell to R. L. Henry, September 12, 1914, the Papers of Carter Glass, University of Virginia, Charlottesville, Va.; hereinafter cited as the Glass Papers.

7. C. Poe to Josephus Daniels, October 5, 1914, the Papers of Woodrow Wilson, Library of Congress, Washington, D.C.; hereinafter cited as the Wilson Papers.

8. J. W. Hamer to Woodrow Wilson, October 8, 1914, *ibid.*

running riot in the South," warned Sen. Morris Sheppard of Texas. "May God in his infinite wisdom point us some path to safety." [9] "The deliberate judgment of our most capable thinkers," added a group of Austin bankers, "is [that] without prompt and substantial help from the national government, Texas will soon confront a condition of general bankruptcy. The condition grows more threatening every day." [10]

It was no time, southern leaders in all walks of life declared, for halfway measures or reliance upon voluntary solution. It was a time, they said, for bold, even unprecedented, action by the federal government, which alone could cope with a problem so enormous. On September 18, 1914, a spokesman for the National Farmers' Union offered a simple plan that promised a comprehensive solution. Let Congress, he suggested, first reinforce the market by offering to buy three or four million bales of cotton at twelve cents a pound; then let Congress give definitive relief by imposing a tax of ten cents a pound on all cotton produced in 1915 in excess of one half the crop of 1914. [11] Hailed by leaders from all parts of the South, the Farmers' Union plan at once became the region's solution for the cotton crisis.

A controversy of large proportions developed rapidly in the wake of the discussions that followed the publication of the Farmers' Union plan, as spokesmen for the Wilson administration condemned the proposal and southern leaders in Congress prepared for their first important battle with the administration. The Secretary of Agriculture, David F. Houston, attempted to halt the burgeoning movement for decisive federal action by issuing a stern rebuke to the southern leaders on September 28, 1914. The federal government, he warned, would not yield to this unprecedented demand for special privileges and an unconstitutional regulation of agriculture. "It is not a question of sympathy—the cotton growers have the sympathy of the whole world in their distress," he added, "but a question of sound business and good government." [12] Meeting in Washington the following day, a conference of southern governors, senators, and congressmen replied with a series

9. Sheppard to Wilson, October 29, 1914, *ibid.*

10. William R. Hamby *et al.* to E. M. House, October 13, 1914, the Papers of Edward M. House, Yale University, New Haven, Conn.; hereinafter cited as the House Papers.

11. S. G. McLendon to Woodrow Wilson, September 18, 1914, Wilson Papers.

12. New York *Times,* September 29, 1914.

of resolutions demanding immediate action along the lines of the Farmers' Union plan.[13]

Thus the stage was set for the decisive congressional phase of the struggle. It opened in the first week of October, when Rep. Robert L. Henry of Texas, speaking for the newly formed cotton bloc, appealed directly to the President and the Secretary of the Treasury on October 2 [14] and three days later introduced a cotton relief bill in the House of Representatives. It instructed the Secretary of the Treasury to issue $500,000,000 in currency for deposit in national and state banks in the cotton states; in addition, it required the banks to lend the money to cotton producers at 3 percent interest against the security of cotton valued at ten cents a pound.

"Mr. Speaker," Henry declared in an impassioned defense of his bill,

the people of the South are prostrated in this present crisis. . . . What we need is . . . the strong arm of this Federal Government to be extended to the 30,000,000 people in the South who produce 15,000,000 bales of cotton. . . . *So we resort to the issuance of United States notes by the Federal Government, the only sovereignty and agency that has the power and upon whom rests the duty to supply the people with an adequate amount of currency in such crises as these.* . . . That is the proposition. I know that gentlemen will say that this is populism and amounts almost to anarchy in our financial system. . . . But I maintain that this Government was set up for the benefit and protection of the people. Sirs, in a crisis like this I have crossed the Rubicon, I have burned my bridges, and am ready to *fight for the principle that this Government shall issue its currency and preserve the progress and prosperity of the southern people.*[15]

The battle over relief for the cotton states raged with increasing intensity in Washington all during the first three weeks of October 1914, as most of the southern agrarian representatives and senators rallied behind the Henry bill or some variation of it and the administration and its loyal spokesmen in Congress joined with the Republican minority to head off the southern

13. *Ibid.,* September 30, 1914.
14. R. L. Henry *et al.,* "Memorandum for the President," October 2, 1914, Wilson Papers; also printed as R. L. Henry to W. G. McAdoo, October 2, 1914, in *Congressional Record,* 63d Congress, 2d sess., pp. 16069–16070.
15. *Ibid.,* pp. 16204–16208.

revolt. There was more involved here than met the casual eye. The superficial issue was the method and form of federal relief; the fundamental issue, however, involved the larger question of the limits of federal activity in the economic field. Still imbued with the New Freedom doctrines of limited governmental activity and the New Freedom opposition to direct federal intervention in behalf of any class or interest, President Woodrow Wilson and his followers were in principle opposed to direct federal support of the cotton market or regulation of crop acreage. The southern agrarians, on the other hand, were the inheritors of the Populist tradition and were in 1914 among the prime exponents in the United States of a program of comprehensive federal aid to agriculture and labor.[16]

We can better understand the cotton controversy when we view it in light of the political situation prevailing in 1913 and 1914. That controversy was no isolated episode; on the contrary, it was a revealing phase of a long struggle between a relatively conservative administration and a powerful pressure group, the so-called southern agrarian radicals, who, along with other advanced progressive groups, were seeking to extend the authority of the federal government into many new areas.

During 1913 and early 1914, the southern agrarians had joined midwestern Republican insurgents in successful forays to force the Wilson administration to increase the income tax imposed by the Underwood tariff bill and to accept amendments that greatly expanded the measure of public control over the banking system provided in the Federal Reserve Act. At the same time, they had struggled vainly for a large-scale rural credit system and for the exemption of labor and farm organizations from the penalties of the antitrust laws, and other such conflicts impended in the future.[17] The controversy over relief for the cotton farmers, however, revealed the ideological gulf separating the administration and the advanced progressive elements in Congress and the country more clearly than did any other episode of the Wilson era.

President Wilson, who had earlier withdrawn largely from

16. For a fuller discussion of the southern agrarian group and their conflict with and contributions to the Wilsonian domestic program, see "The South and the New Freedom: An Interpretation," pp. 298–308, this volume.

17. See A. S. Link, *Woodrow Wilson and the Progressive Era* (New York: Harper & Brothers, 1954), and *Wilson: The New Freedom* (Princeton, N.J.: Princeton University Press, 1956).

public affairs following the death of his wife on August 6, 1914, took charge of the administration forces two days after Representative Henry introduced his relief measure. Addressing a delegation of North Carolinians who came to the White House on October 7, the President declared that the cotton crisis had to be met, not with the heart, but with the head, and "within the limitations of economic law and safe finance." [18] It was an unmistakable warning that he would veto the Henry bill if Congress approved it. The following day, October 8, moreover, Wilson told a group of Georgians that he did not favor plans to reduce cotton acreage in 1915. Such plans, he said, had to be uniform and universal in order to succeed, and he did not see how they were possible. [19]

The President's opposition was a crushing blow, but Henry and a group of southerners prepared a new relief bill on October 7 and 8 in the hope of finding an acceptable compromise. Introduced in the House on October 9, the revised Henry bill directed the Secretary of the Treasury to raise $250,000,000 through the sale of so-called Panama Canal bonds and to deposit the money in southern national and state banks for the use of cotton and tobacco farmers. [20] On October 14, moreover, Sen. Hoke Smith of Georgia, spokesman for a large group of senators from the cotton states, introduced a similar measure, which included also a provision for a prohibitive tax on all cotton grown in 1915 in excess of one half the crop of 1914. [21]

In spite of overwhelming southern popular support and of attempts by southern leaders in both houses to filibuster and prevent congressional adjournment or approval of a war revenue tax bill if some relief for the South were not forthcoming, the President and his lieutenants stood firm against all proposals for direct assistance. In the end, therefore, the southern insurgents

18. New York *Times*, October 8, 1914.

19. *Ibid.*, October 9, 1914.

20. *Ibid.*, October 9 and 10, 1914; R. L. Henry to Carter Glass, October 9, 1914, Glass Papers, enclosing a copy of the revised Henry bill.

21. The Smith bill provided that the Secretary of the Treasury should issue $250,000,000 in bonds, to be given directly to farmers in exchange for cotton at fifty dollars a bale. The bonds would bear interest at 4 percent and would be payable at the end of three years. (New York *Times*, October 15, 1914.)

gave up the fight and permitted Congress to adjourn on October 24, 1914.[22]

The President and Secretary of the Treasury, meanwhile, had been genuinely alarmed by the threat of economic ruin in the South and hard at work on their own program even while they stood off the southern demands for federal intervention to support the cotton market. "I have spent more sleepless nights thinking about cotton than anything else with which I have had to deal since I took charge of the Treasury Department," McAdoo wrote on October 14, 1914.[23] "The thing that is giving us the greatest concern just now," Wilson wrote the following day, "is the situation of the South in view of the tremendous curtailment of the market for her one marketable crop, the cotton. For a little while it looked like bankruptcy, and that is among the disturbing possibilities yet." [24]

To confront the problem and allay the savage criticism of many southerners,[25] McAdoo and other administration leaders worked out a program to save the cotton farmers without launching the federal government upon allegedly dangerous experiments. The first item was a measure written by McAdoo and introduced in Congress in August 1914, which provided for the establishment of a federally owned and operated shipping line, in part in order to carry cotton to European neutrals and to Germany. This, the so-called ship-purchase bill, was defeated by a bipartisan conservative coalition in the Senate in the last days of the Sixty-Third Congress in March 1915. The second item in the administration's

22. For running accounts of the final phase of the controversy in Congress, see the debates in the *Congressional Record,* 63d Congress, 2d sess., vol. 51, part 16; New York *Times,* October 13, 15, 17, 22, 23, and 25, 1914; and New York *World,* October 18 and 23, 1914.

23. W. G. McAdoo to J. Daniels, October 14, 1914, the Papers of Josephus Daniels, Library of Congress, Washington, D.C.; hereinafter cited as the Daniels Papers.

24. Wilson to Mrs. Crawford H. Toy, October 15, 1914, the Ray S. Baker Collection of Woodrow Wilson materials, Library of Congress, Washington, D.C.

25. See, *e.g.,* the statement by Gov. O. B. Colquitt of Texas, printed in the Fort Worth *Star-Telegram* and other newspapers on December 27, 1914. "The President," Colquitt charged, "stood in the road and condemned the South, which made him, to heavier loss and more widespread misery than it has known in three generations. He vindicated an obsolete theory of political economy but he mighty near ruined the country by doing it."

program was a measure prepared by Secretary Houston and sponsored by Rep. A. F. Lever of South Carolina. It provided for a system of federal inspection and licensing of agricultural warehouses, in order to facilitate borrowing by farmers against warehouse receipts. The southern insurgents attacked the Lever bill as a poor substitute for their own relief measure; but the President applied heavy personal pressure and obtained congressional approval a few days before Congress adjourned in October 1914.

The administration's ace in the hole, however, was an ambitious plan, first proposed in early October 1914 by Festus J. Wade, president of the Mercantile National Bank of St. Louis, to mobilize private banking resources in a great cotton loan fund to be used to enable southern farmers to hold their cotton for at least one year. McAdoo and Col. Edward M. House of Texas, the President's leading adviser, at once made the cotton loan plan the cornerstone of the administration's program for southern relief. As House explained to Wilson, "This is an emergency matter of the greatest importance. . . . If this plan goes through, . . . [southerners] will be satisfied that the Administration has met the emergency." [26]

The story of the formation of the cotton loan fund can be briefly told. The first high-level discussions began in Washington on October 9, 1914, when McAdoo and House conferred with Wade and other St. Louis bankers and businessmen and Albert H. Wiggin of the Chase National Bank of New York. Colonel House explained the proposal to the leading Wall Street bankers on October 13 and won their promise to participate. The newly organized Federal Reserve Board gave its blessing on October 24 and, besides, agreed to administer the fund. Finally, the plan went into effect on November 30, 1914, after the completion of the subscriptions and in spite of the strong opposition of New England bankers, who had no desire to abet any scheme to help maintain the price of raw cotton. [27]

26. E. M. House to Wilson, October 14, 1914, Wilson Papers.

27. The above paragraph is based upon E. M. House to Wilson, October 9 and 14, 1914; *ibid.*; the Diary of Edward M. House, Yale University, New Haven, Conn., October 13, 14, and 17, 1914; W. G. McAdoo to E. M. House, October 12, 1914, House Papers; E. M. House to W. R. Hamby, October 14, 1914, *ibid.*; S. R. Bertron to Wilson, October 13, 1914, Wilson Papers; W. G. McAdoo to Wilson, November 6, 1914, *ibid.*; New York *Journal of Commerce,* October 6, 7, and 30, 1914; New York *Times,* October 9, 10, 16, 20, and 25, November 18, and December 9, 1914. For the opposition of the New England bankers, see Josiah Quincy to E. M. House, October 28 and November 9, 1914, House Papers; *Financial Age,* XXX (November 14, 1914), 917; St. Louis *Star,* November 16, 1914;

As it was finally put into operation, the plan established a cotton loan fund of $135,000,000, two thirds of which was subscribed by banks in the North and Middle West, to be administered by a committee of Federal Reserve Board members and private bankers and distributed to banks in the cotton states by state and local committees. The local banks, in turn, might lend the money to farmers against warehouse receipts on a basis of 4.8 cents a pound for middling cotton. Such loans would bear interest at 6 percent, would run for one year, and might be renewed for an additional six months.[28]

Launched with great fanfare as the salvation of the South, the cotton loan fund soon proved a total failure as a means of affording new credit to the hard-pressed farmers. This was true, primarily, because, for all their troubles, the farmers could get better terms than 4.8 cents a pound on cotton through ordinary banking channels, especially through the Federal Reserve System, which went into operation in November 1914. "There is no doubt," one Texan complained,

> but what the cotton loan plan is badly balled up. . . . It is a matter of common rumor in banking circles in Texas that bankers in the North and East have stated that it was not intended by at least some of the subscribers to the fund that the money subscribed should be actually used; that the condition should be made so onerous and unworkable that it would not be used, and that in this way it would serve the purposes of "jollying the South," without really giving them any financial relief.[29]

It was true, besides, because the machinery of the plan was so cumbersome as to make it virtually impossible for the ordinary farmer to obtain a loan.[30] As a result, the cotton loan fund committee had made seven loans, totaling some $28,000, by the time it wound up its affairs and went out of business in early February 1915.[31]

New York *Sun*, November 16, 1914; Boston *Transcript*, November 19, 1914.
  28. New York *Times*, October 28 and December 9, 1914.
  29. Thomas B. Love to E. M. House, December 13, 1914, House Papers.
  30. For an illustration of these difficulties, see the *Financial Age*, XXX (November 21, 1914), 943.
  31. New York *Times*, February 3, 1915.

All told, the cotton farmers suffered an immediate cash loss of some $300,000,000 during 1914, but somehow they struggled through the winter of 1914–1915 and managed to carry over a surplus 4,000,000 bales of cotton. And yet there were signs of returning stability even during the period of greatest despair. The cotton exchanges, for example, reopened on November 16, 1914, with cotton selling at around seven and one half cents a pound. From this point on until mid-February 1915, prices slowly improved in response to increased buying. Spot prices on the New York Cotton Exchange, for example, averaged around eight and one half cents a pound for middling cotton during the last week in January and the first week in February 1915.

An important reason for the increase in prices was the strong revival of foreign purchases toward the end of 1914. Buying on the Liverpool exchange was so heavy during January 1915, for example, that by the end of the month exports were actually running ahead of exports for a comparable period a year before. To southerners, however, the most encouraging sign of all was the renewal of the cotton export trade to the European neutrals and to Germany, following the giving of positive assurances by the British government that it had not made cotton either conditional or absolute contraband and would not attempt to suppress its shipment to Germany.[32] The Germans, like the English, did not begin buying American cotton in quantity until near the end of 1914; but by early February 1915 cotton was moving in a steady stream to Rotterdam and Bremen.

Therefore, just when it seemed that the normal world markets were reopening and that the worst of the cotton crisis was over, the war on the seas erupted in a new phase that threatened to destroy all hopes for southern recovery. Allegedly in retaliation against a British food blockade, the German government on February 4, 1915, announced a submarine blockade of the British Isles and warned that a enemy vessel within the war zone would be destroyed. Invoking the right of reprisal, the British government replied on March 1 and March 11, 1915, by prohibiting *all* neutral commerce to Germany, through neutral or German ports.

32. Ambassador Page to Secretary of State, October 26, 1914, *Papers Relating to the Foreign Relations of the United States, 1914, Supplement* (Washington: Government Printing Office, 1928), p. 289; Ambassador Spring Rice to the Acting Secretary of State, October 26, 1914, *ibid.*, p. 290; New York *Times*, October 26 and 27, 1914.

It was the beginning of an all-out struggle for control of the seas that would eventually draw the United States into the war. But at least until the late autumn of 1916 the British government pursued its campaign of economic warfare with careful regard for American opinion, applying only such pressure against Germany as was compatible with retaining American friendship. That friendship, so vital to an Allied victory, could be retained only if the British blockade did not destroy American prosperity or the prosperity of a section or interest powerful enough to force the Washington government to take effective counter measures.

This was the hypothesis that governed all British policies *vis-à-vis* the United States during the period from 1914 to late 1916. As Sir Edward Grey, the British Foreign Secretary, afterward put it:

It was better . . . to carry on the war without blockade, if need be, than to incur a break with the United States about contraband and thereby deprive the Allies of the resources necessary to carry on the war at all or with any chance of success. The object of diplomacy, therefore, was to secure the maximum of blockade that could be enforced without a rupture with the United States.[33]

Britain's task of blockading central Europe and of channeling the huge American export trade exclusively into Allied ports without provoking a fatal rupture with the United States was not as difficult as might appear at first glance. To begin with, the great bulk of American exports, particularly of midwestern foodstuffs, went normally to the Allied countries or to areas far removed from the scene of hostilities, while strong financial ties bound the United States to the Allied world. In addition, early in the war, the British removed potential sources of friction by making special arrangements with American producers of meat, copper, and oil to purchase all their exports at a generous price.

Thus, by the spring of 1915, the sole remaining *economic* source of potential serious Anglo-American friction was the cotton trade. A reckless Allied policy, say, of preventing the export of cotton to central Europe, without doing anything to support the cotton market, would inevitably engender a strong southern demand for retaliatory action. To the British, the gravest threat of all was the

33. Grey of Fallodon, *Twenty-Five Years, 1892–1916*, 2 vols. (New York: Frederick A. Stokes Co., 1925), II, 107.

possibility that the powerful southern bloc in Congress would combine with pacifist and pro-German groups to create an irresistible demand for an embargo on the export of munitions to the Allies or for positive efforts to break the British blockade.

The British fear was by no means fanciful. Certainly the chief objective of McAdoo's ship-purchase bill was to provide bottoms to carry cotton to Holland and Germany; and by January 1915, administration leaders were talking seriously about using naval transports to carry cotton to Europe.[34] There was, moreover, such strong support in Congress for an embargo on the export of munitions in 1915 and early 1916 that a solid southern support for an embargo bill might have put it across.

The chief objective of British diplomacy *vis-à-vis* the United States in 1915, therefore, was to find a way of shutting off the export of American cotton to Germany without endangering American good will. It was an immensely difficult task, complicated by a powerful demand in Great Britain for the indiscriminate outlawing of all non-Allied cotton exports. But in the end the British Foreign Secretary and his associates succeeded and thereby perhaps guaranteed American acquiescence in the British maritime system. Let us now see how this was done, and what the consequences were.

The first task confronting the British Foreign Office in the late winter and spring of 1915 was to prevent the collapse of the cotton market as a consequence of the inauguration of the all-out blockade of Germany. This the Foreign Office accomplished in three ways. First, it issued its blockade Order in Council of March 11, 1915, without putting cotton on the contraband list and accompanied that Order with assurances that noncontraband goods suspected of having a German destination would not be liable to confiscation but would either be purchased by the British government at the contract price or else returned to its owners. Second, the Foreign Office gave assurances on March 8, 1915, that all American cotton destined for the European neutrals or for Germany by way of neutral ports would either be given free passage or else purchased by the British government, provided the cotton left the United States before March 31, 1915.[35] Third,

34. *E.g.,* W. C. Redfield to Woodrow Wilson, January 18, 1915, Wilson Papers, enclosing Redfield to L. M. Garrison, January 18, 1915, and Redfield to J. Daniels, January 18, 1915.
35. *Papers Relating to the Foreign Relations of the United States, 1915, Supplement* (Washington:

in order to avert the demoralization of the cotton market as a consequence of the inauguration of the blockade, the British government began purchasing cotton in large quantities on the New York and Liverpool exchanges on about March 1, 1915. The result was to push the price of spot middling cotton in New York from 8.25 cents a pound on March 1 to 9.55 cents a pound on March 25, 1915.[36]

Although these measures sustained the cotton market and forestalled a general anti-British movement in the South during the early spring of 1915, actually the most dangerous phase of the Anglo-American tension over the cotton trade impended. As the British tightened their blockade and, more important, gave signs of an intention to make cotton contraband, a wave of hysteria swept over the South during the late spring and early summer. It was stimulated by a fear that the British would suppress cotton exports to Europe altogether and begin a program of confiscation on the high seas, and that this in turn would mean a new demoralization of prices and another year of subdepression for cotton growers already deeply in debt because of heavy losses in 1914.

"The opinion was unanimous," Representative Lever reported to the President at the conclusion of a conference of agricultural leaders in Columbia, South Carolina, in early July,

that the outlook in the South was far more critical and fraught with far more danger than during the season of 1914. It was agreed also that evidence was rapidly coming to light that there is growing among the people—farmers, merchants, bankers and business men, a feeling of unrest and apprehension which might easily develop into a condition of panic. It is felt that the South has never before faced so serious an economic situation and that unless some assurance for the future can be given to the people from those in whom they have confidence, the counsel of wise, conservative leaders will be swept aside by an uncontrollable hysteria such as must develop in men who find themselves facing disaster.[37]

Government Printing Office, 1928), p. 189; hereinafter cited as *Foreign Relations, 1915, Supplement.*

36. Since the British Foreign Office has declined to permit the present writer to examine its archives for the period under discussion, he has no way of knowing precisely how the British officials went about supporting cotton prices at this time or how much cotton they bought on official account. There can be no doubt, however, that they did move into the market in a large way to support cotton prices.

37. A. F. Lever *et al.* to Woodrow Wilson, July 12, 1915, Wilson Papers.

"The marketing of the South's cotton crop this year is a most absorbing topic with her people just now," a Texan added a few days later,

and it is essential to, not only the general welfare, but also the very business LIFE of this section, that the price of cotton shall be as large as any combination of fair and legitimate circumstances can make it. . . . This is a GREAT question . . . with the Southern people, and if cotton does not bring a fair price this fall they are going to be seriously hurt financially. The great majority of them are heavily in debt already, brought over from 1914 on account of the very low price of cotton last fall and winter, and their cotton, even at the very best price attainable, will not be sufficient to liquidate that indebtedness, to say nothing of the debts contracted THIS year to enable them to make a crop.[38]

When the British government, goaded by intolerable pressure at home, moved obviously toward making cotton contraband, the reaction in the South was so violent as to imperil cordial Anglo-American relations. Sen. Hoke Smith, who would soon emerge as the chief political spokesman of the planters, set off the southern campaign for retaliation on May 22, 1915, with a long statement in the press, denouncing the British blockade and warning that Congress would surely apply an arms embargo unless the British ceased their allegedly illegal depredations against the cotton trade.[39] Two weeks later, moreover, Smith appealed to the Washington administration for stern action. "It would be easy for our Government to force Great Britain to recognize our neutral rights," he wrote to Postmaster General Albert S. Burleson, for transmission to the President and the Cabinet. "Great Britain and her Allies are receiving to-day, I am assured, more than one-half of their munitions of war from this country. We need but to notify Great Britain these shipments will cease so long as Great Britain prevents shipments by citizens of the United States legal at the time the war began."[40]

Echoes of the Georgia senator's demands were heard throughout the South in mounting volume during June and July

38. J. W. Madden to E. M. House, July 19, 1915, House Papers.
39. New York *Times,* May 23, 1915.
40. Hoke Smith to A. S. Burleson, June 7, 1915, the Papers of Albert S. Burleson, Library of Congress, Washington, D.C.; hereinafter cited as the Burleson Papers.

of 1915. Charging that Great Britain had deprived southern farmers of a market for more than 3,000,000 bales of cotton, the Georgia legislature on June 28, for example, urged the President to use every means in his power, "diplomatic if possible, retaliatory if necessary," to open the cotton trade to central Europe.[41] As the pro-British senator from Mississippi, John Sharp Williams, warned the President, so powerful was the demand for retaliation that every politician in the South had to be anti-British during that summer of alarm.[42]

The crisis reached the stage of acute tension during the last two weeks of July and the first three weeks of August 1915. Profoundly disturbed by the mounting southern campaign, President Wilson moved swiftly to avert a British declaration making cotton contraband, which action he thought would have a "fatal effect" on American opinion and would probably incite Congress to apply an arms embargo.[43] "The course pursued by Great Britain," he wrote on July 16, in a preliminary warning for direct transmission to the British leaders, "has produced widespread irritation and dissatisfaction through this country, and unless some radical change is made, the situation will become so serious politically that it will be difficult, if not impossible, to find a solution." [44] "Important [that the] British press use influence against action detrimental to cotton," Colonel House added in a cablegram to Sir Horace Plunkett, who was then acting as House's and Wilson's personal liaison with the British Cabinet. "Should Britain do this

---

41. New York *Times*, June 29, 1915. See also "Preamble and Resolution Adopted by the Board of Directors of the New Orleans Cotton Exchange," June 30, 1915, copy in the Burleson Papers; Sen. J. E. Ransdell to A. S. Burleson, July 7, 1915, *ibid.*; resolution of the State Council, Farmers' Union of North Carolina, enclosed in E. C. Faires to Wilson, July 3, 1915, Wilson Papers; resolutions adopted by the Savannah Cotton Exchange, July 8, 1915, copy in *ibid.*; Officers of the Farmers' Union to Wilson, August 13, 1915, *ibid.*; resolution adopted by the Texas Farmers' Union, meeting in state convention August 3–6, 1915, copy in *ibid.*; Sen. Morris Sheppard to Wilson, July 22, 1915, *ibid.*; J. Thomas Heflin to J. P. Tumulty, July 28, 1915, *ibid.*; Hatton W. Sumners to Wilson, July 31, 1915, *ibid.*; the Augusta Cotton Exchange and Board of Trade to the Secretary of State, June 25, 1915, *Foreign Relations, 1915, Supplement,* pp. 191–192; the Galveston Commercial Association to the Secretary of State, July 2, 1915, *ibid.,* p. 192; and the general review article in the New York *World*, July 22, 1915.

42. Williams to Wilson, June 29, 1915, Wilson Papers.

43. Wilson to E. M. House, July 19, 1915, House Papers.

44. Secretary of State to Ambassador Page, July 16, 1915, *Foreign Relations, 1915, Supplement,* pp. 473–474.

Congress would probably retaliate. The matter is of extreme urgency." [45]

Wilson and House, however, were threatening from a position of extreme diplomatic weakness. During the summer of 1915, the United States was embroiled in a controversy with Germany over the use of the submarine against merchant shipping, one so serious that it raised the immediate danger of war between the two countries. The British leaders knew that they would never have a more favorable opportunity to settle the cotton question, once and for all, than during this period of high tension between the United States and Germany. And yet they had been profoundly disturbed by the anti-British campaign in the South; anxious to remove the chief cause of friction in Anglo-American relations, they were prepared to go to extreme lengths to reach a final comprehensive agreement with the American government. "The people who are responsible here," wrote one official from the American Embassy in London, "are greatly concerned about the cotton situation, and apprehensive about losing the friendship and good will of the people of the United States." [46] "It is quite indifferent to us how we stop the cotton . . .," Sir Edward Grey confided to Colonel House, "but hitherto I have hesitated to declare it contraband, for fear of making the feeling in the United States worse instead of better. In any case, we are prepared to enter into any arrangement that will make the price of cotton stable and prevent its collapse." [47]

Such an agreement was feasible because neither Wilson nor any responsible leader in Washington had any desire to challenge the British maritime system during this time when war with Germany seemed daily possible. "I should like to press for the utmost," Wilson explained to Colonel House, "and yet I should wish to be sensible and practical." [48] He explained what he meant about being "sensible and practical" shortly afterward: "It does not seem as if we ought to go to the length of involving the country in war and so cut off the market for cotton altogether." [49]

45. House to Plunkett, July 19, 1915, House Papers.
46. E. G. Lowry to E. M. House, August 5, 1915, *ibid.*
47. Grey to House, August 10, 1915, *ibid.* See the London *Times,* July 23, 1915, and the London *Spectator,* July 30, 1915, for editorial expressions of British concern and eagerness to find a solution acceptable to the southern people and the American government.
48. Wilson to House, July 20, 1915, House Papers.
49. Wilson to Morris Sheppard, July 28, 1915, Wilson Papers.

Meanwhile, unofficial and highly secret negotiations looking toward an Anglo-American understanding were already in progress by the time the President wrote the words quoted above. These negotiations began on July 22, 1915, when Chandler P. Anderson, a former State Department official acting as an unofficial representative of Secretary of State Robert Lansing, conferred with the British Ambassador, Sir Cecil Spring Rice, in Washington. His government, Spring Rice declared, was eager to do anything within reason to support the cotton market. It was, therefore, willing to purchase an amount of cotton equal to the normal German and Austrian requirements, in addition to the usual British purchases; would not interfere with normal cotton exports going from the United States to the European neutrals; and would guarantee a minimum price for cotton, to be determined by mutual agreement.[50]

On July 30, Anderson had further exploratory conversations with Sir Richard Crawford, trade adviser to the British Embassy in Washington. Crawford explained that the British plan to support the cotton market had only one objective, namely, to stop the southern agitation for an arms embargo. He had, therefore, prepared a plan by which the British government would furnish £20,000,000 to a group of banks, with instructions that this money should be used to support cotton at a fixed price per pound. It would, however, be absolutely essential, Crawford continued, to make cotton contraband, in order to give the British government some legal basis for the absolute suppression of the cotton trade to the Central Powers. Anderson replied that although the American government could not officially approve any such arrangement, he would communicate the proposal informally to the Secretary of State. Speaking privately, however, he was willing to say that he thought British support of cotton prices would effectively destroy the southern movement for an arms embargo and avert any serious Anglo-American difficulties over the definition of cotton as contraband.[51]

With such encouragement—for Anderson was in fact speaking for the Washington administration—Crawford now carried his negotiations to a higher level. We lack full evidence on the final

50. The Diary of Chandler P. Anderson, Library of Congress, Washington, D.C., July 22, 1915.
51. *Ibid.*, July 30, 1915.

phase of these discussions. We know, however, that Crawford and Spring Rice conferred at length during early August 1915 with Colonel House, William P. G. Harding of Birmingham, a member of the Federal Reserve Board, and Benjamin Strong, Governor of the Federal Reserve Bank of New York. The upshot was an understanding, or agreement, concluded on about August 13, by which the British government promised to maintain the price of cotton at ten cents a pound after the staple had been put on the list of absolute contraband. The British would do this by using the plan originally devised by Sir Richard Crawford.[52]

There now remained only the task of averting a panic in the South following the issuance of the British order defining cotton as contraband. The Foreign Office issued the order on the afternoon of Saturday, August 21, 1915, after the cotton exchanges had closed. Then on Monday morning, August 23, brokers representing the British government bought cotton so heavily on the Liverpool and New Orleans exchanges that the price increased slightly. On the same day, moreover, Secretary McAdoo, who had been forewarned of British intentions, announced that he was ready to deposit $30,000,000 of federal funds in southern banks, if that were necessary to provide ample cheap credit to enable the farmers to hold their cotton and to market it gradually.[53] At the same time, the President and Harding of the Federal Reserve Board joined McAdoo in telling southerners that they would have abundant credit and urging them to avoid any show of panic.[54]

As a result, there was no financial panic and only a momentary outburst of anti-British denunciation in the South,[55] which was not serious to begin with and soon subsided altogether. This was true largely because heavy British purchases maintained the

52. Page to the Secretary of State, August 13, 1915, copy in the Wilson Papers, and House to Wilson, August 14, 1915, *ibid.*, describe the final negotiations and the terms of the understanding. For an even fuller account, see the New York *Tribune*, November 20, 1915.

53. New York *Times*, August 24, 1915.

54. Wilson to Harding, August 23, 1915, Wilson Papers. Harding read Wilson's letter in an address at Birmingham on August 25, 1915.

55. Hoke Smith to Robert Lansing, August 26 and 29, 1915, the Papers of Robert Lansing, Library of Congress, Washington, D.C.; H. Smith. "Memorandum upon the Order of Great Britain making Cotton absolute contraband," dated September 4, 1914, in *ibid.*; E. Y. Webb to Claude Kitchin, September 2, 1915, the Papers of Claude Kitchin, University of North Carolina, Chapel Hill, N.C.; S. J. Tribble to Wilson, September 7, 1915, Wilson Papers; A. F. Lever to Wilson, September 22, 1915, *ibid.*

price of cotton at slightly above ten cents a pound during the critical month following the issuance of the order making cotton contraband and combined with predictions of a short crop in 1915 to begin a forward movement in late September, which carried prices on the New York Exchange to 12.30 cents a pound for middling cotton on October 29, 1915. From this time forward until 1920, cotton prices continued to rise.

Thus the cotton crisis passed out of sight in the autumn of 1915, and its passing was accompanied by the end of any large-scale organized anti-British movement in the region south of the Potomac. Hereafter, the President's policy of increasing resistance to German pretensions on the seas would be sustained in large measure by southern votes in Congress. And yet we should not overstate the case or be misled by the partisan support that Wilson received from southerners on certain critical occasions between 1915 and 1917. The cotton crisis of 1914–1915 left deep scars upon the South and a residue of intense anti-British sentiment. Combined with the prevailing rural pacifism, southern resentment at the British maritime system made the South one of the chief centers of resistance to military and naval expansion and to strong diplomacy *vis-à-vis* Germany between 1915 and 1917. Like a majority of Americans, southerners went to war in April 1917, not because they wanted to fight or loved the British, but only because they seemed to have no other alternative.

21

The Federal Reserve Policy and the Agricultural Depression of 1920–1921

ECONOMIC depression and its concomitants of falling prices, financial distress, bankruptcy, and foreclosure, it would seem, have been the invariable heritage of the American farmer since the time of the first English settlements in North America over three hundred years ago. The sharp decline in the price of Virginia tobacco on the London market in the 1620s, for example, and the subsequent frantic efforts of the planters to restrict production and raise prices marked the beginning of the economic difficulties of the American producers whom Thomas Jefferson once eulogized as "the chosen people of God." The story of agricultural distress in the early period has been well chronicled;[1] suffice it to say that economic depression has been one of the chief themes in American agricultural history.

During the latter months of 1920, there occurred a decline in agricultural prices that abruptly ended the cycle of rising farm prices which had got under way in 1897; the price decline was

Reprinted from *Agricultural History*, XX (July 1946), 166–175, by permission of the Editor.

1. See especially Lewis C. Gray, *History of Agriculture in the Southern United States to 1860* (Washington: Carnegie Institution, 1933); Percy Wells Bidwell and John I. Falconer, *History of Agriculture in the Northern United States, 1620–1860* (Washington: Carnegie Institution, 1925); and the historical articles in the U.S. Department of Agriculture *Yearbook* for 1940.

all the more disastrous because it came suddenly and without warning. Crops were unusually large in 1920. Corn production reached the all-time record peak of 3,208,584,000 bushels, exceeding even the bumper crop of 1912. Wheat production was only 833,027,000 bushels in 1920 and was considerably below the production record for 1918 and 1919, but it was an above-average crop. The cotton crop in 1920 was 13,440,000 bales, the largest crop since 1915. Because of the high level of wages and prices for fertilizer and farm equipment, the crops of 1920 were produced at the greatest cost the American farmer had ever expended for planting and harvesting his products. "They were incurred willingly," to use the words of Secretary of Agriculture Henry C. Wallace, "because the farmers had been told over and over again that overseas there was a hungry world waiting to be fed and that there would be a strong demand for all they could produce." [2]

The general price level of agricultural products rose steadily during the first half of 1920. Wheat, which was selling at $2.34 per bushel on January 15, reached $2.56 on June 15; cotton advanced from 39.26 cents a pound on January 15 to 41.20 cents on July 15; corn showed an even greater advance—from $1.44 per bushel on January 15 to $1.85 on June 15. The price of hogs, per hundredweight, however, had dropped from 19.30 cents on August 15, 1919, to 13.36 cents on January 15, 1920; but even this price remained steady until November. Wheat began a steady gradual decline in price in July. On October 15, the average price was $2.01 per bushel; within a month, it had declined to $1.66, and by August 1921, it was selling at $1.03. The bottom dropped out from under cotton prices during the last 5 months of 1920. The average spot price of middling cotton on the New York exchange declined from 41.20 cents a pound on July 15 to 15.68 cents on December 15, and by June 15, 1921, cotton was quoted on the New York market at 12 cents a pound. Corn producers, however, suffered the hardest blow: the price of corn declined from $1.85 per bushel on June 15, 1920, to $1.04 in October, 66.8 cents in December, and 61 cents in May 1921. Even then, the bottom of the pit had not been reached, for the year ended with corn selling at 42 cents a bushel! The price of hogs declined rapidly, to be sure—from $13.18 per hundredweight on June 15,

2. U.S. Department of Agriculture, *Yearbook,* 1921, p. 4.

1920, to $11.64 in November, $8.90 in December, and $7.22 in June 1921—but the percentage decrease in the price of hogs was not as great as that of the prices of the other agricultural products cited above.[3] Thus, within from 11 to 16 months, the price of wheat decreased to approximately 40 percent of its highest price in 1920, corn to 32 percent, cotton to 34 percent, and hogs to 50 percent.

Bare figures of the prices of agricultural products, however, fail to convey the full measure of agrarian financial distress. The financial position of the farmer had been strengthened during the inflation of the war years and especially during 1919 and the first half of 1920. Farmers had passed from a period of relative stability into one of dazzling prosperity. The price of land had consequently skyrocketed, especially in Iowa and the great Corn Belt, and land rents had increased from 100 to 200 percent. Thousands of farmers had extended their land holdings at the risk of mortgaging their farms, livestock, and equipment. The disastrous price level of 1920–1921 wiped out most of the gains of the war years, and tens of thousands of independent farmers were now confronted with foreclosures, tenancy, and the loss of their life savings and their homes and farms.

It was a dreary picture, to be sure; and if it were the whole story, it would suffice to illustrate the reality of agricultural unrest. There was, besides, the burden of increased transportation costs and an increased tax load to add to the heavy measure of financial distress. In 1913, for example, transportation and elevator charges accounted for 23 percent of the price of corn shipped from Sioux City, Iowa, and sold on the Chicago market; in 1919, the figure had declined to 20 percent, yet on December 1, 1921, it had risen to 44 percent.[4] Secretary Wallace described the situation in 1921 in the following terms:

The cost of getting farm products from the farm to the consumer's table has increased tremendously during the past three years. The freight charge is very nearly doubled, and in some cases more than doubled. When wheat was selling at $2.50 per bushel, corn at $1.75, cattle and hogs at $16 to $22 per hundred, cotton at 30 cents per pound, the increased freight rate was not a serious matter. It amounted to but few

3. *Ibid.*, 1926, pp. 818, 845, 975, 1101.
4. *Ibid.*, 1921, p. 8.

cents relatively and was a small item in the total price. But with wheat at $1, corn at 48 cents, cattle and hogs at $7 to $10 per hundred, cotton at 17 to 20 cents (all these being primary market prices, not farm prices), the addition of even 10 cents per bushel or per hundred pounds imposes a burden grievous to be borne. When farm prices are ruinously low any addition to the freight charge means added distress. At the present time the cost of getting some farm products to market is greater than the amount the farmer himself receives in net return.[5]

In the face of declining prices, taxes on agricultural land either remained stationary or else increased. Property taxes paid by the farmers increased, in absolute figures, from $532,000,000 in 1920 to $797,000,000 in 1922. On 155 farms in Ohio, Indiana, and Wisconsin, for example, taxes accounted for 9.8 percent of the farmers' net receipts in 1919, 17 percent in 1920, and 33 percent in 1921.[6]

In the midst of the acute financial distress prevalent in the fall of 1920, the farmers turned to the federal government for financial support. On October 13, leaders of the American Cotton Association, who were meeting in Washington, bombarded W. P. G. Harding, Governor of the Federal Reserve Board, with questions regarding the policy of the Federal Reserve System with reference to the extension of agricultural credit. Harding declared that the Board was then in session and that its policies could not be announced at the immediate moment. He told the cotton delegation, however, that he believed orderly marketing of the staple was the solution of their problem, and that they might find it necessary at times to sell their cotton at prices which were below production costs.[7] The following day, certain representatives of the southern and western farmers visited the Secretary of the Treasury, David F. Houston, and demanded credit extensions to aid them in financing the marketing of their crops. Houston indicated that the Treasury Department could do no more than it was then doing to aid the farmers; and he frowned upon the proposal, suggested by agrarian spokesmen, to re-establish the War Finance Corporation to enable Germany and Austria to buy American cotton. J. S. Wanamaker, president of the American Cotton Association, explained the tragic situation and concluded:

5. *Ibid.*, pp. 7–8.
6. *Ibid.*, 1922, p. 7; 1923, p. 8.
7. New York *Times*, October 14, 1920.

"God pity a nation that won't lend money to its people to aid agriculture." [8]

A period of ruinous deflation such as the farmers experienced in 1920–1921 necessitates immediate credit if the farmers are to survive as independent farmers; and of course it was credit that they demanded—credit to meet impending debt payments, to enable them to hold their crops until prices had recovered from the first effects of the panic. Federal Reserve banks discounted agricultural and livestock paper maturing from 90 to 180 days, and this could afford some measure of relief; but there was no federal machinery for providing intermediate agricultural credit of from 6 months to 3 years. The insurance companies, trust companies, etc., which had normally provided this intermediate credit, had largely withdrawn from the lending market and as a consequence the chief burden of "carrying the farmers through" fell upon the commercial banks—and ultimately upon the Federal Reserve System. [9]

The simple fact was that the Federal Reserve banks, because of the narrow restrictions of the Federal Reserve Act, could not meet the crisis. The result was a general and wholesale assault upon the System by numerous agrarian spokesmen during 1920–1922. The charges hurled at the Federal Reserve Board and the Reserve banks were numerous and diverse, general and particular, and once again the latent agrarian hatred of banks and bankers burst forth in full fury against, ironically enough, the crowning achievement of the progressive Wilson administration. Essentially, the root of the farmers' disaffection can be seen in their belief that an inflationary Reserve policy was desirable and possible and that the Federal Reserve Board was chiefly responsible for the deflation of agricultural prices in 1920. One southern agricultural journal, for example, reflected an opinion that was very common when it charged that the Board had refused to extend credit to the farmers on virtually any terms and had made the rediscount rate on agricultural and livestock paper prohibitive. "Never in the history of the world," it declared, "has so much power reposed in the hands of a few men as that now at the

8. *Ibid.*, October 15, 1920.
9. See John H. Rich, *The Federal Reserve Bank and the Farmer and Stockman* (Minneapolis: Federal Reserve Bank of Minneapolis, 1921), p. 4. Rich was chairman of the Minneapolis Federal Reserve Bank.

disposal of the Federal Reserve Board. . . . " [10] The charge that the Federal Reserve Board had deliberately and maliciously set out upon a policy aimed at deflating agricultural prices in 1920 was more serious, but it was made many times by numerous self-constituted agrarian spokesmen and was undoubtedly believed by many farmers. One irate cattle grower in Mississippi even charged that the Board's alleged deflationary program was the work of a few Jewish international bankers who controlled the Federal Reserve System and who were endeavoring to secure a monopoly of the world gold supply.[11]

It is pertinent at this point to summarize the accusations made against the Federal Reserve System. Briefly, they were: (1) The Federal Reserve Board had undertaken a general credit deflation by increasing the rediscount rate on paper secured by farm products and land. (2) The Reserve banks had denied funds to the agricultural sections in order that the money might be employed in speculation on Wall Street. This was a popular taunt of the more ignorant agitators, and Reserve spokesmen made especial efforts to refute it.[12] (3) The small banks in the agricultural areas had been treated unfairly as compared with the large city banks, and the country banks were required to increase the collateral on their borrowings from the Reserve banks to an excessive degree. (4) The statements given out by the Secretary of the Treasury, the Governor of the Federal Reserve Board, and the Reserve bank spokesmen, which had been construed to the effect that commodity prices, particularly the prices of farm products, were too high and that a prewar price level had to be reached within a short time, had contributed to the depression of prices.[13]

Next to George M. Armstrong's broadside, *The Crime of '20,* which was a sizable volume and a semiserious attempt to expose the Federal Reserve policy, the most violent attacks upon the System came from the spokesmen of agrarian interests in Congress. Charges were thrown wildly about during 1920 and 1922, and it will suffice to examine a few of the typical outbursts. Sen.

10. *Southern Planter* (Richmond, Va.), 83 (7): 11 (April 1, 1922).
11. George W. Armstrong, *The Crime of '20: The Unpardonable Sin of "Frenzied Finance"* (Dallas: Press of the Venney Co., 1922), pp. 81–87.
12. See Rich, *The Federal Reserve Bank and the Farmer and Stockman,* p. 6.
13. Ivan Wright, *Bank and Credit Agriculture* (New York: McGraw-Hill Book Co., 1922), pp. 271–272; and Benjamin Haggott Beckhart, *The Discount Policy of the Federal Reserve System* (New York: H. Holt and Co., 1924), pp. 475–476.

Furnifold M. Simmons of North Carolina, himself no flaming radical, opened the congressional attack upon the System on December 20, 1920, by declaring that the Reserve banks had placed special restrictions upon loans made on crops. "It is not in the public interest that the products of the farms of this country should be sold for one-half the cost of their production," he asserted. He further charged that the response of the Reserve banks to the plea for extensive agricultural credits had been that they, the banks, were endeavoring to reduce prices, and that the member banks should do nothing which would tend to enhance the price of agricultural products. While Congress was considering a proposal to help the farmers export their surpluses, Simmons continued, the Federal Reserve Board had promulgated stringent rules of credit and had prevented the farmers from holding their crops until a government-sponsored export corporation could be organized.

There can be no doubt . . . that when the farmer was confronted by a situation of having to sell his product, if he sold it at all, in a market which had been driven down and beaten down until it did not carry a price that would amount to one-half of the cost of production of the crop, that situation was further accentuated when the Federal Reserve Board indicated to the Federal reserve banks and to the member banks that it was undesirable that money should be lent for the purpose, as they phrased it, of withholding crops from the market.[14]

The leadership of the anti-Reserve forces in Congress, however, soon passed from the conservative Senator from North Carolina to Sen. J. Thomas Heflin of Alabama, the long-haired Klan embodiment of postwar southern demagoguery. From time to time during 1921, Heflin rose pompously to condemn the entire System as the wilful agent of agricultural destruction. On one occasion, for example, he declared:

The conduct of the Federal Reserve Board for several months past has been miserable, inexcusable, and indefensible. It has been criticized and condemned by farmers, merchants, and bankers, and others all over the country, and its conduct will go down in the history of this decade

14. U.S., Congress, *Congressional Record*, 66th Congress, 3rd session, December 20, 1920, 60 (1):551.

as a crime against agriculture, commerce, and honest banking in the
United States. . . . Today the Federal Reserve Board holds its foot upon
the neck of the grain industry, the cattle industry, and the cotton industry
and other industries of the United States, while Wall Street and Chicago
look on and applaud. . . .
Mr. President, when a board institutes a policy that destroys the business
of thirty-odd millions of people in my section and thirty-odd millions
of people in another section of the country—the western section of the
United States—it is certainly a criminal act.[15]

Another typical outburst of the agrarian spokesmen in Congress was the statement of Rep. Phil D. Swing of California on
May 23, 1922.

You can "bear" the market or you can "bull" the market. The Federal
reserve bank deliberately set out to "bear" the market. They succeeded
so well that they broke the market—not only broke the market but broke
the farmers as well. We there saw the strange spectacle of the farmer
citizens of this country being ruined by being forced to sell their products
on a glutted market, at less than what it cost to grow them, as a direct
result of a policy adopted by their own Government—a Government
created to aid them, not to harass them. I say it was criminal, it was
damnable for this all-powerful agency of our Government to deliberately
crucify the farmers of this country.[16]

What shall we say of these various accusations? What was
the actual role that the Federal Reserve Board and banks played
during the period of agricultural deflation and distress? In the
first place, what, exactly, was the part the Federal Reserve Board
played in bringing about the general deflation in the price level
during 1920 and 1921? It is clearly evident that the spiral of
inflation which had beset the country in early 1919, following
the removal of most wartime price controls, alarmed the members
of the Board. Writing late in that year, Governor Harding announced the Board's determination to set the machinery of the
Federal Reserve System into motion in order to bring about a
mild and gradual deflation. "The expansion of credit set in motion
by the war must be checked," he warned. "Credit must be brought
under effective control and its flow be once more regulated and

15. *Ibid.*, 67th Congress, 2d session, December 19, 1921, 62 (1): 517.
16. *Ibid.*, May 23, 1922, 62 (7):7517.

governed with careful regard to the economic welfare of the country and the needs of its producing industries." Too drastic a deflation, he declared, would defeat the purpose of a well-regulated credit system "by the needless unsettlement of mind it would produce and the disastrous reaction that such unsettlement would have upon productive industry." [17]

The alarm of the Federal Reserve Board had been occasioned by the disturbing flurry of speculation in stocks and bonds and foreign trade operations and also by the continuous inflation of prices and credit through 1919. It was significant that the credit basis for this speculation had been in part the government bonds which the member banks discounted and the Reserve banks were legally required to rediscount. It was evident, especially to the officials of the Reserve banks, that an advance in the discount rate was essential to restrict credit and restore prices to a reasonable level. [18] Consequently, the Board set out in the latter part of 1919 to increase gradually the Reserve discount rate and when Secretary Carter Glass consented, the rates in the twelve regional banks were increased approximately one-half of one percent. The discount rate on agricultural and livestock paper stood at from 5 to 5½ percent during November and December 1919.

TABLE 1

Discount Rates on Agriculture and Livestock Paper Maturing within 91 to 180 days, for Dates on which Changes Occurred, 1919–1921

Reserve Bank	Nov 20. 1919 %	Feb. 2 1920 %	June 1 1920 %	July 1 1920 %	Nov. 1 1920 %	Jan. 1 1921 %	Mar. 1 1921 %	May 1 1921 %	June 1 1921 %	July 1 1921 %	Aug. 1 1921 %	Oct. 1 1921 %	Dec. 1 1921 %
Boston	5	6	6	7	7	7	7	6	6	6	5½	5	4½
New York	5	6	7	7	7	7	7	7	6½	6	5½	5	4½
Philadelphia	5	6	6	6	6	6	6	6	6	6	5½	5½	4½
Cleveland	5¼	6	6	6	6	6	6	6	6	6	6	5½	5
Richmond	5	6	6	6	6	6	6	6	6	6	6	6	5½
Atlanta	5½	6	6	6	7	7	7	7	6	6	6	6	5½
Chicago	5½	6	7	7	7	7	7	7	6½	6½	6	6	5
Saint Louis	5½	6	6	6	6	6	6	6	6	6	6	6	5
Minneapolis	5½	6	7	7	7	7	7	7	6½	6½	6½	6½	5½
Kansas City	5½	6	6	6	6	6	6	6	6	6	6	6	5
Dallas	5¼	6	6	6	6	6	7	7	6½	6	6	6	5½
San Francisco	5½	6	6	6	6	6	6	6	6	6	5½	5½	5

Compiled from the *Federal Reserve Bulletin.* 1919–1921, *passim.*

17. U.S. Federal Reserve Board, *Annual Report,* 1919, pp. 71–72.
18. Henry Parker Willis, *The Federal Reserve System* (New York: Ronald Press Co., 1923), pp. 1298–1301.

According to Governor Harding, the Board was reluctant, early in 1920, to approve a discount rate higher than 6 percent for any of the Reserve banks. In order to determine the views of a larger number of the bankers than were represented by the twelve members of the Federal Advisory Council, the Board invited the three "Class A" directors of each Reserve bank to confer with the Council and the Board on May 18, 1920. This was the famous conference which certain agrarian critics denominated as "the crime of 1920." In his address before this conference, Harding outlined the recent history of the tremendous expansion of bank credits which had occurred since 1917 and emphasized that there had been a greater expansion of bank credit from April 1, 1919, to April 1, 1920, than had occurred during the 19 months of the war. "Our problem, therefore," he declared, "is to check further expansion and to bring about a normal and healthy liquidation without curtailing essential production and without shock to industry. . . . " John Skelton Williams, Comptroller of the Currency and afterwards a caustic critic of Harding, declared that each bank should be "a missionary for thrift" and warned that "a proper and reasonable degree of contraction" was necessary. Toward the end of the conference, according to Harding, there was some discussion as to the possibility of increasing the Reserve discount rate, but nothing definite was decided on the matter at the time.[19]

Before the Washington conference had gathered, however, the Board had approved in February an increase in the discount rate on agricultural and livestock paper to the general level of 6 percent for all twelve Reserve banks. In light of the charge by agrarian spokesmen that the Federal Reserve Board embarked upon a policy to deflate agricultural prices by raising the discount rate on agricultural and livestock paper, it is significant that, with two exceptions, no change in the rate occurred after July 1, 1920. Table 1 explains the discount policy of the System with regard to agricultural paper during 1919–1921.

What shall we say of the charge that the increase in the discount rate of farm paper was responsible for the deflation in farm prices? It was the opinion of the Congressional Joint Commission of Agricultural Inquiry, which was allegedly heavily

19. W. P. G. Harding, *The Formative Period of the Federal Reserve System* (Boston and New York: Houghton Mifflin Co., 1925), pp. 171–172.

"loaded" against the Federal Reserve System, that during the early months of 1920 the Reserve banks "were confronted with a choice between continuing the high discount rates and the consequent pressure and hardship upon the commercial and agricultural industries of the country on the one hand and a policy of lower discount rates involving a possible financial crisis in the midst of an industrial crisis." [20] Furthermore, the Joint Commission believed:

It seems probable that a change in the policy of the Federal reserve system with reference to discount rates would have accomplished a reversal in part of the psychological and economic factors which at this time were moving in the direction of lower prices, and at the same time would have tended to induce on the part of banks a more liberal attitude toward furnishing additional credit.

One wonders whether political considerations or economic fact dictated this conclusion. Certainly it is obvious that the rise in the discount rate on the paper secured by farm products and equipment in no wise operated to halt the rising prices of farm goods during the spring and summer of 1920; and it is just as doubtful that the increase in the discount rates played any part, one way or the other, in the deflation that followed during the fall. As for the Joint Commission's charge that the increased discount rates operated to restrict agricultural credit granted by member banks,[21] it will be shown that such definitely was not the case.

Ogden L. Mills presented a significant dissenting opinion that, in my opinion, offers a fairly conclusive answer to the Joint Commission's innuendo that there was a connection between increased discount rates and falling farm prices. Mills thought that the suggestion was out of harmony with the balance of the report and inconsistent with the facts brought out by the investigation. Higher discount rates, he asserted, did not cause the break in prices; and, he continued, "it is inconceivable that their reduction could have counteracted the economic forces that were leading to inevitable deflation." In addition, he pointed out the following

20. U.S., Congress, Joint Commission of Agricultural Inquiry, *Report of the Joint Commission of Agricultural Inquiry*, 67th Congress, 1st session, *House Report* 408, serial 7922; (Washington: Government Printing Office, 1921-1922), pt. 2, p. 14.
21. *Ibid.*, p. 7.

facts: (1) Reserve discount rates were below market rates throughout all of 1920. (2) There were some 28,210 banks in the United
States, only 9,840 of which were members of the Federal Reserve
System. Any number of the nonmember banks were unhampered
by competition and charged rates allowed by local custom and
law. "For instance, what efficacy can the decrease in the rediscount
rate of a Federal reserve bank from 7 to 6 percent have on a
western or southwestern bank charging 8, 10, or 12 percent?" (3)
Banks in the agricultural counties received increased credit of 56.6
percent from May 4, 1920, to April 28, 1921, while during the
same period borrowings from Reserve banks in nonagricultural
counties decreased 28.5 percent. "If the statement which I question
be true," Mills added, "it would seem to follow that a lower
rediscount rate would have tended primarily to maintain industrial
prices to the further disadvantage of the farmer." (4) While it
could not be conclusively proved that credit stringency was not
an initial contributing factor to price deflation, there was no evidence to demonstrate that it was. "I do not believe that increased
interest rates and contracting credit were the primary causes of
the sharp price deflation which characterized the second half of
the year 1920." No relationship could be established between
increased discount rates and the drop in the price of any single
agricultural commodity. The price deflation movement was
worldwide; it began in Japan with the break in the silk market
in 1919. The opinion that increased discount rates was one of
the primary causes of the decline of agricultural prices in the
United States, Mills concluded, was "so contrary to economic facts
and to the purposes of the Federal reserve system, that any expression of opinion which seems to support it, even indirectly, should
not be permitted to pass unchallenged." [22]

The causes of the decline in agricultural prices must be found
elsewhere: in the alarming decline in agricultural exports, in the
overexpansion in production and the absence of crop controls,
in the inability of Central Europe to buy American farm commodities, in the decline in governmental purchases, in the fact that
some contraction and deflation had to come after the war and
postwar inflation, and in the large quantities of crops carried over

22. *Ibid.*, pp. 158–159.

from 1919 to 1920—all of which served to glut the domestic and foreign markets and to depress the price level in general.[23]

Critics of the Federal Reserve policy were on sounder ground when they leveled their charges against the progressive rate instituted by certain Reserve banks in 1920. At the request of the Federal Reserve Board, Congress on April 13, 1920, approved the so-called Phelan amendment to the Federal Reserve Act, which provided that, subject to the approval, review, and control of the Federal Reserve Board, discount rates might be graduated or progressed on the basis of the amount of the advances and discount accommodation already extended by the Reserve banks to the borrowing banks.[24] Acting under this authorization, the Reserve banks in Atlanta, Saint Louis, Kansas City, and Dallas—all centered in agricultural districts—instituted progressive rates.

The progressive rate operated to penalize the bank that was borrowing excessively in direct proportion to its excess borrowing.

The theory upon which the progressive rate was applied was that inasmuch as the resources of the Federal reserve bank consist wholly of the contributions of the member banks to the deposits and capital of the Federal reserve bank, that all any member bank can be considered as entitled to borrow with due regard to the interests of all other member banks is its proportion of the amount it could borrow if all the banks were borrowing their full proportion at the same time. . . . If it borrows more than this amount, it is borrowing at the expense of the other banks, and, therefore, should pay a rate of interest in proportion to the excess which it borrows above the amount which it is entitled to borrow on the foregoing theory; that is, in excess of its basic line.[25]

The inauguration of the progressive rate naturally evoked a considerable burst of anger from many of the small country banks that had been borrowing in excess of their reserves. These complaints, in general, may be summarized as follows: (1) The progressive rate caused the imposition of exorbitantly high rates of interest and discount on loans by member banks; and (2) its application resulted in excessive pressure upon member banks borrowing from Federal Reserve banks to reduce their borrowings.

23. For the best discussion of the causes of the agricultural depression of 1920–1921, see *ibid.*, pt. 1, "The Agricultural Crisis and Its Causes."

24. U.S. Federal Reserve Board, *Index-Digest of the Federal Reserve Act and Amendments,* third edition (Washington: Government Printing Office, 1924), p. 32.

25. *Report of the Joint Commission of Agricultural Inquiry,* pt. 2, p. 55.

A few unfortunate incidents occurred, such as the case of the Alabama bank which neglected to maintain its reserves and borrowed so heavily that it was charged a rate of 87½ percent! The penalties in excess of 12 percent were afterward refunded by the Atlanta and Kansas City banks. The rebates amounted to $9,108.66 in the Atlanta district and to less than $300 in the Kansas City district.

Probably the only serious indictment that the historian can make against the progressive rate was that it was, in the words of H. Parker Willis, a "serious and regrettable departure from the theory of the Federal Reserve Act" and a clumsy and ineffective method of checking the credit operations of weak member banks.[26] Certainly there is evidence enough to prove that the operation of the progressive rate in no wise caused a perceptible restriction of credit in agricultural areas. The number of banks affected, in the first place, was small and insignificant. Moreover, the average discount rate charged by the New York Federal Reserve Bank during 1920 was higher than the rate charged by the Dallas bank and the same as that charged by the Atlanta bank; in 1921, the

TABLE 2

*Estimated Amounts of Paper Rediscounted with Federal
Reserve Banks Based on the Production
and Sale of Farm Products,
1919–1920*

Bank	1919 1.000 dollars	1920 1.000 dollars
Boston	2,642	4,979
New York	no data	no data
Philadelphia	2,971	3,580
Cleveland	612	1,753*
Richmond	102,000	325,000
Atlanta	91,300	230,000*
Chicago	47,263	128,408
Saint Louis	220,000*	665,000*
Minneapolis	75,000	225,000
Kansas City	123,481	229,432
Dallas	28,997	44,911
San Francisco	35,000	122,000
Total	729,266	1,980,063

* Data for 11 months only.
Source: U.S. Federal Reserve Board, *Annual Report*, 1920, p. 16–17.

26. Willis, *The Federal Reserve System*, p. 1342.

TABLE 3

*Total Amount of Agriculture and Livestock Paper
Combined, Held by Each Federal Reserve Board on
the Last Friday of Each Month, 1919–1920*

Month	1919 1,000 dollars	1920 1,000 dollars
January	59,001	56,905
February	63,917	67,195
March	67,373	74,665
April	66,881	106,382
May	58,991	140,691
June	68,256	168,038
July	63,604	202,520
August	57,901	216,278
September	60,205	224,424
October	55,475	240,649
November	52,550	245,599
December	51,068	246,938*

* Figures of Thursday, Dec. 30.
Source· U.S. Federal Reserve Board, *Annual Report,* 1920, p. 18.

TABLE 4

Federal Reserve Notes in Circulation, 1919–1921

Bank	Oct. 31, 1919 1,000 dollars	Feb. 27, 1920 1,000 dollars	June 25, 1920 1,000 dollars	Sept. 24, 1920 1,000 dollars	Dec. 30, 1920 1,000 dollars	Feb. 28, 1921 1,000 dollars	May 31, 1921 1,000 dollars
Boston	212,096	259,702	280,617	298,249	291,196	265,726	256,653
New York	750,715	826,287	859,232	855,701	864,516	797,588	715,912
Philadelphia	216,293	242,540	248,785	272,347	280,960	259,163	230,645
Cleveland	243,740	283,835	315,789	350,647	350,725	310,029	268,402
Richmond	138,592	129,535	122,109	140,145	155,162	150,143	126,498
Atlanta	141,976	145,778	140,592	147,003	175,166	164,582	157,090
Chicago	460,397	508,925	531,449	555,188	548,191	496,964	459,838
Saint Louis	130,760	138,778	126,289	133,283	136,610	123,933	107,943
Minneapolis	83,848	81,787	77,728	81,668	80,067	71,007	61,313
Kansas City	95,571	102,214	97,622	107,421	111,874	100,141	83,168
Dallas	61,152	77,089	82,351	88,782	79,474	65,840	49,940
San Francisco	217,736	223,514	234,155	249,362	270,745	243,438	234,467
Total	2,752,876	3,019,984	3,116,718	3,279,996	3,344,686	3,048,554	2,751,869

Source: U.S. Federal Reserve Board, *Annual Reports,* 1919–1921, *passim.*

average rate charged by the New York bank was higher than that charged by the Reserve banks in Atlanta, Saint Louis, and Dallas.[27] But the damage had been done, and political ammunition had been furnished to such spellbinders as Senator Heflin who delighted in bemoaning the fate of the "innocent" little banks which the System "tried to crush."

It has been necessary to examine the discount policy of the Federal Reserve System because of the amazing amount of contemporary misunderstanding with regard to it, and because, also, it was and is an important part of the System's credit policy. Observers of a latter day are more interested in the fundamental question: Was there actually a contraction of credit in rural areas by the Reserve and member banks? Had the System contracted agricultural credits, had it limited unduly the rediscounting of agricultural and livestock paper, or had it reduced the amount of currency in circulation, then a damaging bill of particulars might have been drawn up by the agrarian spokesmen against the Federal Reserve Board and the regional banks.

The truth of the matter is that agricultural credit during 1920 was expanded tremendously in order to meet the crisis precipitated by the sudden decline in farm prices in the fall. The total figures for 1919 and 1920 are given in Table 2.

The figures in Table 3 on the total amount of agricultural and livestock paper held by *all* the Federal Reserve banks on the last Friday of each month during 1919 and 1920 illustrate better the steady expansion, month by month, of agricultural credit that was taking place during the latter part of 1920. It should be reiterated that the figures cited in this table represent the total holdings of agricultural and livestock paper in all the Reserve banks at the end of each month—not, of course, the amount rediscounted during the month.

It is well known that, under the Federal Reserve System, the volume of currency in circulation expands proportionately to the volume of credit extended by the member banks. The figures in Table 4 afford, therefore, another yardstick of measuring the volume of credit expansion or contraction during 1919–1921.

27. Edmund Platt, Acting Governor of the Federal Reserve Board, submitted a thorough and comprehensive account of the operation of the progressive rate to the Senate in 1923. See this report in *Congressional Record*, 67th Congress, 4th session, January 27, 1923, 64(3): 2555–2590.

TABLE 5

Rediscounts between Federal Reserve Banks, 1919–1921

Bank	1919 Rediscounted or sold by 1.000 dollars	1919 Discounted or purchased by 1.000 dollars	1920 Rediscounted or sold by 1.000 dollars	1920 Discounted or purchased by 1.000 dollars	1921 Rediscounted or sold by 1.000 dollars	1921 Discounted or purchased by 1.000 dollars
Boston	20,045			969,884		204,150
New York		40,000	375,000	479,581		595,500
Philadelphia	826,521		371,600	144,579		5,000
Cleveland		229,017		1,406,172		194,503
Richmond	842,946		700,000		500,000	
Atlanta	82,690	5,000	307,997	52,000	65,145	
Chicago		1,328,338	255,000	168,500		
Saint Louis		140,209	309,499	13,000		
Minneapolis		428,613	293,500	40,000	117,000	
Kansas City	56,500	5,000	411,636	20,000	9,008	
Dallas	404,975	57,500	436,013	143,000	306,000	
San Francisco				23,500		

Source: H. Parker Willis and William H. Steiner, *Federal Reserve Banking Practice* (New York and London: D. Appleton and Co., 1926), p. 537.

The figures in Table 5 on the rediscounts between the Federal Reserve banks during 1919–1921 are significant, especially because they reveal that in 1919 several of the Reserve banks in agricultural districts, notably Chicago, Saint Louis, and Minneapolis, were purchasing the paper of the Reserve banks in industrial and commercial districts. In 1920 and 1921, the figures further reveal, the situation was entirely reversed and the Reserve banks in the industrial districts sent huge sums of money to the rural districts. The Federal Reserve Bank of Cleveland, for example, lent more in the South and West in 1920 than it did to its own member banks, which included the large banks in Pittsburgh, Cleveland, and Cincinnati. This, of course, was the way the Federal Reserve System was originally designed to operate; but these movements of inter-Reserve discounts should be sufficient evidence to prove that the South and West were not drained of credit and money at a time they so desperately needed it in order that Wall Street financiers and stockjobbers could speculate with greater ease.

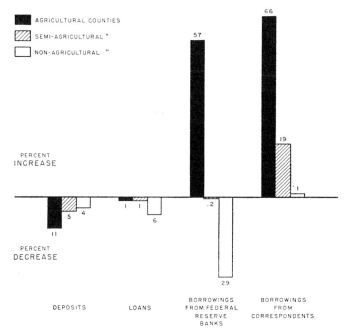

FIG. 1. Percent Change between May 4, 1920, and April 28, 1921, in Loans and Discounts, Total Deposits, and Borrowings of Member Banks in Agricultural, Semiagricultural, and Nonagricultural Counties.

Source: *Report of the Joint Commission of Agricultural Inquiry*, pt. 2, p. 102.

Finally, the evidence in Figure 1 reveals graphically the over-all credit situation in 1920 and 1921 with regard to agricultural and nonagricultural counties. There was an increase of borrowings from the Federal Reserve banks in agricultural counties of 57 percent from May 4, 1920, to April 28, 1921, while there was a corresponding decrease of 29 percent in the borrowing of member banks in nonagricultural counties for the same period.

By way of conclusion, let us first note what the unfriendly Joint Commission of Agricultural Inquiry, after a thorough investigation of the facts, concluded:

An analysis of the figures in these studies seems to justify the conclusion:

1. That the expansion of bank loans in rural districts during the period of inflation ending June 1920 was relatively greater than in the industrial sections, taken as a whole.

2. That the action of the Federal Reserve Board and the Federal reserve

banks during the 15 months preceding April 28, 1921, did not produce a greater curtailment of bank loans in the rural districts than in the financial and industrial sections.

3. Credit was not absorbed by the financial centers at the expense of rural communities for the purpose of speculative activities.

4. That the pressure of the forces of liquidation and depression in the agricultural sections was reflected in a reduction of deposits. This reduction of deposits, particularly demand deposits, was relatively larger in the agricultural and semiagricultural counties in the United States than in the industrial counties.[28]

The conclusions of the Joint Commission seem to be generally warranted, although it should be noted that the second statement implies that there *was* actual curtailment of agricultural credit during 1920 and the early months of 1921. Such emphatically and obviously was not the case. Not only were the agricultural areas not injured any more than were the industrial areas by the Reserve policy, but there was, as we have seen time and again, a great expansion of credit by the System to meet the needs of the farmers during the critical deflationary period.

The upshot of the agitation during 1920 and 1921 was the appointment in 1921 of the Joint Commission, which reported its findings the following year and gave the System a reasonably clean bill of health. The Commission concluded that what the farmers needed most of all by way of credit was some system of Federal intermediate credits, which the System could not supply, and which would provide credit to farmers for a period of from 6 months to 3 years. Consequently, the Commission framed the measure that became in 1923 the Intermediate Credits Act.

Insofar as the anti-Reserve agitation of the agrarian spokesmen was concerned, it seems that, as so often happens, Governor Harding, the Board, and the Reserve banks were made the scapegoats of the agricultural depression by small local bankers who had grossly overborrowed, by demagogic politicians who were serving their own ends primarily, and by the farmers in general who did not understand what had happened with regard to the credit situation, but who were suffering greatly in the economic chaos of the period.

28. *Report of the Joint Commission of Agricultural Inquiry*, pt. 2, p. 117.

22

What Happened to the Progressive Movement in the 1920s?

IF the day has not yet arrived when we can make a definite synthesis of political developments between the Armistice and the Great Depression, it is surely high time for historians to begin to clear away the accumulated heap of mistaken and half-mistaken hypotheses about this important transitional period. Writing often without fear or much research (to paraphrase Carl Becker's remark), we recent American historians have gone on indefatigably to perpetuate hypotheses that either reflected the disillusionment and despair of contemporaries, or once served their purpose in exposing the alleged hiatus in the great continuum of twentieth-century reform.

Stated briefly, the following are what might be called the governing hypotheses of the period under discussion: The 1920s were a period made almost unique by an extraordinary reaction against idealism and reform. They were a time when the political representatives of big business and Wall Street executed a relentless and successful campaign in state and nation to subvert the regulatory structure that had been built at the cost of so much toil and sweat since the 1870s, and to restore a Hanna-like reign of special privilege to benefit business, industry, and finance. The

Reprinted from *The American Historical Review*, LXIV (July 1959), 833–851; copyright 1959, Arthur S. Link.

surging tides of nationalism and mass hatreds generated by World War I continued to engulf the land and were manifested, among other things, in fear of communism, suppression of civil liberties, revival of nativism and anti-Semitism most crudely exemplified by the Ku Klux Klan, and in the triumph of racism and prejudice in immigration legislation. The 1920s were an era when great traditions and ideals were repudiated or forgotten, when the American people, propelled by a crass materialism in their scramble for wealth, uttered a curse on twenty-five years of reform endeavor. As a result, progressives were stunned and everywhere in retreat along the entire political front, their forces disorganized and leaderless, their movement shattered, their dreams of a new America turned into agonizing nightmares.

To be sure, the total picture that emerges from these generalizations is overdrawn. Yet it seems fair to say that leading historians have advanced each of these generalizations, that the total picture is the one that most of us younger historians saw during the years of our training, and that these hypotheses to a greater or lesser degree still control the way in which we write and teach about the 1920s, as a reading of textbooks and general works will quickly show.

This paper has not been written, however, to quarrel with anyone or to make an indictment. Its purposes are, first, to attempt to determine the degree to which the governing hypotheses, as stated, are adequate or inadequate to explain the political phenomena of the period, and, second, to discover whether any new and sounder hypotheses might be suggested. Such an effort, of course, must be tentative and, above all, imperfect in view of the absence of sufficient foundations for a synthesis.

Happily, however, we do not have to proceed entirely in the dark. Historians young and old, but mostly young, have already discovered that the period of the 1920s is the exciting new frontier of American historical research and that its opportunities are almost limitless in view of the mass of manuscript materials that are becoming available. Thus we have (the following examples are mentioned only at random) excellent recent studies of agrarian discontent and farm movements by Theodore Saloutos, John D. Hicks, Gilbert C. Fite, Robert L. Morlan, and James H. Shideler; of nativism and problems of immigration and assimilation by John

Higham, Oscar Handlin, Robert A. Divine, and E. David Cronon; of intellectual currents, the social gospel, and religious controversies by Henry F. May, Paul A. Carter, Robert M. Miller, and Norman F. Furniss; of left-wing politics and labor developments by Theodore Draper, David A. Shannon, Daniel Bell, Paul M. Angle, and Matthew Josephson; of the campaign of 1928 by Edmund A. Moore; and of political and judicial leaders by Alpheus T. Mason, Frank Freidel, Arthur M. Schlesinger, Jr., Merlo J. Pusey, and Joel F. Paschal.[1] Moreover, we can look forward to the early publication of studies that will be equally illuminating for the period, like the biographies of George W. Norris, Thomas J. Walsh, and Albert B. Fall now being prepared by Richard Lowitt, Leonard Bates, and David Stratton, respectively, and the recently

1. Theodore Saloutos and John D. Hicks, *Agrarian Discontent in the Middle West, 1900–1939* (Madison, Wis.: University of Wisconsin Press, 1951); Gilbert C. Fite, *Peter Norbeck: Prairie Statesman* (Columbia, Mo.: University of Missou.i Press, 1948), and *George N. Peek and the Fight for Farm Parity* (Norman, Okla.: University of Oklahoma Press, 1954); Robert L. Morlan, *Political Prairie Fire: The Nonpartisan League, 1915–1922* (Minneapolis, Minn.: University of Minnesota Press, 1955); James H. Shideler, *Farm Crisis, 1919–1923* (Berkeley, Calif.: University of California Press, 1957); John Higham, *Strangers in the Land: Patterns of American Nativism, 1860–1925* (New Brunswick, N.J.: Rutgers University Press, 1955); Oscar Handlin, *The American People in the Twentieth Century* (Cambridge, Mass.: Harvard University Press, 1954); Robert A. Divine, *American Immigration Policy, 1924–1952* (New Haven, Conn.: Yale University Press, 1957); E. David Cronon, *Black Moses: The Story of Marcus Garvey and the Universal Negro Improvement Association* (Madison, Wis.: University of Wisconsin Press, 1955); Henry F. May, "Shifting Perspectives on the 1920s," *Mississippi Valley Historical Review*, XLIII (December 1956), 405–427; Paul A. Carter, *The Decline and Revival of the Social Gospel* (Ithaca, N.Y.: Cornell University Press, 1956); Robert M. Miller, "An Inquiry into the Social Attitudes of American Protestantism, 1919–1939" (Ph.D. dissertation, Northwestern University, 1955); Norman F. Furniss, *The Fundamentalist Controversy, 1918–1931* (New Haven, Conn.: Yale University Press, 1954); Theodore Draper, *The Roots of American Communism* (New York: The Viking Press, 1957); David A. Shannon, *The Socialist Party of America: A History* (New York: Macmillan, 1955); Daniel Bell, "The Background and Development of Marxian Socialism in the United States," *Socialism and American Life*, edited by Donald D. Egbert and Stow Persons, 2 vols. (Princeton, N.J.: Princeton University Press, 1952), I, 215–405; Paul M. Angle, *Bloody Williamson* (New York: Alfred A. Knopf, 1952); Matthew Josephson, *Sidney Hillman: Statesman of American Labor* (New York: Doubleday, 1952); Edmund A. Moore, *A Catholic Runs for President: The Campaign of 1928* (New York: Ronald, 1956); Alpheus Thomas Mason, *Brandeis: A Free Man's Life* (New York: The Viking Press, 1946), and *Harlan Fiske Stone: Pillar of the Law* (New York: The Viking Press, 1956); Frank Freidel, *Franklin D. Roosevelt: The Ordeal* (Boston: Little, Brown and Co., 1954); Arthur M. Schlesinger, Jr., *The Age of Roosevelt: The Crisis of the Old Order* (Boston: Houghton, Mifflin Co., 1957); Merlo J. Pusey, *Charles Evans Hughes*, 2 vols. (New York: Macmillan, 1951); Joel Francis Paschal, *Mr. Justice Sutherland: A Man against the State* (Princeton, N.J.: Princeton University Press, 1951).

completed study of the campaign and election of 1920 by Wesley M. Bagby.[2]

Obviously, we are not only at a point in the progress of our research into the political history of the 1920s when we can begin to generalize, but we have reached the time when we should attempt to find some consensus, however tentative it must now be, concerning the larger political dimensions and meanings of the period.

In answering the question of what happened to the progressive movement in the 1920s, we should begin by looking briefly at some fundamental facts about the movement before 1918, facts that in large measure predetermined its fate in the 1920s, given the political climate and circumstances that prevailed.

The first of these was the elementary fact that the progressive movement never really existed as a recognizable organization with common goals and a political machinery geared to achieve them. Generally speaking (and for the purposes of this paper), progressivism might be defined as the popular effort, which began convulsively in the 1890s and waxed and waned afterward to our own time, to insure the survival of democracy in the United States by the enlargement of governmental power to control and offset the power of private economic groups over the nation's institutions and life. Actually, of course, from the 1890s on, there were many "progressive" movements on many levels seeking sometimes contradictory objectives. Not all, but most of these campaigns were the work of special interest groups or classes seeking greater political status and economic security. This was true from the beginning of the progressive movement in the 1890s; by 1913, it was that movement's most important characteristic.

The second fundamental fact—that the progressive movements were often largely middle class in constituency and orientation—is of course well known, but an important corollary has often been ignored. It was that several of the most important reform movements were inspired, staffed, and led by businessmen with very specific or special-interest objectives in view. Because they

2. Wesley M. Bagby, "Woodrow Wilson and the Great Debacle of 1920," manuscript in the possession of Professor Bagby; see also his "The 'Smoke-Filled Room' and the Nomination of Warren G. Harding," *Mississippi Valley Historical Review*, XLI (March 1955), 657–674, and "Woodrow Wilson, a Third Term, and the Solemn Referendum," *American Historical Review*, LX (April 1955), 567–575.

hated waste, mismanagement, and high taxes, they, together with their friends in the legal profession, often furnished the leadership of good government campaigns. Because they feared industrial monopoly, abuse of power by railroads, and the growth of financial oligarchy, they were the backbone of the movements that culminated in the adoption of the Hepburn Act and later acts for railroad regulation, the Federal Reserve Act, and the Federal Trade Commission Act. Among the many consequences of their participation in the progressive movement, two should be mentioned because of their significance for developments in the 1920s: First, the strong identification of businessmen with good government and economic reforms, for which the general public also had a lively concern, helped preserve the good reputation of the middle-class business community (as opposed to its alleged natural enemies, monopolists, malefactors of great wealth, and railroad barons) and helped to direct the energies of the progressive movement toward the strengthening instead of the shackling of the business community. Second, their activities and influence served to intensify the tensions within the broad reform movement, because they often opposed the demands of farm groups, labor unions, and advocates of social justice.

The third remark to be made about the progressive movement before 1918 is that, despite its actual diversity and inner tensions, it did seem to have unity; that is, it seemed to share common ideals and objectives. This was true in part because much of the motivation even of the special-interest groups was altruistic (at least they succeeded in convincing themselves that they sought the welfare of society rather than their own interests primarily); in part because political leadership generally succeeded in subordinating inner tensions. It was true, above all, because there were in fact important idealistic elements in the progressive ranks—social gospel leaders, social justice elements, and intellectuals and philosophers—who worked hard at the task of defining and elevating common principles and goals.

Fourth and finally, the substantial progressive achievements before 1918 had been gained, at least on the federal level, only because of the temporary dislocations of the national political structure caused by successive popular uprisings, not because progressives had found or created a viable organization for perpetuating their control. Or, to put the matter another way, before

1918, the various progressive elements had failed to destroy the existing party structure by organizing a national party of their own that could survive. They, or at least many of them, tried in 1912; and it seemed for a time in 1916 that Woodrow Wilson had succeeded in drawing the important progressive groups permanently into the Democratic party. But Wilson's accomplishment did not survive even to the end of the war, and by 1920 traditional partisan loyalties were reasserting themselves with extraordinary vigor.

With this introduction, we can now ask what happened to the progressive movement or movements in the 1920s. Surely no one would contend that after 1916 the political scene did not change significantly, both on the state and national levels. There was the seemingly obvious fact that the Wilsonian coalition had been wrecked by the election of 1920, and that the progressive elements were divided and afterward unable to agree upon a program or to control the national government. There was the even more "obvious" fact that conservative Republican presidents and their cabinets controlled the executive branch throughout the period. There was Congress, as Eric F. Goldman has said, allegedly whooping through procorporation legislation, and the Supreme Court interpreting the New Freedom laws in a way that harassed unions and encouraged trusts.[3] There were, to outraged idealists and intellectuals, the more disgusting spectacles of Red hunts, mass arrests and deportations, the survival deep into the 1920s of arrogant nationalism, crusades against the teaching of evolution, the attempted suppression of the right to drink, and myriad other manifestations of what would now be called a repressive reaction.[4]

Like the hypotheses suggested at the beginning, this picture is overdrawn in some particulars. But it is accurate in part, for progressivism was certainly on the downgrade, if not in decay, after 1918. This is an obvious fact that needs explanation and understanding rather than elaborate proof. We can go a long way toward answering our question if we can explain, at least partially, the extraordinary, complex developments that converged to produce the "obvious" result.

3. Eric F. Goldman, *Rendezvous with Destiny* (New York: Alfred A. Knopf, 1953), p. 284. [The "allegedly" in this sentence is mine, not Professor Goldman's.]

4. H. C. Peterson and Gilbert C. Fite, *Opponents of War, 1917–1918* (Madison: University of Wisconsin Press, 1957); Robert K. Murray, *Red Scare: A Study in National Hysteria, 1919–1920* (Minneapolis, Minn.: University of Minnesota Press, 1955).

For this explanation we must begin by looking at the several progressive elements and their relation to each other and to the two major parties after 1916. Since national progressivism was never an organized or independent movement (except imperfectly and then only temporarily in 1912), it could succeed only when its constituent elements formed a coalition strong enough to control one of the major parties. This had happened in 1916, when southern and western farmers, organized labor, the social justice elements, and a large part of the independent radicals who had heretofore voted the Socialist ticket coalesced to continue the control of Wilson and the Democratic party.

The important fact about the progressive coalition of 1916, however, was not its strength but its weakness. It was not a new party but a temporary alliance, welded in the heat of the most extraordinary domestic and external events. To be sure, it functioned for the most part successfully during the war, in providing the necessary support for a program of heavy taxation, relatively stringent controls over business and industry, and extensive new benefits to labor. Surviving in a crippled way even in the months following the Armistice, it put across a program that constituted a sizable triumph for the progressive movement: continued heavy taxation, the Transportation Act of 1920, the culmination of the long fight for railroad regulation, a new child labor act, amendments for prohibition and woman suffrage, immigration restriction, and water power and conservation legislation.

Even so, the progressive coalition of 1916 was inherently unstable. Indeed, it was so wracked by inner tensions that it could not survive, and destruction came inexorably, it seemed systematically, from 1917 to 1920. Why was this true?

First, the independent radicals and antiwar agrarians were alienated by the war declaration and the government's suppression of dissent and civil liberties during the war and the Red scare. Organized labor was disaffected by the administration's coercion of the coal miners in 1919, its lukewarm if not hostile attitude during the great strikes of 1919 and 1920, and its failure to support the Plumb Plan for nationalization of the railroads. Isolationists and idealists were outraged by what they thought was the President's betrayal of American traditions or the liberal peace program at Paris. These tensions were strong enough to disrupt the coalition, but a final one would have been fatal even if the others had never existed. This was the alienation of farmers in the Plains and western states produced by the administration's refusal to impose price controls on cotton while it maintained ceilings on the prices of other agricultural commodities,[5] and especially by the administration's failure to do anything decisive to stem the downward plunge of farm prices that began in the summer of 1920.[6] Under the impact of all these stresses, the Wilsonian coalition gradually disintegrated from 1917 to 1920 and disappeared entirely during the campaign of 1920.

The progressive coalition was thus destroyed, but the components of a potential movement remained. As we will see, these elements were neither inactive nor entirely unsuccessful in the 1920s. But they obviously failed to find common principles and a program, much less to unite effectively for political action on a national scale. I suggest that this was true, in part at least, for the following reasons:

First, the progressive elements could never create or gain control of a political organization capable of carrying them into national office. The Republican party was patently an impossible instrument because control of the GOP was too much in the hands of the eastern and midwestern industrial, oil, and financial interests, as it had been since about 1910. There was always the hope of a third party. Several progressive groups—insurgent midwestern Republicans, the railroad brotherhoods, a segment of the AF of L, and the moderate Socialists under Robert M. La Follette—tried to realize this goal in 1924, only to discover that third-party movements in the United States are doomed to failure except in periods of enormous national turmoil, and that the 1920s were not such a time. Thus the Democratic party remained the only vehicle that conceivably could have been used by a new progressive coalition. But that party was simply not capable of such service in the 1920s. It was so torn by conflicts between its eastern, big-city wing and its southern and western rural majority that it literally ceased to be a national party. It remained strong in its sectional and metropolitan components, but it was so divided that it barely succeeded

5. On this point, see Seward W. Livermore, "The Sectional Issue in the 1918 Congressional Elections," *Mississippi Valley Historical Review,* XXXV (June 1948), 29–60.

6. See "The Federal Reserve Policy and the Agricultural Depression of 1920–1921," pp. 330–348, this volume; and Herbert F. Margulies, "The Election of 1920 in Wisconsin: The Return to 'Normalcy' Reappraised," *Wisconsin Magazine of History,* XXXVIII (Autumn 1954), 15–22.

in nominating a presidential candidate at all in 1924 and nominated one in 1928 only at the cost of temporary disruption.[7]

Progressivism declined in the 1920s, in the second place, because, as has been suggested, the tensions that wrecked the coalition of 1916 not only persisted but actually grew in number and intensity. The two most numerous progressive elements, the southern and western farmers, strongly supported the Eighteenth Amendment, were heavily tinged with nativism and therefore supported immigration restriction, were either members of, friendly to, or politically afraid of the Ku Klux Klan, and demanded as the principal plank in the platform legislation to guarantee them a larger share of the national income. On all these points and issues, the lower and lower middle classes in the large cities stood in direct and often violent opposition to their potential allies in the rural areas. Moreover, the liaison between the farm groups and organized labor, which had been productive of much significant legislation during the Wilson period, virtually ceased to exist in the 1920s. There were many reasons for this development, and I mention only one: the fact that the pre-eminent spokesmen of farmers in the 1920s, the new Farm Bureau Federation, represented the larger commercial farmers who (in contrast to the members of the leading farm organization in Wilson's day, the National Farmers' Union) were often employers themselves and felt no identification with the rank and file of labor.

It was little wonder, therefore (and this is a third reason for the weakness of progressivism in the 1920s), that the tension-ridden progressive groups were never able to agree upon a program that, like the Democratic platform of 1916, could provide the basis for a revived coalition. So long as progressive groups fought one another more fiercely than they fought their natural opponents, such agreement was impossible; and so long as common goals were impossible to achieve, a national progressive movement could not take effective form. Nothing illustrates this better than the failure of the Democratic conventions of 1924 and 1928 to adopt platforms that could rally and unite the discontented elements. One result, among others, was that southern farmers voted

7. For a highly partisan account of these events, see Karl Schriftgiesser, *This Was Normalcy* (Boston: Little, Brown and Co., 1948). More balanced are the already cited Freidel, *Franklin D. Roosevelt: The Ordeal,* and Schlesinger, *The Age of Roosevelt: The Crisis of the Old Order.*

as Democrats and western farmers as Republicans. And, as Professor Frank Freidel once commented to the author, much of the failure of progressivism in the 1920s can be explained by this elementary fact.

A deeper reason for the failure of progressives to unite ideologically in the 1920s was what might be called a substantial paralysis of the progressive mind. This was partly the result of the repudiation of progressive ideals by many intellectuals and the defection from the progressive movement of the urban middle classes and professional groups, as will be demonstrated. It was the result, even more importantly, of the fact that progressivism as an organized body of political thought found itself at a crossroads in the 1920s, like progressivism today, and did not know which way to turn. The major objectives of the progressive movement of the prewar years had in fact been largely achieved by 1920. In what direction should progressivism now move? Should it remain in the channels already deeply cut by its own traditions, and, while giving sincere allegiance to the ideal of democratic capitalism, work for more comprehensive programs of business regulation and assistance to disadvantaged classes like farmers and submerged industrial workers? Should it abandon these traditions and, like most similar European movements, take the road toward a moderate socialism with a predominant labor orientation? Should it attempt merely to revive the goals of more democracy through changes in the political machinery? Or should it become mainly an agrarian movement with purely agrarian goals?

These were real dilemmas, not academic ones, and one can see numerous examples of how they confused and almost paralyzed progressives in the 1920s. The platform of La Follette's Progressive party of 1924 offers one revealing illustration. It embodied much that was old and meaningless by this time (the direct election of the president and a national referendum before the adoption of a war resolution, for example) and little that had any real significance for the future.[8] And yet it was the best that a

---

8. For a different picture, see Belle C. La Follette and Fola La Follette, *Robert M. La Follette*, 2 vols. (New York: Macmillan, 1953); and Russel B. Nye, *Midwestern Progressive Politics, 1870–1950* (East Lansing, Mich.: Michigan State College Press, 1951). Both works contribute to an understanding of progressive politics in the 1920s.

vigorous and idealistic movement could offer. A second example was the plight of the agrarians and insurgents in Congress who fought so hard all through the 1920s against Andrew Mellon's proposals to abolish the inheritance tax and to make drastic reductions in the taxes on large incomes. In view of the rapid reduction of the federal debt, the progressives were hard pressed to justify the continuation of nearly confiscatory tax levels, simply because few of them realized the wide social and economic uses to which the income tax could be put. Lacking any programs for the redistribution of the national income (except to farmers), they were plagued and overwhelmed by the surpluses in the federal Treasury until, for want of any good arguments, they finally gave Secretary Andrew Mellon the legislation he had been demanding.[9] A third and final example of this virtual paralysis of the progressive mind was perhaps the most revealing of all. It was the attempt that Woodrow Wilson, Louis D. Brandeis, and other Democratic leaders made from 1921 to 1924 to draft a new charter for progressivism. Except for its inevitable proposals for an idealistic world leadership, the document that emerged from this interchange included little or nothing that would have sounded new to a western progressive in 1912.

A fourth reason for the disintegration and decline of the progressive movement in the 1920s was the lack of any effective leadership. Given the political temper and circumstances of the 1920s, it is possible that such leadership could not have operated successfully in any event. Perhaps the various progressive elements were so mutually hostile and so self-centered in interests and objectives that even a Theodore Roosevelt or a Woodrow Wilson, had they been at the zenith of their powers in the 1920s, could not have drawn them together in a common front. We will never know what a strong national leader might have done because by a trick of fate no such leader emerged before Franklin D. Roosevelt.

Four factors, then, contributed to the failure of the progressive components to unite successfully after 1918 and, as things turned out, before 1932: the lack of a suitable political vehicle, the severity of the tensions that kept progressives apart, the failure of progressives to agree upon a common program, and the absence of a

9. Here indebtedness is acknowledged to Sidney Ratner, *American Taxation: Its History as a Social Force in Democracy* (New York: W. W. Norton & Co., 1942).

national leadership, without which a united movement could never be created and sustained. These were all weaknesses that stemmed to a large degree from the instability and failures of the progressive movement itself.

There were, besides, a number of what might be called external causes for the movement's decline. In considering them, one must begin with what was seemingly the most important: the alleged fact that the 1920s were a very unpropitious time for any new progressive revolt because of the ever-increasing level of economic prosperity, the materialism, and the general contentment of the decade 1919 to 1929. Part of this generalization is valid when applied to specific elements in the population. For example, the rapid rise in the real wages of industrial workers, coupled with generally full employment and the spread of so-called welfare practices among management, certainly did much to weaken and avert the further spread of organized labor, and thus to debilitate one of the important progressive components. But to say that it was prosperity per se that created a climate unfriendly to progressive ideals would be inaccurate. There was little prosperity and much depression during the 1920s for the single largest economic group, the farmers, as well as for numerous other groups. Progressivism, moreover, can flourish as much during periods of prosperity as during periods of discontent, as the history of the development of the progressive movement from 1901 to 1917 and of its triumph from 1945 to 1956 prove.

Vastly more important among the external factors in the decline of progressivism was the widespread, almost wholesale, defection from its ranks of the middle classes—the middling businessmen, bankers, and manufacturers, and the professional people closely associated with them in ideals and habits—in American cities large and small. For an understanding of this phenomenon no simple explanations like "prosperity" or the "temper of the times" will suffice, although they give some insight. The important fact was that these groups found a new economic and social status as a consequence of the flowering of American enterprise under the impact of the technological, financial, and other revolutions of the 1920s. If, as Professor Richard Hofstadter has claimed,[10] the urban middle classes were progressive (that is, they

10. Richard Hofstadter, *The Age of Reform: From Bryan to F.D.R.* (New York: Alfred A. Knopf, 1955), 131 ff.

demanded governmental relief from various anxieties) in the early 1900s because they resented their loss of social prestige to the *nouveaux riches* and feared being ground under by monopolists in industry, banking, and labor—if this is true, then the urban middle classes were not progressive in the 1920s for inverse reasons. Their temper was dynamic, expansive, and supremely confident. They knew that they were building a new America, a business civilization based not upon monopoly and restriction but upon a whole new set of business values—mass production and consumption, short hours and high wages, full employment, welfare capitalism. And what was more important, virtually the entire country (at least the journalists, writers in popular magazines, and many preachers and professors) acknowledged that the nation's destiny was in good hands. It was little wonder, therefore, that the whole complex of groups constituting the urban middle classes, whether in New York, Zenith, or Middletown, had little interest in rebellion or even in mild reform proposals that seemed to imperil their leadership and control.

Other important factors, of course, contributed to the contentment of the urban middle classes. The professionalization of business and the full-blown emergence of a large managerial class had a profound impact upon social and political ideals. The acceleration of mass advertising played its role, as did also the beginning disintegration of the great cities with the spread of middle-and upper-middle-class suburbs, a factor that diffused the remaining reform energies among the urban leaders.

A second external factor in the decline of the progressive movement after 1918 was the desertion from its ranks of a good part of the intellectual leadership of the country. Indeed, more than simple desertion was involved here; it was often a matter of a cynical repudiation of the ideals from which progressivism derived its strength. I do not mean to imply too much by this generalization. I know that what has been called intellectual progressivism not only survived in the 1920s but actually flourished in many fields.[11] I know that the intellectual foundations of our present quasi-welfare state were either being laid or reinforced

11. *Ibid.*, pp. 5, 131, 135 ff. For a recent excellent survey, previously cited, see Henry F. May, "Shifting Perspectives on the 1920s." Schlesinger's previously cited *Age of Roosevelt* sheds much new light on the economic thought of the 1920s.

during the decade. Even so, one cannot evade the conclusion that the intellectual-political climate of the 1920s was vastly different from the one that had prevailed in the preceding two decades.

During the years of the great progressive revolt, intellectuals—novelists, journalists, political thinkers, social scientists, historians, and the like—had made a deeply personal commitment to the cause of democracy, first in domestic and then in foreign affairs. Their leadership in and impact on many phases of the progressive movement had been profound. By contrast, in the 1920s, a large body of this intellectual phalanx turned against the very ideals they had once deified. One could cite, for example, the reaction of the idealists against the Versailles settlement; the disenchantment of the intellectuals with the extension of government authority when it could be used to justify the Eighteenth Amendment or the suppression of free speech; or the inevitable loss of faith in the "people" when en masse they hounded so-called radicals, joined Bryan's crusade against evolution, or regaled themselves as Knights of the Ku Klux Klan. Whatever the cause, many alienated intellectuals simply withdrew or repudiated any identification with the groups they had once helped to lead. The result was not fatal to progressivism, but it was serious. The spark plugs had been removed from the engine of reform.

The progressive movement, then, unquestionably declined, but was it defunct in the 1920s? Much, of course, depends upon the definition of terms. If we accept the usual definition for "defunct" as "dead" or "ceasing to have any life or strength," we must recognize that the progressive movement was certainly not defunct in the 1920s; that on the contrary at least important parts of it were very much alive; and that it is just as important to know how and why progressivism survived as it is to know how and why it declined.

To state the matter briefly, progressivism survived in the 1920s because several important elements of the movement remained either in full vigor or in only slightly diminished strength. These were the farmers, after 1918 better organized and more powerful than during the high tide of the progressive revolt; the politically conscious elements among organized labor, particularly the railroad brotherhoods, who wielded a power all out of proportion to their numbers; the Democratic organizations in the large cities, usually vitally concerned with the welfare of the so-called lower classes; a remnant of independent radicals, social workers, and social gospel writers and preachers; and finally, an emerging new vocal element, the champions of public power and regional developments.

Although they never united effectively enough to capture a major party and the national government before 1932, these progressive elements controlled Congress from 1921 to about 1927 and continued to exercise a near control during the period of their great weakness in the legislative branch, from 1927 to about 1930.

Indeed, the single most powerful and consistently successful group in Congress during the entire decade from 1919 to 1929 were the spokesmen of the farmers. Spurred by an unrest in the country areas more intense than at any time since the 1890s,[12] in 1920 and 1921 southern Democrats and midwestern and western insurgents, nominally Republican, joined forces in an alliance called the Farm Bloc. By maintaining a common front from 1921 to 1924, they succeeded in enacting the most advanced agricultural legislation to that date, legislation that completed the program begun under Wilsonian auspices. It included measures for high tariffs on agricultural products, thoroughgoing federal regulation of stockyards, packing houses, and grain exchanges, the exemption of agricultural co-operatives from the application of the antitrust laws, stimulation of the export of agricultural commodities, and the establishment of an entirely new federal system of intermediate rural credit.

When prosperity failed to return to the countryside, rural leaders in Congress espoused a new and bolder plan for relief: the proposal made by George N. Peek and Hugh S. Johnson in 1922 to use the federal power to obtain "fair exchange" or "parity" prices for farm products. Embodied in the McNary-Haugen bill in 1924, this measure was approved by Congress in 1927 and 1928, only to encounter vetoes by President Calvin Coolidge.

In spite of its momentary failure, the McNary-Haugen bill had a momentous significance for the American progressive movement. Its wholesale espousal by the great mass of farm

12. It derived from the fact that farm prices plummeted in 1920 and 1921 and remained so low that farmers, generally speaking, operated at a net capital loss throughout the balance of the decade.

leaders and spokesmen meant that the politically most powerful class in the country had come full scale to the conviction that the taxing power should be used directly and specifically for the purpose of underwriting (some persons called it subsidizing) agriculture. It was a milestone in the development of a comprehensive political doctrine that it was government's duty to protect the economic security of all classes and particularly depressed ones. McNary-Haugenism can be seen in its proper perspective if it is remembered that it would have been considered almost absurd in the Wilson period, that it was regarded as radical by nonfarm elements in the 1920s, and that it, or at any rate its fundamental objective, was incorporated almost as a matter of course into basic federal policy in the 1930s.

A second significant manifestation of the survival of progressivism in the 1920s came during the long controversy over public ownership or regulation of the burgeoning electric power industry. In this, as in most of the conflicts that eventually culminated on Capitol Hill, the agrarian element constituted the core of progressive strength. At the same time, a sizable and well-organized independent movement developed that emanated from urban centers and was vigorous on the municipal and state levels. Throughout the decade this relatively new progressive group fought with mounting success to expose the propaganda of the private utilities, to strengthen state and federal regulatory agencies, and to win municipal ownership for distributive facilities. Like the advocates of railroad regulation in an earlier period, these proponents of regulation or ownership of a great new natural monopoly failed almost as much as they had succeeded in the 1920s. But their activities and exposures (the Federal Trade Commission's devastating investigation of the electric power industry in the late 1920s and early 1930s was the prime example) laid secure foundations for movements that in the 1930s would reach various culminations.

Even more significant for the future of American progressivism was the emergence in the 1920s of a new objective, that of committing the federal government to plans for large hydroelectric projects in the Tennessee Valley, the Columbia River watershed, the Southwest, and the St. Lawrence Valley for the purpose, some progressives said, of establishing "yardsticks" for rates, or for the further purpose, as other progressives declared, of beginning a movement for the eventual nationalization of the entire electric power industry. The development of this movement in its emerging stages affords a good case study in the natural history of American progressivism. It began when the Harding and Coolidge administrations attempted to dispose of the government's hydroelectric and nitrate facilities at Muscle Shoals, Alabama, to private interests. In the first stage of the controversy, the progressive objective was merely federal operation of these facilities for the production of cheap fertilizer—a reflection of its exclusive special-interest orientation. Then, as new groups joined the fight to save Muscle Shoals, the objective of public production of cheap electric power came to the fore. Finally, by the end of the 1920s, the objective of a multipurpose regional development in the Tennessee Valley and in other areas as well had taken firm shape.

In addition, by 1928, the agrarians in Congress, led by Sen. George W. Norris, had found enough allies in the two houses and enough support in the country at large to adopt a bill for limited federal development of the Tennessee Valley. Thwarted by President Coolidge's pocket veto, the progressives tried again in 1931, only to meet a second rebuff at the hands of President Herbert Hoover.

All this might be regarded as another milestone in the maturing of American progressivism. It signified a deviation from the older traditions of mere regulation, as President Hoover had said in his veto of the second Muscle Shoals bill, and the triumph of new concepts of direct federal leadership in large-scale development of resources. If progressives had not won their goal by the end of the 1920s, they had at least succeeded in writing what would become perhaps the most important plank in their program for the future.

The maturing of an advanced farm program and the formulation of plans for public power and regional developments may be termed the two most significant progressive achievements on the national level in the 1920s. Others merit only brief consideration. One was the final winning of the old progressive goal of immigration restriction through limited and selective admission. The fact that this movement was motivated in part by racism, nativism, and anti-Semitism (with which, incidentally, a great many if not a majority of progressives were imbued in the 1920s) should not blind us to the fact that it was also progressive. It sought to substitute a so-called scientific and a planned policy for a policy of laissez-faire. Its purpose was admittedly to disturb the free operation of the international labor market. Organized labor and social workers had long supported it against the opposition of large employers. And there was prohibition, the most ambitious and revealing progressive experiment of the twentieth century. Even the contemned anti-evolution crusade of Bryan and the fundamentalists and the surging drives for conformity of thought and action in other fields should be mentioned. All these movements stemmed from the conviction that organized public power could and should be used purposefully to achieve fundamental social and so-called moral change. The fact that they were potentially or actively repressive does not mean that they were not progressive. On the contrary, they superbly illustrated the repressive tendencies that inhered in progressivism precisely because it was grounded so much upon majoritarian principles.

Three other developments on the national level that have often been cited as evidences of the failure of progressivism in the 1920s appear in a somewhat different light at second glance. The first was the reversal of the tariff-for-revenue-only tendencies of the Underwood Act with the enactment of the Emergency Tariff Act of 1921 and the Fordney-McCumber Act of 1922. Actually, the adoption of these measures signified, on the whole, not a repudiation but a revival of progressive principles in the realm of federal fiscal policy. A revenue tariff had never been an authentic progressive objective. Indeed, at least by 1913, many progressives, except for some southern agrarians, had concluded that it was retrogressive and had agreed that the tariff laws should be used deliberately to achieve certain national objectives—for example, the crippling of noncompetitive big business by the free admission of articles manufactured by so-called trusts, or benefits to farmers by the free entry of farm implements. Wilson himself had been at least partially converted to these principles by 1916, as his insistence upon the creation of the Federal Tariff Commission and his promise of protection to the domestic chemical industry revealed. As for the tariff legislation of the early 1920s, its only important changes were increased protection for aluminum, chemical products, and agricultural commodities. It left the Underwood rates on the great mass of raw materials and manufactured goods largely undisturbed. It may have been economically shortsighted and a bad example for the rest of the world, but for the most part it was progressive in principle and was the handiwork of the progressive coalition in Congress.

Another development that has often been misunderstood in its relation to the progressive movement was the policies of consistent support that the Harding and Coolidge administrations adopted for business enterprise, particularly the policy of the Federal Trade Commission in encouraging the formation of trade associations and the diminution of certain traditional competitive practices. The significance of all this can easily be overrated. Such policies as these two administrations executed had substantial justification in progressive theory and in precedents clearly established by the Wilson administration.

A third challenge to usual interpretations concerns implications to be drawn from the election of Harding and Coolidge in 1920 and 1924. These elections seem to indicate the triumph of reaction among the mass of American voters. Yet one could argue that both Harding and Coolidge were political accidents, the beneficiaries of grave defects in the American political and constitutional systems. The rank and file of Republican voters demonstrated during the preconvention campaign that they wanted vigorous leadership and a moderately progressive candidate in 1920. They got Harding instead, not because they wanted him, but because unusual circumstances permitted a small clique to thwart the will of the majority.[13] They took Coolidge as their candidate in 1924 simply because Harding died in the middle of his term and there seemed to be no alternative to nominating the man who had succeeded him in the White House. Further, an analysis of the election returns in 1920 and 1924 will show that the really decisive factor in the victories of Harding and Coolidge was the fragmentation of the progressive movement and the fact that an opposition strong enough to rally and unite the progressive majority simply did not exist.

There remains, finally, a vast area of progressive activity about which we yet know very little. One could mention the continuation of old reform movements and the development of new ones in

13. Much that is new on the Republican preconvention campaign and convention of 1920 may be found in William T. Hutchinson, *Lowden of Illinois: The Life of Frank O. Lowden,* 2 vols. (Chicago: University of Chicago Press, 1957).

the cities and states during the years following the Armistice: for example, the steady spread of the city-manager form of government, the beginning of zoning and planning movements, and the efforts of the great cities to keep abreast of the transportation revolution then in full swing. Throughout the country, the educational and welfare activities of the cities and states steadily increased. Factory legislation matured, while social insurance had its experimental beginnings. Whether such reform impulses were generally weak or strong, one cannot say; but what we do know about developments in cities like Cincinnati and states like New York, Wisconsin, and Louisiana[14] justifies a challenge to the assumption that municipal and state reform energies were dead after 1918 and, incidentally, a plea to young scholars to plow this unworked field of recent American history.

Let us, then, suggest a tentative synthesis as an explanation of what happened to the progressive movement after 1918:

First, the national progressive movement, which had found its most effective embodiment in the coalition of forces that re-elected Woodrow Wilson in 1916, was shattered by certain policies that the administration pursued from 1917 to 1920, and by some developments over which the administration had no or only slight control. The collapse that occurred in 1920 was not inevitable and cannot be explained by merely saying that "the war killed the progressive movement."

Second, large and aggressive components of a potential new progressive coalition remained after 1920. These elements never succeeded in uniting effectively before the end of the decade, not because they did not exist, but because they were divided by conflicts among themselves. National leadership, which in any event did not emerge in the 1920s, perhaps could not have succeeded in subduing these tensions and in creating a new common front.

Third, as a result of the foregoing, progressivism as an organized national force suffered a serious decline in the 1920s. This decline was heightened by the defection of large elements among the urban middle classes and the intellectuals, a desertion induced by technological, economic, and demographic changes,

14. See, e.g., Allan P. Sindler, *Huey Long's Louisiana: State Politics, 1920–1952* (Baltimore: Johns Hopkins Press, 1956).

and by the outcropping of certain repressive tendencies in progressivism after 1917.

Fourth, in spite of reversals and failures, important components of the national progressive movement survived in considerable vigor and succeeded to a varying degree, not merely in keeping the movement alive, but even in broadening its horizons. This was true particularly of the farm groups and of the coalition concerned with public regulation or ownership of electric power resources. These two groups laid the groundwork in the 1920s for significant new programs in the 1930s and beyond.

Fifth, various progressive coalitions controlled Congress for the greater part of the 1920s and were always a serious threat to the conservative administrations that controlled the executive branch. Because this was true, most of the legislation adopted by Congress during this period, including many measures that historians have inaccurately called reactionary, was progressive in character.

Sixth, the progressive movements in the cities and states were far from dead in the 1920s, although we do not have sufficient evidence to justify any generalizations about the degree of its vigor.

If this tentative and imperfect synthesis has any value, perhaps it is high time that we discard the sweeping generalizations, false hypotheses, and clichés that we have so often used in explaining and characterizing political developments from 1918 to 1929. Perhaps we should try to see these developments for what they were—the normal and ordinary political behavior of groups and classes caught up in a swirl of social and economic change. When we do this, we will no longer ask whether the progressive movement was defunct in the 1920s. We will ask only what happened to it and why.

23

Laying the Foundations of the First Presbyterian Church of Princeton

THERE were Presbyterians in New Jersey from almost the first years after the founding of the province by Lord John Berkeley and Sir George Carteret in 1665. The earliest seem to have been Scottish Presbyterians who, fleeing persecution in their homeland, began a substantial migration to East Jersey in about 1679. They settled first in Perth Amboy and then spread to Freehold. To these pioneer Presbyterians were soon added, both in East and West Jersey, Congregationalists, principally from Long Island and Connecticut, who preferred the Presbyterian polity to independency, Huguenots fleeing for their lives after the revocation of the Edict of Nantes in 1685, and others. A Presbyterian congregation was formed in Bound Brook in central New Jersey about 1688, while others sprang up in Maidenhead (now Lawrenceville), Hopewell, Ewing, Pennington, and Trenton between 1698 and 1712.

Presbyterian congregations spread even more rapidly after the beginning of large-scale immigration from northern Ireland, about 1710. That indefatigable missionary from Ulster, Francis Makemie, organized the first presbytery in the colonies, the Pres-

Reprinted from Arthur S. Link, editor, *The First Presbyterian Church of Princeton: Two Centuries of History* (Princeton, N.J. The First Presbyterian Church, 1967), pp. 7–28, by permission of the First Presbyterian Church.

bytery of Philadelphia, in 1706. But Presbyterian growth was so rapid thenceforward that the Church's governmental structure had to be constantly enlarged. A General Synod, embracing three new presbyteries in addition to the Presbytery of Philadelphia, was organized in 1716. The East Jersey Presbytery, organized in 1733, was combined with the Presbytery of New York in 1738, and the Presbytery of New Brunswick was organized to include "all the northward and westward of Maidenhead and Hopewell and into the Raritan River, including also Staten Island, Piscatua, Amboy, Bound Brook, Basking Ridge, Turkey, Rocksitiens, Pequally, and Crosswicks." [1]

At this very time, New Jersey Presbyterians and others were being convulsed by the revivalistic movement known as the Great Awakening. It was a revolt against the cold formalism that had begun to ossify the churches and laid great emphasis upon the personal experience of grace. It swept through all the colonies, from Massachusetts to Georgia, particularly after the arrival in America of the English evangelist, George Whitefield, in 1739. It also divided Presbyterians into two more or less warring groups—the revivalistic "New Lights" and the more conservative "Old Lights." [2]

The winds of the Great Awakening blew with perhaps strongest force in northern New Jersey, due to the fervent leadership in that area of Jonathan Dickinson, pastor at Elizabeth; Aaron Burr, pastor at Newark; and, above all, Gilbert Tennent, pastor at New Brunswick. The New Brunswick Presbytery withdrew or was ejected from the General Synod in 1741 and, together with other presbyteries, formed the "New Light" Synod of New York in 1745, in opposition to the "Old Light" Synod of Philadelphia. The schism was not fully healed until 1758. One outcome of the Great Awakening, among others, was the founding of the College of New Jersey, later Princeton University, in 1746 by Dickinson, Burr, and others.

It is entirely possible that organized Presbyterianism in

1. Quoted in New Jersey Historical Records Survey Project, *Inventory of the Church Archives of New Jersey, Presbyterians* (Newark, N.J.: The Historical Records Survey, 1940), p. 41, to which I am also indebted for more general information about the beginnings of Presbyterianism in New Jersey.

2. See particularly Charles H. Maxson, *The Great Awakening in the Middle Colonies* (Chicago: University of Chicago Press, 1920).

Princeton was also a child of the Great Awakening. Princeton, only a village of some thirty to forty houses in 1750, was then known principally as a way station on the stagecoach line between Philadelphia and New York and was overshadowed by its larger neighbors of Kingston and Lawrenceville. There had been Presbyterians in Princeton presumably since its founding in the 1680s. By 1750 they were apparently a self-conscious group, tired of having to travel great distances to worship at the Kingston and Lawrenceville churches. In any event, someone first spoke for them at a meeting of the Presbytery of New Brunswick in Woodbury on September 3, 1751. The Kingston Church, having lost its pastor in 1749, petitioned Presbytery for "supplies," or preachers. Thereupon some unknown member moved that the supplies should be equally divided between Kingston and Princeton. The Presbytery, on the following day, ruled that it was not expedient to have two places of meeting so close together. However, as a concession to discontented Princetonians, it added that whoever supplied at Kingston might "preach a lecture at Princetown if they can." [3]

How many "lectures" were preached at Princeton in the early 1750s, we do not know. Perhaps the visit of Whitefield to the village in September 1754 [4] increased local religious fervor and the determination to have a separate congregation. In any event, the Presbytery, meeting at Lawrenceville on May 28, 1755, received a petition from Princeton Presbyterians for a supply or supplies and "for liberty to build a meeting house there." Presbytery responded affirmatively on the following day, naming James Davenport and Samuel Kennedy as supplies for certain Sundays.[5]

These two ministers presumably held Presbyterian services, at least intermittently, during the following year. Regular worship began after the removal of the College of New Jersey to Princeton in November 1756, in the Prayer Room of the newly constructed Nassau Hall. This room, about thirty-two by forty feet, occupied the north end of what is now the Faculty Room and contained a fine pipe organ—the first such instrument, incidentally, used

3. "The New-Brunswick Presbytery Book," 1738–56, minutes for September 3–4, 1751; microfilm copy of the original minutes in the Presbyterian Historical Society, Philadelphia, in the Speer Library, Princeton Theological Seminary.
4. Philadelphia *Pennsylvania Journal*, September 12, 1754, cited in *Archives of the State of New Jersey, First Series* (Paterson, N.J. The Press Printing and Publishing Co., 1897), XIX, 408–409.
5. "The New-Brunswick Presbytery Book," 1738–56, minutes for May 28–29, 1755.

in Presbyterian services in America.[6] There was no separate congregation. Local townspeople, renting pews in the Prayer Hall, simply worshipped with faculty and students and enjoyed the preaching of President Aaron Burr until his death in September 1757; of President Jonathan Edwards, the greatest American theologian of the eighteenth century, who survived the rigors of the Princeton climate for only a few months in early 1758; of Acting President Jacob Green in 1758–59; of President Samuel Davies from 1759 to 1761; and of President Samuel Finley from 1761 until his death in 1766.

This was a new order of things for Princeton Presbyterians, but the scanty records of these years do not reveal much about their life as an inchoate congregation. They were undoubtedly greatly stirred by the revival that swept through the college in 1757; and they must have thrilled to the preaching of Samuel Davies, who was renowned as one of the greatest pulpit orators in the world of his time.[7] But they were merely visitors at the college services and probably had no congregational life of their own.

The rapid growth of Presbyterian families in Princeton after the removal of the college must have strengthened the natural desire for separate religious life. Certainly by 1760 Princeton Presbyterians were aspiring to have a sanctuary of their own. What Dr. Schenck described as long and tedious negotiations looking toward construction of a sanctuary began at about this time between leaders of the would-be congregation and the college, which needed a larger auditorium for commencements than that afforded by the Prayer Hall. A group of townspeople, led by Richard Stockton, subscribed the initial funds on January 20, 1762.[8] In the following April, ten trustees of the college signed an agreement, which was confirmed by the full Board on September 29, 1762, with "sundry inhabitants of Princeton for the erection of a church building." [9] It stipulated that a sanctuary might be built

6. Thomas J. Wertenbaker, *Princeton, 1746–1896* (Princeton, N.J.: Princeton University Press, 1946), pp. 38–39.
7. William E. Schenck, *An Historical Account of the First Presbyterian Church of Princeton, N.J.* (Princeton, N.J.: Robinson, 1850), pp. 23–25.
8. John F. Hageman, *History of Princeton and Its Institutions,* 2 vols. (Philadelphia: J. B. Lippincott & Co., 1879), II, 80–81, prints the subscription paper.
9. "Minutes of the Proceedings of the Trustees of the College of New Jersey," 1749–96, minutes for September 29, 1762.

on land owned by the college, that the college would lend £700 toward cost of construction, that one side of the galleries should be reserved for students, and that the college might use the building for three days at commencements and at other times when the President so desired.[10]

There was later some controversy or misunderstanding over the church's legal rights. The Board of Trustees of the college, on October 22, 1783, promised to deed the land on which the sanctuary stood to the congregation, under provisions reserving the right of the college to use the building at specified times and forbidding use of the land as a burial ground.[11] Acting for the Trustees of the college, Dr. John Witherspoon gave a deed to John Little and others representing the congregation for the sanctuary and land on which it stood on February 25, 1785, in return for £720 "Proclamation money." [12] But this deed was never filed, and it was not until 1816 that a deed was given and properly executed.[13] Even it is missing from the courthouse in which it should be found.

The cornerstone of the sanctuary was laid in early 1762, apparently in the spring of that year. The walls were up by September, but work went forward slowly after this date. Indeed, we find the college Trustees, at their meeting on September 28, 1763, appointing a committee to negotiate with the congregation for the return of the land and disposal of the unfinished sanctuary.[14] Perhaps lagging spirits were revived by Whitefield, who preached in Princeton several times in November 1763. Perhaps President Finley, who was now serving as Acting Pastor, rallied his congregation and, as Hageman says, gave the decisive leadership to the cause.[15] Whatever the reason, work on the sanctuary

10. J. F. Hageman, *Princeton and Its Institutions*, II, 81; John Maclean, *History of the College of New Jersey*, 2 vols. (Philadelphia: J. B. Lippincott & Co., 1877), I, 257.

11. This document, signed by John Witherspoon for the Board and Robert Stockton and others for the congregation, is in the Princeton University Library.

12. Deed dated February 25, 1785, in the Papers of the First Presbyterian Church of Princeton, N.J., Speer Library of the Princeton Theological Seminary; hereinafter cited as First Church Papers, Speer Library.

13. J. F. Hageman, *Princeton and Its Institutions*, II, 111–112; John Maclean, *History of the College of New Jersey*, II, 165, printing an extract from the Minutes of the Trustees of the College of New Jersey, April 9, 1816.

14. "Minutes of the Proceedings of the Trustees of the College of New Jersey," 1748–96, minutes for September 28, 1763.

15. W. E. Schenck, *The First Presbyterian Church of Princeton*, p. 30; J. F. Hageman, *Princeton and Its Institutions*, II, 83.

progressed so rapidly after this date that it was substantially complete by the late summer of 1764.

That this was true is evidenced by an item in the New York *Mercury* of October 8, 1764, reporting that the commencement exercises of the College of New Jersey had been held in the new Presbyterian Church on September 26. The preacher in what was probably the first service to be held on the location of the First Presbyterian Church was none other than Whitefield himself. His text was Philippians 3:8, and at the close of his sermon he "gave a very striking and animated Exhortation to the young Gentlemen who were candidates for the Honours of the College." The exercises, this report went on, were "performed to the Satisfaction of all who understood them." They were, it is almost needless to add, in Latin.[16] The second service in the sanctuary of which we have any record was the commencement exercise held on September 25, 1765, at a time when passions were running high over the Stamp Act. The newspaper report of this affair tells us that the young gentlemen who performed evidenced "a spirit of liberty and tender regard for their suffering country," and that most of them appeared dressed in clothing of American manufacture.[17]

It is entirely possible that regular divine services in the new sanctuary began in September of 1764. However, a strong local tradition sets the date at some time during the early months of 1766. The scrupulous chroniclers, Schenck and Hageman, both accept this date, and so must we, too, in the absence of better evidence to the contrary.

The only extant drawing of the sanctuary is the one on the seal of the church, made in 1786.[18] This drawing, in addition to contemporary descriptions and a floor plan reproduced by Hageman, enables us to give a fairly detailed description, lacking only precise dimensions. The building was two-storied, of brick, rectangular in shape, without a steeple, with its long side parallel

16. New York *Mercury*, October 8, 1764, printed in *Archives of the State of New Jersey, First Series* (Paterson, N.J.: The Call Printing and Publishing Co., 1902), XXIV, 431–434.

17. Philadelphia *Pennsylvania Journal*, October 3, 1765, cited in *ibid.*, pp. 631–639.

18. The drawing made in 1813 by the Baroness Hyde de Neuville portrays, not the ruins of the first sanctuary, but the beginnings of the second. For this drawing, see Wayne Andrews, "Patience Was Her Reward: the Records of the Baroness Hyde de Neuville," *Journal of the Archives of American Art*, IV (July 1964), 1.

to what is now Nassau Street. There were double rows of windows all around, and there were two main doors on the street side. Hageman described the interior as follows:

The pulpit was on the side of the audience room. There were 57 pews, 23 of them were squares around next to the wall. There were three aisles running in one direction and two in another. It was built of brick with galleries on three sides. In 1792 Dr. Witherspoon erected a large canopy over the pulpit, with ample drapery of dark colored stuff hanging about it in festoons, fastened by a large gilded, radiating star-shaped ornament.[19]

The floor plan reproduced by Hageman, made not long after the sanctuary was put into use and before the death of President Finley, shows that all fifty-seven pews were occupied by various families, except for part of one reserved for women. Schenck tells us that the leading members in 1766 were Richard Stockton, Ezekiel Forman, Dr. Timothy Wiggins, Jonathan Baldwin, Job Stockton, a Mr. Sergeant (probably Jonathan Dickinson Sergeant), Richard Paterson, Jacob Scudder, and Abraham Cruser. Members apparently paid pew rents in lieu of other contributions, these rents varying from three pounds to twenty-two pounds, ten shillings.

Regular divine services were held at least from 1766 onward, except for an interval during the Revolution, under the leadership of Dr. Finley until his death in July 1766; the Reverend William Tennent and the Reverend John Blair, from 1766 to 1768; and President Witherspoon from 1768 to 1793. Students at the college, attending the Sunday services in addition to the college's own services held in Nassau Hall, occupied most of the galleries, the remaining space there being open to visitors. The floor plan mentioned earlier makes it clear that there was no organ and no space for a choir. Congregational singing must have been limited, according to the prevailing Presbyterian practice of that day, to the singing of psalms.

The congregation was totally unorganized before 1786, there being no Session or Board of Trustees before this date, with the ordinary powers of the Session being vested in the Acting Pastor. It was a curious arrangement for a Presbyterian congregation, but

19. J. F. Hageman, *Princeton and Its Institutions*, II, 82.

the absence of any discussion of it by the New Brunswick Presbytery would seem to indicate a total lack of concern on the part of that judicatory. The congregation, at a meeting on January 5, 1786, resolved to end this ambiguous state of affairs.[20] At a meeting on February 21, 1786, it approved a draft of an act of incorporation prepared by a special committee appointed on January 5. It also elected a Session consisting of Richard Longstreet, James Hamilton, Thomas Blackwell, and John Johnstone,[21] and a Board of Trustees composed of Richard Longstreet, Robert Stockton, Enos Kelsey, James Moore, Isaac Anderson, and William Scudder.[22] The legislature of New Jersey, on March 16, 1786, adopted an act permitting religious societies to incorporate for the purposes of owning property and conducting financial affairs. The congregation thereupon, on May 25, 1786, re-elected its Board of Trustees in conformity with this law, adding John Little to the membership. The trustees then took out articles of incorporation and adopted a seal with a drawing of the sanctuary and the motto, "Speremus meliora [we hope for better things]." [23]

We have no membership or financial records of the congregation between about 1766 and 1792. But the contemporary records give the impression that the decade before the Revolution was a time of prosperity and substantial growth for the congregation as much as for the college. The main cause of this quickening and growth was the coming of John Witherspoon as president of the college and shepherd of the Princeton Presbyterian flock in August 1768.

Witherspoon, born near Edinburgh on February 5, 1724, was a distinguished leader of the orthodox party in the Scottish Church before coming to America. As president of the College of New Jersey from 1768 to 1794, he earned the reputation of "perhaps the greatest educator of the eighteenth century." [24] Even though

20. "Votes and Proceedings of the Congregation of Princeton, 1784", First Church Papers, Speer Library, pp. 7–8.
21. The Session appears to have functioned informally until 1792. At the instruction of the Presbytery of New Brunswick, it began to keep records of its meetings on March 17, 1792. Dr. Thomas Wiggins was the first Clerk. See "Church Book, 1792–1822," First Church Papers, Speer Library.
22. "Votes and Proceedings of the Congregation of Princeton, 1784," p. 14.
23. J. F. Hageman, *Princeton and Its Institutions,* II, 89–90.
24. T. J. Wertenbaker, *Princeton, 1746–1896,* p. 75.

he was a newcomer from Great Britain, he quickly espoused the American cause in the mounting Anglo-American dispute. Elected to the Continental Congress in 1776, he, along with Richard Stockton, another leader in the Princeton Presbyterian congregation, signed the Declaration of Independence. He served alongside Jefferson, Franklin, and others in the Congress from June 1776 until November 1782. He was later a member of the New Jersey legislature and of the state convention that ratified the United States Constitution in 1787. Witherspoon was also unquestionably the leading Presbyterian statesman in America in the eighteenth century, if not the outstanding ecclesiastical statesman in the entire country. He it was who, from 1787 to 1789, gave leadership to the movement for the organization of the national Presbyterian Church. He largely wrote the new denomination's first Form of Government,[25] and he preached the sermon opening the General Assembly at its first, organizational, meeting in Philadelphia in 1789.[26]

We remember Dr. Witherspoon on this occasion, not as a statesman, educator, and founder of the Presbyterian Church in the United States of America, but as the pastor of this congregation for a quarter of a century. The Reverend Ashbel Green, eighth president of the College of New Jersey, who knew Witherspoon well, described him as follows:

In stature, Dr. Witherspoon was of the middle size. He was fleshy with some tendency to corpulence. . . . Like many other clergymen in our country, he laid aside a full bottomed wig, at the commencement of our national independence. . . . His countenance united gravity with benignity, in its general expression. . . . In promiscuous company he had more of the quality called presence—a quality powerfully felt, but not to be described—than any other individual with whom the writer has ever had intercourse, Washington alone excepted. . . . In the pulpit,

25. Drafts in his own handwriting are preserved in the Papers of John Witherspoon, Library of Congress, Washington, D.C.

26. The only scholarly biography is Varnum Lansing Collins, *President Witherspoon, A Biography,* 2 vols. (Princeton, N.J.: Princeton University Press, 1925); but see the sketch by John E. Pomfret in *The Dictionary of American Biography,* 22 vols. (New York: Scribner, 1928–1958), XX, 435–438, and James H. Nichols, "John Witherspoon on Church and State," in George L. Hunt, editor, *Calvinism and the Political Order* (Philadelphia: Westminster Press, 1965), pp. 130–139.

he always wore a band, & when he preached at Princeton, a gown likewise.[27]

Witherspoon had the reputation of a man outwardly stern and inwardly very tender and compassionate. Hageman records that he was assiduous in his duties as pastor to his flock.[28] This may have been true during the early years of his ministry in Princeton. But he obviously had little time or energy for pastoral work after 1776, and one gets the clear impression that his relations with the congregation were neither warm nor intimate during the later years of his Princeton ministry.

Witherspoon preached to his congregation and students twice every Sunday when other duties did not require his presence elsewhere. His sermons, many of which are printed in his collected works and in pamphlet form,[29] were long, closely reasoned lectures embodying as much practical morality as exegesis of Scripture and the Westminster Confession of Faith. He wrote out all his sermons and memorized them for delivery. His public speaking, Green tells us, was somewhat deficient in oratory. "It certainly was not declaratory," Green continues,

nor uttered with a loud voice, nor accompanied with violent or bold gesticulations. His action in speaking never exceeded a graceful motion of his right hand, & the inclination of his body forward, when much in earnest. His greatest defect in public speaking was, the lowering of his voice when he began. . . . Yet take his pulpit addresses as a whole, there was in them, not only the recommendation of good sense & powerful reasoning, but a gracefulness, an earnestness, a warmth of affection, & solemnity of manner, especially toward & at their close, such as was calculated to produce the very best efforts of sacred oratory. Accordingly his popularity as a preacher was great. . . . His public prayers were admirable, plain in language, correct, methodical, abounding in a choice selection of scriptural phrases, & uttered with the appearance of deep devotional feeling. . . . His manner of introducing and administering the sacrament of the Lord's Supper, surpassed any other performance of that sacred service, which the writer has ever witnessed."[30]

27. Ashbel Green, "The Life of the Revd. John Witherspoon D.D. LL.D.," manuscript in the New Jersey Historical Society on microfilm in the Princeton University Library, Princeton, N.J.

28. J. F. Hageman, *Princeton and Its Institutions*, II, 86.

29. John Rodgers, editor, *The Works of the Rev. John Witherspoon*, 4 vols. (Philadelphia: Woodward, 1802); and *The Works of John Witherspoon, D.D.*, 9 vols. (Edinburgh: Ogle & Aikman, 1804–05).

30. Ashbel Green, "The Life of the Revd. John Witherspoon."

The Presbyterian Church of Princeton, because of its close association with the College of New Jersey, was, from the beginning of regular worship in the sanctuary, the temporary church home of an astounding array of future leaders in all walks of life, but particularly in the ministry, politics, and education. One might easily devote a full lecture to this subject, but it is appropriate upon this occasion to point out that the tradition of serving the nation and the world through service to Princeton students began almost from the moment that the sanctuary was first put into use.[31]

The high point of church life each year came with the commencement exercises held always in September during the first century of the college. All roads to Princeton were filled with stagecoaches and horsemen on the day before the exercises. The academic procession began in the morning at Nassau Hall at the words of the president, "Progredimini juvenes!" and wound its way to the church. After the opening prayer, Witherspoon would announce, "Doctors and gentlemen, these young men wish to greet you with an oration." Then followed Latin and English orations, musical performances, and debates, climaxed by the granting of degrees.[32] "Never was there such a commencement at Princeton before and most likely never will be again," wrote one Princeton student soon after the exercises in 1773. "The galeries were cracking every now and then all day—every mouse hole in the church was cram'd full—The stage covered with Gentlemen and ladies amongst whom was the Governor and his lady."[33]

There were other high moments of more purely religious excitement. Religious revivals swept over the college and town periodically in the late 1760s and early 1770s. One, for example, was set off by Whitefield, who preached to the students on Sunday, June 17, 1770, and to the congregation on the following morning.[34] The students invited the Reverend Jedidiah Chapman

31. See particularly T. J. Wertenbaker, *Princeton, 1746–1896*, pp. 111–117, and V. L. Collins, *President Witherspoon*, II, 220–230, for a discussion of Princeton's contribution to the nation's leadership during the last half of the eighteenth century.

32. T. J. Wertenbaker, *Princeton, 1746–1896*, pp. 110–111.

33. William R. Smith to P. V. Fithian, October 3, 1773, in Hunter D. Farish, editor, *Journal & Letters of Philip Vickers Fithian, 1773–1774* (Williamsburg, Va.: Colonial Williamsburg, Inc., 1943), pp. 17–18.

34. Philadelphia *Pennsylvania Journal*, June 21, 1770, in *Archives of the State of New Jersey, First Series* (Paterson, N.J.: The Press Printing and Publishing Co., 1905), XXVII, 182.

of Newark to the campus. He spent a week in Princeton, preaching three times and holding numerous prayer sessions.[35] There were also times of extraordinary effort at money-raising, as, for example, when the college and the Presbyterian congregations of Princeton and New Castle and Christiana, Delaware, co-operated in 1773 to hold a lottery in order to raise £5626 for their mutual benefit.[36] Unhappily, we do not know the outcome of this venture.

The greatest excitement of all, of course, ensued as controversy between the colonies and mother country grew to white heat in the early 1770s. New Jersey was the cockpit of the Revolution, and Princeton was the focal point of the Revolutionary movement in the province, particularly after Dr. Witherspoon openly joined the patriot ranks in 1774.

That Witherspoon had assumed leadership of the patriot cause by this date is vividly evidenced, among other things, by the testimony of John Adams. Adams, traveling from Boston to Philadelphia to attend the First Continental Congress, arrived at Princeton at noon on Saturday, August 24, 1774. He was taken to see Richard Stockton's home, "Morven," and Nassau Hall. "By this Time," his diary record continues,

the Bell rang for Prayers. We went into the Chappell, the President soon came in, and we attended. The Schollars sing as badly as the Presbyterians at New York. After Prayers the President attended Us to the Balcony of the Colledge, where We have a Prospect of an Horizon of about 80 miles Diameter. We went into the Presidents House, and drank a Glass of Wine. He is as high a Son of Liberty, as any Man in America. He says it is necessary that the Congress should raise Money and employ a Number of Writers in the Newspapers in England, to explain to the Public the American Plea, and remove the Prejudices of Britons. . . . The Dr. waited on us to our Lodgings and took a dish of Coffee. He is one of the Committee of Correspondence, and was upon the Provincial Congress for appointing Delegates from this Province to the general Congress. . . . The President says they [his students] are all Sons of Liberty.

Adams spent the following day, Sunday, in Princeton. His laconic remark—"Heard Dr. Witherspoon all Day. A clear, sensible,

35. V. L. Collins, *President Witherspoon*, I, 135.
36. See the notice printed in *Rivington's New-York Gazeteer*, May 13, 1773, *Archives of the State of New Jersey, First Series* (Paterson, N.J.: The Call Printing and Publishing Co., 1916), XXVIII, 505–507.

Preacher"—suggests that he spent most of his time at divine services in the Prayer Hall.[37]

Limitations of space prevent us from reviewing the exciting events leading to the American bid for independence.[38] One of them was the memorable sermon in the Princeton church preached by Dr. Witherspoon on May 17, 1776, the day set apart by the Continental Congress as a day of prayer and fasting. Entitled "The Dominion of Providence over the Passions of Men," it was a clear call for independence.

These events in the morning of our nationhood would soon bring dark days and unforeseen hardships to the little congregation at Princeton, as well as to the college. With Dr. Witherspoon in the nation's service in Philadelphia, there was no pastor in Princeton from 1776 to 1779. The Reverend Samuel Stanhope Smith, Witherspoon's son-in-law and successor as president of the college, returned to Princeton from Virginia, where he had just founded the Hampden-Sydney Academy, as Professor of Moral Philosophy in 1779. He seems to have served as minister to the congregation until Witherspoon returned to active duty in Princeton in 1782.

Meanwhile, the town, college, and church had been reeling under the rude shocks of war. When the college opened in September 1776, Howe was a mere fifty miles away, driving Washington's decimated army before him. Witherspoon adjourned the college on November 29. Washington passed through Princeton three days later, and Howe's forces under Lord Cornwallis arrived on December 7. Cornwallis' troops, largely Hessians, were quartered both in Nassau Hall and the church. The former, along with many local homes, was thoroughly plundered, while soldiers in the church stripped the pews and galleries for firewood which they burned in a makeshift fireplace constructed inside the sanctuary.[39] Washington drove the British forces from Princeton on January 3, 1777, but not before further damage was done by the fierce fighting. "Princeton," Benjamin Rush wrote a few days later, "is indeed a deserted village. You would think it had been deso-

37. Lyman H. Butterfield, editor, *The Adams Papers: Diary & Autobiography of John Adams,* 4 vols. (New York: Atheneum, paperback edition, 1964), II, 112–113.

38. Covered in detail by C. Leonard Lundin, *Cockpit of the Revolution, The War for Independence in New Jersey* (Princeton, N.J.: Princeton University Press, 1940).

39. W. E. Schenck, *The First Presbyterian Church,* p. 33.

lated with the plague and an earthquake. . . . The college and church are heaps of ruins, all the inhabitants have been plundered." [40]

The two buildings were used for various purposes by the American army from time to time from 1777 to 1781. But the American troops were, if anything, more destructive than the Hessians had been. A committee appointed by the congregation, consisting of John McComb, Thomas Stockton, and Enos Kelsey, estimated that the Continental troops did damage to the extent of £491 18s. 8d. between January 3, 1777, and November 30, 1781.[41] Whether any damages were ever recovered from the Confederation government is not known.

Contemporary records are utterly silent about the Princeton church and congregation during the last years of the Revolution. It seems likely that Samuel Stanhope Smith conducted divine services in Nassau Hall after his arrival in 1779. It also seems probably that Dr. Witherspoon resumed his ministry after his return in 1782. But the sanctuary itself was still a shambles, and it does not seem to have been fit for use as late as the summer of 1783, when Congress, fleeing from mutinous troops, settled in Princeton and used Nassau Hall for its sessions.

Dr. Witherspoon had the sanctuary cleaned up and temporary seats and a platform installed in time for one of the most memorable affairs ever held in the Princeton Presbyterian Church—the commencement exercises of the college on September 24, 1783. It brought together one of the most notable gatherings in American history. Dr. Witherspoon presided, and among the guests were Washington, Elias Boudinot, president of the Congress, and the young James Madison. A future president of the college, Ashbel Green, delivered the valedictory address.[42]

This event, in addition to the return of peace, must have strengthened the determination of Princeton Presbyterians to rebuild. A congregational meeting held on March 8, 1784, resolved to open a subscription for repair of the sanctuary and payment of the old debt of £700 to the college. The meeting further

40. Quoted in T. J. Wertenbaker, *Princeton, 1746–1896*, pp. 60–61.
41. "Inventory of Damages done to the Meeting House in Princeton," First Church Papers, Speer Library.
42. Varnum Lansing Collins, *The Continental Congress at Princeton* (Princeton, N.J.: The University Library, 1908), pp. 155–166.

appointed Robert Stockton, James Hamilton, and John Little a committee to put the sanctuary in decent repair—as the minutes of the meeting put it,

the lower part pewed in the same manner as it was before the War. The breastwork of the gallery decently finished. The front of the gallery pewed, as formerly, for the use of the College. The pews shall be rented at the discretion of the above mentioned Committee, in such manner as to discharge the annual interest due to the Trustees, with a surplus, if possible, to go [to] the discharging [of] the principal debt. The highest subscribers to have the first election in the pews, and so in succession according to the several subscriptions.[43]

It was quickly done. A subscription paper, dated March 11, 1784, was circulated, and fifty-two heads of families pledged £375 5s.[44] The work of restoration, undertaken at once, was completed within the year, as Hageman puts it, and regular divine services under Witherspoon's ministry were resumed in 1784.[45]

The following decade was a time of painfully slow rebuilding of the college. Not until 1791 were repairs to Nassau Hall completed, and even then, as Princeton's historian has put it, "an air of poverty hung over the place."[46] The Presbyterian congregation does not seem to have held its own during these years of adversity. Among the earliest Session minutes, there is a record of the communicant members as of November 5, 1792. It listed fifty-three communing members, including five blacks, as they were called.[47] It will be recalled that the first pew list, made probably in 1766, revealed a membership of at least fifty-seven families, not individuals, and that fifty-two individuals, most of them heads of families and presumably also members, subscribed to the reconstruction fund in 1784. Probably not all pewholders in 1766 and contributors to the reconstruction fund and their families were communing members. But after allowing for this fact, it is evident that the congregation suffered a serious decline in membership between 1784 and 1792.

43. "Votes and Proceedings of the Congregation of Princeton, 1784," p. 3.
44. J. F. Hageman, *Princeton and Its Institutions*, II, 88, reproduces the subscription list.
45. For a plan of the ground floor, showing location of pews, see "Votes and Proceedings of the Congregation of Princeton, 1784," p. 23.
46. T. J. Wertenbaker, *Princeton, 1746–1896*, p. 69.
47. "Church Book, 1792–1822," entry of November 5, 1792.

If this conclusion is correct, then the experience of the Princeton congregation was in part a reflection of a malaise and decline that was affecting churches throughout the United States at this time. The Church was in retreat everywhere before Deism and Rationalism and more or less paralyzed by formalism and lack of evangelical zeal. There would be a Second Great Awakening, beginning in 1798, but it lies beyond our period.

There was, moreover, a particular local reason for declining fortunes. Dr. Witherspoon's health began seriously to fail in the late 1780s, and there are numerous intimations in the contemporary records that poor health prevented him from exercising an active ministry. His consequent neglect of the congregation must have been a major reason for its decline.

We also find intimations of a growing desire among the members for a full-time pastor and congregational life separate from that of the college. The Princeton and Kingston Presbyterian churches discussed a plan of union about 1784. It was never consummated, but its execution would have meant the calling of a regular pastor. As we have seen, the congregation elected a Session and Board of Trustees and became formally incorporated in 1786. At the same time, the congregation, after thanking Witherspoon for his past services, requested him to render them pastoral care and promised to pay him some salary.[48] That relations between the acting pastor and the congregation did not improve is evidenced by an interchange that occurred in 1792. Dr. Witherspoon, informing the congregation that he had erected a pulpit in 1783 and a canopy over the pulpit in 1792 entirely at his own expense, requested reimbursement. The congregation replied, somewhat abruptly, on July 2, 1792, that they could assume no responsibility for the pulpit. Somewhat grudgingly, they agreed to pay for the canopy.[49]

Witherspoon went totally blind in 1792. Once during this time he had a seizure in the pulpit and fell prone on the floor after leaving the pulpit enclosure. But the old Doctor hung on tenaciously even while relying more and more upon his son-in-law, Samuel Stanhope Smith, for sermons.

This situation perhaps explains what seems to have been a very great increase at this time in the Session's pastoral and

48. "Votes and Proceedings of the Congregation of Princeton, 1784," p. 14.
49. *Ibid.*, p. 21.

disciplinary activities. On October 11, 1792, it suspended Michael Waddel from communion for fraudulent practices and severely reprimanded John Stockton, a mason, for cruel treatment of his slave. It excommunicated Rachel Waddel, wife of Michael, on November 12, 1792. On April 11, 1794, it considered charges of abusive language made against Aaron Matteson and Captain James Moore. "To which charge," the Session Minutes record, "they both acknowledged they were guilty, and frankly professed that they were sensible of their error, and were sorry for what had happened: upon which a full settlement of their dispute took place, and a friendly reconciliation followed." A more serious case came before the Session on November 9, 1795. As the Session Minutes record it:

A charge was exhibited against John McGregor as having had criminal conversation with a black woman; the black woman, having borne a mollatto child, laid it to him as the father, and public fame charged him strongly with the fact. John McGregor appearing before the Session, denied the charge. The woman appeared not to be a proper person to whom to administer an oath. The Session taking into view all the concurring circumstances, came to the following resolution: That they had not as a church Court sufficient ground to proceed to absolute condemnation: but considering the state of the publick mind upon the subject, and all the appearances on which that sentiment seemed to be formed, they recommended it to him in christian charity to abstain from the healing ordinances of the Church until God in his Providence, should be pleased to cast new light on the subject; and an advice and admonition suitable to the occasion was given him by the Moderator of the Session.

Session's discipline, however, was no substitute for regular pastoral care. How much the congregation suffered from lack of it is evidenced in the Session Minutes for December 1, 1795. The recently installed pastor asked the Session whether it would be wise to commence the visitation of families in order to determine the state of religion among them. "The Session gave it as their unanimous opinion," the Minutes tell us,

that as the Congregation had never been formed to the habits of an organized Church, and were not yet ripe for receiving them in their full strictness, it would be better to introduce a system of private instruction and visitation in families, with catechising in private houses, in the different quarters of the Congregation, and accompanying it with a lecture in each place suitable to the occasion.

The congregation, finally taking matters into its own hands, appealed to the Presbytery of New Brunswick when it met at Oxford on April 23, 1793, to declare the Princeton pulpit vacant. The minutes of the Presbytery embodying the appeal reveal the extent of the estrangement between Witherspoon and his flock:

A petition from the congregation of Princeton was presented & read in which it was stated—That for a long time past they had the Gospel preached, & the Sacraments administered to them constantly by the President of the College, altho not connected with him in a pastoral relation; that the President has now declined performing these ministerial duties to them on account of his advanc'd age & bodily infirmities, & that seeing that they were destitute of the stated means of Grace, they expected the supplies usually given to vacant churches.

Presbytery, undoubtedly out of regard for the feelings of the great Witherspoon, voted to postpone action until it had communicated with him.[50] But it did rule at its next meeting, in Princeton on September 18, 1793, that Dr. Witherspoon had never been the regular pastor of the Princeton church, and it declared the church vacant.[51]

Dr. Witherspoon died at his country home, "Tusculum," on November 15, 1794. Meanwhile, the congregation had been searching for a pastor. It called John Abeel, a young Dutch Reformed minister, in 1793, but he declined.[52] During the next two years, the pulpit was filled by various supplies sent by Presbytery and by Samuel Stanhope Smith. Finally, the congregation voted in September 1795 to call the young Samuel Finley Snowden of the Class of 1786 of the College of New Jersey, who had been licensed by the Presbytery of New Brunswick only the year before.[53] Snowden accepted and was ordained and installed on November 25, 1795.

The beginning of Snowden's ministry marked the end of one

50. "The New-Brunswick Presbytery Book," 1782–98, minutes for April 23, 1793.
51. *Ibid.*, minutes for September 18, 1793.
52. "Church Book, 1792–1822," entry for September 2, 1793.
53. *Ibid.*, entry for September 14, 1795.

era and the beginning of a new one in the history of the Presbyterian Church of Princeton. The first era, from about 1751 to 1793, saw the foundations of congregational life securely laid. An inchoate congregation had taken form, constructed a sanctuary, survived the vicissitudes of war, and courageously struggled to repair the damages of war. But it is also clear that the congregation during this long period was an appendage of the college, that it suffered because it did not have a full-time pastor, and that the members not only realized their need but were also determined to have their own pastor and govern their own affairs in their own way, independent of the college. The calling of Snowden marked the realization of this understandable desire and an entirely new beginning of regular, well-ordered congregational life.

24

Samuel Taylor Coleridge and the Economic and Political Crisis in Great Britain, 1816–1820

IN 1815, Great Britain emerged from the Napoleonic Wars the victor in what had been nearly a quarter of a century of uninterrupted warfare with France. Carthage, as Halévy puts it, had vanquished Rome. The question of British supremacy of the seas had been decided at Trafalgar a decade before; British armies, in conjunction with their allies, had crushed the armies of Imperial France and had frustrated Napoleon's ambitions of dominating the continent. British prestige abroad had never been so great. Triumphant in Europe, the British people nonetheless might have looked upon the domestic scene with dread and foreboding in 1815, for at home a social and economic revolution of unpredictable proportions was in the making. The five years after the Congress of Vienna were to witness the testing of the British economic and social structure.

Great Britain, during the wars with France from 1793 to 1815, had experienced great agricultural and industrial expansion. Since the middle of the eighteenth century the country had imported bread grains from abroad; but the three world wars during the subsequent sixty-five years had stimulated artifically the production of grain in England. The farmers, encouraged by high prices

Reprinted from *Journal of the History of Ideas,* IX (June 1948), 323–338, by permission of the Editor.

and the hope of easy profits, had increased their production and overexpanded their land holdings. Spurred on by an optimism that seems unfailingly characteristic of them, landowners had since 1793 invested heavily, and at a time when prices were highly inflated, in more land and new machinery. The local banks had in large measure financed this expansion by extending credit beyond the bounds of safety.

The storm broke in England in 1815, first upon the farmers and landlords, and next upon businessmen and industrialists. The price of wheat declined from seventy-one shillings, nine pence a quarter in March to fifty-five shillings, nine pence in December, 1815;[1] for the first time since 1750, European grain prices were substantially lower than British prices. Consequently, the entire price structure, upon the maintenance of which depended agricultural income in general, rent payments, and the ability of the landlords to pay their debts, was dangerously threatened. The answer of the landlords who controlled the unreformed Parliament was the enactment of the Corn Laws in 1815, which prohibited the import of wheat at a price below eighty shillings a quarter.

After the usual short postwar commercial boom, there also occurred a collapse in industrial and business activity in 1816; and there followed an economic depression "of unprecedented range, intensity, and duration"[2] which lasted well into 1821. British industrial potential had increased greatly during the last quarter century and so rapid had been the advances in the industrial field that serious technological unemployment had resulted. For a number of reasons, the volume of British industrial production declined below the war-time level; factories were shut down and thousands of men were unemployed.[3] Unrest and agitation swept over the island; and to make bad matters worse, a short crop sent grain prices soaring again in 1816 and 1817. So violent were the outbreaks of the workers and agricultural laborers that the upper classes feared and actually expected a social revolution.

Samuel Taylor Coleridge, poet, philosopher, and former Jaco-

1. Elie Halévy, *A History of the English People, 1815–1830* (New York: Harcourt, Brace & Co., 1924), p. 5.
2. Robert L. Schuyler, *The Fall of the Old Colonial System, a Study in British Free Trade, 1770–1870* (New York: Oxford University Press, 1945), p. 97.
3. Frederick C. Dietz, *A Political and Social History of England* (New York: Macmillan, 1937), pp. 500–501.

bin, was, during this period, in what might be described as a state of conservative relapse. A friend of Wordsworth and Southey, he had shared with them great enthusiasm for the French Revolution and the libertarian ideals it seemed to represent. Reared in the Established Church, son of an Anglican clergyman, he had defied conventional mores by becoming a minister in the Unitarian church and had distinguished himself by refusing to administer the church's sacraments.[4] Coleridge's literary career and achievements, his philosophy of idealism, his travels and studies in Germany and the influence of Kant upon his thought, his personal and family life, his relations with Wordsworth, Southey, and the other major writers of his time—these subjects have been so thoroughly explored and developed by Coleridge scholars that any discussion of them in this article would be superfluous. Needless to say, Coleridge had by 1815 long since abandoned the revolutionary ardor and Unitarianism of his youth and was now a staunch defender of the Established Church and the Constitution. During the period from 1816 through 1823, he was living in Highgate at the home of Dr. James Gillman. Chronic rheumatism had plagued Coleridge since his youth; prolonged suffering had caused him to begin taking opium; and by 1801, the drug had an incurable hold on him. He had come to Highgate to place himself under Dr. Gillman's care. His income from lecturing and from the publication of his numerous poetical and literary works was chronically insufficient to support himself, his wife (from whom he had separated), and his children. On rare occasions, he was financially solvent; but for the most part, he lived on the bounty of his friends.

Coleridge looked upon the contemporary scene in Great Britain from 1816 to 1820 through the eyes of a comparatively detached and impartial, if somewhat conservative, observer. In many respects he was a unique individual who defies classification. He certainly possessed none of the worldly goods, the ownership of which often makes men reactionary on economic and political issues; yet he labored desperately to stem the rising tide of social unrest among the lower classes and to prevent any violent social eruption. On the other hand, he did not identify himself with the rising industrial and commercial classes; in fact, he lashed out time and again at the laissez-faire political economists who

---

4. E. K. Chambers, *Samuel Taylor Coleridge* (Oxford: The Clarendon Press, 1938), p. 89.

were deftly rationalizing exploitation and greed and oppression of the working people in terms of economic laws. He thought of himself as a metaphysician and philosopher.

What Coleridge had to say about the economic and social questions confronting Great Britain during this period, however, was generally representative of the Tory humanitarian school of thought, which had exerted a varying degree of influence in British affairs since the end of the American Revolution and which, during the period under consideration, had an amazing number and variety of exponents in England. Tory humanitarianism was primarily a composite of emotional reactions and deep-rooted beliefs—a strong evangelical religious impulse, which motivated such antislavery reformers as William Wilberforce; a love of the land, a habit of thought originating in the daily life and work of the country people, so characteristic of William Cobbett; a feeling of revulsion against the unfortunate social concomitants of the industrial revolution and an intense sympathy for the working classes, embodied in Tory labor reformers like the elder Robert Peel, Richard Oastler, or Michael Thomas Sadler. Tory humanitarianism, in short, remained to the end the attitude of rural Englishmen who refused to acquiesce in all the social and economic consequences of the revolution that had transformed England from an agricultural into an industrial nation, dominated by a commercial, materialistic philosophy. Lest it be thought that Coleridge was more of a pioneer than he actually was, it should be borne in mind that many of the things he was saying during the period were also being said, although by persons he often condemned, by other Tory humanitarians. The elder Peel, for example, had been championing the cause of child labor reform since 1800; Thomas Attwood, a Tory banker of Birmingham, expounded the same inflationary credit ideas that Coleridge set forth in 1817; William Cobbett defended the cause of the agricultural laborer as against the landlord; Sir Samuel Romilly and Sir James Mcintosh had already got under way a movement for penal and capital punishment reform. Few periods in British history have been so fertile in social ideas. It is not necessary to labor the point that there was, during this period, a diverse multitude of social and political reformers, most of whom we generally group together and call Tory humanitarians, and that Coleridge was simply one representative of this group.

Coleridge's writings during the period under consideration reveal a penetrating insight into Britain's social and economic problems. Stripped of their philosophical and moralistic trappings, they appear singularly modern in the best liberal economic and sociological tradition of the twentieth century. Coleridge did some serious thinking about the causes of the contemporary economic and social distress of his country. Soon after the conclusion of peace at the Congress of Vienna, he wrote his first "lay sermon" and addressed it to the "higher classes of society." But this first admonition was written before the discontent had become acute, and it was a gentle philosophical discourse which endeavored to prove that the Bible was the statesman's best guide to political action.[5]

In the following year, 1816, however, there occurred an alarming series of riots and campaigns throughout England to destroy property. The agricultural laborers in the eastern counties armed themselves with pitchforks and torches and the uprising was suppressed only by the use of the regular troops. "Then the agitation spread to the manufacturing districts of the north and centre—to the weavers, hosiers, and colliers. . . . Strikes accompanied by violence broke out in two regions widely apart—in the collieries and iron foundries of South Wales and in the district around Glasgow."[6] This widespread social unrest evoked the writing of Coleridge's second "lay sermon" in 1817; it was a hard-hitting analytical inquiry into the causes of the present discontent.[7] It is evident that Coleridge feared the possibility of a violent social revolution during the postwar period. "Well then may we pray, *Give us peace in our time, O Lord!*" he wrote at a time when the depression and social agitation were at their height. "Well for us if no revolution, or other general visitation, betray the true state of our national morality!"[8]

Coleridge began his second "lay sermon" by differentiating carefully between the immediate and the deep-rooted causes of

5. *The Statesman's Manual; or, the Bible the Best Guide to Political Skill and Foresight: A Lay Sermon, Addressed to the Higher Classes of Society* (hereinafter cited as *The Statesman's Manual*), in W. G. T. Shedd, *The Complete Works of Samuel Taylor Coleridge*, 7 vols. (New York: Harper & Brothers, 1853), I, 421–484 (hereinafter cited as *Works*).

6. E. Halévy, *op. cit.*, pp. 9–10.

7. *A Lay Sermon Addressed to the Higher and Middle Classes on the Existing Distresses and Discontents* (hereinafter cited as *A Lay Sermon*), *Works*, VI.

8. *A Lay Sermon*, *Works*, VI, 150.

the social distress and economic stagnation. The immediate causes were, he thought, "too obvious to be overlooked but by eyes at once red and dim through the intoxication of factious prejudice."[9] The present depression had begun with the ending of the war, and that fact was of itself a sufficient proof to him that it was a consequence of the economic dislocations attendant upon the cessation of hostilities.[10] Coleridge thought that one of the important immediate causes of the depression was the bungling financial policy of the government; the government, he declared, had manipulated the taxation structure so as to contribute to the economic maladjustment of the time. Taxation, he wrote, was a part of commerce; the government might in a sense be considered a great manufacturing house. As long as there was a balance between income and the expenditures of the government in amount and degree of dispersion; as long as a due proportion existed between the sums levied and the mass of money in productive circulation, so long also did the wealth and circumstantial prosperity of the nation remain unaffected. Taxes ought to be calculated comparatively, he believed, on the basis, not of how much was taken from the individual, but of how much was left in his possession.[11] This, needless to say, is the theory which underlies any system of progressively graduated taxation.

With this by way of introduction, Coleridge proceeded to locate the root of the contemporary economic distress. In a "direct *ratio*," he thought, to the increase of national wealth caused by the balance between taxation on the one hand and governmental expenditures on the other, would be the economic distress caused by the disturbance of this balance, by the loss, in short, of this perfect proportion. And, he concluded,

the operation of the distress will be at least equal to the total amount of the difference between the taxes still levied, and the *quantum* of aid withdrawn from individuals by the abandonment of others, and of that which the taxes, that still remain, have ceased to give by the altered mode of their re-dispersion.[12]

9. *Ibid.*, p. 172.
10. *Ibid.*, p. 176.
11. Under this system, he continued, the settlement of the national account would be in favor of the natural wealth to the amount of all the additional productive labor sustained or caused by the taxes during the intervals between their "efflux" and their re-absorption into general circulation. (*Ibid.*, p. 173.)
12. *Ibid.*, pp. 173–174.

What was the most important immediate factor in causing the existing economic dislocation? It was, Coleridge asserted, the sudden diminishing of the governmental revenues by the repeal of the war taxes.[13] This act of prejudice and ignorant selfishness on the part of the upper classes had been alone sufficient to disturb the economic balance. And this misfortune was heightened by the rapid demobilization of the army which swelled the ranks of the unemployed at a time when governmental revenues were greatly diminished. And to cap the climax, he added, the economic unbalance had been made even greater by the return to "cash payments" without any change in the value of the coin.[14] The result of this deflation, he thought, was in effect to reimpose the heavy burden of taxes upon the people.[15] It is interesting that, as early as 1817, Coleridge set forth the comparatively modern theory that one result of postwar deflation is to cause the shifting of the burden of war taxes almost wholly to the debtor classes who had borrowed during a period of inflated prices, with the result that a small creditor class is benefited.

All of these immediate causes of depression had conspired to an extraordinary degree, Coleridge wrote, and had worked with united strength to create economic maladjustment, agricultural, commercial, and industrial stagnation, and mass unemployment during the period of transition from war to peace. These were, he thought, the obvious and immediate causes of the existing discontent and the diatribic fulminations of all the demagogues in Britain could not alter the facts.

Coleridge, however, carefully pointed out several factors that he thought were not contributary to the contemporary economic distress. We see, he wrote, in every promiscuous public meeting the effect produced by the bold assertion that the present hardships are due to the number of pensions and sinecures given by the government. Coleridge thought the national income and prosperity

13. The Liverpool government had in 1816 repealed the income tax, which brought the government some £ 15,000,000 revenue annually, because of the power that organized middle-class pressure groups were able to exert on the House of Commons. The tax on malt was also repealed, and this reduced the government's income by an additional £ 10,000,000.

14. In 1817, the Bank of England returned to the practice of making and insisting upon specie payments; and the following year, specie payments throughout England were required by Peel's bill which was adopted by Parliament.

15. *A Lay Sermon, Works*, VI, 175–176.

were entirely unaffected by the giving of pensions and sinecures. Capitalists and merchants likewise had received a great amount of criticism from the "wretched demagogues," he wrote, who would destroy the public credit, which was the vital air of national industry and welfare, if they might goad ignorance into riot and fanaticism into rebellion.[16]

The philosopher at Highgate thought that the chief immediate danger lay in the fact that a multitude of demagogues was stirring the people to revolt. Agitators and demagogues there were, in large numbers, to be sure, like William Cobbett, who reduced the price of his *Weekly Political Register* to twopence a copy in the fall of 1816 and began a campaign for democratic parliamentary reform. "Whether in spoken or in printed addresses, whether in periodical journals or in yet cheaper implements of irritation, the ends are the same, the process is the same, and the same is their general line of conduct," Coleridge wrote indignantly:

On all occasions,—but most of all and with a more bustling malignity whenever any public distress inclines the lower classes to turbulence, and renders them most apt to be alienated from the government of their country;—in all places and at every opportunity pleading to the poor and ignorant.[17]

Coleridge denounced the demagogues for what he charged were their unscrupulous methods and dishonest arguments and because they were unwilling to accept half-loaf reforms and sought "an enlargement of the rights and liberties of the people by inflaming the populace to acts of madness that necessitate fetters." [18] For that reason, he declared, demagogues were nothing less than enemies of liberty of the press, inasmuch as they made that liberty

---

16. *Ibid.*, pp. 179–181.
17. *Ibid.*, p. 166.
18. Coleridge described the methods of demagogues in the following manner: (1) Bold, warm, and earnest assertions, oftentimes unsupported by facts; (2) arguments founded upon passing events, deriving undue importance from the passions of the moment; (3) startling particular facts, dissevered from their context; (4) a display of the defects, without also revealing the advantages, of particular measures; (5) concealment of the ultimate results of policies behind the scenery of local events; (6) statement of things true only under particular conditions; (7) statement of chains of rhetorical questions; (8) vague and commonplace satire; (9) transitions from the audacious charge to the pregnant and interpretative lie; (10) jerks of style, buffoonery, and flowery phrases; (11) the stating of mysterious phrases accompanied by striking stances and modulations of voice. (*A Lay Sermon, Works,* VI, 170–171.)

appear incompatible with public safety; and, by the same token, they were enemies of all liberty.[19]

But Coleridge, be it noted, was not disposed to write off the agitation which he severely condemned as the result of the fulminations of demagogues only. He hated and detested Jacobinism, it is true; he was forced to admit a woeful deterioration of the lower classes, "spite of Bible Societies, and spite of our spinning jennies for the cheap and speedy manufacture of reading and writing."[20] Yet the chief blame for the trouble did not lie with the lower classes, he thought; it lay with the gentry. "I see an unmanly spirit of alarm, and of self-convenience," he wrote, "under many a soft title, domestic comfort, etc., etc. in our gentry."[21]

Coleridge, however, was too much a philosopher not to realize that the immediate causes of any difficulty were ephemeral and would change with varying circumstances. He was, first of all, apparently troubled by the implications of the Industrial Revolution; and although he professed to be a friend of commerce and industry, he saw many of the system's inherent defects. One of the things that alarmed him was the fact, as he saw it, that business and the acquisition of wealth had displaced philosophy as the pastime of the upper-class man. He believed that "all the epoch-forming revolutions of the Christian world" had "coincided with the rise and fall of metaphysical systems"; and yet it was plain that speculative philosophy was becoming, as he wrote, *"terra incognita"* to the average intellectual.[22] In July 1817, he expressed emphatically this opinion in an abstruse letter to Lord Liverpool on the causes of the economic distress; the letter, in fact, was so metaphysical that the Prime Minister hardly understood it.[23]

19. *Ibid.*, p. 168.

20. A reference to the monitorial type of education given students in the schools conducted by the British and Foreign School Society, controlled by the dissenting groups, and the Anglican National Society for the Education of the Poor. Under the system, advanced pupils taught pupils in the lower grades.

21. Coleridge to the editor of the *Morning Chronicle*, January 25, 1818, published in Earl Leslie Griggs, editor, *Unpublished Letters of Samuel Taylor Coleridge*, 2 vols. (London: Constable, 1932), II, 224; hereinafter cited as *Unpublished Letters*.

22. *The Statesman's Manual, Works*, I, 428.

23. Coleridge wrote that "As long as the principles of our gentry and clergy are grounded in a false philosophy, which retains but the name of logic and has succeeded in rendering metaphysics a term of opprobrium, all the Sunday and national schools in the world will not preclude schism and Jacobinism in the middle and lower classes." (Coleridge to Liverpool, July 28, 1817, published in Charles Duke Yonge, *The Life and Administration of Robert Banks, Second Earl of Liverpool*, 3 vols. [London: Macmillan and Co., 1868], II, 300–306.)

After defining the importance of speculative philosophy in a civilized society, Coleridge proceeded to probe into what he called the deep-rooted causes of the depression. He summarized them in the following sentence:

They appear to me . . . resolvable into the *overbalance of the commercial spirit in consequence of the absence or weakness of the counter-weights;* this over-balance considered as displaying itself, 1, in the commercial world itself: 2, in the agricultural: 3, in the Government: and, 4, in the combined influence of all three on the more numerous and laboring classes.[24]

The checks to the overvaluing of wealth, he continued, such as the ancient feeling of rank and ancestry (*noblesse oblige*), a genuine intellectual philosophy, and widespread religious feeling were to varying degrees ineffective in stemming the tide of acquisitive impulses. Prejudices against the acquisition of vast wealth had been overcome; philosophy and theology were no longer existent;[25] and religion, the most effective deterrent to the acquisitive spirit, was rapidly being undermined by the Unitarians and Quakers.[26]

Coleridge's criticism of industry and commerce went much deeper than this, however. Brought face to face with the realities of the industrial system, he refused to accept it as a thing of beneficence and progress. He reveals in his writings a haunting desire to return to the "good old days," to escape from the crass materialism of a commercial age, to return to the mythical time when every man was his own master and no man oppressed his fellows. Here of course is evident the philosophy and predilections of Tory conservatism.

Coleridge had only contempt for the political economists, Mill, Ricardo, Malthus, and the like, who declared that unemployment, starvation, poverty, and suffering for the working classes were inevitable; who wrote that economic depressions were to be regarded as so much superfluous steam ejected by the escape

24. *A Lay Sermon, Works,* VI, 182.
25. And, he added, this was all the more important when it was remembered that "an excess in our attachment to temporal and personal objects can be counteracted only by a pre-occupation of the intellect and the affections with permanent, universal, and eternal truths." (*Ibid.,* p. 184.)
26. Coleridge had little use for the Unitarians, many of whom were Jacobins and had formed Coleridge's early audiences. He did, however, profess to admire the Quakers, but concluded by holding them up as conspicuous examples of people supposedly religious yet prosperous and cunning businessmen. (*Ibid.,* pp. 186–198.)

pipes and safety valves of a self-regulating machine, and that in a free country all things would find their level. Persons were not things and should not be regarded as cogs in an inexorable machine, Coleridge retorted. What good could come of a system, he asked, in which friends betrayed friends for the sake of profit, in which thousands of children were ruthlessly exploited by industrial masters? The commercial spirit had even taken hold of the agriculturalists, he added; and he lamented the extension of the enclosure movement because he thought it resulted in the degradation of independent farmers. The dreadful poor rate system, moreover, was a natural result of the commercial spirit.

Thus, faced with the dilemma of whether the blessings of the new dispensation outweighed the evils thereof, he was forced to conclude that the evils of the system far overbalanced the advantages,[27] and that the

extension of the commercial spirit into our agricultural system, added to the overbalance of the same spirit, even within its own sphere; aggravated by the operation of our revenue laws; and finally reflected in the habits, and tendencies of the laboring classes; is the groundwork of our calamity, and the main predisposing cause, without which the late occasions would some of them not have existed, and the remainder not have produced the present distresses.[28]

It was a discouraged philosopher who pondered the causes of the discontent in Great Britain in 1817. He could relate with passion the roots of the trouble, but the test of providing a remedy was too much for him. Thomas Spence had a solution, though it was perhaps impractical for the age, but Coleridge rejected Spencian land communism with vigor. His own proposals, however, were singularly weak. He wrote, for example, that more good would be done by the abolition of the national lotteries than by economies tenfold greater effected by the government.[29] Manufacturers must consent to regulations, he insisted; the gentry must concern themselves with the education of their clients and must regard their estates as offices of trust in the sight of God and country. In short, he concluded, "Let us become a better

27. *Ibid.*, pp. 207–212; 218–222.
28. *Ibid.*, p. 215.
29. *Ibid.*, pp. 224–225.

people, and the reform of all the public (real or supposed) grievances, which we use as pegs whereon to hang our own errors
and defects, will follow of itself." [30]

Coleridge was not, however, so disheartened by the contemporary scene that he refused to labor for reform. Perhaps he
accepted a kind of inevitability, or believed that the problems
he discussed might never be solved. He expressed this idea when
he wrote, "Let us palliate where we can not cure, comfort where
we cannot relieve." [31] But when Sir Robert Peel in 1818 introduced
into the House of Commons a bill for the regulation of child
labor in the textile factories, Coleridge immediately threw himself
into the fight for reform. Here was at least an opportunity for
palliation, he thought. At first, he feared that Peel had brought
forward his bill unwisely, without due preparation of the public
mind, and he even seemed to suspect that Peel was insincere
in his efforts for child labor reform.[32] Nonetheless, Coleridge
industriously set himself to the task of converting public opinion
to the idea of factory legislation. He would try, he wrote to a
friend, to get several articles published in the *New Times* or the
Courier; and he would even attempt to convert the owners of the
Courier to the idea of reform, for (he wrote) the new editor of
the newspaper was a timid fellow and would not dare take part
in the discussion without their consent.[33]

Coleridge's contempt for the political economists increased
when they opposed Peel's bill. "I dare affirm," he wrote, "that
few superstitions in religion have been so extensively pernicious
to the intellectual and moral sanity of this country and France,
as those of (so-called) Political Economy." When it suited the
interests of the rich, he continued, they easily discovered that
political economy was an abstract science which could be violated
with impunity. But when "morals, health, humanity, plead—O!
they are then inviolable truths. Free labor must not be interfered
with, etc." [34]

30. *Ibid.,* p. 225.

31. *Ibid.*

32. Coleridge to Charles Augustus Tulk, February 21, 1818, *Unpublished Letters,* II,
233–234.

33. *Ibid.*

34. Coleridge to William Mudford, April --, 1818, published in W. F. Prideaux, editor,
Letters Hitherto Uncollected by Samuel Taylor Coleridge (London: Printed for Private Circulation,
1913), p. 18.

It was typical of Coleridge that he did not realize what a useless act Peel's bill actually was, since it made no provision for periodic inspection of the factories. He was not interested in details of legislation, however; he was motivated largely by a religious and Tory humanitarian impulse in his fight for factory reform. He often wrote of his sympathy for the "poor cotton factory children," and on one occasion confessed that their sufferings had weighed upon his mind since early manhood.[35] But his detestation of the political economists was nothing as compared to his fury against the factory owners who were trying to defeat the bill. It was a question, he wrote, "Whether some half-score of rich capitalists are to be prevented from suborning suicide and perpetuating infanticide and soul-murder."[36] The thought of children working fourteen or fifteen hours a day "on their legs, in a foul and heated atmosphere," outraged his humanitarian ideals.[37]

In April 1818, Coleridge entered the fight in earnest and published two hard-hitting pamphlets in favor of factory regulation. It is true that his public declarations were considerably milder than his private correspondence, but they were nonetheless effective. The first pamphlet, far the most important, endeavored to answer the arguments of the laissez-faire anti-reformers. Coleridge began by remarking that he would not bother to answer the arguments of the opponents of the bill to the effect that children from six to sixteen years of age who worked from thirteen to fifteen hours a day were healthier physically and morally than children who did not work at all. If that were true, he said, either all the known laws of biology were false, or else God in some miraculous fashion had extended his special protection to the factory children. If replies to this argument were needed, he added, the testimonies already given by doctors and clergymen would be sufficient.

Coleridge next proceeded to deal with what he considered more formidable arguments, viz., that it was improper for the legislature to interfere with free labor; that such measures as the proposed bill would lead to innovations that would be hard to

35. *Ibid.*

36. Coleridge to J. H. Green, May 2, 1818, published in Ernest Hartley Coleridge, editor, *Letters of Samuel Taylor Coleridge,* 2 vols. (Boston and New York: Houghton Mifflin and Co., 1895), II, 689.

37. Coleridge to C. A. Tulk, February 21, 1818, *Unpublished Letters,* II, 235.

stop; that such reforms were calculated to increase discontent to a greater degree than they would be expected to palliate the grievances; and that the masters would voluntarily and gradually introduce reforms in the factory system.

As for the objection that it was improper to interfere with free labor, Coleridge replied that the argument was unhistorical because there had been numerous instances of such legislative interference under the British Constitution. Besides, he asked, how could the labor of children of impoverished parents be called free labor? It had been admitted that one result of child labor was disease and premature death for the children involved; if this, therefore, were free labor, "the employer would purchase, and the labourer sell, what the former had no right to buy, and the latter no right to dispose of: namely, the labourer's healthy life, and well-being."

As for the second objection, that the passage of Peel's bill would give rise to numerous other claims of a like nature, Coleridge replied (in the words of Peel himself) that if the alleged claims were as valid as the claims of the factory children, then "in God's name let them be conceded!" Some opponents of the bill had argued that it was a mere palliative, better calculated to excite discontent than to effect any considerable diminution of the evil. Coleridge gave short shrift to this objection, which he declared was "one of the approved means of reconciling indolence and selfishness" with the warmest pretensions to humanity and sensibility. It was a wicked doctrine, he thought, that declared that men should do nothing because they could not do everything they wished. And, he added, how could the opponents of the bill declare so confidently that it would not prove a blessing to the "poor little *sufferer*" who worked in "a heated stifling impure atmosphere, fevered by noise and glare, both limbs and spirits outwearied." Finally, as for the argument that the manufacturers would themselves introduce the reforms, Coleridge simply pointed to the obvious fact that the masters had not yet taken such forward steps and that they could not reasonably be expected to do so.[38]

Coleridge's second pamphlet, written on April 24, 1818, was an examination of the testimony given in behalf of and in opposi-

---

38. *Remarks by S. T. Coleridge on Sir Robert Peel's Bill,* reprinted in Lucy E. Watson, *Coleridge at Highgate* (London: Longmans, 1925), pp. 171–180.

tion to the factory act. It was an effort to counteract the unfavorable disposition toward the bill that the adverse evidence had created.[39] The most interesting and significant characteristic of both of these circulars was what we would today term the sociological approach that Coleridge made to the problem. The historian is reminded of a striking and much later analogy in American history, when Louis D. Brandeis in 1908 utilized successfully sociological data in defending before the Supreme Court an Oregon statute regulating the hours of women in industry. It is interesting also to note that Coleridge abandoned his preferred role of philosopher and spoke the language of the people when he entered the lists of the protagonists of reform.

The factory act passed the House of Commons in April 1818, and was at once sent to the House of Lords. Coleridge at first expected that it would be accepted by the Lords without controversy; but when James Maitland, the Earl of Lauderdale, let it be known that he would oppose it, Coleridge let loose his pent-up wrath against him. Lauderdale, "that *Scotch* coxcomb," pretended to be a political economist, and that made matters all the more reprehensible to Coleridge, who charged that the lord only desired to display his "muddy three inch depth in the gutter (?Guttur) [sic] of his Political Economy." [40]

Coleridge also feared that the advocates of laissez-faire might succeed in blocking the reform measure in the Lords and he wrote his barrister friend, Henry Crabb Robinson, for information to prove that legislative interference in labor relations was consistent with ancient British practice. The letter has since become a classic; it reveals how passionately and sincerely Coleridge was devoted to the cause of social reform.

Another mendicant letter from S. T. C.! [he wrote]. But no, it is from the poor little children employed in the Cotton Factories, who would fain have you in the lists of their friends and helpers; and entreat you to let *me* know for and in behalf of them, whether there is not some law prohibiting, or limiting, or regulating the employment either of children or adults, or of both in the White Lead Manufactory. [It had been said in the House of Commons that there was no such law, he

39. *The Grounds of Sir Robert Peel's Bill Vindicated by S. T. Coleridge*, published in *ibid.*, pp. 181–187.

40. Coleridge to J. H. Green, May 2, 1818, in E. H. Coleridge, editor, *Letters of Samuel Taylor Coleridge*, II, 689.

continued.] Now, can you help us to a more positive answer? Can you furnish us with any other instances in which the Legislature has directly, or by immediate consequence, interfered with what is ironically called "Free Labor"? (i. e., DARED to prohibit soul-murder and infanticide on the part of the rich, and self-slaughter on that of the poor!) or any dictum of our grave law authorities from Fortescue to Bacon, and from Bacon to Kenyon and Eldon: for from the borough in Hell I wish to have no representative, though on second thought I should have no objection to a good word in God's cause, though it should have slipped from the Devil's mouth. In short, my dear sir, the only objection likely to produce any hesitation in the House of Lords respecting Sir Robert Peel's bill . . . will come from that Scottish ("der Teufel *scotch* man all for snakes!") plebian earl, Lord L———, the dangerous precedent of legislative interference with free labor, of course implying that this bill will provide the first precedent. . . . But a little legal information from you would do more than twenty S.T.C.s, if there exists any law in point in that pithy little manual yclept the Statutes of Great Britain.[41]

The factory act passed soon afterwards, however, and Coleridge's fear of insuperable opposition in the upper house did not materialize.

Prosperity had momentarily returned to Great Britain in 1818; but the following year, depression struck again, especially in the textile industry. It provoked tremendous popular agitation in northern England for manhood suffrage; and the social unrest culminated in the massacre by regular troops of protesters at St. Peter's Fields outside Manchester. The result was to increase the social tension in the country almost to the breaking point. Coleridge looked upon the turbulent scene with foreboding, and again the fear of social revolution haunted his mind. He expressed his emphatic disapproval of the policies of the Liverpool government which, he declared, were being carried out with the aid of the "Ultra-whigs." [42] After the Peterloo massacre, he wrote of his alarm over the "storm louring and muttering in our political atmosphere." He thought that civil war was a very real possibility and dreaded the prospect of it.[43] But the government acted decisi-

41. Coleridge to Robinson, May 3, 1818, published in Thomas Sadler, editor, *Diary, Reminiscences, and Correspondence of Henry Crabb Robinson*, 2 vols. (Boston: Fields, Osgood, & Co., 1870), I, 385–386.

42. Coleridge to the editor of the *Morning Chronicle*, January 25, 1818, *Unpublished Letters*, II, 224.

43. Coleridge to Mrs. Aders, October 28, 1819, E. H. Coleridge, editor, *Letters of Coleridge*, II, 702.

vely and used the entire force of organized law and authority to prevent a spread of the riots; and of course eventually the storm passed over England, and Coleridge must have rejoiced at its passing.

The remainder of the period of crisis after Peterloo passed eventfully, to be sure, but with little public or private comment from Coleridge. Perhaps he felt that he had already made sufficient contribution in providing a way out of the economic, social, and political labyrinth and that his remedy (a return to positive Christianity, a greater emphasis upon speculative philosophy, and an alleviation of the dire social consequences of the industrial revolution) would not, regardless of what he did or said, be accepted by the people.

One of the most interesting features of Coleridge's writings and pronouncements during this period was the very narrow focus of his political attention. At a time when the masses were loudly and, at times, violently demanding manhood suffrage and parliamentary reform, he assiduously avoided the question. His, however, was a voice crying in an age of commercialism for a return to idealistic, non-materialistic Christian values. What he had to say was significant because he was representative of a group of varied and diverse persons who were making their influence felt in Britain during his lifetime and afterwards. He and his brothers in spirit clung tenaciously to the ideals of an age that had passed. Of course, the mythical Golden Age had never really existed; but that is beside the point. They thought, or convinced themselves, that it had; and their eloquent protests against the misfortunes inflicted upon the working people by the factory system were in the best traditions of Tory humanitarianism.

INDEX